Penn
Arts & Sciences

Thank you
for your
support!

Andrea
Gordis

Legacies of the Rue Morgue

CRITICAL AUTHORS & ISSUES

Josué Harari, Series Editor

A complete list of books in the series
is available from the publisher.

LEGACIES OF THE RUE MORGUE

SCIENCE, SPACE, AND CRIME FICTION IN FRANCE

ANDREA GOULET

PENN

UNIVERSITY OF PENNSYLVANIA PRESS

PHILADELPHIA

Published by
University of Pennsylvania Press
Philadelphia, Pennsylvania 19104-4112
www.upenn.edu/pennpress

Printed in the United States of America on acid-free paper
1 3 5 7 9 10 8 6 4 2

Library of Congress Cataloging-in-Publication Data
Goulet, Andrea, author.
Legacies of the Rue Morgue : science, space, and crime
fiction in France / Andrea Goulet.
    pages   cm. — (Critical authors & issues)
Includes bibliographical references and index.
ISBN 978-0-8122-4779-4 (alk. paper)
    1. Detective and mystery stories, French—History
and criticism. 2. French fiction—19th century—History and
criticism. 3. French fiction—20th century—History
and criticism. 4. French fiction—21st century—History and
criticism. 5. Science in literature. 6. Space and time
in literature. 7. Poe, Edgar Allan, 1809–1849—Influence.
I. Title. II. Series: Critical authors & issues.
PQ637.D4G68   2016
843'.087209—dc23   2015024072

For Jed, Jonah, and Maya

CONTENTS

Prologue: Poe

Why France? readers of Edgar Allan Poe's "The Murders in the Rue Morgue" may ask.[1] What led the American tale-teller of gothic suspense to set the first modern detective story in contemporary Paris and to name it, morbidly, for a fictional street in the real Quartier St. Roch?[2] As Baudelaire enjoyed pointing out, Poe had never set foot in France when he wrote the first Dupin mystery, published in the April 1841 issue of *Graham's Magazine*.[3] But he had feathered the path of his worldly ambitions with French or French-sounding pseudonyms ("Henri Le Rennet"), characters ("The Duke de l'Omelette"), and epigraphs (La Bruyère's "Ce grand malheur, de ne pouvoir être seul") for years.[4] Still, the specificity of "The Murders in the Rue Morgue"'s location and its linkage of criminality to nationhood goes beyond the mere patina of glamor associated with Paris. This was a city where the *Gazette des Tribunaux* spread grisly details about domestic crimes to a readership in the thousands,[5] and where a former thief, Eugène François Vidocq, could become director of the Sûreté Nationale, establish a detective agency, and publish his memoirs to worldwide renown.[6] By referencing the *Gazette* and Vidocq in his tale of ratiocination, Poe was speaking in 1841 what may now be called "Global French," a language that paradoxically reaches transnational proportions through local particularity.[7]

Local: a double murder in a home situated between the first *arrondissement*'s Rue St. Roch and Rue Richelieu; Global: shifting demographics and topographies of crime in modern metropolitan areas like Paris, London, and New York. Local: witnesses in the apartment building are questioned for testimony; Global: interpreters are called in, as these inhabitants of Paris hail from Italy, England, Spain, Holland, and France (Dupin calls them "denizens of the five great divisions of Europe"). Local: an amateur detective faces off with the Prefecture of Police; Global: nation-states of the early nineteenth century negotiate between vigilantism and official institutions of judiciary power.[8] Local: Dupin consults both the *Gazette des Tribunaux* and *Le Monde* ("a paper devoted to the shipping interest, and much sought by sailors"); Global: the nineteenth century witnesses a transatlantic explosion of print press publishing. Local: on the floor of the scene of the crime are found four Napoleons, an earring of topaz, three spoons made of *métal d'Alger*; Global: the coins and trinkets invoke France's colonial reach and hint at its centrality to the mystery's solution. Local: this seems to be a Parisian crime, born of urban danger; Global: it has in fact been committed by an orangutan brought to France from the East Indian Islands on a Maltese vessel, through a transnational circulation of commerce that brings with it a fear of the exotic Other that will only increase throughout the century.[9] Local: a Boston-born writer publishes a short story in a Philadelphia periodical; Global: "The Murders in the Rue Morgue" will become a shot heard round the world, inaugurating a genre whose locations will move, over a century and a half, from the Anglo-American-French triangle to Japan, Scandinavia, Africa, Latin America, and—at least on paper—other planetary worlds.

  This book takes Poe's tale as the starting point for that genre, defined broadly to encompass modern crime fiction, from popular *feuilletons* of the nineteenth-century sensationalist press to twenty-first-century novels in the Série noire and including the classic, detective-centered *roman policier*. The premise that Poe singlehandedly invented detective fiction as a distinct genre is, of course, a reductive one—and can be disputed with ease. First, one might note the archaic roots of the genre's epistemology: from Oedipus through the Chinese Judge Ti, premodern heroes have uncovered mysteries through induction from traces and clues.[10] On the other hand, the enormous proliferation of criminal fictions in the nineteenth century was specifically shaped by modern modes of policing the industrialized city.[11] Second, one might apply to Poe's tale the approach used by Bruno Latour in his study of Pasteur's seemingly ex nihilo microbial discovery: nothing, not even the world's "first modern detective story," is entirely new.[12] Kevin Hayes, for example, has demonstrated that Poe picked up many of the "Rue Morgue" details from a previously published story by a British novelist known as Mrs. Gore; these include descriptions of the Rue St. Roch *quartier*, the apartment building's *mansardes* and *loge de concierge*, even the name of Paris's Prefect of Police.[13] Certainly, crime-centered fiction was already in *l'air du temps*, with Honoré de Balzac's judiciary novel *Une ténébreuse affaire* appearing serially in *Le Commerce* in early 1841 and Eugène Sue's huge—and hugely popular—novel of the *bas-fonds* on the near horizon: *Les Mystères de Paris* was published in the *Journal des Débats* from June 1842 to October 1843. Given the seminal impor-

tance of Sue's novel and the fact that the *roman policier* was not separated out
from the tangle of *feuilleton* fictions as a distinct genre until much later, why
give interpretive privilege to Poe's single short story? After all, the crowded
field of influence on modern crime fiction includes, at least, the following
elements: the rise of mass printing (with its *canards*) and of the popular press
(with its *faits divers*);[14] the anti-death penalty discourse of important writers
like Victor Hugo; the *romans judiciaires* of Balzac and others who took readers behind the scenes of justice and injustice; the symbolic transfer of James
Fenimore Cooper's native American clue-tracking onto the urban topography
of Paris;[15] the rise of sensational fictions in which science and the supernatural vie to explain mystery; and the new methods and technologies of the *police scientifique*.[16] And yet, Poe stands out. His tale's simple structure—moving
from criminal mystery to solution through investigation—set the mold for
detective-centered narration; and his Chevalier Dupin, cited explicitly by
Gaboriau and Doyle as the precursor to their own fictional detectives, reached
archetypal proportions as soon as Poe laid out the steps of his deductive reasoning. To readers in France, Poe's tale came across as radically original, as
something truly new from the master of uncanny amalgamations of analysis
and unreason.[17] It was not, in fact, only the form of "The Murders in the Rue
Morgue" that gave it inaugural status; I hope to suggest that Poe's 1841 story
contained in seed everything that has flowered in French crime fiction from
the mid-nineteenth century to today—from its uneasy relation to rationality to the local/global logic of a nation dealing with internal crime and colonial violence. To put it baldly, then, Edgar Allan Poe invented French crime
fiction.

But more precisely, the text of "The Murders in the Rue Morgue" registers a specific spatial imaginary—one that brings the philosophical and
scientific concerns of the nineteenth century to bear on the narration of
crime and its investigation. This was, as crime historian Dominique Kalifa
demonstrates, the age of "l'enquête," dominated by the epistemological thrust
of investigative inquiry in fields ranging from the judicial to the journalistic.[18] Scientific inquiry, meanwhile, expanded to include notions of deep
geological time, while carrying positivism into the realm of the occult, so
that rationality and spiritism (along with their literary analogues of realism
and the fantastic) emerged as interrelated entities rather than oppositional
poles. Though Poe's Dupin stories may seem to represent the triumph of
the analytic spirit over a troubling unknown, they have as much to do with
the shadows of the uncanny as with the author's "mathematical spirit." And

though the *romans policiers* that followed Poe are deeply invested in myths of rationality, they cannot escape the nagging, haunting origin-point of violent death.

I aim to highlight a fundamental connection between this aspect of French crime fiction and the nineteenth-century scientific disciplines that were themselves grappling with the limits of abstract reason and the troubling specters of the long-dead past. On the one hand, Comtean positivism extended the rationalist claims of a Cartesian nation whose confidence in an Empire bolstered by cartographic mastery had been unsettled by the defeat of Napoleon I. But while it was being enjoined to look forward, science was also looking back: the first half of the century saw the rise of new historical disciplines, what William Whewell in 1837 called the "palaetiological" or reconstructive sciences of geology and paleontology, whose discoveries were revealing a deep and violent national past. The chapters that follow trace what I call crime fiction's "spatio-scientific" imaginary, one that anchors Dupin's deductive reconstitutions (whether of a crime or of his companion's thoughts) in the nineteenth century's ambivalent engagement with algebraic and cartographic orders of rationality, on the one hand, and new geological and paleontological conceptions of history, on the other.

Let us begin, however, more generally with the notions of space and place.

In the modern crime genre, location matters. As a 2007 *New Yorker* essay puts it, "In most of the crime novels coming out now, it's a matter not of what happens but of where."[19] If interest in new sources of crime fiction has continued to grow unabated over the last century, it is partly because tangible notations about geography, topography, and architecture give readers a sense of place or the *frisson* of displacement. The titles of at least three recent studies of the globalized genre testify to the enduring appeal of locale specificity: *Crimes of the Scene: A Mystery Novel Guide for the International Traveler* (1997); *Scènes de crimes: Enquêtes sur le roman policier contemporain* (2007); and *Scene of the Crime: The Importance of Place in Crime and Mystery Fiction* (2008).[20] For all the talk of pure ratiocination as the motor of detective stories, their mental puzzles would be forgotten if not for Maigret's Parisian brasseries and Smilla's Scandinavian snow.

All the more telling, then, that in 1841, "The Murders in the Rue Morgue" not only foregrounded setting, but actively narrativized a shift from abstraction to situatedness. Poe's story famously begins with a long discussion of analytical ratiocination as pure game, unconnected to any particular site. It then jumps to the narrator's meeting with Monsieur C. Auguste Dupin at "an

obscure library in the Rue Montmartre" of Paris, but the city recedes quickly
into the background when the two men (their souls kindled by the "wild fervor" of imagination) move to an old house "in a retired and desolate portion
of the Faubourg St. Germain" (243). There, the narrator and Dupin hunker
down in a bibliophilic coupling that ignores the world outside: "Our seclusion was perfect. We admitted no visitors. Indeed the locality of our retirement had been carefully kept a secret from my own former associates; and
it had been many years since Dupin had ceased to know or be known in
Paris" (243). Such hermetic separation from (knowledge of) the city begins
to dissolve, however, when Dupin and the narrator venture into its streets
at night. For even though the men consider their nocturnal perambulations
a mental retreat from the city, Paris in all its specificity and materiality re-
asserts itself: the holes and ruts of the paving-stones around the Palais Royal,
a cobbler on the rue St. Denis, the comedic Théâtre des Variétés—these are
the links in Dupin's famous chain of inductions. By the time the *Gazette des
Tribunaux* brings the Rue Morgue murders to the attention of Monsieur
Dupin, he is anything but an abstracted whist-player or an armchair detective
à distance; abandoning his earlier seclusion, Dupin tells the narrator that they
must go see the premises, where he will examine the entire neighborhood and
the apartment house with minute attention. It is only, in the end, through an
active engagement with specific location—by combining on-site observation
of architectural layout with, precisely, his knowledge of Paris as a world-
linked capital—that Dupin is able to solve the "analytical" mystery.

Indeed, despite Dupin's "abstract manner" (254), he is not one to reduce
a case to mere mathematical formula or mapped diagram—as, for example,
Joseph Rouletabille will attempt to do in Gaston Leroux's locked room mysteries of the early twentieth century. For Dupin to interpret, to know, to
exercise his extraordinary analytical faculties, he must walk in the city and
enter, bodily, into the spaces of crime. Poe's investigator thus cuts across the
two categories of spatial practice Michel de Certeau distinguished in 1980:
between an all-seeing, mastering "geometrical" mind and an ordinary walker,
Wandersmänner, who submits to imposed trajectories.[21] Just as he sees "diagonally" (a star, he claims, is best perceived by sidelong glances), Dupin cuts
diagonally across State regulations, using his influence with the Prefect of
Police to gain admission to the scene of the crime, while butting heads with
him over its solution. The Prefect "is all head and no body" (266), but Dupin's
feet walk the pavement and his hands disentangle a tuft of bestial hair from
the clutching fingers of a corpse.

Even the narrativization of Dupin's deductive process takes on the specific spatial contours of the Paris crime's location. In order to explain the steps of his reasoning to the narrator, Dupin proposes a mental return to the room in which the murders occurred: "Let us now transport ourselves, in fancy, to this chamber" (255). The particularities of that mental return are both precise and material, as Dupin recounts the inspection of the apartment's doors and keys, furniture, frames, and fastenings in order to test the hypothesis that the assassin had no possible mode of egress. Further inquiry leads to a rusted nail in a window casement and a set of shutters "of the peculiar kind called by Parisian carpenters *ferrades*—a kind rarely employed at the present day, but frequently seen upon very old mansions at Lyons and Bourdeaux [sic]" (257). In even this smallest of architectural details, we find not only the cross-linguistic reference, but also a double displacement—from province to Paris and from the past to the present—that imbues Poe's text with the citationality that Philippe Hamon sees as constitutive of narrative space.[22] Hamon writes that the "spatial effect" on narration often involves "transferences, transformations, or quotations," with writers perceiving "the city or the house as the visible stratification, or as a 'reuse' . . . of other constructions" (35). From its *loge de concierge* to its chimneys, stairs, and landings, the apartment house in the Rue Morgue features the verticality of pre-Haussmann Paris architecture, while superimposing onto that realist verticality a fantasmatically exaggerated intermingling of five nationalities in the same space. The urban setting's reorientation of horizontal geographical difference onto vertical architectural layout symbolically reinforces the movements of Poe's orangutan, who crosses oceans from the Indian Archipelago to end up committing an act whose reconstruction involves the minute examination of "the mode of descent" from a fourth-floor window (257). Thus verticality and horizontality play off each other, with the Parisian apartment house as the point of intersection between urban stratification and global span.

It would be wrong, of course, to reduce Poe's story of bestial, brutal strangulations to a series of shapes and lines. Indeed, one of the central arguments of this book is that abstracted conceptions of detective fiction all too easily suppress the visceral violence at the heart of the genre. In the strictest traditional definitions of the *roman policier*, Reason dominates Instinct, Order reclaims Disorder, and the bloody corpse becomes the "figure on the carpet"—an enigma to be analyzed, observed, and resolved. In their classic study, for example, Boileau and Narcejac emphasize the explanation of mystery as the *roman policier*'s primary mission; in order to combat the anxieties of "l'incompréhensible," defined as "la violence sans explication," the detective novel invokes mathematical models and scientific discourse to turn mystery into solution.[23] As the genre developed and was codified in the early twentieth century, the abstract problem-solving function of detective fiction (and fictional detective) was seen to separate off from more sensationalistic forms; blood, terror and suspense, the markers of the *roman noir*, were considered pollutants in a purified fictional sphere of abstract reasoning. But such sublimation not only artificially hews the detective story away from its tangled roots in *feuilletonesque* pulp: it also artificially sets mathematical and scientific reasoning against the bodily, material world.

Maurizio Ascari's 2007 *A Counter-History of Crime Fiction: Supernatural, Gothic, Sensational* provides a welcome genealogical map of the "hybrid zones" between crime fiction and the antirational traditions from which it has classically been distinguished. Although my heuristic emphasis on Poe would seem at first glance to contradict Ascari's thesis, I actually agree with his "refusal of any monogenetic account of the origin of literary genres."[24] Indeed, rather than present Poe as a stand-alone genius, I aim in this Prologue to explore "The Murders in the Rue Morgue" as a particularly suggestive indicator of the cross-fertilizations and tensions Ascari rightly attributes to the "plural genre" of crime fiction. If, as Ascari contends, the "'foundation myth' identifying Poe as the father of detection was created to support a normative view of the genre" (10), I hope to turn the myth inside out, by showing Poe's text to be as non-normative—that is, as counter-rational, gruesome, and conflicted—as any of the sensational murder narratives that were excised from the most purified accounts of the *roman policier*.

Indeed, if "The Murders in the Rue Morgue" is to be taken as prime exemplum for the modern crime genre, it should not be solely because of its prefatory reflections on analytical deduction in the games of whist and draughts. Just as central to the story's staying power are its more troubling details: the bloodied bit of a woman's scalp attached to a torn handful of clotted hair, the "excessive violence" involved in stuffing a mutilated cadaver into the sooty confines of a narrow chimney, and the Borneo beast, whose invasion rips away any sense of safety in the streets and homes of Paris.[25]

Chimney and chamber, street and sailing vessel: the very situatedness of Poe's violent elements reminds us that location matters. When Dupin investigates "the bloody transactions which *took place*" (261, my emphasis), he does so through tangible engagement with the scene of the crime.[26] If there is a gap in Poe's text, as Martin Priestman has argued, between Foucault's "struggle between two pure minds" and the grisly brutality of murder,[27] Dupin straddles that gap. Priestman rightly identifies Poe's two later Dupin stories, "The Mystery of Marie Rogêt" and "The Purloined Letter," as the source of the "armchair detective" tradition, in which ratiocination supersedes sniffing around the premises.[28] But in the "Rue Morgue," even when Dupin is sitting at a distance from the scene of the crime, he narrates a mental return to it that materially recapitulates his corporeal engagement with objects, cadavers, and architecture. No "codfish" Prefect, this investigator has a body attached to his head.

Even Dupin's apparently abstracting moves—those that appeal to geometrical science or dusty academic reference—involve bodily touch. Take, for example, the facsimile sketch Dupin makes of Mlle de L'Espanaye's neck bruises. By mapping the bruises onto the "plane surface" of a paper and making a model out of a cylindrical "billet of wood, the circumference of which is about that of the throat," Dupin seems to sanitize the bloody attack, to reduce it to the clean lines and shapes of mathematics.[29] But once again, the mediating factors fail to suppress the tangible and the human: Dupin asks the narrator to place each of his fingers "in the respective impressions" made by the killer's hand, as though the indentations on the victim's throat had somehow kept their dimensionality on the drawing's flat surface. He could have had recourse instead to a measuring-stick and medical statistics on the size range of the human hand, but it was by asking his friend to engage his body, to place his own hand on the traces of another, that Dupin leads him to the conclusion of a nonhuman attacker. By the time the French naturalist Cuvier's authoritative tome on Natural History is invoked, the narrator is ready to compare fingers to fingers, hair to hair. The size, strength, and brutality of "the beast of Cuvier" mean more than its place in an abstract classificatory system[30]—and the scientific tome is granted as much authority as the shipping newspaper *Le Monde*, whose report serves as Dupin's final piece of paper evidence before he produces a sailor's greasy hair ribbon and then the sailor himself. Dupin has pried a tawny tuft of mammalian hair from the victim's hand, he has fingered the sailor's greasy ribbon, he has poked at window nails and pressed at sash springs, he has leafed through the pages of academic tomes and popular news gazettes, and he has walked the *pavés de Paris*. His space, then, is a Lefebvrian "social space"—neither imagined, unreal, purely geometrical, or ideal; it is lived through contact and experience.[31]

This empiricist thrust is evident even in Dupin's criticism of the Parisian police methods of investigation. The gendarmes had mistakenly assumed, scoffs Dupin, that there had been no possible mode of egress from the Rue Morgue chamber; their "perceptions had been hermetically sealed against the possibility of the windows having ever been opened at all" (258). The metonymic slide from the space of the room to the space of bodily perception reminds us that Dupin himself had left the hermetic space of the home he shared with the narrator in order to explore the streets, staircases, landings, chimneys, and windows of the rue Morgue murder scene. If threshold spaces will retain their hold on the crime fiction imaginary for a century and a half to follow, it is in part because the investigation of the "Murders in the Rue Morgue" hinged on the sites of access and communication between inside and outside, private and public, domestic and foreign. For of course the very intrusion of the "beast in the nursery," that is, the savage orangutan in the domestic compartment of female innocents, was made possible by the porous boundaries of the French nation state in its commercial, colonial global role.[32] Neither mind, nor chamber, nor nation remains sealed in Poe's story.[33] The Rue Morgue's refusal of what would become a myth of the *chambre close* thus opens up the genre, from its very beginnings, to an emerging global modernity.

CHAPTER I

Introduction: Mapping Murder

[G]eography shapes the narrative structure of the European novel.
—Franco Moretti

Through its spatial logics, Poe's *Rue Morgue* bequeathed to its generic descendants two irresolvable tensions: between abstract intellection and bodily violence, and between (inter-) national politics and domestic privacy. The chapters in this book trace those tensions as they have played out in the crime fiction of modern France, land of Cuvier and Napoleon—two figures who dominated nineteenth-century thought and whose cultural "ghosts" continue to mark this particular national generic tradition. Indeed, and as this chapter will propose, the double chronotope of geological and political revolution has emerged as a thread that binds and characterizes representations of violence in French crime fiction throughout its modern history. This book's longitudinal approach allows us to track the crime genre in relation not only to that revolutionary context but also to the broader spatial transformation that theorists like Paul Virilio and Bruno Latour have identified in France's self-consciousness: from the nineteenth-century nation-state to a twenty-first-century node of transnationality, from the mapped metropolis of internal revolution to a matrix of actantial assemblages, from industry to informatics, from the physical geography of the *polis* to virtual (de)-territorialization.[1]

The book is divided into two main Parts, "Archaeologies" and "Cartographies," separated by an interstitial chapter, "Street Names." Each of the three sections moves longitudinally from the *romans-feuilletons* of the 1860s and 1880s through the popular novels of the prewar and interwar periods of the twentieth century, ending with examples of today's crime novels that take up and renew the themes established at the genre's start. Along with the chronological move from the Second Empire to the twenty-first century, a spatial entropy is also at work in the book's main sections. Each begins with a chapter on particular settings in Paris (Hausmannian digs in the quarries and catacombs, *terrains vagues* of the barrier regions, the crime-ridden streets of La Cité) and ends with chapters that explore the expansion and breakdown of national boundaries as postmodern globalization makes its mark on the French *polar*.

And yet each section responds differently to the questions that underlie this project. What role does space play in crime fiction's representations of violence? Do fictional locations reflect shifting sites—literal or metaphorical—of national anxieties about crime? Can we "map" French crime fiction along the binary lines of Parisian metropole and rural periphery? How does the specific topography of Paris—its streets, its divisions into *quartiers* and *arrondissements*, its prisons and courtrooms—impact narrative form? What function do maps and place names play in crime novels? What is the relation between scientific discourses of inquiry and the detective genre's epistemological thrust? How do changing scientific discourses—from paleontology and Pasteurian microbiology to animal studies and neuro-network theory—impact literature from the nineteenth century to today? Does France's specific political history distinguish its crime fiction from that of other world regions? Where do political insurrection and domestic drama intersect in the crime imaginary? How did early crime novels blur the lines between detective fiction's abstraction and the *noir*'s bloody violence? Which themes and tropes of the nineteenth century's popular press *feuilleton* have survived to mark today's Série noire? How have new technologies (trains and telephones in the nineteenth century, virtual reality and globalized computation in the twenty-first) changed the geographies of crime fiction? Does the *néo-polar* of our time represent a new spatioperceptual relation between subject and world?

From its start, this project has been theoretically informed by studies of spatiality that call into question the objective neutrality of visual and textual representations of space. These range from Gaston Bachelard's *The Poetics of Space* (1964) and Henri Lefebvre's *The Production of Space* (1974) to Derek Gregory's *Geographical Imaginations* (1994), Edward Casey's *The Fate of Place* (1998), and Verena Conley's *Spatial Ecologies* (2012). Not only has the field of postmodern geography reminded us that spatiality is culturally constructed and ideologically marked, it has also reiterated the fundamental interrelation of space with time. In *Representing Place: Landscape Painting and Maps*, Edward Casey writes of "this commixture of the placial and the historical":

Preliminary distinctions between geography (space) and history (time) cannot withstand scrutiny, for "Place is finally inseparable from period, because the ramified character of places includes their own past history. The apparently pure synchrony of geography is inevitably complicated by the vagaries of diachronic development."[2]

Though this point is relevant to all types of representation, the literary genre of crime fiction has a particular investment in the crossings of space and time. Both structurally and thematically, crime fiction explores the uneasy intersections between the scene of the crime and its history. Whether classic *roman policier* or sensationalist pot-boiler, novels about crime and investigation consider how a traumatic past imprints itself on the space of the present—and how that past can be reconstructed through an investigation that itself unfolds temporally and in precise locations. A spatial approach to the genre allows us to track the shifting ways mystery (epistemological quest) endeavors to deal with history (real violence, whether criminal or political, individual or national). The organization of this book may seem to follow a Cartesian grid, with its associations of pure intellection and rationalized space: Part I, "Archaeologies," follows a vertical axis to underground space; Part III, "Cartographies," maps the horizontal axis of urban layout; and Part II, "Street Names," marks the point of intersection of the two axes. Yet each of these sections can be more fully understood as tracing a chronotope, a spatial motif that involves its own complex grapplings with historicity—a violent historicity that always returns to disrupt the genre's rationalist grids.

In this introductory chapter, I provide an overview of the book's three sections in order to demonstrate how shifting scientific and philosophical discursive contexts, from Cuvierian geology to Deleuzian deterritorialization, have imprinted the spatiotemporal logics of the crime fiction tradition in modern France.

I. Stones, Bones, and Ghosts: Crime's Archaeological Imaginary

In the beginning was Cuvier.

Indeed, if there is anything I have learned in researching this book, it is that naming the nineteenth century "l'Âge de Cuvier" is hardly an overstatement. As Poe's reference to the naturalist in "The Murders in the Rue Morgue" suggests, Georges Baron Cuvier was internationally renowned, as famous in the 1830s and 1840s as someone like Stephen Hawking is today. Cuvier was recognized world-wide not only for comparatist anatomical studies like the one Dupin cites in "The Murders in the Rue Morgue", but primarily for his geological work on fossils, which revolutionized ways of understanding the past's relation to the present.[3] In particular, Cuvier's stratigraphic model of underground terrain allowed inhabitants of the modern city to visualize the past in layers under their feet; his catastrophist theory of terrestrial revolution mapped onto France's own political cycles of violent upheaval; and his inauguration, at the start of the nineteenth century, of paleontology as a new scientific field paved the way for discoveries of human prehistory and evolutionary thought.[4] These are the three elements of Cuvier's work that Chapters 2 and 3 explore in relation to popular detective fiction from the 1860s to World War I.

The chapters build on a familiar analogy between paleontologist and detective: just as Cuvier boasted, in his 1812 "Discours préliminaire" to the *Recherches sur les ossements fossiles de quadrupèdes*, of reconstructing an entire lost species from a mere fragment of bone, the ingenious detective can deduce an entire criminal sequence from a minor physical clue. The analogy appeared early on, with both Émile Gaboriau and Arthur Conan Doyle describing fictional detectives' investigative methods in terms of paleontological reconstruction of the past.[5]

For science historian Claudine Cohen, the Cuvierian method should be seen as the dominant epistemological mode of nineteenth-century thought; along with Darwin, Cuvier taught modern intellectuals how to reconstitute lost worlds. In *La Méthode de Zadig*, Cohen links Cuvier's scientific reconstruction to the theoretical model of Voltaire's oriental sage Zadig, who deciphered the traces of the past in order to revive it through narration.[6] Cohen's generalization of reconstitutive method is compelling, and it aligns with Carlo Ginzburg's now classic identification of an "evidential paradigm" that manifested itself in the fin-de-siècle triply: through art historian Giovanni Morelli's attention to details like a painted ear; in the detective Sherlock Holmes's deductions from fingerprints and cigarette ash; and in the psychoanalyst Sigmund Freud's symptomatic reading of apparently trivial side matter. Ginzburg's essay traces the roots of this modern conjectural paradigm, citing ancient oriental fables and Mesopotamian divination texts and going as far back as the primordial hunter, who sniffs the earth to reconstruct "movements of his invisible prey from tracks on the ground, broken branches, excrement, tufts of hair, entangled feathers, stagnating odors."[7] This nose-to-the-ground epistemological mode, which Ginzburg opposes to a more abstract and mathematical "Galilean paradigm," reappears in modern form through historical sciences like paleography—sciences whose reconstruction of the past evokes, again, the work of the detective.[8] As we have seen with Dupin's groping of the orangutan's tuft of red hair in *Rue Morgue*, direct sensory contact with tangible clues plays a key role in the fictional act of deduction. But from the start, this "evidential" approach has always worked in close—and not necessarily oppositional—dialogue with the abstract, armchair version of intellectual deduction; the detective may be a hunter and historian, but he is also a mathematician. As erudite as Ginzburg's essay is, its sweeping, transcultural associations risk evacuating the materiality/abstraction tension within detective fiction and ignoring the violence at the heart of the genre. The descendants of Dupin and Lecoq are not merely tracking prey for sustenance or deciphering clues to determine a long dead painter's identity; they are compelled to investigate criminal acts that have violently torn the fabric of society. If the figure of Cuvier looms large in crime fiction, it is not just because he was able to reconstruct lost species with ingenuity; it is also because his scientific methods exposed cataclysmic violence in the very rocks on which our culture is founded. The bones and fragments that testify to death and destruction in our past are buried in layers that threaten to puncture our present.

Beyond the primary analogy between paleontologist and detective as investigators of the past, then, what links fossils to forensics, cataclysm to crime? In Chapter 2, I identify a number of popular crime fictions that literalized the Cuvierian chronotope by setting criminal activity in the underground spaces of Paris's quarries and catacombs. Flourishing during the Second Empire, these "catacomb fictions" (including Berthet's 1854 *Les Catacombes de Paris*, Guéroult and Coudeur's 1859 *Les Étrangleurs de Paris*, Zaccone's 1863 *Les Drames des catacombes*, and Imbert's 1867 *Les Catacombes de Paris*) mobilized geological notions to undercut the modernizing ideology of what historian Colin Jones calls the Second Empire city's "Hausmannian horizontality," its ahistoric, progressivist rectilinearity.[9] They did so, moreover, not just by counterproposing a simple vertical topography of historical regress, but rather by mapping a jagged, Cuvierian geohistory onto the narrative form itself. Berthet's serial novel *Les Catacombes de Paris*, for example, allegorizes the seismic effects of earlier political revolutions on modern urban crime through the prism of scientific debates between cataclysmic deluge and continuist history.

By the second half of the nineteenth century, Lamarckian transformism and Darwinian evolution theories had won the day, but Cuvier's disruptive, seismological model of underground violence continued to haunt the popular imaginary well after Sue's Rodolphe narrowly escaped drowning in a criminal's cave in *Les Mystères de Paris* (1842–43). Both Guéroult and Couder's *Les Étrangleurs de Paris* and Zaccone's *Les Drames des catacombes*, for example, feature dramatic climactic scenes of underground flooding, with crumbling rocks overturned by torrential waters and criminals caught in a recurring cycle of cataclysmic violence. By the time Jules Lermina wrote *Les Loups de Paris* in 1876, Berthet's triple alliance of domestic crime, political Revolution, and cataclysmic geology seems to have become a distinctively French cliché, one that Gaston Leroux will upend with his strange underground adventure of 1903, *La Double vie de Théophraste Longuet*. This novel, set also in the Paris catacombs but peopled by an archaic civilization left over from medieval France, marks a transition from the geological fictions analyzed in Chapter 2 to the "Skull Stories" of Chapter 3, with their revisions of historicist method.

By noting the imprint of France's turbulent geological history on the popular crime serial of the late nineteenth century, we can nuance a seemingly self-evident thesis: that modern crime fiction is about modernity. From Régis Messac's 1929 study of the *roman policier* as the "genre de la ville moderne" to Jacques Dubois's influential 1992 book *Le Roman policier ou la modernité*, detective fiction has been taken as inextricable from the secularized, rationalized, and industrialized society that produced it. For Dubois, the *roman policier* is not just co-temporal with a Baudelairian, Benjaminian modernity; it is modernity itself. The genre's urban settings, its roots in the popular press of the Second Empire, its train station marketing, and its links to phototechnology are as definitional as its formal conventions and violent plots. But what this incontrovertible strain of analysis has largely left unnoticed is the paradoxical discovery of radical <u>pre</u>modernity in modern spaces and by modern means. At the very moment that popular crime fiction was coalescing into a self-identified genre, Haussmann's renovation projects were uncovering archaic stones and fossilized bones under the city of Paris. Meanwhile, the newly formed sciences of geology and paleontology were reaching their epistemological heights through the identification of the "deep time" of millennial prehistory in the very rocks whose strata support the structures of high civilization.[10] The double context of nineteenth-century urban renewal and the rise of Earth Sciences allows us to see the modernity of crime fiction as deeply invested in its apparent opposite.

Let us return here, briefly, to Poe's *The Murders in the Rue Morgue*, in which the brutal savagery of the double murder combines with a tuft of reddish hair and an enormous handprint to unnerve the narrator into slack-jawed repetition: "Dupin! . . . this is no *human* hair" and "This . . . is the mark of no human hand" (260). Dupin responds to the narrator's fear by turning to the cool and civilized pages of science:

> "Read now," replied Dupin, "this passage from Cuvier."
> It was a minute anatomical and generally descriptive account of the large fulvous Ourang-Outang of the East Indian Islands. . . .
> "The description of the digits," said I, as I made an end of reading, "is in exact accordance with this drawing. . . . This tuft of tawny hair, too, is identical in character with that of the beast of Cuvier."
> (260–61)

Dupin's appeal to the French naturalist reinforces the text's distancing of beast from human: not only does the narrator's (re-)reading of the scientific tome stage the highest level of civilized rationality, but Cuvier's classification also upholds a species distinction later disputed by Lamarckian transformism and Darwinian evolutionism.[11] Still, this *crime* story can hold the troubling human/beast connection at bay only incompletely, for its reconstruction of the murders imputes to the ape such human motives and emotions as "wrath," "fury," "phrenzy," and "fear"—as well as, more surprisingly, the "conscious[ness] of having deserved punishment"! (265) Such moral, even judicial, conscious-ness hints at the kind of radical dissolution of the man/animal divide that Jacques Derrida proposed in his 1997 lecture "L'Animal que donc je suis," which has spawned a new field of "animal studies"; as Cary Wolfe points out, the philosophical challenge to the notion of the non-human animal "is linked complexly to the problem of animals' ethical standing as direct or indi-rect subjects of justice."[12] Though Poe's killer orangutan ends up safely im-prisoned in the Jardin des Plantes zoo, it continues to mark the fictional crime genre with an association, however disavowed, between human vio-lence and bestial savagery.[13]

The direct descendent of Poe's orangutan may be less Jacques Lantier, who is driven to murder by atavistic impulse in Zola's 1890 *La Bête humaine*, than the strange half-man half-ape Balaoo appearing in Gaston Leroux's 1911 crime story of the same name. As a Derridean "animot" *avant la lettre*, the anthropithecus Balaoo undercuts any man/beast distinction by combining murderous violence with reasoned tenderness, prehensile hind limbs with a tailored suit.

In Chapter 3, I situate Leroux's *Balaoo* within a subgenre of fin-de-siècle crime fictions inspired directly by the paleontological discoveries of the second half of the nineteenth century. Gaston Leroux and Maurice Leblanc are generally read as standard bearers of modernity: as their heroes hop trains, ride bikes, and communicate by telegraph and telephone, they seem to embrace the accelerating complexity of twentieth-century life and thus enter what David Bell and Dominique Kalifa have identified as a second phase of modern crime fiction, one that moves from urban center to the proto-globalized space of intercontinental travel.[14] But as they face a transnational future, Leroux and Leblanc reflect also on France's national past, by setting some of their heroes' most important adventures in regional coastal settings whose cliffside caverns hold clues to history and prehistory. The readings in Chapter 3 demonstrate that Leroux's *Le Parfum de la dame en noir* and Leblanc's "La Contesse de Cagliostro" engage with an archeological imaginary in order to crystallize crime's relation to history in opposite ways: Leroux uses paleontology to expose an anti-historical fear of the past's reach into the present, while in Leblanc, buried bones in a cave support archival historicism through a contrary fear of temporal stasis. In both cases, the act of unearthing traces from a buried past is what enables the narrative confrontation with violence.

Upon discovering crushed crania next to fossilized weaponry, scientists debated the brutality of primitive humans, a brutality inseparable from their surroundings: cave-formations that themselves revealed the violent upheavals of geological rupture. As the Neanderthal skull revealed the troubling "deep time" of human prehistory under European cities and in coastal caves, popular *feuilletonistes* connected France's past, present, and future through scenes of violence set in the vertical strata of the underground. New notions of primitivism and urban criminality eventually combined with Darwinian evolutionary theory to create science fiction genres whose overlap with the *roman policier* constitutes one of the central theses of this book.

Indeed, novels of prehistory (like Rosny's 1892 *Vamireh* and 1909 *La Guerre du feu*) and ape-man fictions (like Lermina's 1905 *To-Ho, le tueur d'or*) belong to the same *roman-feuilleton* universe as what Daniel Compère calls "le roman d'aventures policières."[15] Although journalist-authors like Elie Berthet and Jules Lermina, who wrote hundreds (!) of serial novels cutting across all popular genres, are not well known today, their experiments with the crime novel form connect us to the trickle-down scientism so formative in late nineteenth-century thought. In particular, along with Gaston Leroux and the other novelists discussed in Chapters 2 and 3, they allow us to discern what might be called a geo-paleontological imaginary of crime: a set of associations with the primitive underground that shaped notions of violence and its spaces.[16]

It is, of course, impossible to discuss criminality and underground space in nineteenth-century Paris without reference to Victor Hugo's monumental novel of 1862, *Les Misérables*. The Paris sewers in *Les Misérables* are many things: cloacal spillways for the city's moral and medical hygienization (Prendergast); politicized convergence points for the horrible and the sublime (Grossman); and muddy, material archives for historiography in its nineteenth-century form (Blix).[17] This last, "archeological" function of Hugo's underground space is, further, marked directly by the science of geology: "Rien de plus difficile à percer et à pénétrer que cette formation géologique à laquelle se superpose la merveilleuse formation historique, nommée Paris" [There is nothing more difficult to pierce and to penetrate than the geological formation upon which is superposed the marvelous historical formation called Paris].[18] Through Jean Valjean's journey into the city's intestinal crypt, personal redemption for a criminal past is linked to the skeletons of national history and their relationship to present-day violence. The aboveground rebellion from which Valjean delivers Marius in 1832 manifests itself as the aftershock of earlier political—and, figuratively, geological—upheavals, as Valjean follows the "sentine redoutée qui a la trace des révolutions du globe comme des révolutions des hommes, et où l'on trouve des vestiges de tous les cataclysmes depuis le coquillage du déluge jusqu'au haillon de Marat" [dreaded bilge that bears the traces of the revolutions of the globe as well as the revolutions of men, and in which we find the vestiges of all cataclysms, from the shells of the deluge to the rag of Marat] (1705). Hugo reinforces here a connection Cuvier himself had made between cataclysmic geohistory and the French Revolution(s). And strangely, along with the diluvian shells and revolutionary rags, are buried the bones of an animal whose violence we have seen marking the pages of Poe: "le squelette d'un orang-outang disparu du Jardin des Plantes en 1800, disparition probablement connexe à la fameuse et incontestable apparition du diable rue des Bernardins dans la dernière année du dix-huitième siècle" [the skeleton of an orangutan that had gone missing from the Jardin des Plantes in 1800, a disappearance likely connected to the famous and indisputable apparition of the devil in the rue des Bernardins the last year of the eighteenth century] (1697). In these two lines we find a strange little crime mystery, a *fait divers* with an animal victim and supernatural solution situated so precisely (year, street) through urban legend that one cannot help but recall the popular plots of the century's *romans-feuilletons*—such as Berthet's *Les Catacombes de Paris*, which takes inquiries into criminal violence through the archaicizing detour of devils and ghosts. Like the popular fictions analyzed in these chapters, Hugo's better-known text uses the urban geological underground to evoke deep connections between violence and history. *Les Misérables* is, in the broadest sense, a "crime novel," one whose real and fantasmatic topographies a) reflect a social order that links political troubles to the *bas-fonds* of the criminal underworld, and b) signal the persistent traces of France's violent past on its present terrain.

In the more strictly defined *roman policier*, an investigator interprets those traces. He measures footprints, analyzes ash—or, in the case of Rouletabille in Leroux's *Parfum de la dame en noir*, inspects a prehistoric skull that is particularly troubling because it serves not only as a reminder of humanity's distant, archaic violence but also as a mirror to its continual threat in the present. Rouletabille's Oedipal investment in a supposedly abstract, rational investigation reminds us that crime fiction is about trauma and its aftereffects. The past always leaves traces on the present, but when that past is violent those traces exert a phantomatic power. Ginzburg was right to link Freud to the detective, for (unlike art historians or soothsayers), the psychoanalyst unearths a traumatized past, the layers of which have been disturbed by a catastrophic or criminal event.

* * *

In fact, Leroux's 1909 novel can be seen as a hinge between periods: if the nineteenth century was marked by a Cuvierian chronotope, in the twentieth century that geological imaginary entered the realm of the psyche. Freud's work introduced the notion of human consciousness as a vertical territory, with surface and depth engaged in an agonistic relation of eruption, disruption, repression, and return. The fundamental anfractuosity of Freudian spatialization emerges in the image of the mind as a layered terrain, with its strata and substrata, fissures and breaks, eruptions into violence.[19] This geological mastertrope has influenced many French thinkers, including Claude Lévi-Strauss, whose 1955 anthropological memoir *Tristes tropiques* remains culturally relevant beyond its primary structuralist scope. Inspired by childhood *randonnées* on a limestone plateau in the Languedoc, Lévi-Strauss described Freud's theories as the application of geological method, with the analyst penetrating the psychic surface to discover the telluric forces bubbling underneath.[20] During the same decade, Gaston Bachelard, in his 1958 *Poétique de l'espace*, spatialized the psyche as a home, with its underground cellar identified as buried madness, "la folie enterrée"—the subterranean site of secrets and crimes.[21] Bachelard cites Poe's *The Cask of Amontillado* as a "récit de caves criminelles," but of course the entire detective genre that Poe founded with his 1841 *Murders in the Rue Morgue* taps into both Bachelard's metaphorics of the underground and Lévi-Strauss's insight on the geological analyst—with the detective as the one who digs up the truth, connecting buried bones to violent history.

For the authors I am analyzing here, that history is buried in the particular terrain of the French nation. Indeed, my research for this book confirms that national identity is at stake in even the most private-seeming investigations into the criminal underground. In modern French crime fiction, fresh corpses lie in the same jumbled terrain as the skeletons of a national past. That image is literalized in the penny-dreadful cover of a pre-World War I Lord Lister adventure, "Dans les catacombes de Paris," in which old bones from the Revolutionary nineteenth century are thrown together with new victims of the fledgling century (see Chapter 2). Seventy years later, Didier Daeninckx's 1985 novel *Métropolice* turns the tunnels of the Paris Métro into a similarly layered chronotope. When a main character of Daeninckx's novel discovers one tunnel opening onto the ancient *carrières d'Amérique*, he learns with surprise of that abandoned space's violent history as the deadly refuge of Communards fleeing massacre in 1871. In this way, the nation's buried traumas continue to haunt the spaces of modernity. Indeed, every time an investigator cracks the earthy crust covering over the past, he (or increasingly in the twentieth century, she) finds that the personal is political. As Bernard Stiegler and Jean-Paul Demoule have put it, "l'archéologie, au-delà de sa progression dans l'espace et dans le temps, est aussi partie prenante de la constitution des identités nationales" [archaeology, beyond its progression in space and in time, is also a prime stakeholder in the constitution of national identities].[22]

It would be a mistake, however, to see those national identities as static or mired only in nineteenth-century tropes of cyclic revolt. As the twentieth century progressed, national identity in French crime fiction went beyond themes of internal revolution and came increasingly to involve trans-border issues of colonialism and globalization. This expansion is particularly evident in the texts analyzed in Part III, which traces an entropic cartography of crime from Emile Gaboriau to Maurice Dantec. But even in the "vertical" space of Part I's archeological fictions, digging into the past involves a double shift: from a nineteenth-century interest in France's paleontological prehistory (overlaid with its more recent Revolutionary past) to the twentieth century's focus on the national traumas of world war and Occupation; and from nineteenth-century conceptions of France as a body threatened from the outside by the irruption of criminal apes and sailors, to a twentieth-century understanding of the nation as fully imbricated in a global network.[23]

Among the theses of this book is the interconnectedness of spatial and scientific logics—and, indeed, the twentieth-century shift toward globalized politics itself follows the epistemological path of the reconstructive sciences. When geology and paleontology were at their height in the late nineteenth century, "l'archéologie de la violence" served to disinter ancient wars; but a century later, archeological techniques were brought to bear on more recent global atrocities like genocide and human rights violations: "On aurait préféré que notre époque ne s'intéressât qu'aux Néandertaliens, aux *Homos erectus* et aux Néolithiques; il aura fallu que notre siècle fasse aussi l'archéologie des génocides" [Though we would have preferred our era to interest itself merely in neanderthals, *homo erectus*, and neolithics, our century will also have forced us to perform the archeology of genocides] (Stiegler and Demoule, 12). Thus, in both practical application and epistemological thrust, postwar sciences of the underground participate in the national memory-work that trauma theorists and historians like Henry Rousso ascribe to the late phase of the twentieth century.[24]

A renewed interest in the buried crimes of a nation certainly contributes to the success of an author like Didier Daeninckx, who has won many prizes, including the Grand Prix de Littérature Policière in 1985 and the Prix Paul Féval de Littérature Populaire in 1994. Though the example of *Métropolice* refers back to the end of the nineteenth century, Daeninckx is best known for lifting the scabs off fresher wounds of the French national body. The Série noire best-seller *Meurtres pour mémoire* (1984) has garnered the most attention for its investigative exhumation of World War II Occupation atrocities and the massacre of Algerians in 1961 Paris. Claire Gorrara situates Daeninckx and his detective-historians within the politicized "*roman noir engagé* of the 1980s."[25] More broadly, by having his fictional investigations into modern crime expose national secrets buried in historical archives, Daeninckx participates in what Dominique Viart calls the late twentieth-century "roman archéologique."[26]

*   *   *

In a sense, any detective novel is "archeological" in its double temporality of present investigation and past crime. But a particularly compelling set of crime

fictions literalizes the Todorovian temporality through the material thematics of the underground: these are real skulls and bones, buried in the geological layers of modern France. And in a sense, any text participates in the uncanny
absence-presence of a Derridean "hauntology," in which past and present co-
exist in a spectral relation.[27] But because detective fiction enacts a puzzling-
out of secrets that somebody wants to keep buried, the genre is particularly
"phantomatic," in the sense employed by Nicolas Abraham and Maria Torok
in their post-Freudian work on trauma analysis: the hidden business of a violent past reappears in the present as gaps of knowledge to be cryptologically
deciphered.[28]

     With these genre logics in mind, Chapter 4 ("Crypts and Ghosts") ana-
lyzes novels by Sébastien Japrisot and Fred Vargas whose underground terrain combines the historical and the psychoanalytical aspects of the
archeological imagination. Unlike other novels by Japrisot, such as *Comparti-
ment tueurs* (1962) and *Piège pour Cendrillon* (1963), his *Un long dimanche de
fiançailles* (1991) is neither a classic nor an experimental *roman policier*; its
"crime" is an army secret buried with soldiers' bodies in a World War I no-
man's-land, and its "detective" a young woman, Mathilde Donnay, who loved
one of the disappeared men. Yet this popular novel, adapted into an Oscar-
nominated movie in 2004, is more than just a romantic testament to stubborn
young love. Through the spatial logics of its underground crypts and war-torn
fields, Japrisot's novel extends the geological analogy to the realms of
language and psychoanalysis. Using Abraham and Torok's theory of cryptonymy and Derrida's essay "Fors," which introduced their 1976 book
Cryptonymie, Chapter 4 explores *Un long dimanche*'s representation of national topography and the textual recreation of a buried past. Though the
novel's French terrain is crisscrossed aboveground by letters and trains, seekers and hiders, it is below the surface that identities are switched and messages exchanged. These substitutions create a tangled *fil* that Mathilde and
the reader must navigate as detectives, in order to uncover a "cyst" in the
French national body: the encrypted secret of the shameful expulsion of its
own young soldiers.

     The crimes of war are similarly inscribed in France's terrain and entwined
with personal investigations in the addictive novels of Fred Vargas. Herself a
trained archeologist, Vargas inserts the spatial logic of phantomatic *revenance*
into her gripping tales featuring police commissioner Adamsberg and the three
historians known as *les Evangélistes*. In *Debout les morts* (1995), the Evangelists
inhabit a "baraque pourrie" [rotten shack] whose three crumbling stories are

described in explicitly geological terms: as stratigraphic layers corresponding to the historians' specializations in, first, the prehistoric age, then the medieval period, and finally the Great War of the early twentieth century. Vargas (whose brother is a World War I historian) uses her crime novels to explore the archive fever that compels scholars, detectives, and readers of the *policier* to dig into the past for its gruesome and troubling traces. Her "polarchéologies" (the term was coined by Anne de Leseleuc, also a contemporary crime novelist with archeological training)[29] take us into the cryptic terrain of cemeteries (*Un lieu incertain*, 2008), folk legends (*L'Homme à l'envers*, 1999), and ghosts (*Pars vite et reviens tard*, 2001). Unlike Georges Simenon, in whose straightforwardly rationalist novels a ghost can only appear as a meaningless figure of speech,[30] Vargas harnesses the phantom's full psychoanalytic and historical powers: "on se raconte une histoire pour purger l'inconscient collectif" [We tell ourselves stories to purge the collective unconscious], says Vargas,[31] and her *Dans les bois éternels* (2006) incorporates a particularly chilling version of Abraham and Torok's "transgenerational phantom."

Modern archeological crime fictions like those by Daeninckx, Japrisot, and Vargas are themselves "haunted" by their generic past. Starting with Gaboriau's reference to Poe's Dupin, the *roman policier* has always revealed a self-consciousness about its indebtedness to previous generations. In the 1960s, Léo Malet described his novelistic investment in a Paris lost to earlier years and in a genre that tries to recover that past: "Ça crevait les yeux . . . en même temps que le cœur: j'ai écrit des romans 'archéologiques'" [It was heartbreakingly obvious: I wrote "archeological" novels].[32] Rather than see the geological catacomb fictions of the Second Empire (Chapter 2) and the paleontological crime stories of the fin-de-siècle (Chapter 3) as cut off from their modern-day descendants by an obsolete scientism, I see them as sedimentary deposits whose *topoi* and themes will continue to irrupt into the genre's surface, even as it moves into new conceptual and geographical territories. The symptoms go beyond today's Série noire winks and nods to popular texts of an earlier era, as when the young heroine of Maurice Dantec's cyberthriller *La Sirène rouge* (1993) reveals her interest in archaeology by reading J.-H. de Rosny's 1909 paleolithic era prehistoric novel *La Guerre du feu*, or when Pierre Bourgeade gives us an absurd update of Poe's orangutan through the public combat of chromosomically near-human apes in *En avant les singes* (2001). The spatiocryptographies of Sébastien Japrisot and the geophantomatics of Vargas reformulate an archaic territorial logic of the criminal underground, moving the genre from the scientific paradigms of geology and paleontology to the wider psychological and political symbolics of archeological inquiry.

II. Street Names: Urban Toponymics and History's Return

The first thing a reader of Poe's 1841 tale learns about the crime is its location: "The Murders in the Rue Morgue." The story's title reappears slightly modified in the *Gazette des Tribunaux*'s report, read by Dupin and his associate, as "The Tragedy in the Rue Morgue" (a "most extraordinary and frightful affair") (247). Both versions put Poe's readers smack-dab in the sensationalist atmosphere of the French popular press, with its *canards*, criminal *faits divers*, and gruesome *"affaires,"* often themselves identified by the Paris street at which an attack has taken place. One of the best known of these was "L'Affaire de la rue du Temple," the murder of a merchant-woman first reported by the daily newspaper *La Presse* on June 8, 1838, in an account that emphasized the shocking encroachment of violence into a middle-class domestic space. Among the readers of the *Presse* account was Eugène Sue, who transposed details from the trial of "L'Affaire de la rue du Temple" into *Les Mystères de Paris* (1842–43); later, Constant Guéroult (in 1880) and Pierre Bouchardon (in 1929) updated the Affaire in their own semifictionalized accounts. By the latter half of the nineteenth century, identifying criminal cases by street address had become a journalistic go-to in both factual and fictional narratives.

Chapter 5 identifies a chain of French "street-name mysteries," from the popular serials of the late nineteenth century, such as René de Pont-Jest's *Le numero 13 de la rue Marlot* (1877) and Georges Grison's *13, rue des Chantres (Au 2me étage)* (1885) through Léo Malet's World War II classic *120, rue de la Gare* (1943) to twenty-first-century versions of the localizing device [Vladan Radoman's *6, rue Bonaparte* (2000), Didier Daeninckx's *12, rue Meckert* (2001)]. In their specificity, the street addresses of these titles act as realist anchors in contemporary maps, while self-consciously situating the latter-day novels in a generic tradition begun by Poe with the *Rue Morgue*. As J. Hillis Miller has argued, topographical considerations are inseparable from toponymical ones;[33] in crime fiction, moreover, place names—and their politically motivated shifts—can provide the key to a murder's mystery. From Pont-Jest to Radoman, plots and narration crucially converge on altered street-names: obsolete maps lead characters astray, neighborhood residents cling to outdated addresses, narrators reflect on the politics of urban nomenclature. In these texts, the spatial or cartographic trope of street-names leads consistently to a temporal logic: a double looking-back by modern crime fictions at (1) their generic origin; and (2) the historical past that marks and continues to disrupt the surface of their urban locations. By signaling, discreetly, a political unconscious, street toponymics represent an intersection between the crime novel's own vertical and horizontal axes, with the layers of national history implicitly inscribed in the current maps of the city. The street address also functions in these novels as a pivot between public and private space, between revolutionary fervor *dans la rue* and domestic violence inside the *salons* and *boudoirs* of the French apartment house.[34]

If throughout the last century and a half, street-name mysteries have used urban toponymic change to reflect on the tension in crime fiction between public and private spheres of violence, it is also true that they have done so with shifting emphases. Chapter 5 begins by analyzing late nineteenth-century crime *feuilletons* in which street names signal a repression—and eventual return—of the revolutionary political context from the domestic sphere of crime fiction. The preponderance of liminal domestic spaces in the era's crime illustrations—scenes in *Le Journal illustré*, for example, of open doors to apartments with gawkers peering in at a murdered corpse—testify to the staying power of class anxieties related to pre-Haussmann urban architecture. Though those scenes seem to offer a view into private, domestic space, they end up textually linked (despite authorial disavowals) to the politicized national violence of the city street.

As Paul Virilio has argued, *la rue* emerged in post-revolutionary France as the primary site of articulation for State power and the restive populace; but by the twentieth century, the generalized militarization of space had taken away the street's iconic symbolic status.[35] So where does that leave the "street-name mystery"? In its second section, Chapter 5 proposes that Léo Malet's *120, rue de la Gare* reconnected the personal and political by anchoring private crime in the context of World War II through the cartographic slippages of Occupied urban space. When it appeared in 1943, Malet's novel revived the popular crime genre by importing *noir* atmospherics from America into the French terrain. Claire Gorrara writes that *120, rue de la Gare* combined plots and themes from Dashiel Hammett's *The Maltese Falcon* (1929) with "a rich network of French intertextual allusions to provide an implicit social critique of German occupation" during a key "period of crisis in French national identity" (*The Roman noir*, 22). My study of street toponymics in Malet's novel shows how it exposes the deep connection between urban nomenclature and ideological power; by exposing the disruptive role of history in the crime novel's cartographic space, *120, rue de la Gare* prepares the terrain for today's more directly *engagé* novels, which explicitly link crime to national political history.

The final section of Chapter 5 focuses on two twenty-first-century "street-name mysteries"—Vladan Radoman's *6, rue Bonaparte* (2000) and Didier Daeninckx's *12, rue Meckert* (2001)—that revive, with self-conscious irony, the emblematic myths of Napoleonic France. By allowing the jagged time of violent history to puncture the detective's urban labyrinth, these novels connect crime to the Lefebvrian political space of uneven development that Kristin Ross identified as key to postmodernity in her well-known essay "Watching the Detectives."[36] In this way, they also lead us to explore the symbolic schisms of "vertical" investigation of the past in relation to crime fiction's ideological investment in cartographic regimes.

III. Cartography and the (Ir)Rationality of Crime

In "The Murders in the Rue Morgue," Dupin's fearless night walks and the narrator's naming of Paris streets testify to a cartographic impulse of mastery, through knowledge, of urban space. This is the detective genre's Cartesian urge, its "transcendental topology."[37] But as we have seen, Poe's story inhabits a rather more slippery terrain, between its prefatory ode to the powers of the analytical mind and its final identification of exotic animal brutality in the heart of the modern city. Abstract, cartographic mastery turns out to be a ruse—and indeed, Jacques Derrida calls the story's first pages a "feint," "a false short treatise on analysis" (199).[38]

When I began work on this book, I gave it the provisional title *Mapping Murder*. The idea was to reorient interest from the questions "whodunit?" and "why done it?" to "where does crime (fiction) take place?" in order to analyze shifting geographies of the genre of violence in France—from the *arrondissements* of the Second Empire to the *banlieues* of today, and from nineteenth-century Paris/province distinctions to twenty-first-century globalized networks of crime, identity, and information. A library search informed me, however, that *Mapping Murder* had been taken: it is the title of a book (and now a television series) by forensic psychologist David Canter, who has established an international reputation as police consultant on high-profile cases like those of the UK "railway rapist," the Lockerbie bomber, and the D.C. Beltway Sniper.[39] At a cursory glance, Canter's trade book seemed to me irrelevant because of its reductive positivism. My project, after all, is about a complex novelistic imaginary rather than the tracking of actual killers. Of course, the irony in my academic ostrich approach inscribes me in a long-standing tradition of nice ladies who read Christie next to their tea-cozies but abhor true crime. Since one of the goals of my analysis in these chapters is to explore the strategic repressions of violence in the crime genre, from documentary *feuilleton* to puzzle-mystery, I decided to look again at Canter's book about actual acts of violence and their analytical mapping. I am glad I did, for it turns out that *Mapping Murder: The Secrets of Geographical Profiling* usefully raises certain issues that have become central to this study of crime fiction's spatiality: cartography's appeal to objectivity, its necessary distortions, and its relation to temporality.

Canter begins his book by claiming that geographical profiling is the most effective science of criminal prediction because "the most objective and observable aspect of any crime is *where* it happens" (6). He organizes the book's chapters around reproduced maps and diagrams he has drawn to identify where murderers and rapists have struck. Canter self-assuredly asks the reader to trust his ability to dispel anxiety through superior analytical method; his maps, it seems, prove that no criminal act occurs at random. It is hard not to read such an assertion as steeped in naïveté, especially given the distinction Canter sees between his own authoritative, "objective" maps and those made by the criminally insane. In a chapter on the "Mental Maps of Crime," Canter reproduces a map a Malaga rapist has drawn of the southern Spanish coast and tells us that its subjective foreshortening and emphasis on certain sites "reveal something of [the criminal's] mental geography" (132). The move to distinguish his own rational cartographic analysis from that of a warped mind is a classic one, and Canter seems willfully unaware of what spatial theorists and postmodern geographers have been telling us for years: maps always distort.[40] From John Ruskin and Gaston Bachelard to Yi-Fu Tuan and Edward Soja, modern and postmodern theorists of space have punctured the myth of maps as neutral representations of reality; the map is always already a fiction. Canter's blindness to the necessary subjective omissions and choices of his own maps can be justified by his crime fighting goals; less easy to dismiss as innocuous are the narrative cheats he employs in order to claim mastery over the frightening specter of random violence. As much as any detective novelist, Canter presents his investigations a posteriori in this book, writing about crimes that have already been solved (and, for the most part, by far more relevant, sometimes random evidence than his maps).[41] Canter is, after all, a narrator—invested in the fiction of his own analytical mastery but admitting far less self-awareness than Poe, who wrote in a private letter about the deceptive "air of method" in his tales of ratiocination: "In the 'Murders in the Rue Morgue,' for instance, where is the ingenuity of unravelling a web which you yourself (the author) have woven for the express purpose of unravelling?"[42] In the end, Canter's maps partake of Poe's "feint" of rationality; their aim to establish referential authority belongs to a fictional tradition begun in 1869, when Émile Gaboriau included in *Monsieur Lecoq* a printed map of the story's scene of the crime.

Chapter 6 reads Gaboriau's crime scene map as foundational—not only because it has been followed by dozens of such maps in novels from Gaston Leroux's *Le Mystère de la chambre jaune* (1907) to Umberto Eco's *The Name of the Rose* (1980), but because it spatializes the abstraction/materiality split evident in Poe's *Rue Morgue*. Lecoq's map of a seedy cabaret at the edge of Paris functions as both sociological document and metafictional reflection. On the one hand, it establishes the peripheral *terrain vague* as a privileged site for criminal activity and in this sense, is grounded in a particularly French history of urban renewal, criminality, and investigation that moves from Haussmannization to the postmodern space of the *banlieue*.[43] On the other hand, Gaboriau's written text reinscribes the map's space into an epistemological field of hermeneutic interpretation, allowing for an abstracted reading of the detective's (and the detective writer's) work. Functioning both historically and symbolically, Gaboriau's map of the *terrain vague* registers the genre's irresolvable tension between criminal violence and the desire for cartographic, rational, and judicial mastery.

By giving his fictional detective the tools of a mapmaker, Gaboriau taps into what Christian Jacob identifies as the perduring "authoritative, ontological power" of maps (xiii).[44] Tom Conley reminds us that cultural anxieties in the West have been quelled by the act of cartography at least since Renaissance mapmakers converted *terrae incognitae* into scriptic art and Descartes grounded the myth of self-possession in perspectival space.[45] By the end of the nineteenth century in France, the best efforts of urban reformers and the *police scientifique* had failed to rid Paris and the countryside of violent pickpockets, highwaymen, and throat-slashers, so it is not surprising that fictional detectives had recourse to spatial and scientific forms of control.[46] But—as evidenced by the very seriality of the genre—violence always returns. And just as Dupin had to step into the streets to unravel the mystery of the *Rue Morgue*, later fictional detectives must leave their purified spheres of intellection.

Gaston Leroux's early twentieth-century detective Rouletabille represents the height of this pull between the ideology of Rationalism and the ragged realities of space, time, and crime. Especially in *Le Mystère de la chambre jaune*, Rouletabille sets himself up as a rational abstractor, drawing "les bosses de la raison" around a mental model of mystery in order to solve it. But, as David Platten and Jacques Dubois have noted, Rouletabille's actual practice represents a deviation from the ideal "science of deduction."[47] Platten cites narrative trickery in the novel as undercutting Rouletabille's confidence in Cartesian reason, while Dubois notes a number of cheats or "ruses" used to shore up the myth of detective as genius-analyst; these include the betrayal of Poe's locked room "archetype" (159). Dubois puts the gap into spatial terms, calling Rouletabille's fictional world a "utopia," in which the detective inhabits a sort of textual no-man's land between mental adventure and physical, social adventure.

But neither Platten nor Dubois mentions the actual maps that are reproduced in Leroux's novels, maps that by their very nature mimic and make visible the central spatial conflicts in these texts. Maps are at once abstract and material, discursive and presentational, sovereign and suborned, totalizing and contingent, objective and subjective, neutral and oriented, coded and deviant, utopic and situated, imaginary and real.[48] Plenty of fictional genres other than the *roman policier* have used maps, of course—think for example of Tolkien's fantasy Middle Earth and Faulkner's Yoknapatawtha County.[49] But crime fiction maps cannot help but register the anxieties of violence even while allowing fictional investigators the appeal to Cartesian mastery. When the conventionality of mapmaking is joined to one of the most conventionalized of literary genres, spatial and textual reference collide over the common aim to make sense of disorder.

In their 2010 book *The Culture of Diagram*, Michael Marrinan and John Bender propose the notion of "diagram" as both process and object in the world, a conceptual mode that has less to do with inert pictorial representations and more in common with atlases, which Lorraine Daston and Peter Galison suggest should "be seen as a hybrid of the idealizing and naturalizing modes."[50] The echoes between this description and the crime novel genre should by now be obvious; but Marrinan and Bender's concept of the "diagram" is even more useful in its specifics, for it carries within its definition three elements that are also central to the fictional crime scene map in the French tradition: *métier*, mathematics, and multivalence. The stories of Lecoq and Rouletabille are *Bildungsromane*—and their cartographic activities are in-

separable from the development of their professional *métiers*. The appeal to
mathematics is a constant throughout the genre (and, as we have seen, in its
criticism as well). And the claims of Cartesian mastery always get constellated
through narrative practice, in the maps and the texts; these investigations are
never really unipositional nor can the detectives avoid getting down and dirty,
as did Dupin in *Rue Morgue*.

As fictional mapmakers in the nineteenth and early twentieth centuries,
Lecoq and Rouletabille can be seen to shuttle between the two spatial modes
Derek Gregory describes in *Geographical Imaginations*: (1) "geography and the
world-as-exhibition": the impulse to render visual a specifically modern
constellation of power, knowledge, and spatiality; and (2) "cartographic anxiety," the questioning or critique of the hierarchical rationalist and nationalist
premises of that impulse.[51] One of the aims of the chapters in Part III is to
show that the French *roman policier* tradition constitutes a particularly powerful
articulation of that rationalist/nationalist pairing—this is, after all, the land
of Descartes, but one whose anxieties about violence correlate deeply to fears
of broken state boundaries, especially as the nation enters the twentieth century.

Thus Leroux's 1909 *Le Parfum de la dame en noir* moves beyond the domestic locked room and estate layout diagrams of *Le Mystère de la chambre
jaune*, to bring in the historical and political dimensions of national identity.
In its final section, Chapter 6 explores the diachronic violence that marks
Leroux's printed maps of the Château Hercule and of the southern coast of
France and Italy, with its blurred frontier lines. Chapter 7 then extends the
transnational dimension by analyzing two mid-twentieth-century novels
whose cartographic spaces seem well-bounded but that signal instead a troubling openness: the printed maps of the Paris arrondissements featured in Léo
Malet's *Nouveaux mystères de Paris* (1954–59) explode the locked room motif
outward, into a paradoxical "open closure" both formal and political; and the
map of an English town in Michel Butor's experimental *L'Emploi du temps*
(1956) unsettles the notions of center and periphery, border and boundary that
anchor the nationalist ideology of the locked room mystery.

Malet's importation of the American *noir* tradition revived the international triangle of the genre's roots, while his proto-Oulipian experimentation
and surrealist political engagements led to his use of the crime map less as an
index of verisimilitude than as a self-aware formal constraint. Chapter 7 connects the "open closure" of Malet's maps in *Les Nouveaux mystères de Paris* to
the anarchic spatiality of the collection's first story, "Le soleil naît derrière le
Louvre." If in Marshall Berman's 1940s New York "all that is solid melts into

air," Malet's mid-century Paris suffers an even more violent form of spatial entropy, similarly spurred by modernization.[52] Malet's descriptions of the Louvre *quartier* allegorize a shift from stable urban consolidation to an age of global expansion: while the Louvre, the Bibliothèque Nationale de France, the Bourse, and the coin and medal shops of the area traditionally conserve cultural and monetary capital, their disruption by criminal displacements (art theft and global trafficking) opens the city up to the emergent spatiality of postmodern *réseaux*. Malet's text thus serves as a precursor to the *noir* anarchy of 1990's authors like Daniel Pennac, who fills his popular Malaussène Saga with melees and mayhem, or Jean-Claude Izzo, whose Marseille Trilogy set the "total chaos" of the criminal underworld in the Mediterranean harbor city, whose deep regionalism fundamentally intersects with the global network.[53]

Michel Butor's *nouveau roman policier* would seem at a far remove from the sociological crime fiction that runs from Malet to Izzo, but for all of its formalism and self-referentiality, *L'Emploi du temps* also reflects on the racial, national, and class divisions that lead to violence in urban spaces. Its map of Bleston continues the *terrain vague* topos Gaboriau inaugurated, identifying an uneasy zone threatened (from within and without) by the unassimilable bodies of vagrants, travelers, and immigrants. More than Robbe-Grillet (whose *Le Voyeur* and *Les Gommes* also played with detective fiction conventions), Butor sets the stage for today's *banlieue* films and fictions, which explore the stereotype of immigrant youth as threat to both urban order and the national fabric of France. *L'Emploi du temps* also explores and explodes the realist spatiotemporality of the *roman policier* through its aporetic narrative chronology and visual cartography. On its two-dimensional map of Bleston, we find "Geology Street," a reminder of the telluric geohistorical forces that have shaped the crime fiction genre from its very beginnings. Indeed, even the most abstract "cartographic crime fictions" have their spatial logics punctured by history and the traces of a national past.

*   *   *

In order to elucidate two dominant spatial strands in the development of popular French crime fiction, the chapters in this book have been divided into parts corresponding to vertical (archeohistorical) and horizontal (cartological) axes; yet, as I have hoped to indicate in this chapter, close textual analysis reveals that each novel inhabits, in different ways, the chronotopic intersections of criminal violence. When, as in Chapters 6 through 8, crime-map fictions call on cartographic authority, it is as much a "feint" as Poe's appeal to pure rationality at the start of the *Rue Morgue*. But as the twentieth century progressed and the conventions of both mapmaking and novel-writing exposed their ideological underpinnings, that authorial feint became increasingly self-aware. Classical cartography implies (1) the suppression of subjectivity: "La géographie scientifique et surtout la cartographie moderne peuvent être considérées comme une sorte d'oblitération, de censure que l'objectivité a imposées à l'imaginaire" [Scientific geography and, especially, modern cartography can be considered as a sort of obliteration, a censure imposed on the imaginary by objectivity] (Roland Barthes); and (2) a totalizing, antihistorical spatiality: "La carte, scène totalisante où des éléments d'origine disparate sont rassemblés pour former le tableau d'un 'état' du savoir géographique, rejette dans son avant ou son après, comme dans les coulisses, les opérations dont elle est l'effet ou la possibilité" [The map, a totalizing stage on which elements of diverse origin are brought together to form the tableau of a 'state' of geographical knowledge, pushes away into its prehistory or into its posterity, as if into the wings, the operations of which it is the result or the necessary condition] (Michel de Certeau).[54] Such insights informed the experimental fictions of authors like Georges Perec, whose 1974 *Espèces d'espaces* implicitly (and somewhat playfully) exposes the ways the realities of global power expansion are obfuscated by the arbitrariness and topological abstraction of world maps.[55] This rationalized abstraction is undermined—or "punctured"—in the crime novels of Malet and Butor (Chapter 7) and Dantec and Radoman (Chapter 8) by the violent histories inscribed in urban and national spaces. By playing with the rational detective's desire (present already in *Monsieur Lecoq*) to circumscribe crime through mapping, these "cartographic crime fictions" should perhaps be understood, rather, as anti-cartographic, as they remind us fundamentally of what Edward Casey has called the "commixture of the placial and the historical," the inevitable disruption of rationalized geographical synchrony by the vagaries of time.[56]

While tracing the different strands of the French crime genre over the last century and a half—*roman policier, crime-feuilleton, roman noir, polar*—in relation to the spatial logics of geology and cartography, I have tried to keep in mind that these are scientific modes of thought which themselves have shifting histories and which are never fully disarticulated from one another. The final chapter of Part I, on the archeological fictions of Japrisot and Vargas, can be seen to explore twentieth-century updates of a geological imaginary.

And the final chapter of Part III, on the schizocartographies of Dantec and Radoman, goes even farther: it reads texts that break free of the vertical/ horizontal paradigm, entering into a multidimensional spatiality attuned to technological "post-"or "hyper-"modernity. In *The Geography of Identity* (1996), Patricia Yaeger describes a dark, pessimistic turn in the narration of space in the late capitalist moment:

> we must recognize that Foucault and Baudrillard are partially right in their despair; in its copious physicality, ordinary space resists traditional patterns of narrative. Space is a fragmentary field of action, a jurisdiction scattered and deranged, which appears to be negotiable or continuous but is actually peppered with chasms of economic and cultural disjunctions.[57]

The politicohistorical "chasms," or crypts, that disrupt the spatial field are made increasingly explicit in twentieth- and twenty-first-century crime fictions, in a way that reconnects the genre's geological imaginary (Part I) to its carto-graphic one (Part III). Narratives of mystery have always been about what is concealed, encrypted, and occulted in rationalized representations. By looking at the shifting ways space and time intersect in the genre, we as readers gain a point of entry into the central tension between the abstract epistemology of de-tection and the political, psychological traumas that pulsate below the surface.

As globalization renders regional and state-centered circumscription less tenable, those traumas take on increasingly transnational contours. This book's final section (Chapter 8) analyzes one chronotope of late twentieth-century crime fiction that captures particularly well the boundary crisis of French na-tional identity in relation to the world: the Serbo-Croatian violence of the 1990s Balkan wars that led to political and cartographic chaos. In Maurice Dantec's bestselling cyberpunk thrillers *La Sirène rouge* (1993) and *Babylon Babies* (1999), Balkanization has forced French nationals into the violent space of "Zéropa-land," a deterritorialized Europe traversed by international data traffickers and schizophrenic mappers on both sides of the criminal/ investigator divide. Serbian-French author Vladan Radoman's 2000 trilogy *Ballade d'un Yougo* (*Bleu Mistral, Orphelin de mer, 6 rue Bonaparte*) extends the Deleuzian themes of schizophrenia and deterritorialization through its apoca-lyptic vision of a psychotic doctor/investigator/assassin in France's Mediter-ranean coast city of Nice. In Dantec's and Radoman's novels, the cartographic motifs of road maps and mappemondes expose the fragmentation of national

identity, the delusions of Empire, and the complete breakdown of any Cartesian mastery that may have guided the classical detective. These explosive crime
novels thus extend the genre's entropic move from *chambre close* in a Paris street
to the technonetwork of postmodern world-space.[58]

For all their schizo-topological newness, however, Dantec's and Radoman's *romans policiers* are still in dialogue with the genre founded by Edgar
Allan Poe in 1841. Winking allusions to nineteenth-century conventions like
the blindfolded ride of a victim through city streets or the inspection of clues
at a murder site keep alive the *neo-noir*'s roots in earlier, earnest tales of deductive mastery. And French national history continues to rear its head, for
example, in the figure of Napoleon, whose multiple identities in Radoman's
text recall the coins, "four Napoleons" scattered on the floor of Poe's *Rue
Morgue* alongside spoons of *métal d'Alger*—as though the French Empire were
always already split and fragmented by its relation to the outside world. From
my book's Prologue, which highlights the global aspects of Poe's "The Murders in the Rue Morgue," to its concluding chapters on the crime genre's explosion beyond the French frontiers, I try to combat the idea of the detective
novel as an insular European phenomenon. Instead, I propose that the very
particularity of France's history links its crime fiction to a global network; in
this way, I hope that my study will complement and contribute to current work
being done on the genre's rise in postcolonial and non-Western contexts, as
well as to spatial and geocritical studies of narrative more generally.[59]

In his recent book, *Énigmes et complots* (2012), sociologist Luc Boltanski
promotes the thesis that the *roman policier* is directly linked to the emergence
of the French nation-state as a European power. To make this claim, he acknowledges Poe as precursor to detective fiction, but de-emphasizes the early
American context in order to focus on the genre's coalescence at the end of
the nineteenth century and into the 1930s within the English and French political regimes of parliamentary democracy.[60] I certainly agree that the French
nation-state has always been and continues to be at stake in its criminal
fictions. But as I hope to have demonstrated, there is no need to set Poe aside
for such a reading, for his short story contains in condensed form all of the
tensions that have shaped this popular genre: private/political, domestic/exotic,
intellectual/visceral, spatial/temporal, abstract/bodily, closed/open, past/
present, and domestic/global. The fertile paternity of the Chevalier C. Auguste
Dupin cannot be cut off from the logics of the rue Morgue.[61]

PART I

ARCHAEOLOGIES

CHAPTER 2

Quarries and Catacombs: Underground Crime in Second Empire *Romans-feuilletons*

Geological imaginations have their histories too.

—Doreen Massey

Unlike New York City, which was built on a uniform geological stratum, and unlike London, which has cut relatively little into its base of sedimentary rock, the city of Paris rests precariously on an extensive subterranean network of vaults and shafts that tunnel through a terrain of stratigraphic complexity.[1] With over 300 kilometers of underground passages, nearly one-tenth of Paris's superficial area lies over empty quarries whose exploitation has exposed the city's geological particularities—and its prehistoric origins. Excavations in the Île de la Cité site began even before Paris was Paris: "Lutetia was one of relatively few Roman cities in northern Gaul in which building could be done in locally quarried stone: the deposits of limestone (for stone) and gypsum (for plaster) within a five-kilometre radius of the Île de la Cité was to provide the raw materials of construction until modern times (the last limestone stone quarry closed in 1939) and over the centuries created vast, cavernous underground complexes."[2] Interest in the "catatmosphère" of Paris's underground spaces continues today, as evidenced by the popularity of sewer and catacomb tourism and other acts of "cataphilie" like secret cinemas and illicit raves.[3]

In the long span of Paris underground history, the nineteenth century stands out as a key moment for its coalescence of modernity and primitivism, urban progress and criminal violence. Framed by the transfer of the Cimetière des Innocents at the end of the eighteenth century and the construction of the Métro at the start of the twentieth, the nineteenth century gave subterranean space a new set of symbolic associations that added class stratification to the mythology of the labyrinth. For David Pike, in his book on underground space in Paris and London, "It all began with the nineteenth century."[4] Though underground catacombs and mines had certainly existed since the twenty-sixth-century B.C.E., "it was only with the development of the nineteenth-century city, with its complex drainage systems, underground railways, utility tunnels, and storage vaults, that the urban landscape superseded the countryside of caverns and mines as the primary location of actual subterranean spaces. This convergence gave rise to a new way of experiencing and conceptualizing the city as a vertical space that is still with us today" (Pike, 1).

The above- and below-ground verticality of nineteenth-century Paris is not merely a question of abstract geometry; underground excavation created an archaeological imaginary that can be seen in conflictual counterpoise with what historian Colin Jones calls the city's "Haussmannian horizontality."[5] Napoleon III's civil engineer conceived his vast urban renewal project as forward-thinking, resolutely modernizing—so that when reminders and remainders of the city's Roman and medieval past emerged from city digs, they "tended only to survive if they could be remoulded so as to play a part in the Haussmannian cityscape, their historic aspect largely subsumed under the functionalist, a-historic trappings of the city of modernity" (Jones, "Vacquer," 166). Thus Second Empire ideology relegates the stratigraphic underground to the role of ugly necessity, hidden below the modern city's newly opened horizontal vistas, its broad boulevards and level topography.

And yet, there is a paradox here. For it was this very project of urban renewal that revealed, through construction digs, the city's ancient substratum— and that led, along with the nineteenth-century emergence of the paleontological sciences, to the discovery not only of Paris's classical past, but of its radically prehistoric past.[6] If reminders of Roman decadence and medieval chaos interfered with the progressivist rectilinearity of Haussmannian thought, imagine how much more troubling was the evidence of radical primitivism— bones from millennia past—buried in the very spaces of civilized humanity. Despite ideological repression, those bones jut out, forcing an irruption of the deep past into sites of high modernity. And they make a mark, a violent mark, on the popular texts of the time.

By studying the corpus of "catacomb crime fictions" that flourished during the French Second Empire in the context of geological and paleontological science, we can rethink the ways in which political history has imprinted itself on the underground imaginary. How, specifically, did the radical notion of "deep time" affect modern conceptions of human violence? And what implications did those have for nineteenth-century France's understanding of its own turbulent, revolutionary history? Scholars like Claudine Cohen have suggestively linked nineteenth-century Cuvierian geology to the "catastrophist imagination" of Romanticism, with its interest in archeological ruins and crumbling worlds (*Fate of the Mammoth*, 114–18). Cohen cites Chateaubriand, Balzac, Musset, and Michelet, as well as English horror novelists of the Victorian period. But there is another generic strand—the popular crime *feuilleton*—that registers, with a difference, the geological imagination of France in the Age of Cuvier. If "high" Romanticism's archeological meditations focus on fragility and the inevitable passing of time (Blix) or on a soothing and serene temporality (Shortland), the "low" crime fictions of popular French journals combine Cuvierian catastrophism with emerging notions of human prehistory to imprint a jagged and violent temporality onto the rocks under modern Paris.[7]

Prehistoric Paris

In 1881, when diggers restoring the Hôtel des Postes unearthed prehistoric mammal bones in the rocky soil of Paris, paleontologist Albert Gaudry reported that it was not the first time underground excavation had revealed the modern city's animal prehistory. Gaudry notes that the teeth of ice-age mammoths had been uncovered in the excavations dug for construction at various Paris locations: the Salpêtrière, the Necker hospital, the sand pits of the rue du Chevaleret, and the rue de Grenelle, where were also found "des débris de rhinocéros, d'hippopotames, de *bos primigenius*."[8] The "bos" is an auroch or ancient ox, and Gaudry's use of its Latin name clinches his scientific authority while reinforcing for lay readers the exoticism of such animals, their distance from our modern world. They disappeared, after all, 15,000 years ago. But that temporal distance seems to be erased by the dig's exposure of spatial coexistence, as Gaudry playfully concludes his report with this remarkable phrase: "le mammouth s'est promené rue Pagevin" [The mammoth strolled about on the rue Pagevin].

The anachronism evokes a comical image of an ancient woolly beast plunked down in the middle of a city street. But this is not just any street. La rue Pagevin, built in the late eighteenth century near Saint-Eustache, carried its own social and literary associations in the nineteenth century.[9] In Balzac's *Ferragus* (1833) this small street near Les Halles has walls strewn with graffiti and reeks of crime and insecurity, while in Hugo's *Histoire d'un crime* (1852) it is the site of a bloody barricade during Napoleon's coup d'état. So Gaudry has chosen for his mammoth a modern street rife with crime, a violence less than civilized. He thus makes a subtle link between the geological space of underground Paris and the above-ground lawlessness that threatens its modern order. According, then, to this logic made possible by popularized paleontology, nineteenth-century victims of urban violence may well be suffering the consequences of treading on ground embedded with the bones of a violent past. Bones upon bones. It is an ill-defined relation: localized curse? atavistic regress? In either case, this notional continuity of criminal brutality across centuries relies on a spatial identity revealed by a new forensic science of the earth.

"[P]aleontological theories are narratives, scenarios, speculative hypotheses."[10] And among the central hypotheses debated in mid- to late nineteenth-century paleontological discourse is the very idea that the prehistoric world was violent.[11] We all recognize the cliché: before the dawn of civilization, fur-clad men stomped into cave-dwellings, clubbed one another on the head, and left with women draped over their shoulders. But before this cartoon image of caveman brutality became embedded in our popular consciousness, it was put forth as a serious scientific assumption based on the archaeological discoveries of the Second Empire. European digs of the 1860s uncovered human bones mixed with flint weapons and animal remains; their coexistence pointed to a hunter society, while the isolation and low population of caves implied noncommunal living.

The resulting stereotype of prehistoric life as nasty, brutish, and short was spread by popular texts combining science and fiction to depict daily dramas among the cave set. The earliest of these prehistoric fictions include Pierre Boitard's 1861 *Études antédiluviennes: Paris avant les hommes* and Samuel Berthoud's 1865 "Les Premiers habitants de Paris," in *L'Homme depuis cinq mille ans*. Both titles testify to the compelling interest of Paris—the metropolitan locus of bustling modernity—as a layered space whose disinterred bones reveal a past marked by violent brutality, whether animal or human. Camille Flammarion's *Le Monde avant la création de l'homme: Origines de la terre, orig-*

ines de la vie, origines de l'humanité came out in 1886, after Louis Figuier's *La Terre avant le Déluge* (1862) and *L'Homme primitif* (originally published in 1870, reprinted in 1873 and 1882).[12] The popularity of *L'Homme primitif* was doubtless due in part to its extensive set of illustrations that show rock-wielding cavemen attacking trumpeting mammoths, while hunters strew bones across muddy cave floors. Certainly, Figuier's book contributed greatly to the notion that the prehistoric Parisian was not a gentle sort.

In fact, *L'Homme primitif*'s scientific hypotheses of caveman brutality directly inspired the blood-filled plots of Elie Berthet's *Paris avant l'histoire*, a novel from 1884 that I propose to analyze here as an important intertext for the nineteenth century's popular stories of crime in the urban catacombs. Cave fictions are not crime fictions, for the notion of crime is contingent on civilization's laws. But Berthet's œuvre, which includes both *Paris avant l'histoire* and *Les Catacombes de Paris* (1854), suggests a continuity in the French imagination between the primitive and the modern dwellers of underground spaces. The continuity, of course, is that of violence, so that it becomes possible to ask—as did Tarde, Freud, and others—whether the modern criminal is an atavistic holdover of prehistoric man. Undoubtedly, as this chapter will demonstrate, popular fictions of the Second Empire and Belle Époque described criminal characteristics in terms of the caveman stereotype. But perhaps more interesting than physiognomy or criminal psychology, both of which have been extensively explored in recent research, is the spatial connection made possible by the new science of paleontological geology. In *Paris avant l'histoire*, Berthet reflects his contemporaries' excitement about the discovery of prehistoric human existence. Even more titillating was the idea that the caveman lived in what is now Paris. Not merely removed to rural or coastal areas still associated with primitivism, prehistoric people and animals inhabited what had become by Berthet's time the ultimate urban space of modernity. Think again of Gaudry's exclamation: "le mammouth s'est promené rue Pagevin!"

Berthet: *Paris avant l'histoire*

Elie Berthet's 1884 *Paris avant l'histoire* (first published in 1876 as *Romans préhistoriques: le monde inconnu*) is an account of prehistoric humanity dedicated to Gabriel de Mortillet, "professeur d'anthropologie préhistorique." The text includes illustrations of real fossil artifacts on display at the Musée St. Germain and cites scientific sources including authorities like Henri Sébastien

Le Hon (*L'Homme fossile*, 1867), Gabriel de Mortillet (*L'Anthropopithèque*, 1869), and Louis Figuier (*L'Homme primitif*, 1870).[13] But Berthet's is an avowed work of fiction, whose particular tropes and obsessions (rape, triangulated desire, physiognomies of good and evil) reflect the ideologies of popular crime fiction in the French fin de siècle.

In *Paris avant l'histoire*, the brutality—even, perhaps, the criminality—of primitive man is linked specifically to his subterranean dwellings. Indeed, out of Berthet's four-part "novel of past epochs" (5), only the second part, entitled "Parisians in the Stone Age" characterizes prehistoric men as both cave-dwelling and unredeemably violent, "livrés aux passions les plus féroces, aux instincts les plus brutaux" [driven by the most ferocious passions, the most brutal instincts] (6). These club-wielding inhabitants of natural grottoes are to be distinguished from an earlier and far more peaceful incarnation, the "sylvan man" of the tertiary geological period.

In Part I, "Un rêve: L'homme tertiaire, l'homme sylvain," Berthet describes the dream vision accorded to him by a female fairy guide to an epoch preceding modern times by two hundred forty thousand years.[14] The sprite allows the narrator to behold a sort of *tableau vivant*, in which monkey-like humans scramble up trees to their nest dwellings above. Described as peaceful beings, these arboreal primitives are herbivorous and physiognomically marked as gentle: "l'œil, come il convient à un frugivore, ne manquait pas de douceur, et son expression paraissait plus sauvage que cruelle" [its eye, as befits a frugivore, was mild, and its expression seemed more wild than cruel] (13–14). Though they squabble occasionally over (vegetarian) food, the "sylvan men" are not shown to engage in any violent acts against nature or one another; indeed, the narrator witnesses no drama other than a mother's attempts to calm her baby by cradling and feeding him. This is a far cry from what he will "observe" in Part II, the fictionalized account of "Stone Age Parisians."

Moving from an unspecified and dreamy landscape to the precise location of the caves of Montmartre, Berthet shifts also from peace to brutality. It is almost as though "The Parisians of the Stone Age" partake already of the future modern city's turbulence; or, inversely, that the very foundation rocks of Paris imbue their inhabitants with the thirst for blood. For one thing, the landscapes described in Parts I and II exist in sharp contrast: while sylvan man lived near a freshwater lake whose azure waters peacefully reflect the sky and gently cradle the sweet-smelling pink pads of an ancient lily (9), the "Parisian" of the Quaternary Age abuts a violent version of the future city's river:

La Seine . . . ne ressemblait pas alors à ce fleuve paisible, civilisé, comme endormi, qui . . . coule maintenant sous de magnifiques ponts. Elle était errante et vagabonde entre les falaises . . . et son lit se déplaçait fréquemment. Elle avait l'ampleur, la fougue, et l'impétuosité des grands fleuves de l'Amérique.

[The Seine did not then resemble this river so peaceful and civilized, as though it were asleep, that runs today beneath magnificent bridges. It meandered restlessly between the cliffs, and its bed frequently shifted. It had the scale, the fiery spirit, the impetuosity of America's great rivers.] (30)

The prehistoric Seine's muddy and turbulent waters course with the blood of ferocious rhinos and hippos. And amid all this animal carnage, asks the narrator rhetorically: where is humankind? "Dans la caverne," comes the answer.

The underground grotto, described as strewn about with foul-smelling bones and filled with the smoky stench of grilled animal flesh, embodies the pre-Parisian's brutal character: "Le logis paraissait tout à fait digne de ses grossiers habitants. La grotte était raboteuse, irrégulière, et la faible lumière venant du dehors ne pouvait l'éclairer jusqu'au fond" [The dwelling looked worthy of its crude inhabitants. The cave was rough, irregular, and the feeble light coming in from outside was unable to reach its back walls] (40). You are what you eat, perhaps, but you are also where you live. Part I's idyllic maternal scene is here replaced by a particularly brutal version of domestic invasion: in a section called "Le Rapt," a visiting hunter named "Roux" enters the protagonist family's cave, shares a meal with them, and grunts with sated appetite before indicating interest in the adolescent daughter "Daine." When Roux learns that Daine has been promised to another man ("Blond"), the red-haired hunter clubs her father to death, beats her mother to a bloody pulp, and carries off the girl to rape her in the wild.

A number of elements of this violent scene echo nineteenth-century crime serial conventions. One is the idea of an invasion from the outside of an enclosed domestic space. The cavern is meant to protect its inhabitants from wild animals, but human trust allows murder to occur in the very space of family comfort. A second is the description of that post-violence space as a "crime scene," à la detective novel: when Blond arrives to visit his betrothed, he sees the traces of the violent attack (the father's cadaver, the mother's bloodied head, the younger children caterwauling with hunger) and—like a future investigator—he tracks Roux's footprints to save the girl and wreak his revenge. Third, naming the killer-rapist Roux and his noble enemy Blond reinforces, while backdating, nineteenth-century stereotypes of race and criminality.[15]

What I find particularly interesting about Berthet's fictionalized account of the prehistoric era is the fascination with primitive brutality as inhabiting the very space that will become modern Paris, with all *its* contradictorily barbarous civilization. At one point in the narration of Blond's observation of rhinoceroses fighting amid the trumpeting of woolly mammoths, Berthet pauses to exclaim, "And all this not far from the square where the Pont Neuf is located today!" (69). He later devotes a long footnote to Albert Gaudry's 1881 *Compte rendu de l'Académie des sciences* (*Constitutionnel* du 28 juin), cited earlier. Here is the longer description of the discovery of prehistoric animal bones in the very center of Paris, excavated during the reconstruction of l'Hôtel des Postes:

> Au surplus, ce n'est pas la première fois que l'on trouve des débris du mammouth sur le sol parisien. On a déjà rencontré ses restes sur plusieurs points de la grande ville, sans parler de la banlieue. C'est ainsi qu'on a recueilli des dents de mammouth dans les fouilles faites pour des constructions, à la Salpêtrière, à l'hôpital Necker, dans les sablières de la rue du Chevaleret, dans celle de Grenelle, où l'on a rencontré en même temps des débris de rhinocéros, d'hippopotames, de *bos primigenius*. Récemment encore, on a fait la même trouvaille rue Lafayette et rue Doudeauville, au coin du boulevard Ornano.

> [And besides, it is not the first time that mammoth fragments have been found on Parisian soil. They had already appeared in many areas of the city, not to mention its suburbs. This is how were recovered mammoth teeth in the excavations dug for construction, at the Salpêtrière, at the Necker hospital, in the sand pits of the rue du Chevaleret, in the one on Grenelle street, where were found at the same time the fragments of rhinoceros, hippopotamus, and *bos primigenius*. Even recently, similar finds have been documented on rue Lafayette and rue Doudeauville, at the corner of the boulevard Ornano.] (82)

Berthet's identification of a network of addresses leaves us with a vision of ancient bones as the extensive substructure to the modern city. It combines, moreover, with the book's image of the primitive Parisian to invoke a vestigial ferocity that somehow connects the city's exposed underground spaces to its above-ground *travaux*. As we shall see, catacombs and quarries became privileged fictional sites of violent crime during the 1860s through the 1880s. This was in part due to their labyrinthine inaccessibility—but also, I propose, because they are the modern "caves," the porous underground spaces destined for brutality and butchered bones.

Berthet's melodramatic *Paris avant l'histoire* contributed to the cultural imaginary of the criminal underground by contrasting the bloodthirstiness of the cave dweller both with the tree-dwellers before him and with the "newer prehistoric" people described in Part III, "La Cité Lacustre." In this section, devoted to the pre-Bronze age of polished stone, Berthet describes the communal living of two tribes, the lake-dwelling Cormorans and the land-hunters, the Castors. These "Gaules" are much closer than cave dwellers to modern Parisians, in both physique ("The young traveler embodied the purest example of the *aryan* or *persian* race, from which our ancestors the Celts seem to be descended," 117) and behavior:

> On touchait . . . à cette période de l'humanité où certains sentiments élevés commençaient à se dégager des instincts grossiers de l'époque primitive. Les hommes étaient mûrs pour la civilisation, qui allait se développer lentement par la découverte et par l'usage des métaux.

> [We were arriving at that period of humanity when certain elevated sentiments were beginning to pull away from the course instincts of the primitive era. Mankind was ripe for civilization, which would slowly develop through the discovery and use of metals.] (188)

No longer motivated by brutal instinct and individual desire, these tribes use (semi-) civilized dialogue to avert violence. At the start, for example, Berthet sets up an apparent recreation of the love triangle drama from Part II, but this time, rather than kill each other, the two robust men discuss their situation long enough to realize that in fact they love two different women, sisters from the Cormoran tribe. A partnership ensues, though soon economic difference will reawaken hostility: one man has acquired bronze weapons and therefore secures his mate, while the land-hunter can only offer meat and fails to win his loved one's hand. The dramas that follow reinforce Berthet's idea of the Bronze Age as the dawn of civilization. When a character covets another's bronze weapons, he does not club the owner to death, as a caveman would have: in one case, he helps the owner in order eventually to inherit the treasure; and in another, he returns to his tribe to organize a modern-style battle, complete with alliances, negotiations, and peace treaties. The private crime of the caveman's "domestic invasion" is thus replaced by tribal warfare—a more communal, organized, and "civilized" form of violence.

The spatiality of this shift in violence is unambiguous. Men living in subterranean caves are hairy and impulsive club-wielding brutes. Men who live outdoors—whether in trees, as in the pre-Quaternary age, or in huts, like the lake- and land-dwellers of the nascent Bronze Age—are either instinctively peaceful or have managed to use collaboration and dialogue to avoid the most direct forms of violence. At the dawn of the civilized era, writes Berthet, people no longer use the "cavité souterraine" for living (149); this space is judged suitable now only for burying the dead. Thus, we have an early version of Berthet's nineteenth-century Paris, in which civilized humans live in aboveground buildings while tombs and catacombs are reserved for cadavers. But what happens when the order is disrupted by the intrusion of cave-dwellers into the subterranean space of the modern city? The catastrophic answer appears in Berthet's *Les Catacombes de Paris*, which, although written earlier, is already infused with the associations between primitivism, crime, and subterranean space that he develops with the help of paleontological science in *Paris avant l'histoire*.

Berthet: *Les Catacombes de Paris*

Though first published in 1854, Berthet's popular crime novel *Les Catacombes de Paris* is set in the late eighteenth century, beginning in 1770. In the novel's first lines, Berthet invokes the city's dark criminal history as located at La Place de Grève, "lieu . . . de souvenirs sanglants" [site of bloody memories].[16] In this sinister place, Parisians of all ranks have gathered to watch the execution of a common criminal. Why such avid interest? asks Berthet. After all, the accused is no titillatingly noble poisoner or regicide priest. No, Lubin Pernet is a vulgar thief, a former quarryman who had led a band of robbers in the vast plains of the southern "banlieue," from Vaugirard to the Jardin des Plantes. Pernet

and his band have not actually victimized many Parisians, but their nocturnal actions have succeeded in sparking terror in the people's imagination:

> pas un ivrogne ne se rompait le col dans les excavations dont ces
> plaines étaient semées, pas un soldat querelleur n'était trouvé mort
> dans un fossé, que les habitants du voisinage n'attribuassent ces
> événements aux "voleurs de Montsouris."

> [Not one drunkard had broken his neck in the excavations
> scattered throughout these plains, nor a quarrelsome soldier been
> found dead in a ditch, without the inhabitants of the quarter
> blaming these events on the "thieves of Montsouris."] (T.1, 4)

Apparent accidents take on the tinge of murder by their very locations: *les
excavations, un fossé*—the underground spaces that fill proper Parisians with
unease (even "horreur," 4), while being mastered by Pernet in his experience
as a quarryman. For years, his band of robbers had evaded police detection
by hiding in the vast tunnels and caves of the underground quarries until he
is finally apprehended in la Tombe-Issoire, a place whose name belies its above-
ground location by evoking both the underground space of a tomb and its
associated theme of a haunting past: "Issoire," explains Berthet, was the name
of a famous brigand from the Middle Ages.

The throughout this popular narrative (and indeed, into our century, with
Fred Vargas's "archeological fictions"), catacombs and ghosts will combine in
a constellation of anxiety both Freudian and geological. The past lies underground, until it wells up or erupts into our upper stratum. In Berthet's text,
the Marxist-materialist overtones are evident: once Pernet has lost his income
and social function as a quarryman, he is forced to rob the "classes privilégiées" (3), who then watch his execution from high balconies and rooftops,
after having symbolically re-interred him: in the Chatelet prison, Pernet is kept
in a horrible cell more than thirty feet below the ground (17).

The sordid conditions of Pernet's imprisonment win him a noble defender,
the young and handsome lawyer Philippe de Lussan, whose proto-revolutionary
beliefs establish the tale's political stakes from the beginning. In direct contrast with his chevalier father, de Lussan believes that social ascension should
be assured by talent rather than by royal favor. When the story skips ahead
four years from its Prologue at the Place de Grève to a house in la Rue d'Enfer

in 1774, Philippe de Lussan has been actively pamphleteering against the king (Louis XV), but his rebellion seems at first unconnected to the city's imminent problem: it is crumbling.

In the Luxembourg area, a house had just collapsed with a crash, crushing all of its inhabitants under the weight of its debris (36). This is the fourth such accident to have occurred in just a few months in the same quartier and as crowds come by to look at the ruins and debris, talk turns to the cause. "Certains bourgeois sensés parlaient bien de cavités souterraines, inexplorées jusque-là, qui s'étendaient sous cette portion de Paris et qui, s'ouvrant tout à coup, engloutissaient les édifices dont ils étaient surchargés" [Certain sensible members of the bourgeoisie spoke of the subterranean cavities, until then unexplored, that extended below this portion of Paris and that, opening up all at once, swallowed up the buildings which had overloaded them] (37). This rational explanation jibes with the city's history, as presented for example in Louis Sébastien Mercier's *Tableau de Paris* of the 1780s. In that text, Mercier had warned of the fragility of the city's construction over the "abîmes" of the quarries:

> Il ne faudrait pas un choc bien considérable, pour ramener les pierres au point d'où on les a enlevées avec tant d'effort, huit personnes ensevelies dans un gouffre de cent cinquante pieds de profondeur, et quelques autres accidents moins connus, ont excité enfin la vigilance de la police et du gouvernement.

> [It would not require a very strong shock to return the stones to the space from which one had raised them with such effort; eight men buried in the depths of a hundred-and-fifty-foot hole, and certain other less familiar accidents have finally incited vigilance from the police and the government]. (36)[17]

In terms of actual city catastrophes, fires far outnumbered infrastructural collapse, but Mercier's brief discussion of the underground quarries hints at their phantasmatic power: "Que de matière à réflexions, en considérant cette grande ville formée, soutenue par des moyens absolument contraires! ces tours, ces clochers, ces voûtes des temples, autant de signes qui disent à l'œil: ce que nous voyons en l'air manque sous nos pieds" [What food for thought, as we consider this grand built city, held up by absolutely contrary means! these towers, these steeples, these temple vaults, all signs that say to the eye: what we see in the air is lacking below our feet] (36). The high/low contradiction emerges here as a symbol of humankind's simultaneous elevation and debasement, or more specifically and in Marxist terms, of the modern city's material substratum as the fragile support of the upper classes. In Berthet's text, written with post-revolutionary retrospection, the threat from the underground quarries takes on multiple metaphorical meanings. For in addition to the "bourgeois sensés" who ascribe the rue d'Enfer's house collapse to the simple mechanics of an underground cavity, there are plenty of superstitious and suspicious folk who imagine other hypotheses. Some think there lurks an evil spirit, an anti-Christ, maybe the "devil of Vauvert" who has returned to haunt the city after having been exorcised centuries earlier (37).[18] Others blame Louis XV's corrupt court. In this way, hauntology meets conspiracy in the collective fear of underground urban space.

When Philippe de Lussan questions a waitress about the recent catastrophe, she expounds on Paris's caves and subterranean tunnels as a space of dark mystery:

> on parle surtout de grandes caves qui s'étendent sous ce côté de
> Paris et dans lesquelles jamais chrétien n'a pénétré. Il y a là dedans
> on ne sait qui, on ne sait quoi; mais ça fait toutes sortes de malices,
> ça sort, ça entre, ça effraye les uns et les autres, et finalement ça
> peut bien aussi jeter bas les maisons, je pense.

> [One hears especially of enormous caves that extend beneath this
> side of Paris and into which no Christian has ever penetrated. We
> know not who, we know not what, exists inside; but *it* plays all sorts
> of tricks, it leaves, it returns, it scares this or that person, and in the
> end it might also tear down the houses, I should think.] (T.1, 46)

With this link of the subject pronoun *ça* to an uncanny power, the story veers toward conventions of the fantastic tale (like Maupassant's *Le Horla*) and taps into a nineteenth-century fear of an internally haunting other. The underground literally tugs at the city's surface, as the waitress adds that women hauling up water out of deep wells have felt a mysterious pull on the rope from below; and a priest has told her that provisions are disappearing from the subterranean recesses below the Saint-Sulpice church. But the serving-girl's superstitions are dismissed by Philippe de Lussan, who explains away these uncanny events as the misdeeds of criminals.

The plot of Berthet's text is organized around a number of descents into the quarries (now called Catacombs, adds the narrator—indicating again the temporal lag between the story's setting and its composition). First, Philippe and his dissolute (but loyal) friend Chavigny descend ninety circular steps to explore the caves as a potential safe spot for their pamphleteering against the king. The allegorical possibilities of the underground space are hinted at by its history, ancient and recent: "comme cette pierre, qui s'altère et noircit au grand air, avait conservé là sa teinte primitive, ce souterrain, œuvre des Gaulois ou tout au moins des Parisiens aux premiers temps de la monarchie française, semblait avoir été creusé depuis quelques mois à peine" [Because this rock, which alters and darkens when exposed to air, had conserved its primitive tint, this subterranean tunnel, the work of Gauls or at the very least of Parisians in the first moments of French monarchy, seemed to have been hollowed out only months earlier] (92). What had remained stable from the monarchy's beginnings is now being altered, as a mysterious entity hacks from below at the rocks that built Paris. Indeed, Philippe and Chavigny soon come to understand the physical cause of the above-ground "écroulements": somebody has been sabotaging the underground pillars so that "up above," on the earth's crust, houses, temples, and palaces risk sinking into the abyss (97). Although Philippe likens his own free-thinking press to the noble cause of Christian martyrs who had taken refuge in the "depths of the earth" (95), he is appalled at the possibility of an actual subterranean plot to destroy the city above. Philippe's is a tempered revolt, a critique of the current king's corruption rather than of the entire monarchic system. When his own father, the Chevalier de Lussan, procures for him the king's pardon for the pamphleteering, Philippe is momentarily silenced, while internally judging the libertine lifestyle shared by chevalier and king. He thus becomes complicit with the system and will spend the rest of the narrative working on a doubly heroic mission: to save Paris from its structural threat from below and to save his beloved Thérèse de Villeneuve from the mysterious brute who has abducted her into his subterranean, labyrinthine lair.

Ghost, demon, *genius loci*, specter, monster: the kidnapper's identity remains shrouded in superstition until near the end of the story, when he is revealed to be the pale, red-haired Médard, son of Lubin Pernet, the thief whose execution had begun the novel.[19] Because Philippe had defended Lubin, his son has sworn to protect him; this does not, however, keep him from desiring Philippe's fiancée—and a large part of the story's dénouement relies on the murky question of whether Médard has raped his prisoner Thérèse.

Rape, triangulated desire—these, as we have seen in *Paris avant l'histoire*—
are themes dear to Berthet's *feuilletonesque* heart. And they connect the modern catacomb story to its prehistoric past. Indeed, Lubin, the underground
dweller of bone-filled caverns, is described in terms similar to those that Berthet
will use for the Quaternary caveman: he has a rough beard, coarse red hair,
bare feet, eyes like a cat, and a gloomy den. But there is one difference; this
human artifact of the "age of brutality" is slender and enervated, with a ghostly
pallor that testifies literally to his life in the sun-free catacombs and figurally
to his role as a haunt to the aboveground city.

For Médard (*Méd*, medieval + *dard* = an arrow from the past?) represents
a threat to the city far greater than that of the counterfeiters, Freemasons,
Templars, and smugglers who also use the underground space of the former
quarries for their dubious dealings. Indeed, unlike those part-time catacomb
users, the "cave-man" Médard comes to be associated textually with a cataclysmic catastrophe of geological proportions.

Near the end of the story, Philippe and a German associate named Hart-
mann pursue the shadowy Médard through the upper and lower galleries of
the underground labyrinth, trying desperately to track the "demon" to his lair,
where he had sequestered the lovely Thérèse. It is in this climactic chase scene
that the narrator, for the first time, mentions the bones that lie under Paris:

> Et ils s'enfoncèrent dans la galerie. Dès les premiers pas, ils
> s'aperçurent que ce passage n'avait pas été creusé par la main
> des hommes et quil devait être l'ouvrage de quelque torrent
> souterrain. . . . La route était encombrée de grosses pierres arrondies
> par le travail des eaux; la roche, déchirée d'une manière bizarre,
> laissait voir çà et là des débris fossiles, des coquillages et de grands
> ossements d'animaux antédiluviens.

> [They plunged into the gallery. After the first few steps they per-
> ceived that this passage had not been hollowed by the hand of man,
> but must have been the work of some subterranean torrent. . . . The
> path was encumbered by large stones, rounded by the force of the
> waters; the rock walls, strangely torn, revealed traces of fossil
> remains—shells, and large bones of antediluvian animals.] (T.2, 268)

Like Jules Verne, whose *Voyage au centre de la terre* appeared in 1864, Berthet
uses the terminology of the geological sciences, describing a gallery hollowed

out by ancient torrents, formation of stalactites, and infiltration of water through fissures in strata of stone. The violence of ancient torrential streams is emphasized, as "les roches elles-mêmes témoignaient par leur désordre et leurs formes bizarres de la puissance du choc qu'elles avaient dû supporter dans ce *cataclysme* mystérieux" [the rocks themselves testified by their disorder and the strangeness of their forms, to the mightiness of the shock they must have sustained in this mysterious *cataclysm*] (T.2, 270, my emphasis). And it is at this moment that Médard, a modern-day relic of this earthly convulsion, struggles with and violently kills Philippe's German helper.

Berthet's use of the term "cataclysm" can only recall Cuvier's catastrophist theory of the earth's transformation over centuries, which he based on fossil evidence of violent water-floods that reordered the geological layers of the Paris Basin. A deluge threatens Berthet's underground characters as well, for right after Médard kills the German, he and Philippe must run from a rumbling flood that leaves the quarry tunnels inundated and the two men knee-deep in water. As Berthet explains in a footnote, the flooding of the quarries in 1744 was no fictional invention, but a documented historical event (T.2, 305).

But Berthet does not merely anchor his dramatic plot in the recent history of the eighteenth-century underground. Rather, his mention of the fossil remains of antediluvian animals directly connects his own Revolutionary century to the "deep time" of geological history. Indeed, we might take Claudine Cohen's description of Cuvier's revolutionary overtones as the basis for our own political reading of Berthet's underground drama. Cohen writes:

> In the "terrible events" of antediluvian epochs [in the 1825 version
> of Cuvier's *Discours préliminaire*, originally published in 1813],
> one can almost hear an echo of the most recent but no less terrible
> revolutionary events that France had recently lived through. The
> reader is warned at the outset that just as today the world in
> which we live "is never disturbed unless by the ravages of war or
> by the oppression of powerful men, . . . nature has had its civil
> wars and the surface of the globe has been upset by successive
> revolutions and various catastrophes." In 1825, in the reign of
> Charles X, recalling the "terrible revolutions" of the past in
> particularly suggestive terms was probably no accident. (*Fate
> of the Mammoth*, 123)

Among the "particularly suggestive" terms that Cohen cites is, of course, "cataclysm," the violent upheaval of earth (and State) that will come to be associated by Berthet with the modern-age caveman Médard.

Médard has planned his own enormous catastrophe, the destruction of above-ground Paris by the sabotage of its underground supports. He shows Philippe the ready-to-crumble spots that he has undermined—under Val-de-Grace, Luxembourg, the Observatoire—and announces a great catastrophe:

> De grands malheurs, . . . une partie de Paris, un monceau de ruines. . . . Les familles écrasées . . . partout des larmes et du sang . . . partout des pleurs et des cris . . . et mon père, qui est mort, serait vengé!

> [Great disasters . . . half Paris a heap of ruins—families crushed to death—everywhere tears of blood—everywhere moans and cries of anguish—and my father, who is dead, would be avenged!] (T.2, 207)

That this vengeance has social overtones beyond the story of a saddened, sick individual is evidenced by Médard's anger at the "fat bourgeois" people who put his father to death and by the narrator's original description of Lubin's execution, with its emphasis on the spatialized hierarchies: "la populace et la petite bourgeoisie" crowd around the scaffold while "les classes privilégiées" watch from their rented balconies and roofs (T.1, 2-3). Coming from underground Paris, the space of geological revolutions, Médard will topple the class system that led to his father's descent from quarry-work to crime and from citizen to scapegoat.

As Rosalind Williams reminds us in *Notes on the Underground*, by the mid-nineteenth century subterranean space carried Marxist overtones of substructure labor and revolutionary potential.[20] Berthet sets his own story of "underground man" on the eve of Revolution, as Louis XVI succeeded his father to the throne. The noble Philippe de Lussan's horror at the decline of the monarchy becomes an important thread in the novel, as he interacts not only with Médard's threat from below but with the part-time inhabitants of the subterranean strata: the smugglers and counterfeiters, briefly, but more important, the Knights Templar and their leader, the Abbé de la Croix. In the narrative logic of *Les Catacombes de Paris*, the eighteenth-century French state has been weakened from above (Philippe's chevalier father as a lazy libertine, the king as ineffectual and corrupt) and below (primitive creatures, secret societies, and quarry-land crime). Things are about to crumble.

One can extend this (geologically) allegorical reading of Berthet's text by contrasting Médard's violent plan to destroy the city with the goals of the Abbé de la Croix, who uses the buried substructure of the ancient Palace of Thermes to hold secret meetings of descendant Knights of the Temple. As the Abbé explains to Philippe, the dissolute monarch signals an imminent end to the very material superstructure of the State:

> Regardez autour de vous; la décomposition envahit l'état social
> . . . . la nation se détourne avec dégoût de ce qu'elle a respecté
> pendant tant de siècles. L'édifice craque de toutes parts; les illusions
> ne sont plus possibles, il va crouler . . .
>
> [Look about you; decomposition is invading the social state . . . the
> nation turns with distaste from that which it has respected for so
> many ages. The whole edifice gives way in all directions; illusions
> vanish, collapse is inevitable]. (T.2, 66)

But his notion of collapse is quite different from Médard's. While the sallow caveman plans a catastrophic "great and awful terror" (in which we hear the overtones of the Revolutionary Terror), the Abbé plans a less cataclysmic transition: the secret illegitimate son of Louis XV will return to claim the throne and restore an enlightened monarchy. And who is this secret son? Why, Philippe de Lussan himself! Our hero listens with horror as the Abbé assures him that the nation is dotted with Freemasons, Rosicrucians, and Templars who will support "the future king." But he is even more horrified by Médard's planned catastrophe, which directly threatens the lives of his beloved Thérèse as well as half the Paris population.

Through this contrast of two revolutionary possibilities, I would argue, Berthet transposes onto eighteenth-century politics the mid-nineteenth century's scientific debate between Cuvierian catastrophism and Lamarckian gradualist transformism.[21] The former explains the Earth's subterranean irregularity as the result of violent floods and volcanic upheavals, sudden "revolutions" that Cuvier himself compared to France's recent political history. The latter theory, supported by Lamarck and Buffon, as well as Lyell and Darwin, maintained instead that geological history is marked by continuous time, with intermediary gradations linking successive species and ages. So, cataclysmic deluge or "continuist" history? This is the question posed by geological discoveries and archaeological research—and "it would be up to the generation of naturalists between 1830 and 1860 to try to resolve the contradictions between fixism and evolution, discontinuity and plan of creation, catastrophes and uniformity of geological and biological change" (Cohen, 127). By the time Berthet writes his *Catacombes de Paris*, Lyell's gradualist theories have won the day; and significantly, in this political fable disguised as popular crime fiction, Médard, man of the fossil-filled caves, will be forced to abandon his cataclysmic plot and Philippe will implicitly accept the mantle of gradual monarchist transformation. Evolutionary theory thus meets revolutionary history, as paleontology informs a genre—crime fiction—that reads meaning into bones and other bodily remains (see Figure 1)

Catacombs and Catastrophism; Crime and Time

As Kalifa notes, Elie Berthet stands within a larger "criminal topography" of the underground that developed in the popular imaginary of the Second Empire:

> The bases of the Trocadéro, the plaster kilns of Clichy, the Montmartre quarries and *carrières d'Amérique* on the right bank, the immense excavation that extends, on the left bank, from Grenelle and Montrouge all the way to the Jardin des Plantes, form according to some a veritable underground nation, criminal in nature and accessible by any of numerous stairways situated at the Val-de-Grâce, at the *barrière du Maine*, at the Puits-qui-parle or else at the *place d'Enfer*. Analyzed through the typical prism of the *bas-fonds* or through the hugolian metaphor of the "*dessous*" and the social cavern, the existence of an immense and criminal subterranean Paris became a common cliché that popular novelists like Elie Berthet, Constant Guéroult, and Pierre Zaconne took upon themselves to transmit. (*Crime et culture*, 24)

In addition to Berthet's *Les Catacombes de Paris* (1854) and Constant Guéroult and Pierre de Coudeur's *Les Étrangleurs de Paris* (1859), Pierre Zaccone's *Les Drames des catacombes* (1861) and Théodore Labourieu's *Les Carrières d'Amérique*

Figure 1. Elie Berthet, *Les Catacombes de Paris*. Bibliothèque Nationale de France, Gallica.

(1868) set their crimes in the quarrylands of Paris.[22] We might also add to this list the Rocambole series by Ponson du Terrail, with its underground adventures "Les Démolitions de Paris" and "Le Souterrain" appearing in *La Résurrection de Rocambole* through the 1860s.[23] Even into the later part of the century, at least one anonymous author backdated his catacomb crime story into the Hausmannian era: *Les Mémoires de M. Claude, chef de la police de sûreté sous le Second Empire* (1881) mentions a "criminal" network of subterranean tunnels between the *barrière des Bonshommes* and the heights of the Trocadéro.[24] And indeed the fictional tropes of underground criminality continued well into the fin-de-siècle and Belle Epoque, with Jules Lermina's *Les Loups de Paris* (1876), Gaston Leroux's *La Double vie de Théophraste Longuet* (1904), and the Fantômas series by Pierre Souvestre and Marcel Allain (especially *Le Bouquet tragique* [1912] and *Le Voleur d'or* [1913]). A less-known serial from the pre-World War I period, the Lord Lister adventures, continued the subgenre with its installment entitled "Dans les Catacombes de Paris."[25]

It is unsurprising that many of these texts have fallen into oblivion, as they generally lack originality and stylistic rigor. For the most part, the catacomb fictions rehash an amalgam of clichéd motifs and conventions that go back to Eugène Sue's 1842 *Les Mystères de Paris*: innocent young women threatened with abduction, noblemen disguised as commoners and vice versa, torture and imprisonment in underground caves by gangs of ugly bandits sworn to a cruel leader.[26] The very repetition of these melodramatic tropes, of course, only reinforces the evocative power of the *bas-fonds* in the minds of modern Parisians.[27] But perhaps more interesting than the recurring plots and themes themselves is the way they are linked formally in these texts to a particular *feuilletonesque* temporality that is anything but linear. In fact, if we trace the geological elements of the Second Empire underground crime texts, we find a Cuvierian catastrophism that maps itself onto the temporal fits and starts of the crime serial.

Les Carrières d'Amérique (Théodore Labourieu, 1868)

This little-known novel was published in the 1860s, but jumps backward at its start to 1820, a time when the vast gorge "at the end of which is still found today the entrance to the plaster-quarries hollowed out of the sides of the buttes Chaumont" (1) is still being mined for Paris's construction materials.[28] Despite its social utility, the gorge is already being "repurposed" to nefarious ends, for after honest quarrymen leave daily, a criminal band led by the shape-shifting Protée takes over the underground space. Protée and his men are social outcasts above ground, but they regain mastery in these "endroits dangereux, leur asile et leur empire" [dangerous places, their haven and their empire] (5). More than that: the uneven terrain of the quarries, with their grottos and ravines, tunnels and gypsum pillars, are integral to the bandits' tenebrous affairs: "habitués aux ténèbres, familiers avec le terrain" [creatures of shadow, familiar with the terrain], two of Protée's lieutenants—the giant Issakar and the crafty "Renard"—kick off the tale by stealthily following a man named Jean, who has carried a bundled infant into the depths of the quarry at night. Issakar and Le Renard take advantage of the quarry's layout to stay hidden, "s'embusquant dans chaque anfractuosité de rochers, se dissimulant derrière chaque pilier, à mesure que l'inconnu s'avançait sous la voûte" [lie in ambush in each rocky crevice, hiding behind each pillar, while the stranger advanced beneath the vault] (5). The underground quarryland here is no smooth and ordered undifferentiated space. Rather, it is defined by anfractuosity: twists and turns of the labyrinth; intricate cavities and irregular surfaces; passages jumbled by cracks and crevices.

The geological complexity of this subterranean space allows the criminals to designate two secret vaults: the ironically named *magasin*, a depot for stolen goods—and, below it, the *sépulcre*, a naturally formed prison cell for informants, traitors, and various victims (8). *Magasin* above *sépulcre*: commerce above death. Such vertical spatialization both recapitulates the above-ground hierarchies of the modern capitalist city and reveals their instability by creating a series of chasms and upthrusts, with corresponding possibilities of both brutal descent and sudden ascent. When the bandits disfigure and blind the innocent Jean with a bucket of quicklime, he falls through a hole in the ground to a lower level of the subterranean gallery. Much later, Jean is able to dislodge a rock from his cell and climb up to the *magasin*, from which he accesses stairs to a trap door in the floor of an aboveground cabaret. Labourieu's narrator explicitly compares the multiple depths of this underground space to the levels of Dante's Hell (14), but there is no mythic atemporality here. Instead, we have constant reversals of high and low, as the longwinded narrative recounts violent upheavals both within the criminal hierarchy and between the bandits and their aristocratic prey.

And it does so through flashbacks and temporal jumps as awkward and laborious as the author's name. As with so many melodramas of the time, Labourieu's crime novel organizes its plot around the questioned legitimacy of a child born to noble state. The infant brought by Jean to the quarry in 1820 is the daughter of the Marquise de Saint-Semay, but her father is thought to be Monsieur de Saint-Semay's doppelganger cousin. We learn in Part I that the marquise has been murdered, but that the crime will not be avenged until fifteen years later. With a sudden forward jump, Part II re-starts the story in 1835 while occasionally reminding the reader of names and events presented earlier. Parts of the two sections thus jut into each other, just as stalactites, fossils, pillars, and crumbling rocks thrust across the quarry's complex and shifting vertical layers. And like the catastrophic deluges and volcanic eruptions that radically altered the stratigraphic order of Paris's geological underground, the 1820 murder of the Marquise and torture of Jean mark the subsequent plot twists with their inaugurating violence. The narrator even codifies that moment, referring often to "le drame de 1820," much as historians refer to key dates of French revolution and revolt.

In a way, then, the anfractuosities of the story's underground topography shape its narrative construction. Just as spatially there are ever-crumbling holes and ever-deeper wells, temporally there are ever-receding back stories. Near the end of *Les Carrières d'Amérique*, for example, Jean's lover admits in 1835 to having poisoned the marquise in 1820, but only out of vengeance for a crime committed years earlier still! (203) A chain of violence emerges retroactively, as with France's political history at the end of the nineteenth century, which looks back on successive Revolutions, each understandable in light of earlier grudges, intrigues, and violent acts. One might, here, even talk of a Cuvierian chronotope, a spatiotemporal model based on catastrophic events that disrupt linear order. Violent upheavals within the criminal world and between bandits and aristocrats cut into Labourieu's narrative sequence, resulting in an awkward jumble of flash-backs and repetitions, flash-forwards and hints. Meanwhile, the subterranean "empire" of the criminal band is shaped by cataclysmic events that force parts of the geological strata to jut upwards and thrust downwards. This connection between the narrative temporality and the stratigraphic underground lies not only in their shared anfractuosity (one figural, one literal), but also in Cuvier's foundational analogy between the Earth's geological revolutions and France's political Revolutions. Both inaugurated a nonlinear model of history disrupted by violence.[29]

Of course, many *romans feuilletons*, not only those dealing with crime, display awkward temporal jumps. But Labourieu's prose is especially strained and his plots especially farfetched when they try to deal with the layered chronology of Paris's subterranean space. A few times, the reader is told of the trap doors and hidden passages that lead from a cabaret on the rue du Temple down into the subterranean caves where stolen loot is melted and marked for resale (67, 72, 83). It is into these caves that the bandit gang throws some of its victims (86–87), before transporting them from under the rue du Temple over to the subterranean "sépulcre" in the Carrières d'Amérique (the Buttes Chaumont quarter) (101). This is the trajectory Jean will follow, when in 1835 he is again attacked by the bandits, as he had been fifteen years earlier. Beaten up and unconscious, Jean is moved to the Carrières alongside—and here is a gratuitous gruesome detail I find telling: the cadaver of a man who had been killed earlier (101). At this point, the narration takes a detour from Jean's tale to explain the cadaver's back story, ending with "c'était son cadavre que l'on a vu étendu sur le tiroir du billard du café du boulevard du Temple, avant qu'il retournât aux carrières . . . et que Jean devait retrouver bientôt aux mêmes souterrains" [it was this corpse that we have seen laid out on the billiard-table drawer in the café of the boulevard du Temple, before Jean had returned to the quarries . . . and that Jean was to come upon again in the same subterranean tunnels] (183). Not only are past and present awkwardly sutured, the two bodies of men—one recently rendered unconscious, the other less recently killed—are juxtaposed in the same subterranean space. Just as layers of fossils in geological strata get jumbled together by catastrophic natural events, living and dead bodies are thrown together by violence in the *Carrières d'Amérique*. The "cachot" or "oubliette" where Jean had been buried ("avait été enterré") along with the dead man (although we're back in the narrative present of 1835, Labourieu is forced here to use the *plus-que-parfait* because of his explanatory detour) is itself located next to the cell of another prisoner who had been the victim of an earlier "drame" (192–93). Thus awkward syntax itself signals an ever-receding chain of violence lodged in the rocks under Paris.

Let me here indulge in a detour of my own, from Labourieu's quarry novel to the cover image of a pre-World War I Lord Lister adventure that captures visually, I believe, this Cuvierian logic of bodily juxtaposition (Figure 2). The lurid cover of *Lord Lister, le Grand Inconnu, no.17: "Dans les Catacombes de Paris"* depicts an underground cavern. In the foreground of this dark subterranean vault, a harried woman runs, with unkempt hair flowing behind her and a lantern held before her, toward a scene that suggests successive acts of violence past, present, and future. Past: skulls and skeletons are scattered across the cavern floor, their bones disjointed and bare. More recent past: one intact skeleton lies in an open coffin. Even more recent past: next to the coffin, a clothed man lies dead or unconscious on the ground, his fingers stiffly clenched.

Figure 2. *Lord Lister, le Grand Inconnu.* Collection Bibliothèque des Littératures Policières (BiLiPo).

Present: the dead victim is straddled by a man struggling to defend himself from an attacking strangler (both are dressed in rather proper attire). Future: behind the struggling pair, another man approaches, wielding a glinting white knife above his head and preparing, apparently, to kill the strangler. The juxtaposition of modern (flat-top derby hat, contemporary gentlemanly attire) with ancient (the skeletal remains could be prehistoric or merely old enough to have decomposed to bare bones) in the dark enclosure of the rocky cave brings together violence past and present. With geology's discovery of fossilized bones strewn violently across stratigraphic layers of rock, it had become increasingly difficult to subscribe to a linear model of history that comfortingly differentiated modern (civilized) man from a brutal prehistoric past. Indeed, cataclysmic Earth theories implicitly refute a positivistic belief in human progress.[30] As if to register the fact that violence (human or geological) continues to cut into and disrupt a teleological temporality that would have us surpass the pre-modern, *Lord Lister's* cover tumbles old bones and skeletons-to-be into the same catacomb space.

Labourieu's *Les Carrières d'Amérique* does the same: at the tale's climactic moment, it throws the innocent Jean into the "profondeurs des souterrains" alongside both a recently beaten victim of the bandit gang and a putrefying cadaver (222). Three stages of violence, as it were, are juxtaposed in this "horrible tableau" of bodies buried underground (224)—but it doesn't stop there. A character announces: "puisqu'on est en train de découvrir des cadavres aux carrières d'Amérique, prenez garde à mon tour que je prenne le falot du plâtrier pour vous faire découvrir d'autres abîmes plus terribles encore" [since we are now discovering cadavers in the America quarries, make sure I take the plasterer's lamp so that I can show you other, even more terrible, abysses] (225). More bodies, more bones, more victims of a violence that will always mark the subterranean space of Paris, as modern as it might seem. By the end of the nineteenth century, of course, at least two layers of bones under Paris were literally visible: the photographer Nadar had famously captured haunting images of the bodies transferred a hundred years earlier from the Cimetière des Innocents to the catacombs,[31] and various published lithographs displaying fossil finds had made paleontological discoveries accessible to the public.[32] Labourieu's "horrible tableau," like the one in the Lord Lister cover, adds present and future skeletons to this jagged chain of seismological violence. Crimes with roots in the past are being committed today in Paris's sewers and catacombs. And just as serial novels are always "to be continued" (Labourieu's 1868 installment ends with "We will see what happens *à la suite . . .*), so will human brutality always return. There can be no forward progress when wars, murders, or geological cataclysms thrust the bones of their victims from past to future.

In late nineteenth-century France, it certainly must have felt as though wars—revolutions, revolts—would keep on coming, again and again without end. The political implications of a jagged chronology, exposed by geological excavations, appear in the obsessive class confusion at the origin of just about every popular crime story of the late nineteenth century: wrongly disavowed aristocrats return to claim their names, crafty commoners take advantage of social upheaval to don upper-crust disguises, low-class criminals join forces with a corrupt bourgeoisie to topple nobility—and of course, stolen infants raise the recurrent specter of illegitimacy while plot chronologies jump backward and forward in time. In the case of Labourieu's *Les Carrières d'Amérique*, the dubious paternity of the Marquise's infant girl is implicitly linked to the question of legitimate royal succession when Jean, in 1835, is forced by the story's villains to forge and back-date a letter wrongly identifying the noble girl's father, on yellowed paper stamped with fleurs de lys "datant de Louis XVIII" (207).[33] This back-dating suggests that the very structure of these popular crime stories links the anfractuous topography of the geological *souterrain* to the complex temporality of France's political history.

Les Étrangleurs de Paris (Guéroult et Couder, 1859); Les Drames des catacombes (Zaccone, 1861); Les Loups de Paris (Lermina, 1876)

Among the most dramatic images arising from Cuvierian geology is that of the cataclysmic flooding of underground cavities. Cuvier himself was careful to distinguish such recurrent floods from the Biblical deluge, but both experts and amateurs in the first half of the nineteenth century tried to reconcile rock history with scripture. By mid-century, though, Cuvier's student Louis Agassiz proposed that apparent flood deposits had actually been formed by glaciers and by century's end, the scientific community largely accepted a secular geochronology. Still, the terrifying topos of a water-filled cave continued to haunt the popular imaginary, making its own periodic appearances in popular crime fictions of the underground.

The most famous of these—and arguably the most copied—is the scene in Eugène Sue's 1842 *Mystères de Paris* where Rodolphe de Gerolstein is imprisoned under a filthy tavern in the Cité by the criminals La Chouette and

Le Maître d'École. Though Sue makes no explicit mention of geological formations, his underground space echoes the stratigraphic layering of the Paris
basin through its verticality: after violently throwing Rodolphe into a "cave"
just under the cabaret, Le Maître d'École drags him to the entrance of a second, deeper cavern, shoves him in, and traps him there under a heavy door.[34]
At this point, Rodolphe realizes that he is at river level and the waters of the
Seine are rising quickly around him. Terror—and melodramatic hyperbole—
ensue. Rodolphe's initial anguish at the thought of the watery death that
awaits him turns quickly, though, to religious resignation: "il avait beacoup
vécu . . . , Dieu le savait! ne murmurant pas contre l'arrêt qui le frappait, il vit
dans cette destinée une juste punition d'une fatale action non encore expiée."
[He had, Lord knows, lived a full life! rather than revolt against the judgment
facing him, he saw in this fate a just punishment for a fatal action not yet
expiated] (140). Even as rats claw at his skin and filthy water chokes his throat,
Rodolphe elevates his soul to God, accepting the cavern flood as divine
destiny. (He is, of course, saved at the last moment in order to continue his
providential exploits for many more hundreds of pages.)

With attenuated spirituality, but heightened consequence, similar flood
scenes recur in the later catacomb fictions of the Second Empire. Guéroult
and Couder's 1859 *Les Étrangleurs de Paris*, which shares with Labourieu's *Les
Carrières d'Amérique* both its jagged chronology—awkward jumps and frame-
stories—and its politically inflected plot of *bas-fonds* bandits infiltrating
aristocratic homes and undermining the capital with "les plus sinistres catastrophes," ends its first series of installments with a climactic scene of
water-filled violence.[35] Indeed, water invades the Paris underground from
above and below, with cataclysmic force: while the "étrangleurs" meet in subterranean sewer passages wet with rising river-waters, a violent rainstorm rages
outside (281). The pelting noise of the rain's "véritables cataractes" merges with
gunfire from police officers surrounding the bandits's above-ground hideout.
And though God is nowhere mentioned, Nature brings its own cataclysmic
dénouement to this face-off between forces of social order and its murderous
underminers.

> Les soldats, descendus par la trappe dans la cave de la boutique,
> sondaient les voûtes et allaient peut-être découvrir l'entrée secrète
> du souterrain; alors une commotion violente avait ébranlé le sol, et
> une vaste excavation s'était ouverte, dans laquelle roulèrent avec
> fracas les débris du mur du côté de la rivière.

[The soldiers, who had descended through the trap-door into the tavern's wine cellar, probed the vaulted walls and were perhaps about to discover the secret entrance to the subterranean tunnel, when suddenly a violent commotion had shaken the ground and a vast chasm had opened up, into which came crashing through the debris of the riverside wall.] (295)

This dramatic cave-in allows the criminal band's leader to escape through a sewer vomiting out thick torrents of yellowy water, and the story goes on: "to be continued . . . ," like the torrential waters that periodically overturn rocks and nobles with their (geological, political) revolutions.

In Zaccone's *Les Drames des catacombes* (1861), the even more dramatic and climactic scene of a cavern flood brings with it both divine retribution for criminal acts and the narrative lesson that the past will always return. At the very end of this story of switched identities, paternity theft, and cross-class murder, we find the criminal Robert lured into a subterranean vault by Thérésa, known as "the madwoman of the Catacombs." Fifteen years earlier, Robert had kidnapped and raped the young, noble-born Thérésa, then left her to wander for years through the eerie passageways under Paris. Now, in 1840, armed with the knowledge that Robert has also killed their only son, Thérésa will enact a cruel but just revenge: she shuts herself up with Robert in the undergound grotto, blocking its only exit and digging a passage to allow flood waters to enter. Horrified, Robert turns first to threats and pleas, then to hope in the geological formations of the rocky vault. As the water rises, and thinking that some fissure or exit-hole must exist, he seizes the first rough protuberance he feels. "Mais la pierre, rendue friable par l'humidité qui régnait éternellement dans ces souterrains, ne lui offrit qu'un appui incertain, et, à plusieurs reprises, il retomba lourdement dans l'eau" [But the rock, rendered friable by the humidity that reigned eternally in these underground passages, gave him only unsteady support, and, repeatedly, he fell heavily back into the water] (67). The robust Robert redoubles his efforts, grasping at the vault's outcroppings until his fingers bleed. At last, an opening up to "les galeries supérieures" reveals itself to his hand and he strains to climb out of the flooding cavern to safety. But no, Providence intervenes with just punishment for his crimes: "Mais Dieu veillait . . . car au même instant un craquement épouvantable se fit entendre dans les profondeurs des galeries; la grotte s'ébranla du sommet à la base, et Robert, entraîné par la chute de la muraille, à laquelle il resta cramponné, alla tomber dans l'abîme d'où il ne devait plus remonter"

[But God was watching . . . for at that very moment a dreadful crack was heard in the depths of the tunnels; the cave shook from top to bottom, and Robert, carried off by the falling wall, to which he continued to cling, was to plunge into the abyss from which he could never return] (67). Thus ends, in geological cataclysm writ small, the life of the criminal Robert. The crashing waters and crumbling rock recall Guéroult and Couder's sewer scene, while the theme of divine reckoning rewrites Sue in reverse. If we want to find echoes of post-Cuvierian catastrophism in Zaccone's 1861 tale, they might be in the cyclically recurrent nature of the underground catastrophes that I have already linked to the serial form of the *feuilleton*. Even though the double drowning of Robert and his victim Thérésa is described by Zaccone as the last act of "ce drame des catacombes," the claim is undercut by the addition of a page-long *Epilogue*, in which a tourist group descends a few years later into the same subterranean space "sans être bien rassuré au fond sur les catastrophes qui peuvent l'y atteindre" [without being truly reassured regarding the catastrophes that might await them there] (67). It seems, indeed, that the cycle of violence will never abate (despite, at the end of this Epilogue, the arrest of another criminal, Jacques, by the magistrate who had chased him years earlier). The past reaches forward to grip the present, just as prehistoric floods continue to mark and render unstable the rocks under modern Paris. At the same time as the scientific community in France was trying to reconcile Cuvier's proof of recurring cataclysms with a scriptural Flood of divine reckoning, Zaccone's catacomb fiction imbues its tale of recurring underground violence with trailing tropes of a providential God.

In the following decade, on the other hand, Jules Lermina's 1876 *Les Loups de Paris* pairs a fully secularized discussion of underground violence with explicit scientific discourse on France's geology. It also directly links the typical family melodramas of the crime *feuilleton* to national Revolutionary history. The tale starts in 1822 Toulon, during a series of revolts to overthrow the Bourbons, "encore mal assis sur leur trône" [still seated uneasily on their throne]. The narrator continues: "Depuis deux années seulement, par suite de dissentiments politiques, une rupture avait eu lieu et M. de Mauvillers avait interdit sa maison au fils de son ancien ami." [As a result of political disagreements come to light only two years earlier, a rupture had occurred and M. de Mauvilliers had banned from his home the son of his former friend].[36] Thus we have an initial break—"une rupture," between the royalist Mauvillers and his closest friend's son, Jacques de Costebelle—that threatens to cut into generational continuity, for Jacques and the baron's daughter Marie are in love and about to give birth to a son. Mauvillers does not know this when he has Jacques thrown into the "cachots souterrains de la Grosse-Tour," a prison site whose underground location is accentuated by the vertical rise of the tower above it. Rather than dwell on the well-known tortures of underground imprisonment (think, for example, of Hugo's *Notre-Dame de Paris* and Dumas's *Le Comte de Monte Cristo*), Lermina allows Jacques a quick escape and cuts over in his narrative to an underground hideout for bandits, located in the Gorges d'Ollioulles near Toulon. This "val d'enfer" [valley of hell], which the criminals Biscarre and Diouloufait choose as their lair before reappearing later in Paris as the titular "Loups," is described in terms of geohistorical violence:

> La pierre âpre, noirâtre, brune, se dresse comme une muraille infranchissable. Les anfractuosités de la roche se déchiquètent en dentelures bizarres, et quand le soleil couchant rougit le ciel, on dirait une frange bordée d'or rutilant. Par quel cataclysme cette masse colossale s'est-elle fendue dans toute sa hauteur, comme sous le choc d'une hache géante? Dans quelle convulsion géologique s'est opéré ce déchirement . . . ?

> [The harsh, blackish-brown stone rises up like an impassable wall. The anfractuosities of the rock are shredded into bizarre jagged outlines, and in the reddened sky of the setting sun, they seem fringed in gleaming gold. By what cataclysm was this colossal mass split in two from top to bottom, as though under the shock of a giant axe? Through what geological convulsion was it torn asunder?] (chap. 21)

Note that Lermina here is invoking the catastrophist theory to explain the rock's jagged juts and ragged rifts. As we have seen, Cuvier's studies of underground strata inaugurated a new geohistory that accounts for the disruption of stratigraphic layers by violent natural events. This geohistory has a spatial form: the stratigraphic map, which projects historical time onto vertical space, but with the bi-axial model of time and space complicated precisely by the thrusts and cracks that have jumbled the layers of rock. This is the spatial model of catacomb crime fictions, with their thrusts of violence, jets of Revolutionary ambition, and underground menace to order above. It is the shape of their political imaginary, for though it seems buried deep in the past, the Cuvierian cataclysm necessarily evokes in the nineteenth-century French mind the more recent political "rupture" that inaugurated this tale of violent splits and fractious events.

Indeed, a (somewhat subterranean) lexical network links the volcanic up-heavals of the geological underground to France's political cycles, through Lermina's descriptions of Jacques de Costebelle's revolutionary fervor. As with the ever-receding dated dramas we saw in Labouriau's *Les Carrières d'Amérique*, Jacques's situation in 1822 has its origins in an earlier crisis: he is described as having a "fièvre révolutionniste qui semblait jaillir à nouveau du foyer de 89" [revolutionary fever that seemed to spurt up anew from the hot-bed of '89] (chap. 4). The young man's energies spew out and gush forth, hot and uncontrollable, like volcanic fires: "Jacques inquiétait M. de Costebelle. En vain il avait tenté de régulariser cette fougue, d'endiguer cette énergie" [M. de Coste-belle was worried about Jacques. In vain had he tried to regulate this hot-headedness, to check this energy]. Not only his father, but M. de Mauvilliers tries to tamp down Jacques's ambitious élan—yet it continues to spurt like hot magma, entering into the fissures and crevices of Mauvilliers's own royal-ist household (Marie de Mauvilliers "aimait . . . à ouvrir son âme à toutes les effluves" [enjoyed opening her soul to every effluvium]) (chap.4). It is perhaps not incidental that Jacques's family name, Costebelle ("beautiful coast") an-chors him in the very rocks that define the French nation. The beauty of France's coast is that of the cave-filled, jagged cliffs made rough and craggy by cataclysmic forces as recurrent as the country's modern Revolutions.

But then, if the sympathetic hero Jacques de Costebelle is textually as-sociated with the upheavals of underground space, what are we to make of the low-class criminals who haunt the caves produced by those cataclysmic revolutions? How does Lermina distinguish, in other words, between the in-spired fires of Jacques's revolutionary fever and the nasty, brutish ways of the violent band? One way, typical of the time, is through their animal physiog-nomy. Biscarre has the low forehead, prominent jaws, yellowed eyes, and sharp teeth of a wolf. As for Diouloufait, "le nez épaté, les gros yeux, la bouche lip-pue et largement fendue, les oreilles rouges et s'écartant du crâne en conques disproportionnées, tout contribuait à donner, au premier coup d'œil, la sensa-tion de la brutalité poussée à ses dernières limites" [the flat nose, wide eyes, thick-lipped and gaping mouth, the red ears sticking out from his skull like shells askew, all contributed to cause at first glance an impression of brutality pushed to its last limits]. And yet, for all the apparently natural predetermi-nation of these men's savagery, Lermina reveals his socialist leanings when he describes their descent from poverty into crime. In a narrative detour, Lermina provides a back-story for Diouloufait's murderous impulses, one that again invokes watery catastrophe. At twelve, the young "Loup" was thrown overboard from his father's fishing boat by storm waves crashing against the coastal rocks of the Mediterranean. The child fought against the torrential tides to survive, but his working father drowned, leaving behind a widow who blamed the "catastrophe" on class inequality: "Ce qu'elle voyait, cette femme, c'est que la misère avait tué son mari, et que cette misère était l'œuvre de la société" [What she saw, this woman, was that poverty had killed her husband, and that this poverty was the work of society]. Le Loup, who had been associated with a certain stolid earthiness (his vigorous nature is "sculpted out of full flesh" and when fighting the sea, he calls out for salvation from France's coast: "Father! the land! the land!"), deteriorates from beggar to thief to hardened ex-con. To this sequence, Lermina appends a moral lesson: "De la mendicité au vol, la distance est courte" [it's a short distance from begging to thieving]. In the end, the criminal Loup serves as a tragic counter-image of Jacques, rather than his moral opposite. Both, in fact, are described as martyrs to the uncontrolled forces around them: Le Loup, a "martyr" of the turbulent Sea that destroyed his family and honor; and Jacques, a martyr to the Nation, exclaiming as he is about to die: "Mes amis, mes frères, je tombe pour la France et la liberté . . . , Le martyr vous pardonne" [My friends, my brothers, I fall for France and for freedom; the martyr forgives you] (chap. 8). The combination of cataclysmic waters and national upheavals reveals a geologic imaginary of "révolutions" that motors the criminal *roman-feuilleton*. The violent thrusts, the ambitious jets, the underground menace to order above—all the hackneyed tropes of Lermina's catacomb fiction can be understood in terms of both social instability and geohistory, as though the Earth's own anfractuous form had somehow determined or shaped the political rhythms of nineteenth-century France.

Entering the Twentieth Century: Underground Crime with a Twist

The bandit bands of the fictional underground had their criminal heyday in the troubled Second Empire and early Commune days. But by the Belle Époque, the catacombs' vigorous "stranglers" and "wolves" had given way to anemic larvae and ironic ghosts, in the fictions of Gaston Leroux (*La Double vie de Théophraste Longuet*, 1904) and Souvestre and Allain (*Fantômas: Le bouquet tragique*, 1912).

When Fantômas' arch-enemy Juve finds himself descending an ever-increasing number of steps into a mysterious underground lair, he signals his awareness of inhabiting a literary cliché: "Où diable vais-je dégringoler? c'est le voyage au centre de la terre que je commence!" [Where the devil am I tumbling? it's the journey to the center of the Earth that I'm starting!][37] Vernian adventure gives way quickly to crime fiction, as the policeman recognizes the familiar textual terrain of a narrow, vaulted subterranian gallery and we smile with him when he concludes, "Très bien! . . . Il y a décidément des chances pour que tout cela me conduise en plein repaire de brigands!" [Very well! There's a decidedly good chance that all this will lead me straight into a bandit's lair!] (180). While Fantômas and his creators smirk their way through the over-trod underground, Gaston Leroux evinces a desire to escape its hackneyed associations:

> Quand on se réveille au fond des catacombes, dit M. le commissaire de police Mifroid dans l'admirable rapport qu'il rédigea à l'issue de ce surprenant voyage, la première pensée qui vous envahit l'esprit est une pensée de crainte : la crainte d'être vieux jeu ; j'entends par là l'anxiété subite où l'on se trouve de reproduire tous ces gestes ridicules que les romanciers et dramaturges ne manquent point de faire accomplir aux tristes héros qu'ils égarent dans des souterrains, grottes, excavations, cavernes et tombeaux.

> [When one awakens in the depths of the catacombs, wrote the police commissioner Mifroid in the admirable report he composed at the conclusion of this astonishing voyage, the first thought that comes to mind is one of fear: the fear of being trite; I mean by that the sudden anxiety in which one finds oneself re-enacting all those ridiculous gestures that novelists and playwrights never fail to ascribe to their pathetic heroes whom they've led astray into subterranean tunnels, grottoes, excavations, caverns, and tombs.][38]

Mifroid's concern may well double that of the author's—and Leroux does all he can, in this, his first published *roman feuilleton*, to bring novelty to a by-then clichéd popular genre.

Though *La Double vie de Théophraste Longuet* starts off, for example, with the well-known *roman judiciaire* topos of a visit to the Conciergerie prison, it quickly veers into a realm of strangely mixed temporality where modern technological details—disappearing trains and electric lanterns—combine with troubling hold-overs from the past: the famous eighteenth-century criminal Cartouche takes over Théophraste's identity, while below Paris live "Les Talpa," who have inhabited the catacombs since the Middle Ages. And though Leroux begins by rehearsing all the historical points of entry into the Paris underground—the 1777 cave-in of a house on la rue d'Enfer, the monuments like Val-de-Grace and Saint-Étienne-du-Mont that seemed to raise themselves up on subterranean supports, and the networked caverns under la Tombe-Issoire and the Panthéon—he consciously re-writes the catacombs as a non-realist space through a famously playful chapter title: "Où nous commençons à entrer dans le fantastique, si l'on entend par fantastique tout ce qui ne se passe pas à la surface de la terre" [where we start to enter the space of the fantastic, if one understands by fantastic all that does not occur on the earth's surface] (chap. 35).

Souvestre and Allain likewise disavow the realism of the criminal catacombs, explaining away (at least at first) Juve's entire subterranean adventure, with its long descent and encounter with blind babblers and supposed specters in the vaulted tunnels, as the hallucinatory effect of an unintended opium intake (186). Both authors update the tropes of nineteenth-century crime fictions through de-realization and doubling. The *canard*-like grisly domestic murder at the end of *Théophraste Longuet* is rendered uncanny by Cartouche's habitation of a modern body, while the more elegant jewel thievery and assassinations in *Le Bouquet tragique* are sieved through the protean Fantômas's manipulation of a collective hallucination around the talismanic word "Jap."

And then, of course, we have the underground people: Fantômas's "Larves" and Leroux's "Talpa." Whereas Labourieu and his contemporaries conformed to the sociological categories of "classes laborieuses et classes dangereuses" with their post-Revolution quarrymen-become-criminals, Leroux and Souvestre/Allain create their own, weirder, species of underground dwellers. In *Le Bouquet tragique*, Fantômas reveals that after having been blinded by a gun-shot, he decided literally to enter the shadows by moving into the quarrylands of Montmartre. "C'est alors, continuait-il, que commencent les aventures les plus étranges. Je réunis tous les aveugles de Paris, j'en fais mes esclaves, je fonde, dans ce souterrain, le Royaume des Larves" [It's at this point, he continued, that the strangest adventures commence. I gathered together all the blind people of Paris, I made them my slaves, I founded, in this underground passage, the Kingdom of the Larvae] (364). More unsettling than nineteenth-century bandit gangs, these blind subjects of the supreme Shadow-Master embody the creepy-crawly fear of larval infestation. Half-seen and unseeing, they lurk in the dark depths not only of the rock under Paris, but of the discombobulated minds of Juve, Fandor, and Fantômas's victims above ground. In a way, *Fantômas* deviates from the sociorealist conventions of crime fiction not only through his "Royaume des Larves," but also—and paradoxically—through the overdetermined citationality that surrounds them. Every element of the tale's subterranean descents can be read as pastiche of popular fictions, from Sue's *Mystères de Paris* (with its famous blinding of the Maître d'École) to the Second Empire catacomb novels (with their villain/hero face-offs set in quarry vaults) to Leroux's own recently published *Le Fantôme de l'Opéra* (with its haunting musical passages and seduction of a young woman into the underground lair). By the time Juve is brought a second time against his will into Fantômas's subterranean realm, we are not surprised to find rushing waters above his head (358); nor can we react with naïve terror when the *Bouquet tragique* episode ends with a cataclysmic cave-in:

> avec un fracas formidable la vieille bâtisse s'écroulait . . . Et Jérôme
> Fandor, à demi évanoui, à demi conscient, avait l'impression qu'une
> énorme vague d'eau l'emportait, le roulait comme un fétu! Fantômas,
> en s'enfuyant, venait de faire sauter le réservoir d'eau de Montmartre!
> Sa victoire était-elle donc définitive et complète? Juve et Fandor
> devaient-ils mourir ensemble, broyés?
>
> [with a tremendous crash, the old building collapsed . . . And
> Jérôme Fandor, half-fainted, half conscious, had the impression
> that an enormous wave of water was carrying him away, was rolling
> him like a wisp of straw! Fantômas, while escaping, had just blown up
> the water reservoir of Montmartre! Was his victory, then, definitive
> and complete? Were Juve and Fandor destined to die together,
> crushed?] (381–32)

Even as it cites the tropes of Second Empire catacomb fiction, *Fantômas* dismisses its correlation of geohistory to political Revolution. Fantômas has made himself the Master—and therefore undoer—of cataclysmic history. Thus, the story ends with a question and a wink: the ironized question of eternal return and the knowing wink of cynical seriality.

Leroux's semi-larval population, Les Talpa, also disrupts history and crime story convention, but in a different manner. The anachronistic civilization of the "Talpa" owes its description to both geological and evolutionary science. When the narrator of the subterranean journey encounters an underground lake populated by one-eyed fishes and eyeless ducks, he gives his amazed companion an explanation of Cuvierian proportions:

> Je ne perdis point notre temps à lui faire un cours sur le rôle que chaque genre de terrain pouvait jouer dans un pareil phénomène ; je n'eus garde de lui obscurcir l'entendement de la théorie des couches sablonneuses reposant sur des couches imperméables. Tout de même, il fallut bien qu'il comprît que, dans les couches perméables, les eaux pouvaient former des nappes liquides continues se mouvant avec une certaine vitesse. Ces eaux courantes, entraînant peu à peu les roches et les sables environnants, des rivières souterraines prennent ainsi la place du massif originaire et opèrent de grands vides là où primitivement tout se touchait.

> [I did not waste our time providing a lesson on the role each type of terrain might play in such a phenomenon; I refrained from confusing his comprehension of the theory of sandy sediment layered above impermeable strata. None the less, it was imperative that he understand that in permeable strata, the forces of water can produce continuous liquid layers that move with a certain speed. Since these flowing waters carry along with them, little by little, the surrounding rocks and sediment, subterranean rivers eventually replace the original *massif* while creating large gaps where once all had been contiguous.] (33)

The speaker here, police commissioner Mifroid, claims to have science on his side, but we should not forget the comic, even parodic tone of his discourse: after all, he has been aiming to impress his companion Théophraste Longuet with a series of absurdly erudite outbursts since the start of their journey. In fact, their dialogue recalls nothing less than the philosophical dueling between the Hegelian idealist Lenoir and the buffoonish Tribulat Bonhomet in Villiers de l'Isle-Adam's "Claire Lenoir" of 1887; like Bonhomet, Mifroid puffs himself up by layering theory over theory, jargon over jargon. The particular invocation of geohistory cited above, for example, comes as a defense against Longuet's taunting juxtaposition of Mifroid's Latinate jargon with the quacking of ducks:

Eh ben, mon vieux ! qu'est-ce que tu dis de ça ? C'est autre chose
que tes asellides, asellus, asionus, aquaticus, masticus, mastica,
masticum, puteanus ! Coin ! Coin ! Coin !

[Well, old pal, what do you say to that? It's something entirely
different from your asellides, asellus, asionus, aquaticus, masticus,
mastica, masticum, puteanus! quack! quack! quack!] (33)

At this point, Mifroid explains the hydrogeological theory of stratified terrain,
then ramps up his scientific riposte by another excursus on a Slovenian lake
whose tides expose subterranean caverns housing primitive fish forms. The dialogue between expert babbler and practical naïf continues until Mifroid and
Longuet catch sight of a nude woman bathing in the underground lake; then,
scientific discourse gives way to a series of hilariously overblown paeans to
art, to Venus, to Théophile Gautier—all through the prism of the two men's open-
jawed lust for the comely creature. Comely, that is, until her face becomes visible
and the men see that she has no eyes, overgrown ears, and a piggish snout. She
is a "Talpa," they learn, one of an entire nation of citizens living under Paris
since the fourteenth century, who have made up for their eyelessness by developing enlarged ears and noses, twenty fingers and twenty toes. By the time we
get to the fuller descriptions of the "Talpa nation," we should remember the
narrator's earlier announcement that with the descent into Paris's catacombs,
we have entered the realm of the fantastic—but it is certainly a "scientific-
fantastic," à la Villiers (though with a counter-idealist thrust). For, as with the
Fantômas adventures, this underground journey account comes with a wink.

More specifically, I think that Leroux is skewering the nineteenth-century
catacomb crime genre and its grandiose triple alliance of domestic crime, political Revolution, and cataclysmic geology. Mifroid and Longuet's dialogues
continually reinforce the sense of generic belatedness:

Pour tromper ma faim, monsieur le commissaire, vous devriez bien
me raconter des histoires sur les catacombes. "Mais certainement,
mon ami." "Vous en connaissez de fort belles ?" "De tout à fait
belles."

[To distract me, dear commissioner, you should tell me some
stories about the catacombs. "But certainly, my friend." "Do you
know some very good ones?" "Yes, very good ones indeed."] (31)

And as Longuet foolishly peers at the catacomb walls with a wildly swinging electric lamp: "Je cherche, dit-il, des cadavres. 'Des cadavres?' 'Des squelettes. On m'avait dit que les murs des catacombes étaient tapissés de squelettes'" ["I'm looking," he said, "for cadavers." "Cadavers?" "Skeletons. I'd heard that catacomb walls were covered with corpses"] (31).

The comical tone extends to a brief tug-of-war between the two men over who gets to hold Mifroid's watch in his pocket; Mifroid cedes it to Longuet, saying, "Qu'est-ce que cela, au fond, pouvait me faire, qu'il eût ma montre, puisque je savais où était l'heure ?" [What difference did it make, really, that he had my watch, since I knew where the time was?] (31). Somehow, this spatial localization of time has something to do with the logic of the underground: "Je n'eusse jamais pensé cette dernière phrase hors des catacombes, ... Or, cette phrase renferme une révolution auprès de laquelle les bouleversements sociaux de 1793 sont de petits jouets de peuple en enfance" [I never could have conceived that last phrase outside of the catacombs; yet, that phrase contains within it a revolution compared to which the social upheavals of 1793 are mere playthings for the French people in their infancy.] The underground plays with time and space—in a way that bypasses or dwarfs the human dramas of post-Revolutionary French history. Moreover, the presence of the Talpa nation under modern Paris reveals a decidedly jagged and non-progressist chronology, since the Darwinian evolutionary adaptation of the Talpas' bodies is paired with cultural anachronisms like their use of the fourteenth-century *langue d'oïl*.

In his book *Subterranean Cities*, David L. Pike compares Leroux's Talpa society to the pastoral animal community of Kenneth Grahame's 1908 *The Wind in the Willows*; but beyond the etymological link of Talpa to "mole," I see little in common between the two groups. Indeed, rather than exist outside history as "pre-Edenic noble savages" (Pike, 106), the decisively Gallic Talpa represent a specific French history whose linearity has been shattered by the anfractuosities of the Paris Basin's geochronology. Spatial continuity is combined with temporal discontinuity. To explain the Talpa existence as anachronistic back-eddy in the rocks under Paris, Mifroid turns to a catastrophism actively unlinked from a nineteenth-century-centered human history:

Vous devez imaginer—avec certitude—qu'une famille, dans les premières années du quatorzième siècle, s'est trouvée enfermée dans les catacombes, à la suite d'une catastrophe qui n'a pour nous aucune importance, qu'elle a pu y vivre, qu'elle y a vécu, en effet, et qu'elle a engendré.

[You need to suppose, with certainty, that the members of a family, in the early years of the fourteenth century, and as a result of some catastrophe that need not concern us, found themselves trapped in the catacombs, succeeded in sustaining themselves, continued to live in that space, and indeed bred there.] (34)

The Earth's cycles have created the discontinuities that allow, comically, "gentille dame Jane de Montfort et damoiselle de Coucy" to rub elbows underground with the modern Miford and Longuet (himself possessed by the eighteenth-century rogue Cartouche!).

Pike is right about the Talpa's utopianism—but here, too, Leroux seems to be poking fun at the conventions of the crime *feuilleton*. Note the title that introduces the chapter in which we learn that the Talpa have no private property, no theft, no crime, no law, no justice system at all: "Le peuple Talpa est un peuple comme il n'en existe pas sur la terre. MM Mifroid et Longuet, l'un comme commissaire et l'autre comme voleur, sont parfaitement ridicules" [The Talpas are a people unlike any who exist on the earth. MM Mifroid and Longuet, one as commissioner and the other as thief, are perfectly ridiculous] (35). Leroux has constructed a (literally) topsy-turvy world, in which the Paris catacombs and quarries are inhabited not by clichéd bandit gangs but by strangely crime-free creatures that combine historical retrogression with biological evolution. He thus disjoins Earth history from both Revolutionary politics and banal criminality. In the land of the Talpas, Mifroid and Longuet are rendered ridiculous, but in the tradition of *Candide*, they return to a world of grisly violence when they leave the utopic realm. Again, let us not forget the narration's melo-comic tone as Longuet/Cartouche hacks his adulterous wife to death: "Dans un état d'exaltation sanguinaire comparable à rien dans l'histoire des crimes—même si l'on se donne la peine de remonter aux crimes de la mythologie qui furent cependant de bien beaux crimes" [In a state of bloodthirsty exaltation unlike any in the history of crime—even if one troubles oneself to go back to the crimes of ancient mythology, which were, even so, quite fine crimes indeed] (41).

In the long scheme of things, Leroux seems to suggest, these events don't really matter all that much. The ending of *La Double vie de Théophraste Longuet* is an over-the-top mish-mash of *fait divers* barbarity and fin-de-siècle theories of criminality and atavism. Its final words can only be read as a send-up of feuilletonesque conventions, a light-hearted jab at the continual return of characters one thinks have been killed off:

> Et il expira . . .
> Ambroise pleure, pleure, car il ne sait pas que cet homme, qui vient d'expirer, n'est pas mort ! . . .
> Certes, il est des gens, très bien renseignés, paraît-il, qui disent que lorsqu'on est mort, on est mort ! Ils en sont sûrs ! . . . Félicitations ! Félicitations ! Je ne les contredirai pas aujourd'hui, parce que je suis très fatigué . . . Mais nous en reparlerons demain au fond des tombeaux !

> [And he expired . . . Ambroise laments, laments, for he knows not that this man, who has just expired, is not dead! Certainly there are many who, seemingly well-informed, would claim that once one has died, one is dead! They are quite sure of it! . . . I congratulate them! Congratulations! I will not contradict them today, because I am quite fatigued . . . but we will reopen the discussion tomorrow, in the depths of the tombs!]

As we shall see in the following chapter, Gaston Leroux was soon to take on the historical implications of paleontology more directly in his *roman policier* of 1909, *Le Parfum de la dame en noir*. But here, in his first *feuilleton*, Leroux undercuts the conventions of popular nineteenth-century catacomb fictions through his own quirky use of discontinuous history. Like Souvestre and Allain in the *Fantômas* series, Leroux taps into the geological imaginary in order to subvert what Berthet, Labourieu, and other *feuilletonistes* had established in their sometimes overwrought fictions—namely, the aggrandizing dramatization of modern criminality as both political Revolution and earth-rending cataclysm.

CHAPTER 3

Skulls and Bones:
Paleohistory in Leroux and Leblanc

In the previous chapter on catacomb fictions, we have seen that the chrono-tope of the urban criminal underground flourished especially during the Second Empire. As modern construction exposed ancient bones under Paris, geological discourse merged with Revolutionary history to inflect narra-tives of cyclical violence, under and on the streets of the nation's capital. But within the relative stability of the Third Republic, thinkers began reflecting less on how the deep past imprinted France's own seismic turbulence—and more on how their nation was positioned to face an expanding, industrialized future in the global arena. The Paris/province distinction was losing its clarity through political decentralization and vexed regionalism in the first decades of the twentieth century.[1] Meanwhile, scientific discoveries of human fossils in Europe, America, and the coastal cliffs of France had established beyond doubt not only a geological prehistory but also the more radical existence of humanity's evolutionary past. How did these two contexts—the politics of decentralized national identity and the science of human prehistory— intersect in the pages of France's best-known detective novelists of the early twentieth century? In this chapter, I explore the cliffside settings of Gaston Leroux's and Maurice Leblanc's crime fictions as sites of intersection between national historiography and paleontological discourse. The first two sections of the chapter contrast Leroux's *Le Parfum de la dame en noir* (1909) and Maurice Leblanc's *La Comtesse de Cagliostro* (1924), with each representing, through the image of bones in caves, a different model for France's relation to its own past and future. The chapter then moves to another consequence of paleontological discovery—the debate about primitive humans and evolution—through a reading of Leroux's strange crime story *Balaoo* (1911), in which an ape-man reconfigures notions of animal brutality and human civilization. In the work of these two authors of "modernity," Leroux and Leblanc, we find not only an engagement with the sciences of premodern humanity, but also rearticulations, through geo-paleontology, of France's national self-definition at the start of a new era.

One reason Leroux and Leblanc have typically been associated with modernity is that they made ample use in their tales of new transportation technologies: their heroes Rouletabille and Arsène Lupin respectively hopped trains and rode bicycles to solve or commit crimes, trail criminals, or evade detection. In many of their fictions, Paris is represented as a global hub. It is crisscrossed by train lines and inhabited by foreign transients and world adventurers. Moreover, the motif of transatlantic sea travel seems to situate the authors' detective series squarely in the realm of modern internationality; Leblanc's first Lupin adventure, "L'Arrestation d'Arsène Lupin" (1904), and Leroux's *Le Parfum de la dame en noir* (1909) both feature ocean liners connected through telegraph technology to transnational networks of trade and communication. As is the case with the shape-shifting Fantômas, the categorization of Rouletabille and Lupin as masters of mobility seems undergirded by the spatial logics of urban internationalism.

Yet Leroux and Leblanc, both of whom spent large parts of their childhood in Normandy, also devote many pages of their crime fictions to France's provincial coasts. Two texts in particular, Leroux's *Le Parfum de la dame en noir* and Leblanc's *La Comtesse de Cagliostro* (from *Les Aventures d'Arsène Lupin, gentleman-cambrioleur*), involve seaside settings that would seem to promote insularity rather than openness to modern global networks. With their descriptions of the coastal provinces of Normandy and Provence, these stories might be considered "regionalist" outcroppings of a quintessentially urban genre. As such, they might also imply a nostalgic back-eddy toward the idea of crime as a local, communal matter rather than one of modern policing—and it is true that Rouletabille and Arsène Lupin shun official justice systems in favor of their own idiosyncratic forms of redress. Such a reading of these texts as throw-backs would apparently jibe with Stephen Knight's classic genealogy of detective fiction as arising from eighteenth-century rural roots before entering nineteenth- and twentieth-century city systems.[2] But even Knight's account of the generic move from farms and villages to complex urban space resists a too-easy dichotomization of rural versus urban space as primitive// modern, communitarian//individualistic, and superstitious//rationalized. For one thing, the well-known transfer of tracking detection from the wild woods of Cooper's Leatherstocking novels to the urban streets in Balzac, Dumas, and Sue shows us that natural and urban spaces were often taken as homologous in the modern crime imaginary. More generally, as Stéphane Gerson has argued, "the local and modernity were interlaced rather than inimical in France" even in the early nineteenth century.[3] And certainly, a century later it was becoming more and more evident that regionalism was not incompatible with global modernity.

Thus, even in their provincial fictions, Leroux and Leblanc reconnect apparently peripheral spaces to the internationalist themes associated with modern urbanity. Take, for example, the motif of transatlantic ships cited above. We might note that they explicitly invoke the French provinces through their quaint nomenclature—*La Provence* (in Leblanc) and *La Dordogne* (in Leroux). These names could be read as either ironic regionality in the face of inevitable modern progress or as a nostalgic anchoring of global exchange in local sites of rural economy, but I think instead that Leroux's *La Dordogne* and Leblanc's *La Provence* serve to project nationalistic extension rather than retrogressive regionalism.[4] Just as Leroux's and Leblanc's "regional" novels do not undercut their reputations as Parisian authors, provincial names of transatlantic ships are not incompatible with France's self-presentation as a player on the global scene. Indeed, the ships can be seen to stand for the nation, for "Tout navire arborant le pavillon tricolore est, juridiquement, territoire national; le *jus soli* s'y applique d'une manière qui n'est pas seulement symbolique. La personnalité nationale se manifeste, et se projette, avec toute la charge de son passé et de son être" [Every ship displaying the tri-color flag is, legally speaking, a national territory; the *jus soli* applies in a manner that is not merely symbolic. The national character manifests and projects itself, with all of the weight of its past and its present being].[5]

But what exactly is the relationship—in early twentieth-century crime fictions—of France's national past to its "present being"? *Le Parfum de la dame en noir* and *La Comtesse de Cagliostro* both engage with this question through their particular spatial logics.

The two texts share, for example, an obsession with the ocean as the site of false drownings—a theme that indicates textually an uneasy association of water with History, of the oceanic space with threatening returns of the past. In Leroux's *Le Parfum de la dame en noir*, a story organized around the three ports of Tréport, Marseille, and Menton, both the arch-criminal Larsan and the hero journalist/detective Rouletabille fake their own drownings in order to return undetected; only at the end of the novel does the ocean definitively swallow up the corpse of Larsan, thus effacing his uncanny return from the past. Leblanc's *La Comtesse de Cagliostro* similarly connects danger to waterways, when its villainess the Countess ("La Cagliostra"), accused of having murdered two men by throwing them off Breton cliffs into the sea, is herself stranded in a sabotaged boat by angry avengers. They assume that she has drowned—but in fact, a smitten Arsène Lupin has swum out to save her. After La Cagliostra's apparently miraculous return to life from the ocean depths, she tricks her enemies into again believing her dead, this time by staging her own river barge's accident, with flames visible from the coast. The multiple false drownings in Leroux and Leblanc thus mark the ocean as a place of danger, deceit, and nefarious rebirth. From Eugène Sue and Victor Hugo on, popular crime fiction had associated the urban metropolis (with its anonymous crowds, underground mafias, and unmappable alleyways) as the ideal site for a criminal to disappear and re-emerge with a false identity. But here, the vast sea serves this "laundering" function, as though it were an offshore bank account for the criminal body. The erasure, however, can only be incomplete. At the same time as it opens onto a future of transnational commerce and communication, the ocean returns bodies to France's national coastline, thus thematizing an inevitable return of the past, of History.

In the case of Larsan, the history in question is personal: he is Mathilde's former husband and Rouletabille's hidden father, returning to taint and threaten their newly purified lives. La Comtesse de Cagliostro, on the other hand, represents a European historical past, both in her uncanny genealogy (Russian princes, Italian nobles, French diplomats) and through her involvement in the mystery of France's monastic buried treasure. The coastal settings in Leroux and Leblanc thus crystallize crime fiction's necessary relation to a violent past at once personal and national. But they do so not only through their invocations of an angry sea. More important to the action in both novels, in fact, are the caves in the coastal cliff-sides that introduce to the texts a deeper History in the form of paleontological discourse.

The Sinister Skull: *Le Parfum de la dame en noir*

As fans of the successful Rouletabille cycle know, Leroux's novel *Le Parfum de la dame en noir* provides a continuation of the story begun with *Le Mystère de la chambre jaune*, published two years earlier in 1907.[6] The first novel ended by exposing Jacques Larsan as a villain whose seduction of Mathilde Stangerson had resulted in the birth of a boy, now grown up into the young journalist-investigator Rouletabille. Much has been made of this Oedipal triangle, with Mathilde as unacknowledged mother to Rouletabille and Larsan as his manifest enemy.[7] Certainly, the Freudian overtones of spectral carryover from the past are present at the beginning of *Le Parfum de la dame en noir*. At the sequel's start, Mathilde has married the scientist Robert Darzac, but their newly-wed bliss is threatened by the return of the vengeful and jealous Larsan. His haunting, taunting persistence embodies a narrative refusal to exorcise the criminal; defying classical detective novel form, *Le Mystère de la chambre jaune* had allowed him to escape incarceration. Now, in the novel's sequel, Larsan shows up in glimpses, in a train car mirror, on the station quay . . . despite having been officially declared dead. As a result, the entirety of *Le Parfum de la dame en noir*'s plot consists in attempts to avoid, dispel, and definitively destroy this troubling figure of Mathilde's past indiscretions and Rouletabille's paternal origin. Unexpectedly, in this work associated by many with modernity, the characters' spatial solution to the problem of Larsan's return seems symbolically to require a temporal regression, a return to a historical Past that far predates Rouletabille's personal family romance.

For, leaving behind the modern markers of city and train, the Darzacs and Rouletabille seek refuge in the Fort d'Hercule, an ancient coastal fortress near Menton, at the Mediterranean border of France and Italy. Rouletabille's goal to protect the newlyweds is made possible by the crumbling fort's adherence to the country's coastal topography: over the centuries, Fort d'Hercule's architecture has taken on the contours of a "presqu'île"—an almost-island. Though now connected to the mainland by a narrow isthmus, the fort had originally been completely cut off by its twelfth-century Franco-Italian lords. Eventually, the natural land-bridge had re-formed to link the fort to the coast, so that "Les murs du château d'Hercule épousaient la forme de la presqu'île, qui était celle d'un hexagone irrégulier" [the walls of the Hercules Chateau hugged the contours of the peninsula, which formed an irregular hexagon] (69). The fort's hexagonal shape might tempt us to read it as an allegory or microcosm of France, yet a nationalistic reading is hard to sustain given Rouletabille's separation of his personal mission from State notions of justice, the text's emphasis on the fort's joint Franco-Italian history, and Leroux's cartographic dismissal of State frontiers (in the story's reproduced map of the Menton coastline, no vertical boundary divides France from Italy). More suggestive is the fort's formal resemblance to Rouletabille's central trope for solving a mystery: "closing the circle."[8] The famous "cercle de la raison" that had allowed him to solve the *chambre jaune* mystery is here transposed onto the fort as a seaside version of the *local clos*, so that topographical space and mental strategy map onto each other. But while Rouletabille's protective strategies involve barricading the fort (i.e., "closing the circle"), his plan also relies on a theory that "leaves the circle open," for only if egress and ingress are possible can his hypothesis of Larsan's imposture be confirmed. To Rouletabille's geometrical mind, the *presqu'île* represents, in the end, a conflicted desire: to cut himself off from his own troubling past while retaining the limited connection that will enable him to fight its threat in the present. The semiclosed circle of the fortress combines vulnerability and invulnerability; and just as the mainland's natural isthmus reappears despite attempts to destroy it, Rouletabille's familial link to the criminal Larsan refuses to stay repressed.

Through the central figure of the seaside fortress, then, France's history of defense against maritime attack gets recast as at once mythic and personal—falling, as it were, on either side of national history. Descriptions of the fort's twelfth, fifteenth, and seventeenth-century architecture include military details—a parapet pierced by *meurtrières*, for example—but these are eclipsed by a longer, rhetorically fanciful passage that abjures history in favor of myth. The narrator first celebrates the heroic son of Jupiter and the mythic banks of the Mediterranean, then turns to the Château d'Hercule's more recent history of glorious defense against Saracen looters and Genovese pirates, only to end with a most mundane present of household concerns: where the fort's new guests will sleep, what entrances the servants will use to make the beds, etc. From mythic landscape to coastal fortress to private home, History has been brought down to the scale of the personal by the time Rouletabille takes Les Rochers Rouges as the site of his own Œdipal quest. Even the drawn diagram of the fort, which Leroux inserts in his text, indicates a flattened temporality, as the (vertical) layers of architectural history collapse into a two-dimensional plan. On the site of the Fort d'Hercule, capital-H History converts again to personal story when Rouletabille hears his mother cry with terror from the fort's twelfth-century Tower and he calls back from the seventeenth-century Château Neuf, "Maman! Maman! Maman!" He is frustrated, writes the narrator Sainclair, by his inability to fly from the "New" Tower to the old one, as though stuck in an eternal present. And indeed Rouletabille's personal/mythic battle with the evil Larsan manifests itself throughout the text as a resistance to History.

After all, Larsan—the "skeleton" in Mathilde's personal closet—represents the past as threat; this as opposed to a horizontal or geographical threat, since the story's foreign-born characters visiting France (the Americans Rance and Old Bob, the flirtatious Russian prince) all turn out to be inoffensive. Rouletabille's personal sense of menace from his past, I will suggest, is inscribed onto the seaside site in the form of a rejected archaeological history.

As Sainclair explains, the Fort d'Hercule is located in a region identified by its geological name, les Rochers Rouges, referring to the red sandstone in which human tool and fossil remains had been found by avid scientists in 1874. This actual paleontological site becomes the fictional setting for Rouletabille's investigation into Larsan's identity and threatening plans. But rather than suggest an affinity between the young journalist's *enquête* and the cliffside setting, Leroux contrasts Rouletabille's rational clarity to the foolish digs of a red herring character, the American geologist *Bob*—or as he is called throughout, *le vieux Bob*, the eccentric aged uncle of Rouletabille's hosts who had come to *les Rochers rouges* to unearth fossil bones in the cliffside grottoes and to revive the decades-old debate on the antiquity of man. Introduced as "un vieux géologue [an old geologist] de l'Académie des Sciences de Philadelphie" (57), Old Bob practices a science of retrogression, searching for the most ancient relics of man:

[Les découvertes] attestaient, à ne pouvoir s'y méprendre, que les premiers hommes avaient vécu en cet endroit avant l'époque glaciaire. Sans doute la preuve de l'existence de l'homme à l'époque quaternaire était faite depuis longtemps, mais, cette époque mesurant, d'après certains, deux cent mille ans, il était intéressant de fixer cette existence dans une étape déterminée de ces deux cent mille années. On fouillait toujours aux Rochers Rouges et on allait de surprise en surprise. . . . Or, la rumeur publique (car l'événement avait dépassé les bornes du monde scientifique) répandait le bruit qu'il venait de trouver dans la *Barma Grande* d'extraordinaires ossements humains, des squelettes très bien conservés par une terre ferrugineuse, contemporaine des mammouths du début de l'époque quaternaire ou même de la fin de l'époque tertiaire!

[The discoveries proved beyond a doubt that the first humans had lived in this place before the glacial period. Of course, the fact of man's existence during the quaternary period had already long been proven, but, since that era lasted, according to some, two hundred thousand years, it was critical to pin down that existence to a particular segment within the two hundred thousand years. Excavations continued to be undertaken at the Rochers Rouges, and surprising discoveries abounded. Eventually, even the public scuttlebutt (for the event had transcended the scientific sphere) had it that extraordinary human bones had been unearthed at the *Barma Grande* site: skeletons well conserved by ferruginous soil and contemporary with the mammoths of the early quaternary period or even the end of the tertiary era!] (107)

Old Bob's enthusiasm for the archeological dating process is matched by his competitive investment in antiquity: when told that the Russian Prince Galitch has "Le plus vieux crâne de l'humanité" [the oldest skull of humanity], he responds with fury: "Ça n'est pas vrai! Le plus vieux crâne de l'humanité, il est au vieux Bob! C'est le crâne du vieux Bob!" [Not so! The oldest skull of humanity belongs to Old Bob! It's Old Bob's skull!] (111). The slippage here from external possession ("il est au vieux Bob") to personal anatomy ("c'est le crâne du vieux Bob") is humorously consistent with the old man's deep identification with prehistoric relics:

Il disait: *mon propre squelette*, ne faisant plus de différence, dans son enthousiasme, entre son squelette vivant qu'il habillait tous les jours de sa redingote noire, de son gilet noir, de son pantalon noir, de ses cheveux blancs, de ses joues roses, et le squelette préhistorique de la Terre de Feu.

[He would say: *my own skeleton*, making no distinction, in his enthusiasm, between his living skeleton which he clothed every day in a black waistcoat, black vest, black trousers, white hair, red cheeks—and the prehistoric skeleton from Tierra del Fuego.] (110)

Not just an old man who likes old bones, Bob embodies the antiquarian thrust of paleontological science.[9]

In this, he contrasts directly with the Stangersons, whose anticipatory experiments in modern physics were described in *Le Mystère de la chambre jaune*.[10] Whereas the French father-daughter couple hypothesized a "dissociation of matter" by means of electricity, radiography, solar, or ultraviolet light, the American Old Bob hopes to unearth the past, digging for fossils in cavernous soil. (One might note the chiasmic irony of "New World" historicism, "Old World" futurity). In any case, Leroux shifts the scientific setting of his Rouletabille novels from laboratory physics to skulls and bones—i.e., phrenology and paleontology. For Jacques Dubois, these two "indicial" sciences represent a unifying methodological bridge between (Rouletabille's) criminal investigation and (the Stangersons') abstract physics (*Le Roman policier ou la modernité*, 168). But one might alternately see the palaetiological sciences as an opposite pole from which Rouletabille recoils, as he tries to find his own path between the abstraction of the Stangerson model and the haunting implications of Old Bob's. For although Rouletabille laughs at the antiquarian's theatrical gaiety, he is also made uneasy by the obsessive unearthing of skeletons in the closet (or "cave") of humanity—we should recall here that throughout the novel Rouletabille's energies in *Parfum* are spent on tamping down the public resurrection of Larsan as specter of the Past.

As a red herring, Old Bob becomes the narrative object of displacement for Rouletabille's anger. In order to solve the mysterious "Attaque de la tour carrée" without alerting Larsan, Rouletabille publicly redirects suspicion onto Old Bob. The accusation seems absurd—to Edith Rance, who believes her uncle to be a harmless old scholar; and to the narrator Sainclair, who has mockingly dismissed Old Bob as a theatrical fool. But as any post-Freudian reader will recognize, humor reveals sites of anxiety—and Leroux's narrative seems quite invested in the recurring joke of Old Bob's "plus vieux crâne de l'humanité." Sainclair points out that he and Rouletabille enjoy the irony of using the entire phrase any time they mention the skull; and elsewhere, he explains, "en vérité, le vieux Bob était drôle à faire pleurer avec son plus vieux crâne de l'humanité" [in truth, Old Bob was tear-inducingly hilarious with his oldest skull of humanity] (112). "Drôle à faire pleurer," an expression turned literal when Old Bob's odd behaviors contribute to Rouletabille's recurring sobbing fits near the end of the book.

In a double gesture of repudiation, Rouletabille at once ridicules Old Bob's theatrical gaiety and grants him some sinister power, referring to him as "le professeur noir" [the black professor] and allowing suspicion for murder to fall on his bewigged head (or skull!) (145). Could Old Bob truly be Larsan in disguise? Though Rouletabille does not apparently believe so, he plants the distracting suggestion—and, moreover, seems himself perturbed by the text's continual identificatory slippages from Larsan's head to his own (through disavowed family resemblance) and from the quarternary fossil skull to Old Bob's. Of course the act of stirring up the past justly bothers Rouletabille, but the narrative emphasis on the *deep* past remains one of this novel's mysterious quirks. The superlative "le plus vieux" [the oldest] returns in gruesome form, for example, to identify the weapon responsible for the only actual death that occurs: one of the Fort's caretakers is impaled by "le plus vieux grattoir de l'humanité" [the oldest scraping-stone of humanity], itself displaced from a cliff-side cave to the château's walled territory. Even more tellingly, the paleontologist Old Bob gets described not just as a clown, but eventually as something more sinister—as an infernal return of the past aligned with the cliff-side caves of the present: "Par quel prodigieux anachronisme, ce moderne croque-mort, avec sa redingote et son chapeau haut de forme, s'agite-t-il, grotesque et macabre, devant cette caverne trois cents fois millénaire, creusée dans la lave ardente pour servir de premier toit à la première famille, aux premiers jours de la terre? Pourquoi ce fossoyeur sinistre dans ce décor embrasé?" [By what prodigious anachronism did this modern-day undertaker, with his waistcoat and top hat, bustle about, in grotesque and macabre manner, at the entrance to this three-thousand-year-old cavern, hollowed out of burning lava to serve as the first roof for the first family in the first days of the Earth?] (143): Grotesque, macabre, sinister—and all for his insistence on entering and disturbing the spaces of the deep past.

Leroux's description of Old Bob is a far cry from Balzac's famous ode to Cuvier, which exalts the French paleontologist as a sublime and inspired sorcerer-poet:

> Emporté par son génie, avez-vous plané sur l'abîme sans bornes du passé, comme soutenu par la main d'un enchanteur? En découvrant de tranche en tranche, de couche en couche, sous les carrières de Montmartre ou dans les schistes de l'Oural, ces animaux dont les dépouilles fossilisées appartiennent à des civilisations antédiluviennes, l'âme est effrayée d'entrevoir des millions de peuples . . . . Cuvier n'est-il pas le plus grand poète de notre siècle?

> [Swept away by his genius, have you ever soared above the boundless abyss of the past, as though borne by the hand of a sorcerer? As one discovers within layer upon layer, stratum upon stratum, under the quarries of Montmartre or the schists of the Urals, these animals whose fossilized remains belong to antediluvian civilizations, one's

soul is astonished to catch a glimpse of human millions. . . . Is not
Cuvier the greatest poet of our century?] (*La Peau de chagrin*, 1831)

Though Balzac's passage contains a hint of unease about Cuvier's discoveries
("l'âme effrayée"), it mainly contributes to the admiring and romanticized notions of geology cited by Lawrence Frank in his 2003 book *Victorian Detective Fiction and the Nature of Evidence*. In this study of British crime fiction
by Poe, Dickens, and Conan Doyle, Frank demonstrates that the figure of
the geologist was shrouded in the aura of the Romantic poet well into the
nineteenth century. He cites as an example Gideon Mantell's prose in *Wonders of Geology* (1838): "the palaeontologist, in his inquiries into . . . fossil remains . . . is enabled to call forth from their rocky sepulchres, the beings of
past ages, and like the fabled sorcerer, give form and animation to the inhabitants of the tomb" (25). The reconstructive science thus serves as an idealized
model for detective forensics, which attempts its own figural resurrection of
the past.

But, as Frank acknowledges, the positive associations with epistemological implications of modern paleontology were not unalloyed. In *Scenes from
Deep Time*, Martin Rudwick argues that as paleontology's claims became more
ambitiously historical, it acquired an epistemological power that many found
troubling.[11] As examples, Rudwick cites caricatures of fossil-finders, like one
from 1822 in which William Daniel Conybeare gently mocks the audacity of
British paleontologist William Buckland's historical reconstructions of the
antediluvian age. In the cartoon, Buckland enters a cave and sees live hyenas
feasting on scavenged bones. "Into the cave crawls Buckland himself, candle
in hand, illuminating this scene from deep time with the light of science,
penetrating the epistemic barrier between the human world and the pre-human,
and looking perhaps as surprised to see the hyenas as they are to see him"
(Rudwick, *Scenes*, 39). The scientific act of illuminating a cave's contents in
order to recreate the past becomes aligned with the deep myths of human hu-
bris: Prometheus' theft of divine fire, Adam and Eve's grab from the Tree of
Knowledge. The nineteenth-century paleontological discovery of human
prehistory not only disturbed the biblical literalists who feared an alternative
to the scriptural seven days of Creation; it also aroused general derision and
suspicion for its historicist, evolutionary implications that the human species itself may be trudging along a path that leads from primitivism to possible extinction. Rudwick cites another cartoon mocking Lyell's idea that

history is cyclical: imagining a future when humans have become extinct and other creatures study him as a relic of the past, it depicts a "Professor Ichtyosauras" holding a human skull and lecturing about "man found only in a fossil state" (48). Looking into the caves of prehistory, writes Rudwick, was seen as a problematic and intrusive act of "epistemic *penetration*," akin to spying through a keyhole into a human past that was otherwise inaccessible to human experience (58).

One might easily overlay this image of epistemic dangers with a Freudian reading of *Le Parfum de la dame en noir* in which the unconscious serves as metaphorical underground: in that case, Rouletabille's rejection of Old Bob's spelunking would be understood as a repression of his own subconscious identification with his criminal father. In fact, Leroux all but makes such a reading explicit when he invokes—by way of a skull—Rouletabille's physical resemblance to Larsan at the story's climactic moment. In classic detective fashion, Rouletabille has assembled all the characters in one room in order to reveal that one of them is Larsan in disguise. As his audience glances about nervously, Rouletabille engages in an odd rigamarole ("[une] bizarre cuisine"), having picked up Bob's prehistoric skull from the paleontologist's desk and starting to wash the blood-colored paint off of its surface (252). "Le plus calme, c'est Rouletabille entre son crâne et sa casserole. Mais quoi! Pourquoi reculons-nous tous soudain d'un même mouvement?" [The calmest of all was Rouletabille, between his skull and his saucepan. But, what's this! Why do we all suddenly recoil in unison?] (253). The spectators' sudden alarm is due to the stark resemblance between Rouletabille and his father Larsan, a resemblance made visible only at this skull-washing moment and located, moreover, in the bone most associated with paleontological discovery: the jawbone. The young journalist's jawbone, described in terms of ancestral menace, textually echoes the prehistoric "mâchoire ensanglanté" [bloodied jawbone] (245) and "crâne ensanglanté" [bloodied skull] (246) that had appeared on Old Bob's desk five pages earlier. Indeed, the blood on those geological artifacts gets displaced onto the external décor in the passage about Rouletabille's disturbing appearance:

Ah! ce profil, dans l'ombre rouge de la nuit commençante, ce front au fond de l'embrasure que vient ensanglanter le crépuscule comme au matin du crime est venue rougir ces murs la sanglante aurore! Oh! cette mâchoire dure et volontaire qui s'arrondissait tout à

l'heure . . . et qui, maintenant, se découpe sur <u>l'écran du</u>
<u>soir</u>, mauvaise et menaçante! Comme Rouletabille ressemble
à Larsan! Comme, en ce moment, il ressemble à son père!
<u>c'est Larsan!</u>

[Ah! that profile, in the red shadow of the nascent sky, that
forehead in the depths of the doorway that the dusk has come to
stain with blood, just as on the morning of a crime the bloody
dawn arrives to redden the walls! Oh! that jawbone, so hard and
stubborn, that had softened earlier . . . but that now juts out
against the screen of the evening sky, evil and menacing! How
Rouletebille resembles Larsan! How, at this moment, he resembles
his father! He is Larsan!] (253, my emphases)

Rouletabille is not Larsan, but in this spatially and temporally uncanny passage, a crime gets cast through the projection of Rouletabille's jawbone, itself
repeating ancestral forms, onto an external screen in order to create a bodily
identification between son and father. Bloody dusk somehow evokes crime's
bloody dawn . . . but which dawn? The one following Larsan's attack on
Mathilde; or the prehistoric dawn of humanity? Modern crime is underwritten
by ancestral violence in this story of skulls and bones, caves and crevices. At
the same time that the distance between Rouletabille's identity and Larsan's
is collapsed ("c'est Larsan!") by the shape of a jawbone, so is the distance between prehistory and modernity collapsed by a skull whose external location
is unsettled by a strange pronoun, "son": "Rouletabille est là, devant nous
avec son eau chaude dans sa casserole, une serviette et son crâne. Et il nettoie
son crâne" [Rouletabille is there, before us with his hot water and his saucepan, a towel and his skull. And he wipes his skull clean] (253). The skull that
once belonged to a prehistoric cave-dweller has passed through the possession
of the paleontologist Bob to settle into the hands of this young investigator—
and perhaps into his head, given the phrase's ambiguity: "son crâne." So as
Rouletabille washes away the blood-red paint from the skull, he is also attempting to cleanse himself of the blood relation, of the archaic violence that
threatens to dissolve the distinction between his rational self and the primitive Other.

    But this is not simply a story of Œdipal angst. And there is too much
emphasis on the skull's materiality to dismiss it as mere symbol. As a relic

of the past, the skull is only present in Rouletabille's ambit through the intervention of a particular science, paleontology, and its implied methodology: historical reconstruction. This is the investigative method that Rouletabille rejects, in favor of his preferred science, pure geometry. In *Le Parfum de la dame en noir*, abstract mind more than bodily skull will provide the answers. Constantly—and famously—referring to his "bonne bosse de la raison," Rouletabille had used an "admirable faculté de raisonner" to invent his own personal algebra for logical crime-solving, one that depends primarily on the notion of "closing the circle" or creating a geometrical frame for apparent mystery. Rouletabille's mathematical bent is paired with suspicion of other modern sciences—like the physics whose volatile gases blind Darzac and allow Larsan to return in disguise—and like paleontology, whose descent into deep time troubles Rouletabille's horizontal spatiality. As David Platten has noted, Leroux subordinates, through the character of Rouletabille, the value of empirical and forensic evidence to the abstract realm of Cartesian reasoning ("Reading-glasses," 260). I would add that in *Le Parfum* it is the specifically historical—paleontological—nature of forensic evidence that Rouletabille rejects in favor of abstract thought. Witness, for example, the turning point in Rouletabille's inquiry. Having entered Old Bob's dusty study, Rouletabille first picks up the geologist's ancient skull and peers with theatrical intensity into its cavities; what follows is the rigamarole of inspections as he checks the skull in profile and looks deeply into its eye sockets, before discarding the relic and turning his energies instead to drawing a geometrical map of the fort estate where they're staying. The narrator Sainclair is puzzled by this seemingly pointless task: "Comment, dans un moment aussi tragique, . . . comment Rouletabille pouvait-il *s'amuser* à faire des dessins avec une règle, une équerre, un tire-ligne et un compas?" [How, at a moment so tragic, . . . how could Rouletabille play at making drawings with a ruler, a t-square, a drafting pen, and a compass?] (179). The geometric tools of compass and ruler allow Rouletabille to suppress the haunting traces of the Past (*la vieille tour, le vieux chateaux, la trace du crime imposssible*) and recast the mystery into an algebraic and cartographic problem. "[I]l faisait un plan" [He was making a map], declares Sainclair, and apparently this two-dimensional map has more to divulge than did the prehistoric skull, for Rouletabille suddenly jumps up from his diagram with a frenzied declaration that the ink he had used was blood. This was the same ink that he had inspected on Old Bob's skull, but only when transferred to the horizontal space of the map does the color's significance become clear to him and does he then solve the mystery by "closing the circle" on Larsan.

Rouletabille's preference for two-dimensional spatiality (as opposed to the three-dimensional cavity-ridden skull with its fossil implication of stratified time) is reinforced in the text by descriptions of the coastal setting that evacuate its military and geological histories in favor of a mythical atemporality: the Mediterranean basin, writes Sainclair, may well be the very spot where Hercules slew the 100-headed dragon: "Aussi," he adds, "je ne suis point bien sûr que les os de l'*Elephas antiquus*, découverts il y a quelques années au fond des Rochers Rouges, ne sont pas les os de ce dragon-là!" [Therefore, I would not be surprised to discover that the bones of the *Elephas antiquus*, discovered a few years ago deep in the Rochers Rouges, were the bones of that very dragon!"] (64–65). By recasting a real archaeological find—the mammoth bone—as mythic fable, the narrator downplays the scientific curiosity about man's past that first brought Rouletabille's hosts to the *Rochers Rouges*. Stratigraphical geology and historical time give way, then, to cartographic space and mythic atemporality in this Oedipal tale of a son's resistance to his sinister Father's return from the past.

Poe, Gaboriau, and Conan Doyle may all have cited Cuvier's fossil reconstructions as analogous to detective work, but Leroux's Rouletabille rejects paleontology and its historicist implications of the past's reach into present and future, in favor of geometrical space and mythic time. In the end, Rouletabille is literally conservative (one of *La Chambre jaune*'s maxims was Lavoisier's "nothing gained, nothing lost")—neither past- nor forward-thinking, but preserving a state of insularity, "closing the circle" against threats from ocean, father, and time.

*   *   *

Through this rejection of historiographical thought, Rouletabille stands in contrast to the more modern "gentleman-cambrioleur" that Maurice Leblanc introduced in his 1905 *Arrestation d'Arsène Lupin*. As a subversive foil to the classic detective (rendered comically by Leblanc as "Herlock Sholmes"), Arsène Lupin might be expected to thumb his nose at the ideological and epistemological certainties of investigation. And indeed, his spatial mobility and anarchic gaiety undermine small-minded notions of social order; but through a particularly grounded relation to his country's past—buried stratigraphically in the coastal *terroir*—Lupin reinforces ideals of national unity that epitomize the investigative positivism of Third Republic historiography.

Arsène Lupin, *historiographe-paléontologue*

Unlike Rouletabille, whose Œdipal mission is both personal and universal— i.e. at once smaller and bigger than the category of "nation"—Lupin is solidly nationalist in his "(anti)heroism."[12] Deeply invested in his country's welfare, Lupin knows its history by heart; known for donating some of his stolen loot to the nation, Lupin is called, with ironic pride, "notre voleur national" [our national thief].[13] Though Francis Lacassin suggested in 1979 that Arsène Lupin's relationship to history is one of lyric intimacy rather than chronological accuracy, adding that Lupin sublimates dusty History into romanesque legend (24), more recent critics have—rightly, I believe—joined Dominique Jullien in identifying Lupin as a strong historiographer. In her 1990 study of "L'Aiguille creuse," Jullien argues that Lupin's investment in the national *patrimoine* finds its logic in modern historiography's archival thrust; after the 1791 opening of the national archives, the analogy between historical and detective investigations is tightened, for now both clearly rely on traces (whether documents or clues) of the past.

> On le voit, l'histoire constitue le nerf de l'intrigue policière. Recherche historique et enquête policière convergent et s'appuient sur une méthode commune: l'examen critique du document. En cela du reste, Maurice Leblanc ne fait que transposer sous forme romanesque une donnée fondamentale de l'historiographie positiviste: l'importance croissante de l'archivistique

> [Clearly, history is at the heart of detective fiction plotting. Historical research and police investigation converge and corroborate each other through their common method: the critical examination of a document. In that respect, moreover, Maurice Leblanc is merely transposing onto fictional form a fundamental fact of positivistic historiography: the growing importance of archival science.] (Jullien, 107)

Lupin is no armchair archivist, however; his "documents of the past" are engraved in sea walls and castle-forts, buried in roman ruins under the lac d'Auvergne, concealed in secret treasure vaults, and interred under Norman fields. The strongly spatialized nature of Lupin's relation to the past is evident in *L'Aiguille creuse* (1909), a novel whose plot relies on coastal topography and arcane architecture for its solution. As David Platten notes in his excellent summary of the novel, the true Château de l'Aiguille is an excavated needle of rock situated off the north coast of France at Etretat: "Complete with hidden entrances and exits, this sorcerer's castle consists of circular rooms each superimposed on the other, in which a precious national heritage, including the *secret des rois de la France* . . . , is stored."[14] Lupin capitalizes on the site's coastal geology by escaping from the castle through an upper chamber of a sea cave, whose ceiling shifts as waters rise and fall. For both Jullien and Windish, *L'Aiguille creuse* exemplifies Lupin's historiographic nationalism, showing him to be an avid and knowledgeable conservator of the *patrimoine*'s treasures.

But I would like to shift attention to a lesser-known adventure, *La Comtesse de Cagliostro* (1924), which similarly invokes sinister caves and buried treasure, while also usefully reminding us that Lupin's is not merely a retrogressive eye; the past for him is useful only insofar as it can be mobilized, recast for future exploits. In Leblanc's fiction, the past is certainly there for the plucking, but only for someone whose identity-shifts and wanderlust mark him as master of mobility and openness to the future. In other words, Arsène Lupin's reconstructions of French national identity may well jibe with a Third Republic discourse of historicism, but it is a historicism that is future-oriented rather than nostalgic. Or in terms of the paleontological-detective model, I would say that if Lupin likes digging up buried clues or "documents," it is less to *conserve* the national past than to put it back into movement and play.

La Comtesse de Cagliostro first appeared in *Le Journal* from December 1923 to January 1924. The story itself is built from the strata of a literary past, as it self-consciously revives the legend of Cagliostro that Alexandre Dumas had popularized for French audiences in 1846; "Le roman d'Alexandre Dumas avait mis à la mode Joseph Balsamo, soi-disant comte de Cagliostro" [Alexandre Dumas' novel launched Joseph Balsamo, the so-called count of Cagliostro, into fashion] (23). Leblanc's narrative gaze, however, remains fixed on the latter-day female Countess who claims a hazy relation to the famed and mysterious eighteenth-century Count. Set in 1894, *La Comtesse de Cagliostro* opens with the young Arsène Lupin, calling himself Raoul d'Andrésy, riding a bicycle and preparing to marry a baron's daughter, Clarisse d'Étigues. Though sweet Clarisse is a perfect match for the twenty-year-old Raoul, he becomes fascinated by the sinister rumors surrounding the Comtesse de Cagliostro; she has been accused of having murdered two men by throwing them off cliffs into the sea, at le Havre and Dieppe, and of having attempted to kill a third with poison. Clarisse's father, the Baron d'Étigues, enters into a vigilante plot to punish the Countess by setting her out to sea off the Normandy coast in a sabotaged boat. The avenging men believe La Cagliostra to have drowned, but in a chapter called "La barque qui coule," the reader discovers that Raoul, in bathing-trunks, had surreptitiously accompanied the boat in order to rescue her and become her lover.

By entering into a liaison with the older, experienced Countess, Raoul rejects the future that his intended Clarisse represents. Not just the individual future of an honorable marriage, but the open Future upon which a historically-motivated society prepares to embark as the twentieth-century approaches, with its bicycles, trains, and transatlantic liners. For La Cagliostra embodies, in this story, modern mobility's opposite: historical stasis. Supposedly born in 1788, La Cagliostra has "conservé" the same ravishing appearance as displayed in a miniature painted portrait from 1816, a photo from 1870, and her current embodiment of 1894 (31). Irrationally, inexplicably, counterhistorically, this conservation of eternal youth inscribes itself on the Countess's face.

Raoul—Arsène Lupin—is initially enticed by this uncanny quiescence, but eventually he will begin to see it as a threat (as opposed to Rouletabille, for whom stasis equals safety). When La Cagliostra seduces the young Lupin after the ocean rescue, she takes him to her houseboat, *La Nonchalante*, aptly named for the sensual and lethargic idyll that takes the lovers along the Seine's riverbanks dotted with ruined castles and abbeys (93). Here, once again, the Countess seems to hold out the tempting promise of historical inertia, as the barge floats listlessly and unengaged near ruined reminders of the past: "La forêt de Brotonne, les ruines de Jumièges, l'abbaye de Saint-Georges, [etc.]" (100). The watery indifference to history lulls Lupin into a month of sex and thievery, but eventually his horror of blood-letting awakens the young man from his torpor and he renounces his murderous lover: "Tu entends, Josine. Je ne veux pas tuer! Voler, oui. Cambrioler, soit! Mais tuer, non, mille fois non!" [Understand this, Josine: I do not want to kill! Steal, yes. Burglarize, sure. But kill? No, a thousand times no!] (118). In the novel's spatial terms, to renounce La Cagliostra's evil nature is to reject *La Nonchalante*'s indolent coasting. For when Lupin finally tears himself away from his lover's sexual tyranny, it is to pedal away from the riverfront on a modern bicycle. "Toute la nuit, prenant les chemins qui se présentaient à lui, [il] pédala, autant pour dépister les recherches que pour s'infliger une fatigue salutaire." [All through the night, taking paths as they arose before him, he pedaled, as much to avoid pursuit as to achieve a salutary state of exhaustion] (178). Thus the modern bicycle, associated from the start with Lupin's honorable love interest Clarisse d'Étigues, replaces the barge; mechanical work replaces sensual liquidity; engagement with history replaces immoral inaction; moving forward replaces languishing in a ruined past.[15]

And indeed, Lupin then embarks on an adventure that involves looking doubly forward and back, unearthing France's history to mobilize it for the future. Like an archeologist or paleontologist searching underground for human and cultural remains, Lupin decides to dig up the "7 chandeliers" treasure, a trove of church donations that had been buried centuries earlier off Normandy's coast by a secret association of monks. Lupin's delight at this underground legacy from the past is expressed in terms that combine historical inquiry with detectival deduction: "Quelle manifique [sic] aventure! J'ai toujours eu la certitude que le passé avait légué au présent de ces trésors fabuleux dont la recherche prend inévitablement la forme d'un insoluble problème" [What a wonderful adventure! I'd always been sure that the past had bequeathed to the present some of these fabulous treasures whose pursuit inevitably takes the form of an unsolvable problem.] If the epistemological "problème" part of his statement seems to connote the kind of abstracted mathematical equation favored by a Rouletabille, it is quickly re-grounded in the physical terrain, as Lupin continues:

Comment en serait-il autrement? Nos ancêtres ne disposaient pas comme nous des coffres-forts et des caves de la Banque de France. Ils étaient obligés de choisir des cachettes naturelles où ils entassaient l'or et les bijoux, et dont ils transmettaient le secret par quelque formule mnémotechnique qui était comme le chiffre de la serrure. Qu'un cataclysme survînt, le secret était perdu, et perdu le trésor si péniblement accumulé.

[How could it be otherwise? Unlike us, our ancestors had no access to the safes and cellars of the Banque de France. They had to make do with natural hiding-places such as these, in which they stashed their gold and jewels, and whose secret existence they transmitted through some mnemonic device serving as entry code. Were a

cataclysm to occur, the secret would be lost, as would the treasure
so painstakingly accumulated.] (130)

The difference between a bank's artificial "caves" and the crevices of natural
terrain is the latter's vulnerability to forces beyond human control: Lupin's
present pursuit of the buried mystery is made possible because the chain of
transmission has not been interrupted by geological events. Though somewhat
casual, Lupin's reference to the Cuvierian notion of cataclysmic geological
events combines with his delight at the buried inheritance to create an archaeological sense of French regional territory. He adds:

si les dix mille pierres précieuses ont été glissées dans l'étrange
tirelire, c'est à quelque chose comme un milliard de francs qu'il
faudrait évaluer ces biens de mainmorte légués par le moyen âge,
tout cet effort de millions et de millions de moines, cette gigan-
tesque offrande de tout le peuple chrétien et des grandes époques de
fanatisme, tout cela qui est dans les flancs de la borne de granit, au
milieu d'un verger normand! Est-ce admirable?

[If the ten thousand precious gems have indeed been slipped into
this strange moneybox, around a million francs would be the
estimated worth of this mortmain [*lit.* dead hand] property
bequeathed to us by the middle ages—all this effort by millions
and millions of monks, this enormous offering by all christian
peoples and the great eras of fanaticism, all of this buried in the
stony side of a granite marker in the middle of an orchard in
Normandy! Is it not amazing?] (129–30, my emphasis)

National glory and regional territory are united through a historicizing link between past and present—"ces biens de mainmorte légués par le moyen âge"—
that is concretely situated in the very rocks of the land. Lupin uses here the legal
term *mainmorte*, first meaning a feudal lord's rights to his dead vassal's goods,
then expanded to ecclesiastical property rights, and now figuratively used as post-
humous control, "mort-main" in English: the dead hand that reaches from the
grave. Thus in its connotative effects, *mainmorte* signals a sort of originary violence. So although Lupin is an anti-detective in this popular crime series, he is
nonetheless engaged in the kind of historicist investigation into a mysterious
and potentially disturbing past that characterizes the classic *roman policier*.

My reading here is informed by the explicit links between the palaetiological sciences and nineteenth-century detective fiction that Lawrence Frank, for example, has identified in the English corpus. The analogy goes beyond the mere Cuvierian reconstruction of past events; it involves a particular archeological methodology, such as Charles Lyell describes in his *Geological Evidences of the Antiquity of Man* (1863). Embedded in cave wall formations and shifting strata, fossil bones and shells provide only fragmentary evidence to the investigator's eye; in order to read "the pages of the peaty record" of an ever receding past, the geologist must accept the epistemological uncertainty that comes of geological disruptions (Frank, 120). He must be, in other words, a skeptical historian—skeptical of fictions of continuity and of handed-down authority (as is Arsène Lupin), but still invested in historical change, as distinguished from the mythic or theological time that conservative antiquarians of the nineteenth-century opposed to paleontological discovery. In this context, we can see the anti-establishmentarian Lupin as an apologist for the historical imagination. With his interest in the *7 chandeliers* treasure, he seems to tell us: look to the past, don't stop the flow of history—resist, in other words, La Cagliostra, with her violent interruptions of men's lives and her troubling physiological stasis.

Lupin is also to be contrasted, as suggested earlier, with Rouletabille's paradoxical anti-historicism. Indeed, if we return to Lupin's use of the term *mainmorte* for the *7 chandeliers* treasure, we are led to another scene in the novel, with its own "main morte," and which highlights the contrast between Leblanc's historicism and Leroux's "closed circle" of mythic stasis. In Leroux, as we saw, primitive skulls serve as sinister red herrings buried in the cliffside grottoes of the southern coast; but the paleontological approach represented by Old Bob ended up being surpassed by Rouletabille's "pure reason." In Leblanc's Normandy, too, we find cliffside grottoes aligned with sinister deeds: la Cagliostra takes advantage of the grottoes and cracks in riverside cliffs to hide her criminal henchmen and their dirty deeds. But "buried" in those caves are not irrelevant fossils from the past; rather, the caves conceal the all-too-present torture by La Cagliostra's thugs of an innocent old woman. In order to investigate the double mystery of the monastic treasure and La Cagliostra's machinations, Arsène Lupin enters the dark and crumbling interior of a cliffside cave, much as Conybeare and other paleontological spelunkers of the previous century had done. Clawing through the cave's debris to follow the indistinct moans of an aged lady, Lupin finds to his horror that the woman's hand bones have been broken one by one by Cagliostra's thugs. This non-

historical "main morte"—the dead hand of a living woman—is what finally incites Lupin to break away from his lover's cruel, sensual, and presentist
grip. Thus, where Rouletabille rejects the bones in a cave because they represent history's threatening reach from the past, Lupin rejects his "bones in the
cave" for the opposite reason: because they are the wrong kind of mainmorte,
attached to a living tortured being rather than buried in the Norman fields as
national link in a historical chain of past, present, and future.

By doing his own digging for buried treasure in the *terroirs* of France's
coastal provinces, in other words, Lupin relies on a historiographical investigative method distinct from that of Rouletabille. Indeed, unlike Leroux's
journalist-investigator, whose rejection of Old Bob's antiquarianism exposes
a conservative statism, Lupin implicitly embraces the doubly back- and
forward-looking thrust of paleontology. Although Gaston Leroux and Maurice Leblanc are typically lumped together under the umbrella of crime fiction modernity, their best-known detective fictions reveal starkly differing
attitudes toward pre-modernity and the palaetiological reconstruction of the
past. And if we dig deeper into the corpus of Leroux's popular crime fiction,
we find that author to be particularly invested in exploring one of paleontology's most troubling implications: the erasure of clear distinctions between
humankind and primitive beast.

Skull Stories: *Balaoo*, the Criminal Ape-Man

Claudine Cohen, in her 2007 book *Un Néandertalien dans le métro*, writes of
the controversy surrounding the discovery of a skull in 1856 that was eventually to be identified as the first prehistoric human fossil, that of "Neanderthal" man.[16] On the cover of that book, Cohen strikingly combines the now
familiar profile of a caveman with a decidedly *un*primitive porkpie hat and
shirt collar. Cohen, a historian of paleontology, playfully uses her book title
to locate the caveman in the metro to evoke hard-fought debates about whether
prehistoric man was an exotically simian brute or, alternatively, just an un-
shaved version of us—of modern, civilized people. In the 1860s through the
1880s, those debates revolved around common features in the shape of the fossil
skull—and still today, the skull remains the site of debate about our common
ancestry with the chimpanzee.

In 2009, for example, paleontologists unearthed the remains of *Ardipithe-
cus ramidus*, a fossilized female nicknamed Ardi and considered, at 4.4 million

years of age, to be the earliest known hominid. Their reports, published in the journal *Science*, detailed the features of Ardi's skull that distinguish her from both apes and modern humans; these include the monkey-like projecting muzzle, a more humanoid ridge above the eye socket, and openings at the bottom of the skull where nerves and blood vessels entered the brain. The resulting picture of Ardi as a mixed-up missing link troubles the binary categories of human and animal: "This is not an ordinary fossil. It's not a chimp. It's not a human. It shows us what we used to be."[17]

A century and a half ago, of course, the simian ancestry of humankind was far from accepted. In France, in particular, although Darwin's 1859 *Origin of Species* was immediately circulated in its original English, Cuvier's authoritative dismissal of human prehistory remained so prevalent that when Pierre Boitard published in 1861 his *Paris avant les hommes: L'homme fossile, etc.*, he only argued for a primitive connection between human and ape through the convoluted and fantastical narrative pretext of an extraterrestrial genie-demon who comes to guide the somnolent author through past epochs. Before commencing their journey into Paris's deep prehistory, the "diable boiteux" quizzes Boitard on the meaning of the relatively esoteric word "paléontologie," to which the author responds: "Les géologues . . . ont donné ce nom à l'étude des animaux qui vivaient avant le déluge, et dont on retrouve les ossements et les débris fossiles enfouis dans les diverses couches de terre qui forment la mince écorce de notre globe" [Geologists gave this name to the study of animals that existed before the great Flood, and whose bones and fossil remains are found buried in the varied strata of soil that form the thin crust of our earth].[18] A pedagogical prefatorial dialogue ensues, in which the cloven-hoofed little demon bursts into laughter at "Georges Cuvier et les géologues de l'Académie des sciences" for their stubborn refusal to accept fossil evidence of human prehistory. Many chapters later, when the two time-travelers eventually reach the "Cinquième époque de la cinquième période paléontologique," they come upon some creatures of a physiognomy so monstrous that the narrator cannot at first recognize them as men (239). Hairy and bloody-lipped, flat-nosed and black, the foul-smelling cave-dwellers wield silex tomahawks and emit gutteral grunts. When the narrator evinces horrified disbelief at the identification of the hairy creatures as "l'homme fossile," the demon responds by connecting them to modern man through the intermediate figure of the ape: "Beaucoup d'individus, même en France, sont presque aussi velus que des singes" [Many individuals, even in France, are almost as hairy as apes] (249). Moreover, he explains, the shape of these creatures' heads matches the skulls found by modern paleontologists, adding with the pseudo-scientific racism of the era that "certains nègres éthiopiens t'offrent encore la même figure" [certain Ethiopian negroes display the same features] (249). Boitard includes on a facing page two drawings of fossil skulls, the first from an ancient Peruvian tomb and the second unearthed in Austria in 1823, as evidence that the French Academy of Sciences has been held back by religious conservatism and blind obeisance to Cuvier.

Skulls remained at the forefront of the human prehistory debate and, indeed, quickly entered the French public imaginary through vulgarizing science journals and museum exhibits. The Paris Exposition Universelle of 1867 devoted a large exhibit to finds in prehistoric archaeology and anthropology, and at the 1900 Paris Expo, a Javanese "Pithecanthropos erectus" skeleton was fully reconstituted for display. In *Dances with Darwin* (2009), Rae Beth Gordon explores the racial investment of these popularizations of paleontological science, in which the particular morphology of primitive skulls is the determining factor used to link apes to present-day Javanese and African natives.[19] Gordon mentions, too, that the Museum of Natural History owned more than 1,300 skulls; that a museum established by the neurologist Paul Broca held 2,500 skulls; and that the author Paul Hyacinthe-Loyson set up an exhibit of skulls at the Théâtre Antoine in 1908 (84, 83).[20] Another odd episode in the history of skull display is the nineteenth-century "crystal skull hoax," in which French antiquities dealer Eugène Boban acquired supposed pre-Columbian skulls carved out of quartz; three of these human skull "artefacts" ended up at the Trocadéro Museum (later named Le Musée de l'Homme) before being exposed as modern fakes. But it was the actual fossil skulls found by paleontologists next to weapons in geological strata in Europe whose primate features raised scientific and popular questions about primitivism, atavism, and human brutality. Already, to nineteenth-century phrenologists and criminal anthropologists, the modern human skull had provided supposedly legible information about brutal tendencies and innate violence.[21] But the fossil discovery of the *pre*historic human skull added a new and radically historical dimension to notions of human violence, reversing the Rousseauistic model of the noble savage and proposing in its place a club-wielding caveman ready to burst atavistically into modern-day society.

It is fascinating to see the fin-de-siècle shift in the French popular press from Cuvierian skepticism to a wide acceptance of both the existence of prehistoric humanity and the Darwinian thesis of evolution. The somewhat lowbrow periodical *Le Voleur* (democratically subtitled "Journal pour tous"), which published the serialized crime fictions of Fortuné de Boisgobey and Émile Gaboriau, also carried a popularizing science column, "La Science pour tous," that allows us to track human paleontology's entry into nonspecialized public discourse. In 1870, the column's unnamed author asks with overt skepticism, "L'homme a-t-il été singe?" [Did man start out as an ape?]. Eight years later, the same column continues to claim that anthropoids are clearly distinguishable from monkeys, despite some common features: "Un organe, toutefois, subit chez les grands singes une modification profonde qu'on ne retrouve pas chez l'homme: c'est le crâne" [One organ, however, undergoes in great apes a profound modification that is not found in man: the skull]. It is precisely the skull, then, that separates man from monkey in 1878. But by 1892, in a *Voleur* article called "L'homme et le singe," the skull is invoked for the opposite argument, i.e., to link them together: writing of a chimpanzee named Edgar (!) who had been brought back to Paris from Guinea, a columnist explains that this primate species "est de tous les grands singes celui qui se rapproche le plus de l'homme par l'ensemble de son organisation. Il a le crâne arrondi" [is, of all great apes, the one that most resembles man in his overall form. He has man's rounded skull]. On both sides of the evolutionary debate, then, the skull remained a primary site of evidence.

It was the skull, too, that inspired popular fictions mixing the species of man and monkey. In his 1935 bibliographical essay on "ape-man novels," Régis Messac noted the translation into French in 1867 of Thomas Henry Huxley's *Evidence as to Man's Place in Nature* as a key moment for the evolution debate in France: "Huxley, usant d'un argument qui allait devenir à la mode, faisait un rapprochement entre le crâne du gorille et les crânes préhistoriques de Neanderthal" [Using an argument that would soon come into fashion, Huxley drew a parallel between the skull of a gorilla and the prehistoric skulls of the Neanderthals].[22] The skull even reappears in the title of a story by Goffredo de Crollalanza: published in an 1885 short story collection *Le Souper rouge*, "La Foire aux crânes" recounts a brutal attack by a monkey on the wife of Professor von Donderblitzen, in imitation of the professor's cadaver dissections (Messac, 33–34). By the first decades of the twentieth century, the theory of the missing link had fully taken hold and popular novelists were imagining more and more confrontations between ape-men and contemporary civilization. The most famous of such fictions is of course Edgar Rice Burroughs's 1912 *Tarzan of the Apes*, but Tarzan himself was of human birth and therefore did not represent a transition species of primate. More directly challenging to the human/animal distinction were the intermediate ape-men of Sumatra that appear in Jules Lermina's 1905 *To-Ho le tueur d'or*: the savage "Orang-Aceh" fight off Dutch invaders at the edge of a forest whose depths hold increasingly simian creatures, in a spatialized reworking of cross-epoch evolution.

Lermina's tale may well have influenced Gaston Leroux, who came out in 1911 with the strange story of *Balaoo*, an ape-man brought to France from the Malaysian jungle by the eccentric scientist Coriolis. A 1913 film version was released under the title *Balaoo the Demon Baboon*, but there is nothing supernatural about Leroux's apeman; he is, in fact, firmly anchored in the sciences of paleontology and evolution. As the narrator straightforwardly explains, late nineteenth-century fossil evidence had identified an intermediate creature between monkey and human whose existence confirms the Darwinian thesis.[23] This *anthropopithèque*, the term used throughout to describe Balaoo, has survived to the modern day, and Coriolis takes it upon himself to trick his colleagues by passing the monkey-man off as man: he shaves Balaoo's face and hands, surgically alters his voicebox to accommodate human speech, teaches him manners and philosophy, and enrolls him in law school in Paris. As a result, Balaoo is considered by all to be an eccentric foreigner—perhaps a Chinese acrobat or an ugly native of Java. One character, struck by Balaoo's sartorial elegance, thinks he might even be considered handsome in far eastern latitudes, but for the exceptionally powerful build of the animal jaws, *la mâchoire animale*. The jawbone combines with other features of Balaoo's skull—"ses yeux bridés, . . . son nez légèrement épaté et . . . sa face aux larges méplats" [his slanting eyes, his slightly flattened nose, and the wide planes of his face]—to reveal his simian side, one that is both primitive and violent.

So far, this "skull story" seems fully in keeping with other ape-man fictions of the time; but a distinguishing generic feature of Leroux's novel is its capitalization on crime fiction conventions. At the story's start, there is little indication that a typical small-town murder mystery will morph midway into a scientifically inflected meditation on transitional species. Readers of *Le Matin* on October 9, 1911, encountered the serial novel's first installment, entitled "Le crime de l'auberge du soleil-noir," in which the inhabitants of Saint-Martin-des-Bois deplore a recent train accident and the brutal murders of their local barber and tailor. Coy avoidance of the titular character proceeds long enough to make possible this back-cover publicity prose in a later book edition:

Quelle nouvelle épouvante faisait donc courir, ce soir, dans le couloir ordinairement désert de la rue Neuve, les pauvres gens du pays de Cerdogne? . . . Des accidents de chemin de fer inexplicables,

des crimes aussi mystérieux que spectaculaires, voilà ce qui terrorise
les habitants de Saint-Martin-des-Bois. La nuit, barricadés dans
leurs maisons, ils entendent des gémissements venant de la rue, puis
une voix sourde qui prononce cette phrase énigmatique: *"Pitié à la
maison d'homme."* Et, un peu plus tard, on retrouve un cadavre
pendu au plafond par un être certainement doué d'une force
surhumaine. Qui est donc ce mystérieux assassin? Pourquoi
commet-il ces crimes apparemment gratuits? Telles étaient les
questions que se posaient anxieusement, en 1911, les lecteurs du
Matin, en attendant chaque jour la suite de leur feuilleton.

[What unknown terror had sent the poor folks of the Cerdogne
fleeing, tonight, into the usually deserted lane of the rue Neuve?
Unexplained train accidents, mysterious and spectacular crimes:
these are what terrorize the inhabitants of Saint-Martin-des-Bois. At
night, barricaded inside their homes, they hear moans coming from
the road, then a muffled voice that utters this enigmatic phrase:
Mercy in the house of man. And, moments later, the discovery is
made of a corpse, hung from the ceiling by a being clearly endowed
with superhuman strength. Who, then, is this mysterious assassin?
Why does he commit these apparently motiveless crimes? Such are
the questions that were anxiously posed in 1911 by the readers of *Le
Matin*, as they daily awaited their serial novel's next installment.]

A hindsight reader of the novel's refrain "Pitié à la maison d'homme" might
identify the speaker's self-exclusion from humanity, but Leroux delays the introduction of Balaoo until the novel's eighth chapter—and even then, he is
first presented merely as "Noel," Coriolis's melancholy manservant and agricultural helper. In the earlier chapters, townspeople suspect instead a family
of rustics named Vautrin: the strong and stocky red-haired Hubert, his albino
brothers Siméon and Élie, and their savage little sister Zoé.[24] Born like a litter
of wolves and living in a hovel at the edge of the forest, the wild Vautrin siblings hint at the novel's later themes of species indeterminacy, as does the hybrid plant species breeding in which the scientist Coriolis is engaged.

But of course it is Balaoo, whose story dominates the Second and Third
Books of the novel, who truly topples distinctions between human and animal. On Coriolis's estate, Balaoo speaks with modesty and admires the scientist's daughter Madeleine from afar, making every effort to distance himself

from his forest origins: "Depuis qu'on lui avait expliqué ce que c'était qu'un anthropopithèque, il exagérait la douceur et la timidité de ses manières, car, pour rien au monde, il n'eût voulu être confondu avec un de la race singe qui est si mal élevée" [Upon learning what an anthropopithecus was, he began to exaggerate the gentleness and shyness of his own behavior, for he wanted above all else to avoid being mistaken for a member of such an ill-mannered primate race] (109). In the forest, however, Balaoo's primeval animality reemerges, as he casts off his shoes to climb trees with his prehensile hind limbs. Soon it becomes clear that Coriolis's civilizing efforts can only go so far: the ape-man continues to emit unpleasantly gutteral moans, scratches himself at the formal dinner table, and—most important—is revealed halfway through the novel as the brutal murderer of the two innocent townsmen. When the magistrate comes to arrest Balaoo in Coriolis's home, he makes the mistake of bantering about the lovely Madeleine's marriage eligibility; the jealous Balaoo responds by strangling him to death right in front of the horrified scientist and his daughter. "Quelle catastrophe!" thinks Coriolis. And yet, he defends Balaoo, likening his violent act to that of glorified war generals: "L'anthropopithèque . . . traîne [sa proie] derrière lui avec un orgueil aussi conscient que, dans le triomphe, le général romain traînant les dépouilles opimes. Ah! quel front relevé il a, ce Balaoo . . . Et bien fait pour la couronne de lauriers. Dans tout singe, il y a un général romain!" [The anthropopithecus drags his prey behind him with a pride as self-aware as that of a triumphant Roman general dragging along his rich spoils! Oh, how upraised it is, this Balaoo's head . . . and how well-fashioned for the wreath of laurels. In every ape, there is a Roman general!] (126). Only Coriolis, it seems, can see the man in the ape. Or, following Darwin, the ape in the man:

Evidemment, cet anthropopithèque allait gêner bien du monde; mais tant pis! . . . tant pis pour les imbéciles qui ne croient pas au transformisme . . . A-t-on jamais entendu une stupidité pareille?

[Evidently, many would be bothered by the existence of this anthropopithecus; but, too bad for them! Too bad for those imbeciles unwilling to believe in transformism. Has one ever heard such stupidity?] (187)

Leroux's explicitly transformist thesis has rightly led Marc Angenot, in his study of prehistoric fictions, to contrast Balaoo with the *non*-human orangutan in Poe's inaugural crime fiction, "The Murders in the Rue Morgue." Balaoo seems equally brutal, but unlike Poe's monkey, the anthropopithèque explicitly and insistently unsettles the man/animal divide. Yes, he represents the evolutionary missing link, but one can go even farther and suggest that because this missing link is brought forward from prehistory into modern France, he becomes even more than just a historical connector between mankind and monkey: he becomes, surprisingly, a Derridian "animot."

Jacques Derrida's 1997 lecture "L'Animal que donc je suis" has become a foundational text for the emerging interdisciplinary field of animal studies. Translated into English as *The Animal That Therefore I Am*, it is cited alongside Donna Haraway's *Primate Visions* and Deleuze and Guattari's writings on "becoming-animal" as a key blow to the longstanding notion that we humans are radically different from the animal Other.[25] Derrida's talk breaks down conceptual divides between the human subject and the millions of animal species that exist in the world by introducing a new word, "animot," whose phonic character recalls the plurality of species but whose spelling reminds us that the word animal is, merely, a word and that we like all other species exist in subjection to the materiality of language. We cannot dominate, for we share our finitude with all other animals. As the theorist of post-humanity Cary Wolfe puts it, Derrida's *animot* forces us to acknowledge "the thickness and finitude of human embodiment and [to understand] human evolution as itself a specific form of animality, one that is unique and different from other forms but no more different, perhaps, than an orangutan is from a starfish" ("Human, all too human," 572). Wolfe here chooses the orangutan as an obvious intermediary between human and animal in order to help us make the leap, but in his lecture Derrida generally avoided discussion of primates to talk instead about cats, cicadas, hedgehogs, and cows—surely because he wants us now to confront what seems to be the even more radical otherness of those species that we pet, step on, ignore, or eat. The one time Derrida implicitly refers to the missing link is when he calls Darwinism a cultural trauma—one of three productive decenterings of humanity, along with Copernicus and Freud (136). Derrida's title explicitly plays on the verb in "je suis": *l'animal que donc je suis* is the animal that I *am* as well as the animal that I follow. For Derrida, to follow the animal is to abandon the space of primacy, of subjective agency and conscious construction of the other. But our ability to conceive of that form of following was itself only made possible by the nineteenth-century proposal that we *follow* animals temporally in the evolutionary process. Through Darwin, we came to know ourselves as

Johnny-come-latelies, not the apotheosis of Divine planning, but mere animals sharing ancestry with apes and frogs and maybe fish. We should not forget that the monkey matters—and that our primate identity was as radical and challenging an idea in the late nineteenth century as is our shared subjectivity with a cicada today.

In *L'Animal que donc je suis*, Derrida identifies a number of characteristics that anthropocentric philosophers from Kant to Lacan have reserved for the human domain. Strangely enough, in Leroux's novel written 100 years ago, Balaoo displays just about every one of these traits of human subjecthood:

a. shame: *"[T]he question of whether an animal can see me naked, and especially whether it can see itself naked, is never asked"; "[S]ince every show of modesty is linked to a reserve of shame, to a reserve that attests to a virtual guilt, does one have the right to rely on this other metonymy in order to conclude that an animal modesty exists and therefore that animals have a sense of nakedness?"* (Derrida, 59, 60–61)

When Balaoo finds himself in the deep forest wearing torn pants and a "paletot en loques," he is deeply embarrassed and concerned not to be seen by someone of the human race until he can change into a less ragged suit (109). And it is shame, too, that motivates Balaoo's first two crimes: not realizing that both the town barber and the tailor were lame, he had killed them for what he mistook to be a mocking imitation of his own waddling gait. Of course, Balaoo's shame is precisely linked to the gap between him and humanity.

b. desire: *"And here we find ourselves already caught in a fleece, in the immense bushy enigma of body hair, of fur, coat, and skin, between Adam and Prom-Epimetheus, in the small pubic forest that seems to surround or protect—but from what?—the nudity of an intensely desirable zone in the body of certain living creatures, one that is also devoted to the reproduction of the species."; "[I]t is also the same thing, that thing that combines within itself desire,* jouissance, *and anguish."* (Derrida, 57, 61)

Balaoo's silent pining for Madeleine leads to a protective jealousy manifested at times through violence; he kills the magistrate for a casual comment

and follows Madeleine and her betrothed Patrice on their wedding day. When
Madeleine is attacked that night in her bedroom, a trail of blood from bed to
window points to Balaoo as her abductor. Meanwhile, the Parisian tabloid
press warns of further dangers to the capital city's female population: "Jeunes
filles, ne quittez pas vos parents! QUATRE JEUNES FILLES DISPARUES.
Un monstre, indigne du nom d'homme, les traîne par les cheveux dans
les arbres, les emporte, comme une proie, sur les toits de la capitale" [Young
girls, do not abandon your parents! FOUR YOUNG GIRLS DISAPPEARED.
A monster, unworthy to be named a man, is dragging them by the hair into
the treetops, carrying them like prey onto the roofs of the capital] (280). It
turns out, however, that these savage abductions have been perpetrated by an
actual gorilla from the Jardin des Plantes zoo. And as for Madeleine, it had
been the albino Élie who had tried to attack her, only to be thwarted by the
heroic Balaoo. Through loyal love and sublimated desire, then, Balaoo distinguishes himself from both the zoo animal and the savage humans—that is,
from those just below and just above him on the evolutionary chain.

> c. speech beyond mimicry: *"[I]t would be* incredible *that a superior
> specimen of the monkey or parrot species should not be able to speak as
> well as well as the stupidest child . . . if their souls were not completely
> different in nature from ours. And we must not confuse speech with
> the natural movements which* witness to *passions and which can be
> imitated by machines as well as by animals. Nor should we think, like
> some of the ancients, that the beasts speak, although we do not under-
> stand their language."* (Descartes, cited by Derrida, 76)

Believing the faculty of speech to define the human species, Coriolis surgically enhances Balaoo's pharynx capabilities and teaches him French, as
well as some Greek and Latin. Meanwhile, an authorial footnote questions
the premise that speech is the sole province of man: according to Philippe
Garner, a professor who studied primate speech by enclosing himself in a cage
in the center of the equatorial forests of America, "les organes vocaux des chim-
panzés sont capables d'émettre vingt-quatre sons différents, pour exprimer
autant d'émotions diverses et parfaitement définies" [the speech organs of
chimpanzees are capable of producing twenty-four different sounds, designed
to express as many different and perfectly defined emotions] (201). Balaoo, we
are told, speaks both human and "ape." Moreover, he holds in the greatest con-
tempt a parrot named General Captain, for it insists on repeating people's

words without understanding what they mean. In a strange chiasmus, Balaoo and Coriolis end up inhabiting each other's linguistic space. At the novel's end, the two protagonists are joined by the servant Gertrude and the kind-hearted savage girl Zoé in a bittersweet return to the forests of Java. Here, the whole group learns monkey-language, and soon our erudite professor Coriolis "avait perdu l'habitude de parler homme et ne transmettait plus sa pensée qu'à l'aide de quelques monosyllabes de langue anthropoïde, et il se sentait avec une âpre jouissance retourner à ce qu'il pensait être le point de départ, la source de la vie humaine: à la race singe" [had lost the habit of speaking human and now only communicated his thoughts through a few monosyllables of the anthropoid language; and with a bitter joy, he felt himself returning to what he believed to be the starting point, the source of human life: the ape species] (310). Meanwhile, the human professor's retrogression is contrasted with the ape-man Balaoo's superior skills: "Seul, Balaoo, qui continuait tous les six mois à retourner à la ville de Batavia pour chercher une lettre de Madeleine, poste restante, et qui n'avait cessé de lire *Paul et Virginie*, avait conservé presque toute sa civilisation acquise" [Only Balaoo, who continued to return every six months to the city of Batavia in order to retrieve a letter from Madeleine, poste restante, and who had never stopped reading *Paul et Virginie*, only he had conserved almost all of his acquired civilization] (310). The cute evocation of Bernardin de Saint-Pierre's primitivist fable of a Rousseauistic harmonious state of nature paradoxically reinforces Balaoo's (philosopher-)human status in the midst of his native jungle.

> d. <u>empathy</u>: *"[For Bentham], the* first *and* decisive *questions would . . . be to know whether animals* can suffer." (Derrida, 27)

In an unusual sort of apologia for animal rights, the vegetarian Balaoo expresses outrage at the sport of hunting. He finds it odd that the townsmen make a big deal of a human cadaver, while they themselves callously kill stags and boars; "Je ne ferais pas de mal à une mouche pour manger! Moi aussi, je tue; mais je tue parce qu'on m'embête, *mais jamais pour manger*, je trouve ça dégoutant, et je ne te l'envoie pas dire" [I wouldn't hurt a fly in order to eat! Sure, I kill, as do others; but I kill in order to stop something from bothering me, *never to eat it*—I find that disgusting, let me tell you!] (154).

In the Paris sections of Leroux's novel, Balaoo cries for the animals imprisoned behind bars at the Jardin des Plantes. He envies their ignorance of the "difference" that separates animal and human; feeling himself in the middle of the divide, Balaoo weeps and prays to his god in one of the stranger passages of Leroux's novel. Balaoo's poetic "plainte," printed in full at the end of the book, begins: "Patti Palang-Kaing! Patti Palang-Kaing! / Pourquoi le Dieu des Chrétiens / N'a-t-il pas mes doigts lié, / Mes doigts de mains de sou-liers? [Why didn't the God of the Christians tie together my fingers, these slipper-fingers of mine?]" (313–14). Yes, he suffers. Yes, he empathizes with the suffering of others. But his empathy only goes so far, as Balaoo refuses to asso-ciate with the filthy lower primates at the zoo. Paradoxically, of course, this limit to empathy serves only to further align Balaoo with humankind. In *L'Animal que donc je suis*, Derrida meditates on the animalizing mechanisms that have underlain anti-Semitism: "The animal remains for Levinas what it will have been for the whole Cartesian-type tradition: a machine that doesn't speak, that doesn't have access to sense, that can at best imitate 'signifiers with-out a signified' . . . , a sort of monkey with "monkey talk," precisely what the Nazis sought to reduce their Jewish prisoners to" (117). Balaoo himself indulges in an all-too-human racist diatribe, railing against the "nègres" and "esqui-maux" as primitive savages unworthy to wear the white man's (or his, Balaoo's!) shirt-collars. Among the members of the Human Race that Balaoo discounts as unworthy brutes are the cave-dwelling troglodytes, whom he describes as squatting on their hams, with hair coming down to their heels. Evolution-ary discourse is thus added to the spatial logic of crime fiction that Leroux has inherited from the nineteenth century. The violent Vautrin brothers, it turns out, use abandoned stone quarries as storage space for their hidden loot; meanwhile, the zoo-ape Gabriel, whom Balaoo has befriended, abducts young virgins of Paris and carries them across the city's rooftops as though he were swinging limb-to-limb in the forest trees. As with Berthet's prehis-toric fiction of the 1880s (see Chapter 2), truly civilized people inhabit the horizontal plane of land-surface, while primitives and savages hop trees or lurk underground.

> e. <u>awareness of life and death</u>: *"At the heart of all these difficulties, there is always the unthought side of a thinking of life . . ."; "That is why the animal doesn't die. That is why its nonresponse cannot be compared to the nonresponse (another very important concept for [Levinas]) by means of which he nevertheless defines death."* (Derrida, 111)

Although Balaoo does not share Coriolis's ethical code, he is aware that he has brought about the deaths of his victims. Moreover, he is aware of his own finitude, threatening suicide (by throwing himself into the Seine), when he learns that Madeleine is to marry Patrice.

> f. dreams *"The question "Does the animal dream?" is, in its form, premises, and stakes, at least analogous to the questions "does the animal think? "Does the animal produce representations?"; "I am dreaming through the dream of the animal and dreaming of the scene I could create here."* (Derrida, 63)

Balaoo's dreams are, as Freud would deem apt, erotic.

> g. second-order deception: *"There is, according to Lacan, a clear distinction between what the animal is quite capable of, namely, strategic pretense (warrior, predatory, or seductive suit, pursuit, or persecution) and what it is incapable of and incapable of witnessing to, namely, the deception of speech within the order of the signifier and of Truth. The deception of speech of course means, as we shall see, lying . . . ; but more precisely deception involves lying as what, in promising what is true, includes the supplementary possibility of telling the truth in order to lead the other astray . . . . According to Lacan it is that type of lie, that deceit, and that pretense in the second degree of which the animal would be incapable."* (Derrida, 127–28)

When Balaoo feigns indifference to his rival's conversation at the dinner table, Coriolis angrily chides him for precisely what Derrida's anthropocentric philosophers claimed as the exclusive domain of humanity: "It's very bad manners to pretend to be dreaming at table and never to attend to the conversation. I say no more!" The irony is that Coriolis rebukes him for this human pretense, just as he had for the "beastly" acts of scratching himself at the table and stealing tarts from the kitchen. When accused of the latter crime, Balaoo defends himself by citing a high-philosophy aphorism: "The clear sense which we possess of our faults is a sure sign of the freedom which we have enjoyed to commit them!" There is certainly a comic aspect to this ape-man's civilized talk, but the scene also displays an uncomfortable conjunction of the all-too-animal and the ultra-human. Balaoo grunts his beastly grunts, while simultaneously displaying just about every supposedly human characteristic cited by Derrida—including, also, self-sacrifice, nostalgia, and of course the fundamental sense of the self (*Je suis*).

But it is not only by giving his title character these strikingly human traits that Leroux challenges the binary distinction of man from animal. He also places, as we have seen, the monkey-man within a whole spectrum of secondary characters who defy categorization. On the "animal" side, we have a fox who argues with Balaoo about the ethics of meat for murder and the ape named Gabriel who escapes from the zoo in men's clothing to steal peanuts from street vendors and eat at Maxim's. On the "human" side, we have the savage Vautrin family that lives like a pack of wolves: the oldest, Hubert, of red hair and stocky build, the two brothers nicknamed the Albinos for their creepy pallor and yellow eyes, and their savage little sister named Zoe, described as being "black as a mole," "nimble as a monkey," and light-footed as a bird when she runs to her "burrow" in the woods. The Vautrin albinos, it turns out, are at least as violent as Balaoo—and in fact, the novel ends with the *anthropopithèque* saving Madeleine from their brutal lust.

By including intermediate characters, Leroux's text mitigates the kind of demonization of the primate Other that we find, for example, in the sensationalistic cover image used for a 1977 edition of the novel (see Figure 3). Here, a frightened Madeleine huddles for safety in the arms of her betrothed, as he calmly aims a gun toward the window of their luxurious train compartment; outside, a dark and hideous ape-man presses his face and hand against the window, looking in. Sanguinary motive is suggested by the red color of Balaoo's garment, echoed above and below by the book's title and the carpet under the cool and civilized feet of the human hero. Leroux's text itself is far more subtle. Yes, the book includes a scene in which Madeleine's fiancé aims his gun at the jealous Balaoo outside their train compartment. But this is right after Balaoo has gone unnoticed by passengers inside the train, as he sits in gentleman's clothing in the fancy dining car. He literally inhabits both the inside and outside spaces of civilization. Moreover, Balaoo's threatening face at the train window parallels an earlier scene in the novel in which the engaged couple are equally surprised and frightening by the leering face of the Vautrin Albino. Like the Tarzan series Edgar Rice Burroughs began in 1912, *Balaoo* dissolves comforting distinctions between white man and his Others, but it does so with a more purposeful evocation of intermediate categories of man and monkey, as the novel slides from tropes of the typical crime novel to philosophical reflection on the implications of evolutionary theory.[26] In her book *Membranes: Metaphors of Invasion in Nineteenth-Century Literature, Science, and Politics*, Laura Otis reads the Face in the Window motif in Arthur Conan Doyle's crime fiction as the projected fear of British imperial

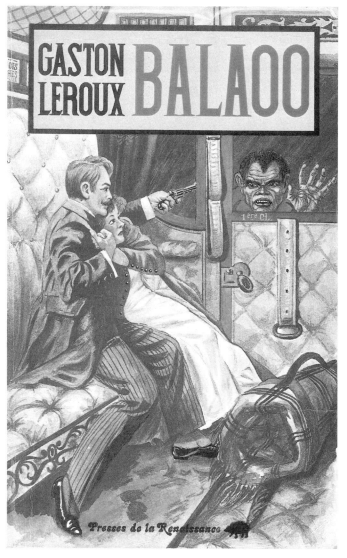

Figure 3. Gaston Leroux, *Balaoo*. Collection Bibliothèque des Littératures Policières (BiLiPo).

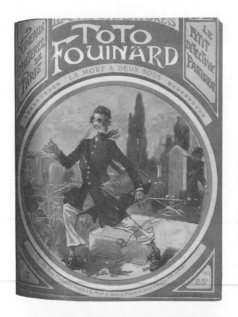

Figure 4. Skulls in Crime Fiction. Collection Bibliothèque des Littératures Policières (BiLiPo).

invaders.[27] An element of colonial allegory certainly pertains in Leroux's *Balaoo*, with Coriolis as scientific imperialist, but more centrally, Leroux forces the recognition of primal violence in ourselves that is raised by the novel's Darwinian thesis. The late-edition sensationalistic cover undoubtedly overstates the case, but it may serve to capture the terror felt when the human is faced with the animal, in the unsteady knowledge that the other side of the train window might instead be this side of the mirror.

Late nineteenth-century and early twentieth-century paleontological discoveries of skulls and bones led to an evolutionary "mirror" that continues to trouble our sense of difference from the other, from the criminal and/or the brute. And the primal violence in the form of the skull will continue to lurk in the dark corners of modern French crime fiction. *Le Carillon des catacombes* (1949); *Le Gang des catacombes* (1959); *La Clef dans le crâne* (mid-1930s); *Le Crâne dans la poubelle* (1954): the titles of French pulp crime fictions at their mid-century height attest, along with their lurid cover images of skulls and bones, to the enduring power of underground spaces and the skeletons found therein[28] (see Figure 4). The next chapter will study the archaeologics of two crime novelists writing a hundred years after Leroux and Leblanc: Sébastien Japrisot and Fred Vargas, who transfer the tropes of the criminal underground from natural caves and quarries to manufactured cemeteries and crypts, in which fantasmatic contents both conceal and reveal the haunting traumas of individual psyche and national terrain.

CHAPTER 4

Crypts and Ghosts: Terrains of National Trauma in Japrisot and Vargas

Et sous la ville sont les autres villes, l'histoire piétinée des hommes
et femmes d'avant et les maisons d'aujourd'hui ont repoussé sur
leurs caves et la chair d'aujourd'hui dressée sur les os dans la terre.
—François Bon, *Impatience*

When Léo Malet claimed to have written "archaeological" novels throughout the 1950s and 1960s, he was not referring to a literal transposition of scientific method into the crime genre. We do not find in his work, for example, the geological allegories of Berthet's *Catacombes de Paris* or the fictionalized paleontologist of Leroux's *Le Parfum de la dame en noir*. After all, by the mid-twentieth century, the positivistic sciences were largely held in suspicion by the philosophical discourses that informed literary production. It was in a broader, more figurative sense that archaeology emerged as a model for intellectual thought from Freud to Foucault, both of whose "excavations" into archaic psychic origins and the historical past of cultures are mental, rather than manual. And yet it would be a mistake to evacuate all concrete associations of archaeology from the work of the analyst and the archivist, for their reconstructions of the past still rely on (1) material vestiges, whether in the form of somatic symptom or linguistic sign; and (2) a topological model of the past as schistic, seismic, and stratified. In the case of Malet, the term "archéologique" should be understood not just as the detective's abstract investigation of past events, but as his entry into the actual spaces of crime, with their own particular topologies. In her study of World War II and postwar Jewishness in French crime fiction, Claire Gorrara cites Malet's story *Du rébecca rue des Rosiers*, in which a secret cellar used to shelter Jews hides a second, "dark, damp crypt" that protects (and eventually entombs) a Vichy *collabo*.[1] This second crypt, writes Gorrara, "can be read as an image of 'repressed' memory, one buried deeply within the national psyche under the official narrative of national resistance and valor" (9). In this way, Malet's story prefigures the "archaeological" crime fictions of today's authors like Didier Daeninckx, whose celebrated *Meurtres pour mémoire* identifies criminality as the brutal legacy of the collective national wounds of war and colonialism.[2] Indeed, the national-historical dimension of such fictions has been well established; and Gorrara fruitfully aligns their criminal investigations with the psychoanalytical notion of repression in a "national psyche." But given the particular topologics of Malet's doubly hidden crypt, we can go even farther: in light of trauma theories like that of Nicolas Abraham and Maria Torok, the fictional crypt signals not only the burial of unspeakable family/national secrets, but also the linguistic displacements and disruptions that turn retroactive investigation into a "cryptonymic" or "decrypting" endeavor.[3]

The psychoanalytic notion of the "phantom," an unspoken trauma transmitted across generations, has provided a suggestive key to interpreting the uncanny ghosts and haunted houses of the Gothic genre.[4] But the *roman policier*, of course, is also about buried secrets and the analytical work it takes to unearth them. Abraham and Torok define the intrapsychic secret as a devastating, often "death-dealing," trauma, so violent that it creates splits and rifts in the topography of the self.[5] In the crime novels analyzed in this chapter, by Sebastien Japrisot and Fred Vargas, violent traumas literally imprint the underground terrain of the French nation, creating crypts and rifts through "the mechanisms of concealment and dissembling that thwart readability" (Rashkin, *Family Secrets*, 33). As a result, the investigator can no longer claim any simplicity of abstraction for historiographical or archival work. She or he must now decode and decrypt entombed secrets, entering into the anfractuous topography that is the consequence of (psychic or bodily, individual or political) trauma. Indeed, these "archaeological" novels consistently connect personal loss to trauma at the collective level, so that shameful, unspeakable family secrets (incest, adultery, illegitimacy) become themselves symptoms of broader national and political systems of violence. Gorrara writes of the "national psyche"; there is also a "national body," pockmarked and buckled by the buried bones of war and crime.

Le nom du lieu: Cryptic Spaces in Japrisot's *Un long dimanche de fiançailles* (1991)

Sébastien Japrisot is the anagrammatic pseudonym for the Marseille-born author Jean-Baptiste Rossi, whose popular crime fictions, especially *Piège pour Cendrillon* (1963) and *L'Été meurtrier* (1978), extend the boundaries of the *roman policier* into the realm of metatextual play and polyphony. In their edited volume dedicated to Japrisot's work, Simon Kemp and Martin Hurcombe emphasize the "playful and subversive" nature of his fiction;[6] David Bellos points out that his generic experimentation matches that of *nouveaux romans policiers* like Robbe-Grillet's *Les Gommes,* Georges Perec's *La Vie mode d'emploi*, and Patrick Modiano's *Rue des boutiques obscures*;[7] Pierre Verdaguer puts him in same category as Jean Lahougue, Jean Echenoz, and Jean-François Vilar for their "resolutely intellectualist" dimension.[8] The well-known statement by the female amnesiac narrator of *Piège pour Cendrillon*, "J'étais l'enquêteur, l'assassin, la victime, le témoin, tout ensemble" [I was at once the investigator, the victim, and the witness], testifies to Japrisot's refusal of classic conventions, including the clear distinction between criminals and investigators. For Jacques Dubois, the ironic subversions evident in Japrisot's audacious fictions represent a "utopic" break with the constraints and repressive ideology of the modern detective genre; by stretching the limits of a code set in the capitalist industrialist age, they offer an alternative stance to bourgeois conservatism while partaking in the twentieth century's general "identity crisis of the subject."[9] Both *Piège pour Cendrillon* and *L'Été meurtrier* feature divided subjects (Do/Mi and Eliane/Elle) and narrative disturbances that unsettle the *policier*'s presumed promise of narrative resolution.

Compared with these earlier novels, Japrisot's 1991 *Un long dimanche de fiançailles* seems downright tame and traditional. Its romantic plot of a young crippled woman whose true love for her fiancé transcends the horrors of World War I lends itself to the "sepia-toned nostalgia" for which Jean-Pierre Jeunet's 2004 film adaptation has been criticized.[10] But, as Kemp points out, the novel's polyphonic construction adds unreliability and conflictual narration to the seemingly simple tale of investigation. Indeed, *Un long dimanche* can be seen as avant-garde in many respects, including its treatment of gender (Mathilde

Donnay is primary investigator, sidelining the male professional detective to a hired, accessory role—and Tina Lombardi acts as a violent avenger for her beloved's sacrifice); its formal quirks (an implied third-person narration by the protagonist, the inclusion of an epistolary chapter); and its language play (puns abound, beginning with character names like "Six-Sous" for Francis— combining *verlan* and the substitution of "sous" for "francs"—and Germain Pire, "Pire que la fouine"). Even more than Japrisot's other successful crime novels, *Un long dimanche* resists categorization as a *polar* (which David Bellos defines as "an umbrella term that includes the Anglo-American genres and subgenres of thriller, detective story, murder-mystery, police procedural, and courtroom drama").[11] It is, perhaps primarily, a war novel, a historical fiction, a romance.

And yet given Japrisot's previous output, analysis of the novel in relation to the *polar* grid is justified—and productive. It allows us, for example, to ask what becomes of the definition of crime in the context of national political violence: what is, after all, the central "crime" in this novel? Is it the self-mutilation by soldiers condemned as traitors by national tribunal? The suppression of President Poincaré's pardon of those men? The cruel order to send France's own soldiers into the no-man's-land facing enemy trenches? Or a bereft and angry lover's murderous revenge for their deaths? And though the novel may seem at first glance less amenable to the kind of psychotextual analysis Shoshana Feldman applied to *Piège de Cendrillon* in her 1983 article, *Un long dimanche de fiançailles* reflects in complex ways on the physical, psychological, and linguistic reactions to trauma, from Mathilde's unexplained childhood paralysis to her fiançé Manech's staggering shell-shock. Most of all, through its structure that follows Mathilde as she layers the pages of official and unofficial testimonies into a mahogany box, the novel allows us to explore the underground logics of investigation, archive, and the Letter.

The novel begins with a fairy-tale phrase: "Il était une fois . . ."[12] Yet *Un long dimanche* devolves quickly into the unpleasant reality of war, as five French soldiers are marched through the Somme region to the front, "aux premières lignes" [on the front lines/in the first lines], after having been convicted of the crime of self-mutilation (13). Boots and mud and wounded hands reinforce the concrete physicality of the scene, while its temporal specificity—January 1917—anchors us in a referential space. Still, Japrisot's punning epigraph, in which Alice in Wonderland sees "nobody" and is praised for her excellent eyesight, has set the reader up for wordplay, so that we might not be faulted for reading the passage's "premières lignes" as both military front lines and as a textual self-reference to the opening lines of the novel itself.[13] Certainly, this is the logic at play in the repeated refrain, "Attention au fil" [watch out for the wire], for while the wounded soldiers are told to mind the telephonic communication wires as they march along snowy ground, so we are reminded to pay attention to the narrative "fil," the textual thread that leads us across the territory of Mathilde Donnay's search for her lover Manech, youngest of the five condemned soldiers.

The "fil" of communication slips between literality and metaphoricity, corporality and textuality, as Mathilde re-traces the steps leading up to Manech's apparent death:

> Il restait ce fil, rafistolé avec n'importe quoi aux endroits où il craquait, qui serpentait au long de tous les boyaux, de tous les hivers, en haut, en bas de la tranchée, à travers toutes les lignes, jusqu'à l'obscur abri d'un obscur capitaine pour y porter des ordres criminels. Mathilde l'a saisi. Elle le tient encore. Il la guide dans le labyrinthe d'où Manech n'est pas revenu. Quand il est rompu, elle le renoue.

> [There was still that wire, mended whenever it broke with whatever came to hand, a wire that snaked its way through all the trenches, through all the winters, now up at the top, now down at the bottom, across all the lines, until it reached the obscure bunker of an obscure captain to deliver criminal orders. Mathilde has seized hold of it. She holds it still. It guides her into the labyrinth from which Manech has not returned. When it breaks, she ties the frayed ends together.] (31)[14]

In the wartime front, the crackling wire "était tout ce qui reliait les hommes au monde des vivants" [was the only link to the world of the living] (48)— and when the living Mathilde "picks it up," she will be confronted with a crime that itself consists in the interruption of a communicative "fil." The French president Raymond Poincaré had pardoned the wounded soldiers, commuting their death sentence to mere forced labor. But his message had been blocked. Communication was cut, as were the lives of five men, sent over the barbed-wire fence of the trenches into a no-man's-land with no escape.

To discover this act of sabotage, Mathilde is forced to construct her own "fil" of letters, newspaper announcements, and conversations, with no guarantee that the thread will lead her to Manech. "Et puis, Mathilde est d'heureuse nature. Elle se dit que si ce fil ne la ramène pas à son amant, tant pis, c'est pas grave, elle pourra toujours se pendre avec" [And Mathilde has a cheerful disposition, too. She tells herself that if this wire doesn't lead her back to her lover, that's all right [*c'est pas grave*], she can always use it to hang herself] (31). Dark humor, indeed. But despite its throwaway tone, the phrase reminds us of the linguistic potential for ambiguity or semantic multiplicity—not just of the "fil," re-literalized here as a hangman's noose—but perhaps even of the "grave" in the defensive "c'est pas grave" of Mathilde's indirect discourse. It's no big deal, thinks the French girl. But to an anglophone reader, the "grave" is also a grave—a tomb, a vault, a crypt. This may seem at first irrelevant, but it becomes clear that the thematics of Japrisot's novel warrant English-French bilingualism for its decoding. For the moment, let me indulge in the pun, as it exposes both a logic of denial ("c'est pas grave," when of course it *is*) and the centrality to the text's hermeneutics of the very question of a grave's existence. Is there a grave? Is there a body? Is it Manech's body?

Only by denying her lover's death—only, in other words, by refusing to mourn, can Mathilde continue to weave her investigative thread. And here, in the construction of a text by the very refusal to mourn, lies an opening to an essay that resonates strongly with Japrisot's novel: Jacques Derrida's *Fors*.[15] Derrida wrote *Fors* in 1976 as a Preface to Abraham and Torok's study of the Wolf-man's cryptonymic—secret-bearing—language. Abraham and Torok's study of Freud's patient itself relies on their distinction between *introjection* and *incorporation*. Introjection refers to the process of working through a traumatic loss. It can be interrupted by incorporation, in which an unbearable reality is confined to an inaccessible region of the psyche: it is "buried alive" in a crypt of the ego. The textual result of this entombment is a "secret-driven narrative" whose ciphered or encrypted language can be analyzed by a psychoanalyst—or by a literary critic.[16]

In this chapter, I aim to expose a similar cryptographic logic, one based on a number of preliminary assertions. (1) *Un long dimanche de fiançailles* begins with secrets buried under the snow and ends with bodies buried under the ground. (2) Though the French terrain is crisscrossed above ground by letters and trains, seekers and hiders, below the surface is where things really happen: in a hidden church crypt under a wartime no-man's-land, identities are switched and bodies exchanged; in the coded letters sent by prisoners nearing death, words are switched and messages exchanged. (3) These substitutions— of bodies and names—create a tangled "fil" which Mathilde and the reader must navigate to uncover a "cyst" in the French national body: the encrypted secret of the shameful expulsion of its own young soldiers, whose bodies are literally buried and reburied in a series of underground spaces. Mathilde thus serves as both patient-refusing-to-mourn and analyst/reader of the novel's own plot; she is both Ariadne holding the thread and Theseus facing the monster in the labyrinth.

To explore the uncanny spatiality of this labyrinth, the snow-covered terrain of the no-man's-land, it is worth returning to the novel's beginning.

Things Buried

On the first page of the novel, the five condemned soldiers are marched "vers les grands reflets froids du soir par-delà les premières lignes, par-delà le cheval mort et les caisses de munitions perdues, et *toutes ces choses ensevelies sous la neige*" [toward the cold glints of night sky beyond the front lines, beyond the dead horse and the lost crates of supplies and all those things shrouded under the snow] (13). The phrase I have emphasized will appear again, only two pages later, when one of the soldiers, nicknamed l'Eskimo but identified here by his dogtag number 2124, is described as still naïve despite his relatively advanced age of thirty-seven: "il croyait à *toutes ces choses* qu'on lui avait dites pour justifier le malheur et *qui sont ensevelies sous la neige*" [he believed in all those things they'd told him to justify this tragedy and that lie shrouded under the snow] (15–16). From the first to the second iteration, the "choses" [things] have shifted from the concrete (weapons and bodies buried under the snow in the no-man's-land) to the textual (hollow lies told by patriotic authorities to justify war's brutality). But there is something strange about the second phrase's syntax. Shouldn't the patriotic discourse justify "le malheur" [tragedy] that consists of bodies buried underground? That is, would it not make sense for the phrase to read: "il croyait à toutes ces choses qu'on lui avait dites pour justifier le malheur des corps ensevelis sous la neige" [he believed in all those things they'd told him in order to justify the tragedy of bodies that lie shrouded under the snow]? Instead, it is the words themselves that are buried underground: "toutes ces choses qu'on lui avait dites . . . et qui sont ensevelies sous la neige" [all those things they'd told him and that lie shrouded under the snow].

Word-things are buried in *Un long dimanche*, just as they are in Abraham and Torok's case study, cited by Derrida: "When the word-thing . . . is buried (in the unconscious, in fact, as the cryptic Unconscious's Thing), it is "interred with the fallacious fiction that it is no longer alive." The inhabitant of a crypt is always a living dead, a dead entity we are perfectly willing to keep alive, but *as* dead, one we are willing to keep, as long as we keep it, within us, intact in any way save as living" (xxi). In the underground war-space covered over by snow in Japrisot's text, the patriotic word-thing functions as an ideology both dead—hollow, futile—*and* alive: kept active in the trusting mind of a provincial soldier even as he is being betrayed by his own nation.

What else is buried under the surface of official discourse? For one thing, the very existence of a burying-place for the soldiers whose mode of death was the result of a cover-up: when Madame Conte writes to Mathilde about Tina Lombardi's own search for her lover Ange, she cites the army's official report as incomplete. "Sur l'avis, il y avait: *Tué à l'ennemi, le 7 janvier 1917,* mais pas où on avait enterré Ange Bassignano. Vous imaginez bien que je l'ai demandé aux gendarmes. Ils ne savaient pas" [On the notice there was *Killed in action, January 7, 1917,* but not where they had buried Angel Bassignano. As you can well imagine, I asked the policemen, but they didn't know] (113). The mystery of the tomb thus propels the novel's hermeneutic thrust.

Midway through the novel, Mathilde learns of two burials: a summary interment by British soldiers at the very trench where the bodies had fallen, followed by a transfer of the corpses to the military cemetery d'Herdelin in Picardie. The earlier, hastier burial takes advantage of the war-pocked terrain of the no-man's-land, as the British troops who have relieved the French at the front cover the five men's bodies with a large brown tarpaulin and put them into a ready-made grave, "un trou d'obus" [shell-hole] (216). By the time they are transferred to the official burial ground, the bodies have been given coffins and crosses. But their new resting place is not much different from the first, a fact signaled textually by the snow that covers the ground at two moments: the day of their death and the day of Mathilde's visit to the military cemetery. At both moments, the inert bodies of the sacrificed soldiers have become "choses . . . ensevelies sous la neige." *Choses*: things, secrets.

And like the word-things that are secretly encrypted in the traumatized psyche of Abraham and Torok's patients, these buried bodies create a particular linguistic anguish. For when Mathilde considers the possibility of having Manech's coffin moved from the military cemetery of Herdelin to a burial ground nearer to her home, she displays the pathological mutism associated with psychic *incorporation*:

un sentiment d'angoisse effroyable a envahi Mathilde, elle en avait la gorge serrée à ne pouvoir articuler un mot. Exactement

comme si Manech, du fond d'elle-même, criait non, non, qu'il ne
voulait pas. Et quand elle a été capable d'articuler un mot, elle a dit
précipitamment . . ."Non, ne faites rien."

[a horrible feeling of anguish swept over Mathilde, clenching her
throat so that she couldn't utter a word. It was exactly as though
Manech, from deep within her, were crying out no, no, he didn't
want that at all. And when she was finally able to speak, she said,
hastily, "no: do nothing."] (241)

Manech—at once dead (officially) and living (in her refusal to mourn him)—
has been "incorporated" into her Self. It is from within her—"du fond d'elle-
même"—that he speaks, cutting off *her* ability to speak the words that will
acknowledge his death. "The Self: a cemetery guard," writes Derrida (xxxv).
Mathilde, in Japrisot's text, becomes herself a cemetery guard, refusing to
unearth the crypt for fear that it contains the body it claims to contain. Her
silence, the "gorge serrée à ne pouvoir articuler un mot," is an oral symptom
of incorporation's refusal to work through by introjection. Derrida situates
introjection literally in the mouth, adding that it is only after having blocked
oral usage that "incorporation passes through a crypt of language (whence the
'linguisticistic' effect), but this is only because the forbidden moment of the
oral function had *first* been a 'substitute' for or a 'figure' of a wordless presence" (xxxviii). In Japrisot's text, as we shall see, encryption will indeed become linguistic (coded words, encoded letters), as though Mathilde's psychic
incorporation (presented here as Manech speaking from within her to block
her own speech) has engendered a narrative whose de-codeability is based on
substitution of bodies, of words, of things. Because there is the possibility that
the cemetery of Herdelin holds a body other than Manech's, the text can continue to weave its investigative "fil."

Names and Numbers

Is Manech's body in the tomb? The answer lies in the notion of identity, a
notion presented from the novel's start as being of the order of the textual or
numeric sign. Japrisot's narration begins by introducing the five men being
marched across the "labyrinth of snow." Instead of proper names, their army
matriculation numbers act as primary identifier: "Le premier . . . portait à son

cou le matricule 2124 d'un bureau de recrutement de la Seine" [The first soldier . . . wore around his neck an identification tag marked 2124, the number assigned to him at a recruiting office in the department of the Seine] (13); "le deuxième soldat aux bras liés avec de la corde était le 4077 d'un autre bureau de la Seine" [The second man's number was 4077, issued at a different recruiting office of the Seine] (16); "Le troisième venait de la Dordogne et portait sur sa plaque de poitrine le numéro 1818" [The third man was from the Dordogne and wore on his badge the number 1818] (18). By the time we get to the fourth soldier, we are used to the stripping away of all other signs of identity:

> le quatrième des cinq soldats sans casque, ni insigne, ni numéro de regiment, ni poche de veste ou de capote, ni photo de famille, ni croix de chrétien, étoile de David ou croissant d'Islam, ni rien qui puisse faire feu plus grand que cœur qui bat, celui-là, le matricule 7328 d'un bureau des Bouches-du-Rhône, né à Marseille parmi les émigrés italiens de la Belle de Mai, s'appelait Ange.

> [The fourth of the five soldiers who had been stripped of their helmets, regimental badges, insignia, jacket and overcoat pockets, who carried not a single family photo, Christian cross, Star of David, crescent of Islam, or anything that would amount to damn-all—had been born in Marseille, in a neighborhood of Italian immigrants called Belle de Mai. He had been assigned number 7328 at a recruiting office in Bouches-du-Rhône. His name was Angel.] (20–21)

In this case, we get a name, Ange, but it holds no natural link to its human referent: "jamais prénom n'avait été plus mal porté" [never had a man been more ill named] (21). Names and nicknames are slippery signifiers, based on metonymic relations (*l'Eskimo* once worked in snowy North America), linguistic word-play (*Six-sous* and *Pire que la fouine*), or simple generalization (the third soldier, a peasant from the Dordogne, is called "Cet homme" [this man]).

The fifth and final soldier is Mathilde's lover, introduced first by a nickname that defines him as a springtime field flower/recent recruit: "Le cinquième le dernier des soldats aux bras liés dans le dos, celui-là était un Bleuet" [The fifth and last of those soldiers with their arms tied behind their backs was a

"Cornflower" (the nickname of the military class of 1917)] (26). A page later, he is given more names and numbers:

> Son prénom était Jean, encore que sa mère et tous les autres, au pays, lui disaient Manech. A la guerre, il était simplement Bleuet. Le matricule qu'il portait en bracelet à son poignet valide était le 9692 d'un bureau des Landes. Il était né à Cap-Breton, d'où l'on voit Biarritz, mais la géographie n'étant le fort de personne dans les armées de la République, ceux de sa section pensaient qu'il venait de Bretagne"

> [His first name was Jean, although his mother and everyone else back home always called him Manech. In the army, he was known simply as Cornflower. The number he wore on the bracelet around his good wrist was 9692, from a recruiting office in the Landes. He was born in Capbreton, within sight of Biarritz, but since geography wasn't the strong point of the Army of the Republic, the men in his section thought he was from Brittany.] (27)

In wartime (il)logic, place-names can be easily substituted, just as can a person's proper name. Bleuet's "real" name is variously designated Manech, Manex, or just plain M, making it reciprocal with Mathilde's name in the young lovers' tree-trunk inscription: "MMM pour qu'on puisse lire, à l'envers comme à l'endroit, que Manech aime Mathilde et que Mathilde aime Manech" [MMM so that it reads, backward or forward, Manech loves Mathilde and Mathilde loves Manech] (233). Their substitutability by the random identity of the first letter of their names seems to Manech and Mathilde to seal and bless their performative linguistic act, a symbolic marriage of M's carved into bark. But it also signals to the reader a fundamental arbitrariness of the identifying sign, through the phonetic homonymy of "aime" [loves] and M.

This arbitrariness is what makes it possible for the bodies of living and dead soldiers in the no-man's-land of 1917 to be substituted. No one knows who they are, so identification must rely on external signs, whether official dogtags or unofficial, idiosyncratic deviations from the uniform norm: a red mitten lent to le Blueuet as he ventures, innocent, into a snowy death-ground; a German boot stolen by l'Eskimo but then traded by his friend Gordes in order to save his life; the bandages on the hands of all five mutilated soldiers.

When Mathilde begins investigating the disposal of the victims' bodies, she grasps avidly at any indications of identifying markers. One of her witnesses, a self-exiled Canadian, passes along to Mathilde the message that the British troops who first buried the men had had little to go on:

> Nat Belly dit qu'ils ont enterré sous une bâche cinq Français tués, qui avaient des pansements à leurs mains. Leurs numéros de régiment, tous leurs insignes avaient été arrachés, probablement par les Boches pour ramener des souvenirs chez eux. Nat ne se souvient malheureusement plus de leurs noms, pourtant ils avaient encore leurs plaques et le chef de patrouille les a notés 'au cas où', mais il ne se souvient plus.

> [Nat Belly says they buried five dead Frenchmen under a tarp, and they all had bandages on their hands. Their regimental numbers and other insignia had been torn off, probably by the Boches, for souvenirs. Unfortunately Nat no longer remembers their names, but they did have their dog tags and the patrol leader wrote down their names "just in case," but Nat can't remember them.] (253)

The memory of names is erased, in this "no-man's-land" where the soldiers have died and are summarily buried. "La terre de personne," rendered in both French and English in Japrisot's text, recalls the Alice in Wonderland epigraph where "personne" [nobody] can become "une personne" [somebody]—and vice versa, for in the "no-man's-land" of trench warfare, an individual soldier (his identity already reduced to a number) can become no man, a cipher. When the five bodies are transferred from the no-man's-land to the official military cemetery, the army attempts to pin down their identities: an officer calls out the names and matriculation years as they appear on their "plaques militaires" (294). But as we and Mathilde learn, the names do not correspond to the men who have died. Cet Homme had traded his papers, boots, and dogtag for the dying Gordes; he'd also found Bleuet/Manech alive and given him the identifying markers of a young dead soldier named Jean Desrochelles. The two are living now under the false identities of two dead men. An even trade, made of mere markers. "Un nom, je peux vous le dire, ne représente rien" [I can tell you this, a name means nothing], says Cet Homme to Mathilde when she finally meets him (351). A name represents nothing; it is not bound by a referential relation to its object.

And yet it signifies. Its polysemic potential is what carries the plot along, what weaves its "fil." Take, for example, the novel's fundamental place-name, Bingo Crépuscule, which is first introduced to Mathilde by the veteran Esperanza: "La tranchée de première ligne où je devais . . . conduire [les soldats] portait un numéro mais, à la guerre, il en allait des tranchées comme des bonhommes, on retenait plus facilement les surnoms. Celle-là, on l'appelait, ne me demandez pas pourquoi, Bingo Crépuscule" [The front-line trench where I'd been ordered to take them had a number, but in war, it's the same with trenches as with men, it's easier to remember nicknames. That one was called—don't ask me why—Bingo Crépuscule] (45–46). Two things to note: first, the trench, a place, is equivalent to the soldiers themselves ("les bonhommes") in that its identifying markers are mere numbers and nicknames; and second, Esperanza's ignorance about the origin of this trench's particular nickname kicks off another of the novel's hermeneutic series—for just as the *fil* of the plot takes the reader and Mathilde closer and closer to the discovery of the soldiers' multiple graves, it also leads us to a number of revelations—some false, some true—about the name Bingo Crépuscule. And just as with the investigation into the soldiers' identities, the investigation into the trench name is plagued by official obfuscation ("Oubliez cette affaire, Esperanza. Oubliez jusqu'au nom de Bingo Crépuscule" [Forget this whole thing, Esperanza. Forget even the name Bingo Crépuscule] 62); hermeneutic delay ("Bingo Crépuscule. Pourquoi ce nom? Je me le suis demandé longtemps, je n'ai jamais trouvé" [Bingo Crépuscule. Why that name? I've wondered about it for a long time, but I never found the answer] 65); and referential instability: one veteran asserts that "c'était pas Bingo, mais Bing au Crépuscule," based on his recollection of a wooden sign nailed onto a stake at the site of the trench (160).

While *Bingo Crépuscule* evokes an English-language game of chance, perhaps underlining the arbitrary fates of soldiers posted to the front, "Bing au Crépuscule" identifies a proper (and properly English) personal name, Bing—or Byng, according to some witnesses—while creating syntactical coherence by giving "crépuscule" [dusk] its temporal concreteness. As the story progresses, Mathilde learns more about this man whose presence at the trench gave it its bilingual name. The sister of a German soldier tells her that a redoubtable English general went by that name (296). In a letter written before her execution, Tina Lombardi explains that "la tranchée de l'Homme de Byng" got its name from the text of a painting by a Canadian soldier (310–11). And four years *after* she has discovered her lover Manech under his borrowed name, Mathilde receives a package from her informant Céléstin Poux, who has now moved to Canada. The package contains the actual "pancarte en bois de Bingo," a wooden sign with its faded letters showing only "BY et CUL, elle trouve que c'est parfait" [BY and CUL (i.e., "ass"), which Mathilde thinks is just perfect] (357). Strangely, the narrative voice continues to spell the name "Bingo," even as the "Byng" spelling is confirmed by the text on the wooden sign; it is as though the text refuses to pin down the referent even as the hermeneutic mystery is solved.

But is it solved? Maybe it only seems to be. Certainly, the reader and Mathilde are given a historical-biographical resolution to the name's origin. On the back of the wooden sign, Mathilde finds the yellowed painting of a British officer at nightfall, with a tiny caption at the bottom: "*Lieutenant général Byng au crépuscule. 1916*" [Lieutenant-general Byng at dusk] (357). Mathilde then looks up this General Byng in the Larousse encyclopedia at her local library and learns that this man had led the Canadian divisions in the war, then afterward become *gouverneur général* of Canada and had also run Scotland Yard before promotion and retirement. She puts Byng's biography into the "coffret en acajou" [mahogany jewel-box/casket] in which all notes, letters, evidence have been stored, alongside a photocopy of Maréchal Fayolle's *Cahiers secrets de la Grande Guerre* (the book that provided Japrisot with his central plot) (358). This title reminds us that the war was built on secrets, that the letters written home from the trenches like Bingo were themselves filled with secret codes, that "Byng au Crépuscule" is itself a war-text holding, potentially, its own secrets. Heeding Cet Homme's reminder that "un nom ne représente rien," we can look beyond the surface of Bingo Crépuscule's referential explanation (i.e., the historical presence of a British general on site). If we attend instead to the materiality of the sign, we note that the central difference between the two versions lies in the phoneme /o/, rendered either as an attached "o" (Bingo) or a separate "au" (Bing au). This unstable sign ensconced in the middle of the name's "body" is at first a closed circle, an "o" like a hole or a crypt—or an incorporated secret. As the novel progresses, it shifts toward the set-off, open "au" (open literally, as the enclosed circle is substituted by two letters that open typographically to the side or the top), as though the crypt were opening and the secret were being let out. And the secret, I would suggest, is the crypt itself—the open/closed space in the name that manifests textually what exists spatially in the terrain of the no-man's-land: an actual underground church crypt that allowed Cet Homme to survive, served as the place for the substitutions of names, bodies, identities, and provides Mathilde with the key confirmation Manech is not in the grave.

The Crypt

In *Fors*, Derrida describes the psychic space of incorporation as a crypt, a cyst, a vault, a safe, a tomb. It is a site whose double function of sealing the loss of the object while marking the refusal to mourn gives it the uncanny spatiality of open closure: "the cryptic enclave produces a cleft in space, . . . in the architectonics of the open square within space, itself delimited by a generalized closure, in the *forum*. Within this forum, a place where the free circulation and exchange of objects and speeches can occur, the crypt constructs another, more inward forum like a closed rostrum or speaker's box, a *safe*: sealed, and thus internal to itself, a secret interior within the public square, but, by the same token, outside it, external to the interior" (xiv). This description, with its emphasis on the circulation and exchange of objects, reminds us of Mathilde's own externalized "casket," the *coffret en acajou* into which she puts every letter, note, news clipping, every document having to do with her investigation. Continually opened and closed, the wooden box at once preserves the links in the *fil* as inert objects (dead bodies) and keeps alive the refusal to mourn Manech.[17]

But perhaps even more directly relevant to the open/closed spatiality of the psychic "crypt" is the underground vault whose existence is gradually revealed to Mathilde. Célestin Poux has told her that the only way for a soldier to survive in the no-man's-land during enemy attack is to find a hole in which to hide: "Pour sortir de là, il fallait tout de suite se trouver un bon trou et, comme l'avait conseillé le capitaine Favourier, la boucler. Il fallait rester dans ce trou toute une nuit, tout un jour, sans jamais plus attirer l'attention de personne" [To make it out of there, you had to find a good hole right away and keep your trap shut, just like Captain Favourier said. You had to stay in that hole all night, all day, unnoticed by anyone] (280). If the topography of the no-man's-land had been flat, it would all (life, story, . . .) have been over in an instant, but "Il y avait heureusement beaucoup de trous et d'entonnoirs, devant Bingo Crépuscule" [luckily there were lots of shell-holes and craters just beyond Bingo Crépuscule] (57). Holes from bombs, ramped-up earth and mud, furrows and rises make this a space of verticality and depth that allows for secrets, for the "encryption" of a body and its substitution by another. The post-war farmer who now tends the fields that used to be Bingo Crépuscule tells Mathilde that the no-man's-land had existed above the ruins of a small chapel with an underground "cave." And Célestin Poux's testimony suggests Cet Homme had taken advantage of that secret underground church crypt, for he had seen the soldier disappear by a pile of bricks jutting out from the snow (262). Finally, when Mathilde hears Cet Homme's own account of his escape, she understands the multiple vertical levels of enclosures and openings that made his survival possible: "j'ai trouvé la cave effondrée tout de suite, parce que j'ai vu ce tas de briques qui sortait de la neige quand les premières fusées ont éclaté. J'étais avec l'Eskimo et le Bleuet dans un trou d'obus trop peu profond pour qu'on y reste" [I found the caved-in cellar almost immediately, because I spotted that pile of bricks sticking out of the snow when the first flares went up. I was with the Eskimo and Cornflower in a shell hole too shallow for us to stay there] (339). The three soldiers had dispersed; then Cet Homme went to the pile of bricks, where he found "un grand panneau de bois, en fait c'était une porte abattue, et dessous, le vide" [a big wooden panel under the snow, a door it was, and underneath was nothing]. Climbing down the steps, he enters a rat-infested, water-filled cave with its own false bottom: when he picks up a large iron slab, the filthy water drained down into a well even farther underground. It is in this enclosed (but open above and below) space that Cet Homme is able to hide through the night and to exchange his identity with Gordes, who has fallen wounded down the steps of the church crypt. The topography of the no-man's-land is full of complex verticals: shallow bomb-holes and furrows, upward juts of beams, bricks, and earth, the deeper crypt with its own lower well. As a cyst in the traumatized body of the French nation, the church crypt is marked by the anfractuosities that Derrida identifies as the "partitions of the [psychic] crypt": "angular pieces, . . . cavities, corridors, niches, zigzag labyrinths, and craggy fortifications" (xx). It is a place for the burial of secrets, a place where the dead and the living can be substituted one for the other.

In this way, it is a place of encryption—in the sense of encoding. The underground church crypt is the vertical site of "open closure" where the textual (i.e. name and number) identity of a soldier has been switched. Mathilde's investigative work leads to the decoding of that moment of substitution. And, as with the analyst who investigates a psychic "crypt," her very act of decoding must follow the "allosemic pathways" (*Fors*, xlii)—the multiply determined phonetic and semantic associations—of written text, as in the soldiers' letters that she sets out to decode. (She is, after all, both the Self-refusing-to-mourn *and* the reader-investigator of an encrypted narrative.)

Codes and Letters

From the start, Mathilde has been reminded that letters from the front are subject to military censorship. When the five condemned prisoners are allowed to write one letter each, they do so under surveillance, with a warning from the lieutenant that any hint of their situation will result in destruction of the letter. It is for this reason that Esperanza makes a copy of each missive—and that he tells Mathilde to be alert for coded messages when she reads them.

But her first act of deciphering comes with a letter written not by one of the condemned men but by the Captain Favourier, who had reminisced to Esperanza about the long hours he had once spent with his stamp collection, fascinated by portraits of Queen Victoria as they appeared on stamps from sites of the British Empire: Barbados, New-Zealand, Jamaica. He had closed his eyes, recounts Esperanza, to murmur, "Victoria Anna Penoe. C'est ça" (60). Later, he had written a letter to explain:

> Je vous disais donc, entraîné là par le cognac et ma nostalgie des timbres-post: "Victoria Anna Penoe." Prétendre qu'à quinze ans j'étais amoureux fou de l'effigie de la plus grande des reines serait un euphémisme. J'enrageais de n'être pas anglais ou australien ou même de Gibraltar. . . . J'ai eu . . . la naïveté d'imaginer qu'Anna, la monnaie des Indes en vigueur là-bas, était le second prénom de ma bien-aimée. Pour Penoe, c'est encore mieux. . . . C'était un deux pence dont je vous laisse l'excitation de chercher l'origine, et une erreur ou un écrasement à l'imprimerie avait fait que le C de pence s'était refermé en O.

> [So I was telling you, inspired by the cognac and my postage-stamp nostalgia, about Victoria Anna Penoe. To claim that at age fifteen I was madly in love with the effigy of the greatest queen of all would be an understatement. I was in despair over not being English or Australian or even from Gibraltar. . . . I naïvely imagined that Anna, the Indian currency in use down there, was my beloved's

second name. As for Penoe, this is even better. . . . The denomina-
tion was two pence—I'll leave you the thrill of discovering the
place of origin—but an engraving error or a smudge during the
printing had closed the C of PENCE into an O.] (79)

In addition to the strange adolescent eroticism ("amoureux fou," "excita-
tion") and the fascination with the exoticism of Empire, we find here a textual slippage, from C to O. A monetary value (pence) becomes a proper name
(Penoe) and the typographical opening of the letter C re-closes into the tight
circle of the O, as though the crypt's walls were being reinforced. And indeed,
this "revelation" of the name's origin seems to do nothing to further Mathilde's
investigation; the captain brings it up as a sort of red herring, as a way to
exculpate himself from the soldiers' deaths ("I'm not such a bad guy, after all"
is the letter's point.) But in the end it will prove useful, for it contains testimony that the five soldiers were still alive the Sunday morning after their
abandonment to the no-man's-land. Mathilde's older family friend Pierre-
Marie tries to convince her that the letter is a fake, but Mathilde finds a way
to discount him by searching an entire catalogue of British stamps until she
finds documentation of the erroneous stamp, issued from the Isle of Mauri-
tius in 1848. She notes the "PENCE" to "PENOE" substitution, adding her
own commentary: "Un état des pertes se trafique. S'en tenir désormais à la
lettre du capitaine Favourier" [A casualty list can be altered. From now on,
stick to Captain Favourier's letter] (150). Letters can lie, but typographical
substitution of one letter for another substantiates this one.

Célestin Poux tells Mathilde all sorts of possible ways for soldiers to insert secret codes into their letters sent from the front. He cites *Le Saut de puce*
[Flea Jump], which consists of reading a new phrase by skipping groups of
two or more words, *La Carte du tendre* [Lover's Lane], in which one reads only
the lines agreed upon in advance, and *L'Ascenseur* [The Elevator], in which
words are aligned on the page so that they can be read from top to bottom or
bottom to top: "à la verticale d'un terme-repère décidé une fois pour toutes,
une phrase secrète" [vertically, beginning with a a previously selected base
word, a secret phrase] (274). It turns out to be the last method that Cet Homme
used in the letter sent to his wife; and since Mathilde only has a handwritten
copy, made by Esperanza, of the original, she is forced to spend hours realign-
ing the words until a phrase sets itself off vertically from the horizontal text.
In Japrisot's novel, we find first the letter reproduced, with the phrase aligned

vertically within the lines, then an explanation: "A la verticale du mot Bernay, on peut lire, de haut en bas: *Je serai Bernay mars. Vend tout. Dis rien. Ecoute personne. Benoît*" [Vertically along the word Bernay, one reads from top to bottom: Will be Bernay March. Sell everything. Say nothing. Heed nobody. Benoît] (331). Thus the key information that sends Mathilde to find her final witness, Cet Homme, relies for decoding on the switch from a horizontal to a vertical axis. In a way, the new vertical alignment alerts us to a spatial verticality that holds the secret to Manech's escape: the underground church crypt, with its upward-thrusting brick steps and downward-draining well; the holes and ramps and furrows that make of the no-man's-land a place of secrets and substitutions. The space of the encrypted letter is also the terrain of the en-crypt-ed soldiers.

The realignment from horizontal to vertical axes of Cet Homme's letter also reminds us of the multidirectionality of textual decryption in general, as described in *Fors*. Rather than follow simple metonymic displacements, Abraham and Torok's analysis of the Wolf-Man's language slips and slides along multi-lingual routes, what Derrida calls "the allosemic pathways" that "pass through nonsemantic associations, purely phonetic contaminations" (*Fors*, xlii). Words are treated as things ("word-things"), material objects whose phonetic characteristics can be reinterpreted according to different languages—primarily, in the case of the Wolf-Man, Russian, German, and English (the languages of his family and childhood). Thus, for example, the German word for necklace, *Halsband*, is read as encrypting a familial relationship revealed by the phonetic near-identity of the English word *husband*.

In Japrisot's novel, a case can be made for reading word-things simultaneously in French and English, for the Gallic terrain is contaminated throughout the text by elements of the British Empire. We have already noted the Lewis Carroll epigraph and the Victorian stamps collected by Captain Favourier, hailing from colonial lands. In an early moment in the novel, Esperanza recalls having watched two of the prisoners attentively examine a small object: "C'était un bouton d'uniforme britannique, orné d'une tête de caribou, avec des lettres gravées sur le pourtour: *Newfoundland, Terre-Neuve*" [It was a button from a British uniform, decorated with a caribou's head, with letters engraved all around the edge: *Newfoundland, Terre-Neuve*] (44). And most important, the Bingo Crépuscule trench is itself a terrain crisscrossed by the feet of British soldiers. As the original farmer of the no-man's-land territory explains, he had returned in the final days of the war to inspect his devastated fields:

J'ai retrouvé mes champs et les ruines de ma ferme en avril 17, après que les Boches, pour raccourcir leur front, s'étaient repliés quarante ou cinquante kilomètres en arrière . . . . Le pays était traversé par des Britanniques de partout, même des Indiens des Indes avec leurs turbans, des Australiens et des Néo-Zélandais, des Ecossais, des Irlandais et des Anglais d'Angleterre. Je n'ai jamais entendu spiker English de ma vie comme en 17 et 18.

[I came back to my fields and the ruins of my farm in April of '17, after the Boches had tightened up their front by falling back about forty or fifty kilometers to their Siegfried Line. The countryside was swarming with Britishers from everywhere, English, Scots, Irish, Australians, New Zealanders, even natives from India with their turbans. In all my life I never heard so much English jabbering as I did in '17 and '18) (290)

Note the linguistic interference, the combination of phonetic memory (*spik* for "speak") and mixed grammar ("-er"), as though the farmer's native tongue were shot through with bubbles (crypts, cysts, . . .) of the alternate communicative network. Remember, too, that it was the British who first buried the bodies of the five dead men at the front, when these allies relieved the French troops at Bingo Crépuscule (itself named for British colonial lieutenant-general Byng). The narrator keeps reminding us, "Attention au fil." *Attention au fil.* What does "fil" sound like? *"Attention aux filles"?* It is, after all, Mathilde who holds the key—and it is Tina Lombardi who first follows the deductive "fil" and takes it to her vengeful conclusion. But if we follow the "allosemic" pathways into the text's bilingualism, we can ask, rather: where does the phoneme lead us in English? "Attention au . . . /fil/." Drop a letter, "Fee." Add a letter, "Field." Pay attention to the "fee": to the British pence in a stamp whose typographical error takes the reader along an erotically charged labyrinth of associations, obfuscations, and eventual revelations. Pay attention to the "field": to the terrain of the no-man's-land, whose anfractuosities enable a substitutive encryption that keeps Manech out of the tomb and keeps Mathilde's "fil" going. *Attention au fil* means, in the end, that we follow language's pathways, that we read the text for its own meanderings and not for a hermeneutic or sentimental resolution. For even though Jean-Pierre Jeunet's film version of *Un long dimanche de fiançailles* concludes with Mathilde's and Manech's reunion, Japrisot's novel adds a final chapter, one that returns to the "Lundi matin"

[Monday morning] of the soldiers's first makeshift grave, thus reminding us that what counts is what is buried underneath the surface (of land, of letters, . . .). *Les choses ensevelies sous la neige.* For *Un long dimanche* is more than just a romantic testament to stubborn young love; it is a reflection on the ways in which the trauma of war effects the dispersal, substitution, and identification of bodies and words (letters in both senses) in a cryptic terrain at once psychic and geographical, at once individual and national.[18]

The short final chapter of *Un long dimanche de fiançailles* follows the steps of British soldiers from Newfoundland as they cross the trench of "l'Homme de Byng" and come upon the bodies of the French dead. They decide to bury the five mutilated men, they read their names on the matriculation tags, they assemble their bodies in a shell-hole, they cover it with a solid tarp, and they add a casket of sorts: a red metal tobacco tin that echoes Mathilde's box and acts as a minuscule substitution-crypt. This box contains the soldiers' epitaph, written by hand with a pencil on a ripped piece of notebook paper. The words of this epitaph, printed in their versified order with narrative interruptions, serve as the novel's conclusion:

> *Cinq soldats français*
> *Ici reposent,*
> *Morts leurs souliers aux pieds,*
> *à la poursuite du vent,*
> le nom du lieu,
> *où se fanent les roses,*
> et une date,
> *il y a longtemps.*

> HOSSEGOR, 1989
> NOISY-SUR-ECOLE, 1991

> [*Here lie*
> *five French soldiers,*
> *who died with their shoes on,*
> *chasing the wind,*
> the name of the place,
> *where the roses fade,*
> and a date,
> *a long time ago.*]

This conclusion refuses the specificity of intradiegetic place and time, re-orienting "le nom du lieu" toward a poetic abstraction and the "date" toward a timeless past. Only the novel's own composition is identified by date, re-minding us not only that this is a fiction but also that what is at stake in that fiction is textuality itself: words buried in a casket, subject to the cryptic dis-tortions of the violent archive.

Geology's Ghosts: Fred Vargas and the Hauntological Terrain of Crime

Today's detective novelists are often themselves archivists, littering their texts with unearthed phrases from the past as they revive a generic tradition. Ja-prisot found the central episode of *Un long dimanche de fiançailles,* in which condemned soldiers are sent into no-man's-land to face death at the hands of the enemy, in Maréchal Fayolle's *Cahiers secrets de la Grande Guerre,* a text made public in 1964 and cited by Japrisot in his novel's flash-forward scene of Mathilde reading. Another World War I episode inspired the title of Fred Var-gas's prize-winning and best-selling 1995 novel *Debout les morts.*[19] The phrase refers to a famous rallying-cry reported by Lieutenant Jacques Pericard who recalled being surrounded by Germans in a trench at Verdun in April 1915; the situation seemed desperate until a badly wounded soldier stood up and cried "Debout les morts!" to his comrades, inspiring them to continue the fight. Fred Vargas's own brother, prominent World War I historian Stéphane Audoin-Rouzeau, explains with his co-authors that the phrase was "raised to the status of national myth" after having appeared in the *Journal des débats* and Maurice Barrès's newspaper, *L'Écho de Paris.*[20] The propagandistic resonance of the rallying-cry was in part due, it seems, to the nation's "deep anxieties about death and the afterlife"; in one version of the oft-repeated tale, it was not just the heroic wounded who arise against *les Boches,* but the dead themselves (55–56). In a way, this phrase about the living dead has itself become a phantom, haunting the terrain of French politics and, eventually, Vargas's crime fiction.

In his work on the detective genre, Pierre Verdaguer cites obsession with the wounds of France's unresolved past as the prime motivation behind the archaeological fictions of Vargas and her fellow antiquarian-cum-crime writer Anne de Leseleuc. National memory underlies these novels, even when they are set in the seeming distance of the prehistoric era, as in Lese-leuc's Marcus Aper series (begun in 1992):

L'intérêt ici est que cette historienne nous signale le parallèle entre l'époque lointaine qu'elle a choisie, et qui est généralement perçue comme l'aube mythique de l'esprit national français, et la période actuelle. On notera que Marcus Aper et Astérix sont des contemporains, vivant à ce moment de l'Histoire qui est censé refléter particulièrement bien le nôtre. C'est aux origines de la mémoire nationale, là précisément où l'historique et le mythique tendent à se confondre, que se retrouverait le convaincant reflet de notre France actuelle.

[What is of interest here is that this historian is showing us the parallel between the past era that she has chosen, and which is generally perceived as the mythic dawn of the French national spirit, and today. Let us note that Marcus Aper and Astérix are contemporaries, living at the precise moment of History that purportedly reflects ours with particular resonance.][21]

Through temporal displacement (in de Leseleuc's case) and archaeo-historical method (in Vargas's), contemporary crime fictions explore the rifts and cracks in France's nation-state identity.

Susanna Lee places Vargas at the near end of a post–World War II shift in crime fiction from maverick, nonconformist detectives to investigators identified closely with the republic's *étatiste* values; Vargas's fictional police commissioner Jean-Baptiste Adamsberg represents the latter, a "modern romantic hero" whose qualities reinforce "an imagined symbiosis and intuitive congruence between the individual and the state."[22] In her reading of Vargas's *L'Homme à l'envers* (1999), Lee contrasts Adamsberg's official, representative function with the isolation of the novel's sociopathic killer, a wolf-tracker motivated to violence by "a pathological and generations-old search for vengeance" (Lee, 73). Such a return from a deep, trans-individual past is typical of Vargas's novels, in which the ghosts and werewolves of archaic legend take on modern form.

But how does that buried past manifest itself in and through Adamsberg's own investigations on behalf of his nation-state? The remainder of this chapter will focus on three novels—*Debout les morts* (1995), *Pars vite et reviens tard* (2001), and *Dans les bois éternels* (2006)—that reflect Vargas's archaeological training through their investment in the stratigraphic layers of the (national and psychic) underground as archival registers of violent trauma.

Debout les morts: *"la terre peut parler"*

Most murder mysteries begin with the discovery of a corpse. *Debout les morts* begins with the disquieting discovery . . . of a tree. The beech tree (an "hêtre") has appeared overnight in the garden of the famous singer Sophia Siméonidis, who is so unsettled by this unexplained entity (a being, an "être") that she asks her neighbors to dig into the dirt below its roots, in the hopes of finding some clue to the intruder's provenance. Her neighbors are neither gardeners nor detectives, but historians—the fictional trio known to Vargas fans as *Les trois Évangélistes*: Marc Vandoosler ("Saint Marc"), Mathias Delamarre ("Saint Matthieu"), and Lucien Devernois ("Saint Luc"). If their nicknames seem like relics from a faded religious era, it is no coincidence; for the three men are professionally and psychologically invested in reviving the past.

The historiographical character of *Les trois Évangélistes* is evident from the start in the very layout of their crumbling mansion: "la baraque pourrie," as they call it, is a five-story behemoth that the historians inhabit according to the chronological order of their specializations. On the *premier étage*, we have the *pre*historian Mathias; one floor up, we find Marc the medievalist, and above him, Lucien, a World War I scholar (whose character is based on Vargas's brother); and finally, in the attic, Marc's godfather, an aging lothario and former police detective. Marc, the medievalist, explains this peculiar layout with mock seriousness, saying that it is based on a system of chronological gradation:

> au rez-de-chaussée, inconnu, mystère originel, merdier général, ...
> Au premier étage, légère émergence du chaos, balbutiements
> médiocres, l'homme nu se redresse en silence, bref, . . . Mathias.
> Montant plus avant l'échelle du temps . . . bondissant par-dessus
> l'Antiquité, abordant de plain-pied le glorieux deuxième millénaire,
> les contrastes, les audaces et les peines médiévales, bref, moi, au
> deuxième étage. Ensuite, au-dessus, la dégradation, la décadence, le
> contemporain. Bref, [Lucien]. Lui, au troisième étage, fermant de la

honteuse Grande Guerre la stratigraphie de l'Histoire et celle de
l'escalier. Plus haut encore, le parrain, qui continue de déglinguer
les temps actuels à sa manière bien particulière.

[on the ground floor, unknown, original mystery, general mayhem
. . . . On the second floor, slight emergence from the chaos,
mediocre first faltering steps, man basically rises, silent and bare:
Mathias. Continuing to climb the ladder of time, leaping over
Antiquity, and moving head-on into the glorious second mille-
nium, the contrasts, risks, and troubles of the Middle Ages, in
short, me, on the third floor. And then, above that, we find
deterioration, decadence, the contemporary. In short, Lucien. Him,
on the fourth floor, capping off the stratigraphy of History—that
of the shameful Great War and that of the stairway. And even
higher up, the godfather, who continues to crack up our own times
in his own particular way.] (61, my emphasis)

While poking some fun at this scheme of grand eschatology, Marc nonetheless reinforces its vertical order, from deep time at the bottom to shallow
present at the top, an order that mimics above ground the geological layers
of the earth below—layers that hold weapons and bones, clues to the past
for those who dare to dig. Most interesting in the *baraque pourrie*'s layout,
in addition to its topographical organization of time, is the particularly geological nature of its description. Marc twice uses the scientific term "stratigraphie" to describe the house's storeys—and again later to describe the layers
of dirt that hold the key to the crime, thus connecting the historians' profession to their amateur investigation of their neighbor's mysterious beech
tree. Once that neighbor herself disappears, possibly victim to the same type
(and place) of burial as the beech-tree, the Three Evangelists must apply
archaeological method to a real terrain. At one point in the dig, they find an
earthen pipe, identified casually as "fin XVIIIe" (52). The dirt outside Sophia
Siméonidis' home seems silent ("muet"), but the prehistorian Mathias "tentait
de faire parler ses tas de silex et d'ossements" [was trying to make the piles of
flint and bone speak to him] (226). Flint and bones—the objects of study for
Earth scientists, but not so typically for investigators of contemporary crime.

   Of course as historians, the Three Evangelists know that nothing in the
present is without roots in the past. So in addition to sifting through the flint
and loam of Sophia's property, they consult another type of document: the

program reviews and newspaper clippings that have been stored, boxed, and dated in the singer's family archives. It is in those dusty cartons, possessed by "archive fever" (on finding a stack of World War I notebooks, "Lucien était ailleurs, inabordable, avalé par la découverte de sa mine et devenu incapable de s'intéresser à autre chose" [Lucien was elsewhere, inaccessible, swallowed up by the discovery of his goldmine and no longer capable of paying attention to anything else], 208), that the unofficial investigators find the key to Sophia's murder: a long-buried tale of professional rivalry that emerges, distorted, in the form of her false friend Juliette Gosselin. Juliette, it turns out, is actually the disgraced opera singer Nathalie Domesco. Fifteen years earlier, when Sophia was hospitalized as a result of a mysterious and brutal attack, Juliette had stepped in as understudy to replace her in performances of *Elektra*; but her inability to match Sophia's vocal skills led to disastrous reviews and an all-consuming jealousy that would continue to haunt her. Ironically, by making Sophia disappear, Juliette dispatches her into the uncanny realm of legend, as the public imagines "Sophia la belle rôdant, la nuit, dans Paris . . .] / La morte-vivante" [Sophia the Beautiful wandering through Paris at night / the living dead] (256).

But Sophia is no immaterial phantom—and the solution to her disappearance relies on earthy matter. The singer's very identity is aligned with rock: when police find the charred remains of a body in a burning car, they identify it as Sophia because of the presence of a volcanic pebble that she had always kept on her person. That igneous remnant of a distant past, a "fétiche volcanique" Sophia had kept in her purse or pocket for twenty-eight years, had served as a talismanic reminder of the Greek singer's first success and was now the only material trace to survive the devastating fire. In a more symbolic sense, the basalt pebble textually links Sophia to her devoted investigators. As Marc tries to unravel the mystery of his neighbor's disappearance, his jumbled thoughts take on the geological traits of volcanic plates:

Ses pensées se cognaient, s'entassaient ou bien s'écartaeint les unes des autres. Comme les plaques de l'écorce terrestre qui s'ingénient à déraper sur le machin glissant et chaud qu'il y en a dessous. Sur le manteau en fusion. C'est terrible cette histoire de plaques qui déconnent dans tous les sens à la surface de la Terre. Impossible de tenir en place. La tectonique des plaques, voilà comment ça s'appelle. Et bien lui, c'était la tectonique des pensées. . . . Quand les plaques s'écartent, éruption volcanique.

[His thoughts knocked about, crashing together and bouncing
apart. Like plates of the earth's crust, striving to slide across the hot
and slippery thing underneath. Over the mantle of molten lava. It's
messed up, this business of slabs that slip and slide all over the
Earth's surface. Impossible to keep in one spot. Plate tectonics,
that's what it's called. Well, for him, it was thought tectonics.
When the plates bounce apart, the volcano erupts.] (117)

And if the layers of Marc's mind risk volcanic disruption as they sift through
the confusing evidence of Sophia's murder, his solid-as-a-rock friend Mathias
is equally vulnerable to the seismic effects of the unknown: Marc thinks of
Mathias as "une sorte de dolmen, une roche massive, statique, sacrée, mais
s'imprégnant à son insu de toutes sortes d'événements sensibles, orientant ses
particules de mica dans le sens des vents" [a sort of dolmen: a massive, static,
and sacred rock, but one that's unknowingly permeated with all sorts of troubling events, orienting its particles of mica toward the direction of the winds]
(175). As for Lucien, it is in linguistic form that fragments from the past arise
to disrupt the surface of a peacetime present; the historian's speech is peppered with World War I locutions (the neighbors to the left are on "the Western front," being drunk is entering "un trou d'obus," preparing to leave the
house is being "mobilisés"). Naturally, it is Lucien who explains the history of
the phrase "Debout les morts," this title connecting patriotism to a deeper anxiety about blurred boundaries between the quick and the dead.

As we have seen through the cryptonymics of Japrisot's Long dimanche, a
buried trauma can leave scars underground and symptoms above—including
on the level of language. In Debout les morts, "La terre peut parler" [the earth
can speak] (228) because it can reveal to a historian's eye, through its loamy
textures and gradations of grit, the timing of buried secrets and their disruptive effects. And the past can "speak," whether through Lucien's verbal tics
or the "truc curieux" that Marc discovers in the written archives: Sofia's name
had been written with an "s" in the middle, turning it into "Sosie Siméonidis,
sosie, double, doublure . . ." [Siméonidis the twin, double, stand-in . . .]—
which leads the investigators to Juliette, the singer's understudy and rivalrous
double (271). Starting with that discovery, Marc had reconstructed Juliette's
movements through a series of underground spaces: the hole under the mysterious beech-tree (which she had buried to trouble Sophia), the cellar of Le
Tonneau (the restaurant under which Juliette had killed her rival), a deep
subterranean well (into which Juliette had thrown Marc, out of an archaic

impulse to imitate medieval assassins), and back to the hole under the *hêtre* (in which Juliette had buried Sophia's corpse, knowing that the dirt there had already been deemed free of bones in the initial investigative dig). Though Juliette's motivations are superficially explained by her professional failure fifteen years earlier, the true temporality of criminal investigation in Vargas is geological in scope: explaining the police's inability to solve the crime, Marc tells his companions, "ils n'avaient donc pas fouillé plus profond que nous . . . quelqu'un d'autre avait creusé après eux, plus loin, jusque dans la strate noire et grasse . . ." [they must not have dug as deeply as we did; someone else had excavated afterwards, deeper, all the way into the black and oily layer of the earth] (273).

Geology and Psychology

In the geological imagination of *Debout les morts*, volcanic forces erupt not only on the side of violent crime, but also in the deductive processes of the investigators themselves. Marc, as we have seen, turns to plate tectonics as a figure for the perpetual *glissades* of his mind, fearing a mental version of volcanic eruption when its parts collide. But he also wonders whether the other historians feel the same subterranean forces at work:

> Et Lucien, il éruptionnait, lui? Ça n'existe pas, éruptionner. Érupter? Non plus. Lucien était plutôt à ranger dans l'activité sismique fumante chronique. Et Mathias? Pas du tout tectonique, Mathias. Mathias c'était . . . la vaste flotte, l'océan. L'océan qui refroidit les laves. N'empêche qu'au fond de l'océan, ce n'est pas si calme qu'on ne croit. Il y en a des merdes aussi là-dedans, il n'y a pas de raison. Des fosses, des fractures . . .

> [And what about Lucien? did he eruptify? that's not a word, eruptify. Erupt? Nope. Lucien was more of the chronic seismic smoldering type. And Mathias? Not at all tectonic, that one. Mathias was the vast sea, the ocean. The ocean that cools lava down. Of course, that doesn't change the fact that in the depths of the ocean, it's never as calm as people might think. There's plenty of shit down there too, no reason why there wouldn't be. Shafts, cracks, . . .] (117–18)

In this language of fissures and fractures, tectonic shifts and volcanic eruptions, we might recognize a Freudian model of the subconscious mind. And
digging into the past involves an exposure of deep mental strata as much as of
dirt and documents.

More specifically, the narration of *Debout les morts*'s climactic resolution
to the crime mystery takes on the form of a psychoanalytic "talking cure"—
for the historian/investigators as well as for the assassin. Marc's verbal reconstruction of Juliette's crime is delayed by the trauma of having been thrown
in the subterranean well, where he was temporarily paralyzed by its cold
waters. Hoping to coax the tale out of his friend, Mathias enjoins him to speak.
Or rather, he *would* enjoin him to speak if he himself were not also suffering
from the traumatic attack: "Si Mathias avait eu plus de force, il aurait dit 'Parle,
Marc.' Sûrement il aurait dit ça, le chasseur-cueilleur" [If Mathias had more
strength, he would have said "Talk, Marc." Surely, the hunter-gatherer would
have said that] (272). The archaic identity of the hunter-gatherer enters into
this modern space of interrupted speech. And if "la terre peut parler," traumatized humans show more resistance; on the final page of the novel, Mathias explains what he had whispered to Nathalie Domesco when he'd begun
to suspect her: "Je disais, 'Parle, Juliette'." Along with the repeated injunction
to speak, we have here a psychic schism or fissure in the form of split person-
ality, as Nathalie/Juliette is called to confess by a neighbor willing to dig
down, down to the dark eruptive strata of the past.

Les cailloux, l'intrus, and the Trans-Generational Phantom:
Pars Vite et reviens tard

Commissioner Jean-Baptiste Adamsberg, the investigative hero of eight Vargas novels written between 1991 and 2011, likes rocks. He is known for bringing pebbles back from the seaside as enigmatic souvenirs for his bemused
colleagues (*Dans les bois éternels*); he solves cases by sifting through the "cailloux" [stones] and "algues" [algae] of his oceanic mind (*L'Homme à l'envers*);
he muses on the mystery of pebbles sunk deep into a subterranean well
(*L'Homme aux cercles bleus*). In *Pars vite et reviens tard*, Adamsberg sees the
ocean's effects on limestone rock formations as a metaphor for the hardships
of criminal investigation: hard-core cops, he says, are like calcified jaw-bones
whose softer parts have been washed away by the violent tide. This insight
comes at the end of a rather technical debate with his colleague Danglard,

who insists that "le calcaire mou n'existe pas en géologie" [soft limestone doesn't exist in geology]. "On s'en fout, Danglard" [We don't care], replies Adamsberg, continuing:

> Il y a des bouts mous et des bouts durs, comme dans toute forme de vie, comme dans moi-même et comme dans vous. Voilà ces rochers. A force que la mer les frappe, les cogne, les bouts mous se mettent à fondre. . . . Les parties dures commencent à faire saillie. Et plus le temps passe et plus la mer cogne et plus la faiblesse s'éparpille à tous vents. A la fin de sa vie d'homme, le rocher n'est plus que crénelage, dents, mâchoire de calcaire prête à mordre. A la place du mou, voici des vides, des absences.

> [There are soft bits and there are hard bits, as in any life form, as in me and as in you. Look at those rock cliffs. By dint of being hit over and over, struck by the sea, the soft bits begin to dissolve. The hard bits start to stick out. And the more time passes and the sea keeps striking, the more the weak spots get scattered. At the end of a man's life, all that's left of the cliff are the jagged bits, the teeth, the stony jawbone ready to bite. Where once were soft spots, now are empty holes, absences.] (34–35)

His conclusion is that "le flic" [the cop] becomes nothing more than a "mâchoire de calcaire," an image that externalizes the psyche onto the violent topography of sea, earth, rocks, and bone. If the psychoanalytic angle here remains discreet, it emerges explicitly in Vargas's 2004 *Sous les vents de Neptune*, which opens on Adamsberg's strange sensation that his own mind is harboring a stowaway, "un clandestin à bord" that intrudes on his peaceful consciousness (22). This uncanny split is presented in the terms of geological violence: "Homme ordinaire au matin, bouleversé au soir, bloqué par un volcan surgi devant ses pas, gueule de feu ouverte sur une indéchiffrable énigme" [An ordinary man by day, shattered by night, jammed up by a volcano that has appeared before him, its fiery maw opening onto an unsolvable mystery] (25). This volcanic intrusion reminds Adamsberg of his own great-uncle, who used to withdraw into the rock crevices of a Pyrénées cliffside to deal with illness:

> Puis l'ancêtre se dépliait et revenait à la vie, fièvre tombée, avalée par le roc. Adamsberg sourit. Il ne trouverait nulle tanière dans

cette vaste ville pour s'y lover comme un ours, nulle anfractuosité
pour absorber sa fièvre et gober tout cru son clandestin. . . . Son
ami Ferez, le psychiatre, aurait sans doute cherché à identifier le
mécanisme de l'irruption.

[Then the ancestor would come back to life and emerge, his fever
gone, swallowed up by the rock. He couldn't find any hiding-place
in this big city to coil up in like a bear, no crevice to absorb his
fever and swallow up his stowaway secret. . . . His psychiatrist
friend Ferez would surely have tried to diagnose an intrusion
mechanism.] (24)

Whether or not Adamsberg pooh-poohs it as psycho-babble, there is some
mechanism of "irruption" at work in Vargas's novels, some geological anfractuosity of the psychic terrain that is transmitted across generations, connecting dead ancestors to modern investigators and allowing the past to intrude
upon the present.

We need to go beyond Freud to see exactly how Vargas's fiction relates
the subterranean geologies of violence to a specifically linguistic model of the
uncanny. As we have seen, the French psychoanalysts Nicolas Abraham and
Maria Torok developed in the 1970s and 1980s a theory of the mind's *topography* as it attempts to assimilate the violent effects of trauma and loss. Among
their best-known contributions to post-Freudian psychoanalysis is the theory
of the "Transgenerational Phantom," defined as the unsettling disruption of
an individual's psyche by the unconscious transmission of secrets from a previous generation. When a deeply shameful act occurs (rape, adultery, incest,
murder) and is not avowed, its unspoken trauma is passed in distorted form
to unknowing descendants: "what haunts are not the dead, but the gaps left
within us by the secrets of others."[23] In "Notes on the Phantom," Abraham
includes the telling example of a man who cannot understand why he has been
drawn to a geological hobby:

[This] carrier of a phantom became a nature lover on weekends,
acting out the fate of his mother's beloved. The loved one had been
denounced by the grandmother (an unspeakable and secret fact)
and, having been sent to "break rocks" [*casser les cailloux*, i.e., do
forced labor], he later died in the gas chamber. What does our man

do on weekends [a generation later]? A lover of geology, he "breaks rocks," catches butterflies, and proceeds to kill them in a can of cyanide. (175)

In the psychic topography of Abraham's patient, the secret fate of his mother's lover remains buried in a subterranean stratum until his analyst de-crypts the symptom by following the linguistic slippage from *casser les cailloux* to the forced labor of an Auschwitz victim. This cryptoanalysis of what Esther Rashkin has called the "transtextuality" of the phantom is precisely the method Vargas's Inspector Adamsberg brings to bear in *Pars vite et reviens tard*.

In that novel, Joss Le Guern, a modern-day town crier who reads aloud handwritten messages at the place Edgar-Quiner in Paris, owes his anachronistic profession to his great-great-grandfather. Although the Breton's ancestor has been dead for a century, he doesn't mind cozying up to a bistro bar counter to discuss the day's business with Joss. As they chat, the ancestor gives occasional advice and muses on how nice it is to be a ghost, since "Quand on est mort, on sait des trucs qu'on savait pas avant" [When you're dead, you know things you didn't know before]. Though a jaded reader of the rational *policier* would easily dismiss the ancestor as the comic projected hallucination of a town drunk, he is presented in the text as a bona fide character, who comes to Le Guern's aid when troubling messages in the mail-bucket warn city residents of an impending apocalyptic pestilence. Serpents and rats, claim the archaic-sounding texts, will slither from the depths of subterranean tunnels to attack the population above. Joss's landlord is a retired professor named Decambrais, whose reconstructive linguistic analysis allows him to identify the historical "couches" [layers] of Joss's mail-bucket warnings: seventeenth-century prophetic texts about the Plague have been typeset incorrectly with f's replacing s's, so that archaic script comes to haunt the modern form. Even farther back, Decambrais finds Latin passages, marked by "l'intrus" of an arabic word (75)—and, as with Abraham and Torok's phantom, the "intruder" gets passed along a chain of transmission: "Des écrits qui se recopiaient les uns les autres, parfois mot pour mot. Différents auteurs ressassant une seule idée, jusqu'au XVII siècle encore, une idée qui se transmettait de génération en génération" [Writings that were copied and recopied, often word for word. Different authors would trot out the same idea, even still in the seventeenth century, an idea that was transmitted from generation to generation] (75–76).

And like Abraham and Torok's "carriers" of the phantom, Joss and his uneasy neighbors are unable to comprehend the implications of these unsettling
textual remnants from the past, these cryptic quotations about a Plague that
they thought had been wiped out centuries earlier.

In this text about texts, the police investigation is kicked off by a second
cryptic relic: the backwards numeral four, an ancient figure for the Plague that
was inscribed in medieval times as a protective talisman against infection but
that appears in modern-day form as grafitti painted on the doors of potential murder victims in Paris. In order to unearth the motive behind this
unsettling series of warnings and killings, Inspector Adamsberg enlists the
help of two "archivists": the medieval historian Mark Vandoosler (one
of the Three Evangelists) and his own psychoanalyst, Dr. Ferez. They discover, first, that the killer is strangling his victims, but staging the murders
to mimic the bubonic Plague; he blackens the corpses with coal and injects
them with a modern version of the *bacille pesteux*, a bacterium described as
a "historial killer," the Black Death as anachronistic intruder (126). As they
ponder the Plague's symbolic meaning for the killer, Adamsberg and Ferez
are led to the psychoanalytical solution of the "transgenerational phantom."
What seems to be a modern-day return of the medieval Plague is actually
"une affaire de . . . famillle" (221). Two generations back, a family has suffered public shaming for having survived a pestilential infection; this social
trauma has been passed on as psychic pathology. Says Adamsberg to his
shrink:

> Et je pense, Ferez, que la famille de ce type a connu cette tour-
> mente, qu'elle y est pasée en partie, les arrière-grands-parents
> peut-être. Que le drame s'est figé dans la saga de famille.
> —On appelle ça un fantôme familial, coupa la médecin.
> —Très bien. Il s'est figé et c'est ainsi que la peste s'est infiltrée
> dans la tête de l'enfant, par la décimation des ancêtres proches,
> inlassablement racontée.

> [So I'm thinking, Ferez, that this guy's family must have
> undergone this kind of suffering, went through it in part, maybe
> the great-grandparents. And that the trauma got hardened into
> the family lore.
> —That's called a familial phantom, interrupted the doctor.

—Fine. So it set in and that's how the plague seeped into the kid's head, through the annihilation of his nearest ancestors, tirelessly repeated.] (222)

For Abraham and Torok, the family secret must remain unspoken in order to haunt the descendant's unconscious mind, but in every other respect, Vargas's criminal case follows the logic of the "transgenerational phantom." In itself, this transfer of psychoanalytic theory into the *roman policier* is not particularly significant; from the genre's start, authors have invoked contemporary scientific and medical theories of criminal insanity to bolster their tales' realism and relevance. But what distinguishes Vargas's texts from many less self-conscious narratives is their embrace of the full crypto-linguistic consequences of the psychoanalytical "phantom" as it intersects with crime fiction's very form. When Ferez explains to Adamsberg that the familial phantom can only manifest itself in the killer because "des perturbations violentes . . . lui ont permis de s'installer" [his own violent disruptions made him vulnerable], he adds: "Les fantômes font leur nid dans les fractures" [Ghosts make their nests in the cracks] (222). Fractures, geological fissures that allow subterranean forces to irrupt to the surface, but in linguistically encrypted fashion. With its multiple "*intrus*" from the past, *Pars vite et reviens tard* allows the narrative of violent trauma to follow the triple paths of linguistic, geological, and psychic fracture.

Haunted Terrains: *Dans les bois éternels*

A man moves into a large crumbling mansion with creaking floors and attic winds. He is welcomed by an elderly one-armed neighbor who warns him never to bring a woman to the home, for every one of its female inhabitants has met with violent death. One woman hanged herself, one jumped from a high window, a third stuck her head in the oven; all were driven mad by the ghost of Saint Clarisse, an eighteenth-century murderess nun who has haunted the attic of this home ever since she herself was violently killed at a young age back in 1771. The one-armed neighbor has himself seen Clarisse in the attic window and even knew some of her latter-day victims, but the house's new tenant remains unconcerned. In fact, he is rather amused by the gruesome tale of this killer phantom, but he has his own living killers to track down, for he is Inspector Adamsberg—and this ghost story is the start to Vargas's tenth novel, *Dans les bois éternels* (2006).

In *A Counter-History of Crime Fiction: Supernatural, Gothic, Sensational* (2007), Mauricio Ascari aims to re-anchor the detective novel in the popular traditions that its classic myth of rationality has suppressed. According to generic convention, ghost stories should play no role other than that of superstitious folly to be dispelled by the superior reasoning of the fictional detective. But as Ascari argues, the idea of a murder victim's vengeful return to the land of the living retains a persistent and powerful hold on the crime fiction imaginary.[24] In a way, *Dans les bois éternels* sustains the classic *policier* tradition by providing, near the end, a rational explanation for the modern-day ghostly steps in Adamsberg's attic. And yet it refuses to dispel definitively the ghostly spirit of Saint Clarisse and her historical victims; indeed, the novel's final pages bring us back to the realm of apparent superstition. This could be read as a tongue-in-cheek framing device, but Vargas's ghost story does more than merely serve as a gothic decoy; rather, it fundamentally imbues the modern crime story with the logic of the phantom—not only because every *roman policier* is about the effects of a traumatic past on the narrative or investigative space of the present, but more specifically in this case, because Clarisse's story is about secrets, language, and layers of dirt.

As Adamsberg's elderly neighbor explains, Saint Clarisse had belonged to a silent sororal order, "un ordre muet": "Il y avait un ancien monastère de femmes ici, au siècle avant avant. C'étaient des religieuses qui n'avaient pas le droit de parler" [There used to be a convent here, in the century before the last one. The nuns weren't allowed to speak] (15). So repressed speech marks the first, primal scene of violence (Clarisse's murder), one that leads in subsequent generations to a linguistic slippage of toponymic order: "On disait la rue aux Muettes," explains the old man, "Et puis ça a donné 'Mouettes'" [They used to call it the street of the Mutes, and then that turned into Mouettes (seagulls)] (16). The aviary term now covers over the initial silence, the stifled speech of the Muettes, nuns whose convent lent their name metonymically to Adamsberg's new address. For Abraham and Torok, "The phantom represents the . . . intergenerational consequences of silence." And in Vargas's novel the consequences of Clarisse's silent order have lodged themselves across generations in the layered space of the crumbling mansion. By using the new name Mouettes, modern inhabitants of the dead-end street repress the etymological origin of silence, thus reinforcing "une impasse" in the topographical sense (the mansion is literally on a cul-de-sac) and the psychoanalytical one (blocking, temporarily, the analytical investigation on which Adamsberg will eventually embark). Significantly, Adamsberg's first act when he moves into the haunted house is to build a wall. Yet his elderly neighbor (whose own body is itself haunted by a "phantom"—the phantom limb whose itch he continues to feel in the place where he had lost an arm decades earlier) keeps the ghost story in the forefront of his (and the reader's) imagination. At one point, the old man explains to Adamsberg why no one has ever tried to destroy the cursed mansion: "Vous comprenez maintenant pourquoi on n'a jamais voulu démolir la maison? Parce que Clarisse serait allée loger plus loin. Chez moi, par exemple. Et nous tous, dans le secteur, on préfère savoir où *elle se terre*" [Now do you understand why no-one ever wanted to demolish the building? Because Clarissa would have just moved somewhere else. Like at my place, for example. And all of us in the area would rather know where she's hiding away] (18, my emphasis). *Où elle se terre*: where she hides out or is lodged, for in the logic of phantom possession, ghosts reside in a particular place. But the old man's locution is interesting, for not only is "se terre" a homonym for "se taire," to be silent; its earthy meaning locates this ghost in the ground. Even though she seems to be a spirit who wafts about in the heights of the mansion's attic, she is also somehow rooted in the terrain, in the layers of dirt which the neighbors are loathe to dig up, for fear of disturbing the cadavers of Saint Camille's victims: "C'est pour ça qu'on ne pioche pas trop profond. On ne va pas provoquer le diable" [That's why we don't dig too deep. We're not about to disturb the devil] (19). Digging for dirt is a risky act, but it is what Inspector Adamsberg does—often literally—every time he takes on a new case, for he knows that "la terre peut parler."

And indeed, in *Dans les bois éternels*, we find the culmination of what might be called the geo-phantomatic logic of transgenerational violence. To solve his modern murder mystery, Inspector Adamsberg traces the dirt under two murder victims's fingernails back to a cemetery, deserted because the guard claims to have seen a gray haunt floating eerily among the tombstones. We have seen the way in which Japrisot's Mathilde functions as a figural "cemetery guard," at once blocking and opening gates to past secrets that haunt the psyche of individual and nation. Vargas's cemetery guard similarly represents a troubled gateway to the terrain that Adamsberg must explore. He does this by calling in, once again, one of the Three Evangelists—this time, the prehistorian Mathias, who examines the layers of dirt under a recently moved tombstone: "Mathias promena sa main sur la surface uniforme de la terre. Puis il sembla accrocher du bout des ongles une *fissure fantôme*, qu'il suivit ensuite lentement" [Mathias ran his hand across the smooth surface of the earth, until his fingertips seemed to hit a snag, a phantom fissure that he then slowly followed] (128, my emphasis). This phantom fissure in the subterranean strata of the village cemetery's dirt signals a crack in the case—and a crack in the psyche, for it turns out that the deranged killer is a "dissociée," someone with a split consciousness: one side law-abiding and unaware of the other side's violent deeds. The medical examiner explains the phenomenon to Adamsberg in terms of a mental topography. Though there seems to be no communication between the two sides of a criminal "dissocié," one can always uncover the hidden "failles" that split the subject "comme une lézarde fend un mur" [like a crack splits a wall] (35). And those "failles" manifest themselves linguistically: "Des mots saugrenus sautent d'un côté du mur à l'autre. L'assassin ne s'en aperçoit pas mais l'analyste peut les surprendre" [Odd words leap from one side of the wall to the other. The murderer doesn't notice but the psychoanalyst can detect them] (35).

At the end of the novel, Adamsberg plays the role of the crypto-analyst, literally sitting the killer on a couch and talking through her symptoms until the violent Other irrupts into the surface of her conscious Self. This is the logic described in Abraham's "Notes on the Phantom": "What comes back to haunt are the tombs of others" (*The Shell and the Kernel*, 172). In Vargas's novel, the tombs are real ones, located in a village cemetery and in a church crypt, where the relics of saints are archived and where a seventeenth-century Latin text, *De sanctis reliquis*, holds the key to the familial schisms that created a violent, "volcanic" Other speaking through the killer's rational Self. By attending to the unfinished business handed down unconsciously across generations, Adamsberg is able to solve a modern-day murder mystery.

But that's not the end of the story. Adamsberg then repeats a patient-on-the-couch scene of analysis, this time with his colleague Veyrenc. Adamsberg and Veyrenc have suffered from a tense professional relationship, whose roots are found in an old-standing territorial feud between their home villages in a valley of the Pyrenées. Though they know, rationally, that this feud should remain dead and buried, they cannot help but carry it on; when asked why he doesn't just leave it in the past, Veyrenc answers in a language formally marked by archaism:

Hélas je ne le puis, Seigneur, car tout m'y porte.
Le sang de mon ancêtre à ce péché m'exhorte.

[Alas I cannot, Lord, I am pull'd by the flood.
To this sin I am call'd by my ancestor's blood.] (92)

Indeed, in a well-known quirk of Vargas's novel, the character Veyrenc himself hosts a hereditary phantom, one that takes the form of a linguistic tic:
this twenty-first-century cop speaks in full alexandrine verse, because his
grandmother had read only Racine. Veyrenc's archaic form of poetic speech
haunts Vargas's modern text just as in *Debout les morts*, Lucien's World War I
locutions insistently irrupt into common discourse. The past makes its mark
on the present through somatic symptoms as well; a strange streak of red in
Veyrenc's brown hair signals a shameful trauma from his past. *Dans les bois
éternels* ends with Adamsberg exorcising that deeply buried trauma from Veyrenc's psyche, as he helps him work through a violent childhood attack by
territorial thugs that had left the sanguinary mark on his hair. And Adamsberg does this by taking a shovel to the original site in order to dig up the
earth and listen to "le chant de la terre" as would an "archéologue" (124). Once
again, it is the earth that reveals a buried trauma, and the detective-archivist-
analyst who reads the return of a phantom Other.

    That Other, manifested linguistically, has its roots in a geologically deep
past. In another example of archaic language, Adamsberg's colleague Danglard uses old-fashioned terms like "la salle du Concile" to denote the officers' common room; "A l'entendre, ces termes désuets étaient remontés du fin
fond des temps pour imprégner les bâtiments, telle une eau antique suintant
via le réseau des caves" [To hear him speak, you'd think these outmoded terms
had risen up from the very depths of time to seep into the buildings like ancient waters oozing through an underground maze] (75, my emphases). In this
geological image, we find echoes of the cataclysmic waters and subterranean
strata that marked the nineteenth-century popular crime fictions analyzed in
Chapters 2 and 3. In a sense, Vargas's texts revive the "transgenerational phantom" of geology in the detective novel, updating a deep-seated theme of cataclysmic violence erupting under the rocks of Paris and emerging in the (literal
and psychic) spaces of modern crime. Though classically seen to dispel superstition and the supernatural, the *roman policier* itself works through a logic of
revenance and crypto-analysis, as the detective always attends to the buried
voice of a traumatized Other in order to reconstitute the past. This may be
why the spatial trope of the subterranean has, as it were, haunted the crime
fiction genre throughout its modern history, from the popular *feuilletons* of

the 1860s, which set violent crime in the quarries and catacombs of the Paris underground, to Didier Daeninckx's 1985 *Métropolice*, set in the tunnels of the Metro.

*   *   *

In these chapters, I have traced the ways in which the geological imaginary— the tropes of layered rock and buried bones made possible by nineteenth-century discoveries in the Earth Sciences—imprints the narrative form of fictional crime. Not surprisingly, we find a gradual internalization or psychologization of subterranean space. Whereas in nineteenth- and early twentieth-century fictions of authors like Eugène Sue and Gaston Leroux, underground caves symbolically threaten the lawful superstratum of the city, by the end of the twentieth century the layered and labyrinthine terrains of the underground threaten instead the coherence of the individual's psyche. From the spatio-cryptography of Sébastien Japrisot to the geo-phantomatics of Fred Vargas, we find new formulations of an archaic territorial logic at work in the crime fiction genre.

PART II

INTERSECTIONS

CHAPTER 5

Street-Name Mysteries and Private/Public Violence, 1867–2001

The first part of this book analyzes a cluster of "underground" crime fictions, in which violence below the surface threatens order above. And in Part III, maps in crime fiction signal a cartographic impulse at work in the detective's navigation of urban space. The distinction here between verticality and horizontality, however, is a heuristic one, since in any text involving the reconstruction of a violent past (i.e., a crime), the layers of history are sure to puncture the flattened space of rational investigation. Still, some narratives emphasize either the schistic rifts of repressed violence or the geographic orders of comprehension that would lay those rifts to rest. A third organizational category, though, has emerged in my preparation of this book. In Part II, "Intersections," this short, single-chapter "interlude" between the book's main Parts, I propose reading a subset of crime novels that crystallize some of the ways in which their two imaginaries intersect. These are what one might call "street-name mysteries," from early *feuilletons* like René de Pont-Jest's *Le Numero 13 de la rue Marlot* (1877) through Léo Malet's World War II classic noir *120 rue de la Gare* (1943) to today's updates of the localizing device, like Didier Daeninckx's *12, rue Meckert* (2001). In each, let me suggest, the titular street address works as a figure for the intersection between the "horizontal" and the "vertical"—between present and past, reason and disorder, domestic crime and the political violence that is always marked by national History.

Poe's (A)political Legacy

Linked by the common *rue* of their titles, street-name mysteries are self-consciously situated in the generic tradition begun by Edgar Allan Poe with

"The Murders in the Rue Morgue." Poe himself could have named his 1841 short story "The Murders of the Ladies l'Espanaye" or "Dupin's Deductions," but instead he tapped into and reinforced a French cultural habit of identifying crimes by location. Early in the nineteenth century, popular news gazettes and illustrated *canards* had already taken to marking the dangerous zones of the city of Paris through the titles of their sensationalistic reports on murder and theft. By the Second Empire and Third Republic, novelists were routinely copying the true crime format and using titles to anchor their plots in the specific geography of the French capital city's well-known *quartiers*: Charles Barbara's *L'Assassinat du pont-Rouge* (1859); Fortuné du Boisgobey's *Le Crime de l'Opéra* (1879); Maurice Jogand's *L'Agent d'affaires de la rue St.-Denis* (1886); Jules Lermina's *L'Étranglée de la Porte Saint-Martin* and *L'Étrange affaire du père lachaise* (1908). In a way, the identification of those areas allowed readers the solace of mapping—and therefore containing—criminal threat. The naming of locations thus partakes in what we have seen in our Prologue and Chapter 1 as the controlling, rationalistic "feint" inherent in Poe's inaugural narrative.

But what is unsuccessfully repressed in Poe's prefatory "feint" is not only pure reason; it is also the historical context of French colonization, which reappears in the story's main body in the form of trinkets, coins, and a violent beast. Today, "The Murders in the Rue Morgue" has inspired at least two recent re-writings that claim in their titles to provide the "true" story behind Poe's fiction: René Réouven's *La Vérité sur la rue Morgue* (2002), which fictitiously ties together Poe's three Paris mysteries into a common source-crime, and Robert Deleuse's *La Véritable affaire de la rue Morgue* (2004), which connects Poe's tale to the Haitian insurrections of the Napoleonic age.[1] Of the two returns to crime fiction's primal scene, the latter is particularly interesting for its implied generic argument: by fundamentally disavowing politics, Poe's story launched a deceptively refined tradition of mysteries interested only in bounded, private, domestic forms of violence.

In his somewhat gimmicky *La Véritable affaire de la rue Morgue*, Deleuse has a French narrator of 1848 investigate a real-life *fait divers* of 1815 from which he believes Poe had cribbed his story. Struck by the fact that the double murder took place on the same day as the Emperor's escape from Elba, Deleuse's narrator takes the simultaneity of State events and private crime as evidence of their interconnectedness—and he soon reveals a cover-up of the *rue Morgue* murders by Napoleon's security advisor Fouché (84). To the incredulous question of whether those domestic murders might be connected to an affair of the State, the narrator's response is a resolute yes (43). It turns out, he explains, that the two female victims were related to anti-Napoleonic dissidents and supporters of the slave revolts of Saint-Domingue (now Haiti). The women had been safe-keeping diamonds for the insurgents' cause; their murder is no common crime, but part of government-sponsored repression of an anti-Napoleonic plot.

How, according to Deleuse's fiction, had Poe effaced the international political motives for an attack on private citizens in Paris? By making the following substitutions: from *rue de la Saunerie* to the fictional *rue Morgue*; from a government cover-up by Napoleon's security advisor to the deductive delays of Dupin's ratiocination; from the colonial context of Haitian insurrection to the vague mention of a visiting sailor; and from Napoleon himself as tyrannical source of the violence to an exotic orangutan as scapegoat assassin. In reproduced newspaper accounts of Napoleon's escape from Elba, the returning Emperor is called a monster, an ogre, a tiger, a tyrant, and then, upon arrival in Paris, "sa majesté l'Empereur." The move from monster to majesty reflects the whitewashing Deleuse sees in detective fiction's inaugural turn away from the Real, its displacement of political brutality onto a plot of rational deduction.

As if to underline the importance of revolutionary context for the mystery genre, Deleuse sets his narrator's own investigation in the days of the Paris revolt in 1848. No disinterested puzzle-solver, the narrator participates "activement" with his friend Charles Baudelaire in the popular insurrection. And yet he has been tempted to play ostrich-in-the-sand by . . . none other than Poe's novel!

Mon séjour en Russie, particulièrement à Saint-Pétersbourg, m'avait coupé des réalités nationales malgré les lettres et les journaux qui m'étaient parvenus. Sans compter que le texte d'Edgar Allan Poe, emprunté à ce fait divers de 1815, avait eu tendance, ces derniers temps, à occuper tout mon esprit. C'était pour cela, d'abord, que je m'étais précipité chez Charles et non pour entendre parler de politique.

[My stay in Russia, particularly in Saint Petersburg, had cut me off from the realities of the nation, despite the letters and newspapers that I had received. Not to mention the fact that Edgar Allan Poe's tale, taken from the real-life events of 1815, had tended, in recent days, to occupy my mind entirely. It was for that reason, not to listen to talk of politics, that I had rushed to meet Charles.] (30)

Deleuse thus inserts into his narrator's life a thematic mise-en-abyme of the larger, implied generic argument: that Poe's novel has artificially cut off crime fiction from politics.

And "politics" equals "streets." In his Postface to *La Véritable affaire de la rue Morgue*, Didier Daeninckx writes that Deleuse has established the "noces éternellement noires du roman et de l'Histoire" [the dark and eternal marriage of the novel to History] by re-anchoring Poe's text in the context of Haitian independence and in the "fevered streets of 1848 Paris" (154). Even more directly, Deleuse substitutes metonymically the street for the revolutionary impulse: "La rue avait voulu une autre république" [The street was demanding another republic] (147). Poe's replacement, then, of the anchored reality of Paris's *rue de la Saunerie* with the purely fantasmatic *rue Morgue* becomes the founding move for what Deleuse sees as the story's laundering of political grit.

Deleuse's connection between urban streets and political suppression tips us off to a key localizing aspect of Poe's literary legacy. Not only did Poe's *ur*-site of Paris inspire a well-known Anglo-French—and increasingly, global—tradition of crime mysteries whose rational investigations hinge on urban location, architectural quirk, and topographical orientation. It also, as we have seen, sparked the lesser-studied strand of "street-name mysteries" that I analyze in this chapter. A brief investigation into the spatial logics of that Second Empire sub-genre reveals Deleuse's fictional attack on Poe's tale as both wrong and right. Deleuse is wrong to imply that "The Murders in the Rue Morgue" can possibly have eliminated politics from its narrative sphere; although the attack on Mme and Mlle Lespanan occurs inside the domestic space of their home, their case automatically enters the public fray of media, police, and crowd curiosity. But Deleuse is also, and more importantly, right in proposing that politics are at stake any time urban street names anchor inquiry. Poe's rue Morgue may be imaginary, but the very identification of his tale by *rue* (the urban street, site of revolutions) and *Morgue* (the place where death becomes public) inaugurates a genre that cannot fully separate private crime from concerns of the State.

Crime Fictions and the "Toponymic Lag"

A second thematic opposition that street crime mysteries cut across is the one between present and past. Indeed, despite the apparent stability of their street-address titles, the fictions themselves are riven by toponymic change. From the *feuilletons* of Pont-Jest to the *noirs* of Radoman, plots and narration crucially converge on the alteration of street names: obsolete maps lead characters astray, neighborhood residents cling to outdated addresses, narrators reflect on the politics of urban nomenclature. The spatial trope of street names thus always leads to a temporal one, as urban location is marked by the shifts of history.

In the serial fictions of the late nineteenth century, that temporal disjunction already takes a particular form. As Dominique Kalifa explains in his work on criminal topographies, popular *feuilletons* of the Second Empire produced a mythical map of urban violence that converged on the center of Eugène Sue's foundational *Mystères de Paris* (1842–43): the Cité. He notes, moreover, that even well after Haussmann's reforms had effectively chased violent crime from city center to periphery, late-century novelists continued to set their murders in the streets of the Cité and the alleyways of "le vieux Paris."[2] There was thus a disjunction between sociological reality and symbolic imaginary, as serials written during the Third Republic either updated earlier crimes, set their murders in the past, or simply revived the mythic force of a pre-Haussmann Paris by continuing to ascribe labyrinthine dangers to the city's cleaned-up center.

At least one late century "street-name mystery," Grison's *13, rue des Chantres* (1885), emplots the disjunction between new and old Paris by kickstarting its mystery through a coach ride from the boulevard Haussmann, where the dapper count Horace de Pringy lives, to "13, rue des Chantres, dans la Cité" (5). The narrator immediately explains that the journey will be a long one, as though signaling the act of temporal displacement that will take the reader back along with Pringy from the modern *boulevards* to the tenebrous, crime-ridden streets of the *Cité*. That is the site, if not of actual crime—then of crime *fiction*. Even today, when readers pick up a crime novel, they are aware of a temporal displacement, with new motifs (globalized theft, virtual violence) being inserted into a framework dating back to the mid-nineteenth century. What I find notable is that even as early as the second half of the nineteenth century, that framework was already figured as both spatial and temporal, through a conversion of real sites like the Cité into markers of a mythic revival.

Kalifa's thesis—of a lag between sociological reality and imaginary topography—compellingly signals the chiasmic force of place names as intersections of fiction and truth, space and time. From the mid-nineteenth to the twentieth century, Kalifa traces a symbolic decentering, recentering, and dispersal of crime in fictional representations of Paris. Phase 1: an acknowledgment of criminality's move outward to the city's periphery. Phase 2: an anachronistic revival of the Cité as picturesque labyrinth of crime. Phase 3: the early twentieth-century opening of Paris to a transnational network of transportation, communication, and crime. This last phase, typified by *Fantômas*'s famous mobility, announces the entropic spatiality of street-name mysteries that I will address in the later sections of this chapter. But for the moment, let us focus on Kalifa's Phase 2, in which crime fiction folds back its spatial imaginary onto an earlier time. A number of Third Republic writers revived the earlier July Monarchy's *vieux Paris* topography of alleyway knifings and labyrinthine escapes; Constant Guéroult, for example, retells a famous murder from 1836 in his 1880 *L'Affaire de la rue du Temple*. This time lag in the spatial imaginary of the Third Republic is typified for Kalifa by what he calls the "anachronistic toponym" of Les Halles (a name that outlived its market function).[3]

The notion of the anachronistic toponym is key to understanding modern crime fiction, with its narrative form of a time delay to which space seems to need to conform. In the nineteenth century, the genre's obsession with "location, location, location" appears in concentrated form in the titles of its street-name mysteries: Adolphe Belot's *Le Drame de la rue de la Paix* (1866), Constant Guéroult's *L'Affaire de la rue du Temple* (1884), Maurice Jogand's *L'Agent d'affaires de la rue Saint-Denis* (1886). Popular titles could also indicate an actual numbered address, as in the case of René de Pont-Jest's *Le Numéro 13 de la rue Marlot* (1877), but the prize for specificity must go to Georges Grison, whose 1885 *13, rue des Chantres* comes with the subtitle *Au 2ème étage*. When one reads these once-popular novels, one finds that the street name itself—that is, the toponym, not just the site—acts as a critical hinge between past and present, politics and privacy, myth and reality.

In the titles cited above, la rue Marlot is the only street name without overt religious associations. The others are rue du Temple, de la Paix (peace), Saint-Denis, and Chantres (cantor)—all apparent carryovers from a pre-Revolutionary system of nomenclature. Their recall of an ancien régime of Church and State attempts symbolically to erase the blood of multiple revolutions from the streets they name. Thus their very status as anachronistic toponyms points us back to the central function of these street-name mysteries: namely, to work through the tense relationship between domestic and political violence in the streets of Paris—between private crimes "de la rue" and public violence "dans la rue."

What's in a Name? Domestic Crime Versus Political Violence in Pont-Jest and Belot

Modern crime fiction—especially in the classic detective story form—has always stood in an uneasy relation to politics, often sidelining the big-H History of world events to home in on private dramas, while at the same time ineluctably touching upon the economic and societal structures that lead to criminal acts. The tellingly awkward structure of Emile Gaboriau's 1869 *Monsieur Lecoq*—an investigation plot that gets interrupted for hundreds of pages by a flashback to Restoration politics—testifies to the genre's attempts to extricate private from public modes of violence. By the twentieth century, we find emerging what Uri Eisenzweig identifies as two "symmetrically opposed" forms of violence: the first, "collective, systematic, and massive, indeed global to an unprecedented degree," and the second, "local, individual, almost sporadic in nature."[4] In other words: wars versus murder. The incompatibility of political and private violence leads in the twentieth century to a generic split between two modes of crime fiction: on the one hand, the Agatha Christie-type parlor game whodunits, which cut off domestic crime from its political context, and on the other hand, the *noir engagé*, which links seemingly random violence to the ideologies of nation and the politics of war.

Before the generic split, however, street-crime mysteries reveal an uneasy coupling of these two modes of violence. Though the murders described in most Third Republic crime novels are born of private drama, they point outward from private interiors to the common scene, shifting focus from the individual to the national scope through the device of their urban geography. We can begin to see the political stakes of street nomenclature in the first sentence of Pont-Jest's *Le No. 13 de la Rue Marlot*:

La rue Marlot, qui a changé de nom ou qui même a peut-être disparu depuis l'époque où s'y est passé le drame que nous allons raconter, était située dans le quartier le plus calme, le plus retiré du Marais, à deux pas de la place Royale, qu'on appelle la place des Vosges, comme au temps des immortels principes. Nos révolutions,

en effet, qui semblent si bien destinées, c'est du moins ce
qu'affirment ceux qui les font, à apporter dans nos lois et dans nos
mœurs des réformes utiles, n'ont guère servi qu'à réformer les noms
de nos rues.

[The rue Marlot, which has changed its name or even perhaps
has ceased to exist since the dramatic affair that we will recount,
was located in the quietest, most remote neighborhood of the
Marais, two steps from the place Royale, which is still called the
place des Vosges, as in the time of immortal principles. Indeed,
our revolutions, which seemed so clearly destined—at least
according to those who waged them—to bring useful reforms to
our laws and our customs, have served almost no purpose but to
reform the names of our streets.][5]

The instability of the titular street's identity—it may by now have changed
names or even ceased to exist—is contrasted with a time of immortal principles, themselves ironically linked to the shifting nomenclature of the place
des Vosges. The narrator then moves on to a rare political comment on the
inefficacy of revolutions, which succeed merely in changing "les noms de nos
rues" rather than bring about useful reform. Victor Hugo had made a similar
point in *Notre-Dame de Paris* when he complained that medieval legislation
meant to ensure street safety in Paris resulted in nothing more lasting than a
name switch from *rue Coupe-Gueule* to *rue Coupe-Gorge* ("un progrès évident"
[a clear step forward], he wryly adds).[6] Though referring back to the fifteenth
century, Hugo's comment targets a nineteenth-century concern with the disjunctions between political revolutions and their toponymic traces. If, as Priscilla Parkhurst Ferguson suggests, Hugo's backward glance can be understood
as tempered nostalgia for the spatial coherence of a prerevolutionary Paris,
Pont-Jest's ironic evocation of "the time of immortal principles" reflects a more
jaded attitude, coming as it does after a century of revolt and revolution culminating in the fiascos of 1870 and 1871.[7]

    This link that Pont-Jest established between urban toponymics and na-
tional politics had already surfaced in Belot's *Le Drame de la rue de la Paix*
(1866), set during the July Monarchy. One of the tale's central characters is an
elderly marquis who clings staunchly to an outdated royalist absolutism. In a
novel by Stendhal or Balzac, such reactionary stubbornness would likely be
indicated by the use of white wig-powder or the dated cut of a jacket, but in

Belot's street-titled drama, the marquis' political conservatism is signified by his refusal to use the new names of the city. When his liberal nephew accuses him of living in the pre-Revolutionary past, the marquis protests by saying:

[Moi?] Pas de mon siècle! Pourquoi? Parce que je dis: le Jardin-du-Roi au lieu de dire le Jardin-des-Plantes, et la rue d'Artois au lieu de la rue Laffitte. Qu'importe, si je m'y promène dans la rue Laffitte et si je prends part de temps à autre aux saturnales auxquelles on s'y livre.

[Me? Not of my century? Why not? Because I say *King's Garden* instead of *Botanical Garden* and rue d'Artois instead of rue Laffitte? What does it matter, as long as I continue to stroll along the rue Laffitte and as long as I partake from time to time in the debauchery of the place?][8]

The marquis may ask, what does it matter? But of course, names do matter, as his nephew and the reader both know. In fact, street names are significant enough in the national imagination of France to have warranted status in our day as *lieux de mémoire* (sites of memory) in Pierre Nora's collection of the same name. In the chapter in Nora's work devoted to street names, Daniel Milo emphasizes precisely the kinds of name changes Belot's marquis evokes: the shift from Jardin du Roi to Jardin des Plantes and la rue Artois to la rue Laffitte reflects the expurgatory work of the Revolution, bent on erasing all markers of religion, monarchy, and noble prestige.[9] Milo's history of toponymic change traces a shift from the "spontaneous" or communal names of medieval streets to the government-decreed denominations of every regime change in the nineteenth century, whether revolutionary, counter-revolutionary, Napoleonic, Restoration, or Republican. Street names are literal "sites of memory" because they mark historical change, but they are also "lieux d'oubli" (sites of forgetting), as certain names are erased and replaced. As a result, nineteenth-century Paris is not so much a neatly layered palimpsest as it is a disquieting patchwork of conflicting ideologies, one whose "mémoire collective" toggles between official decree and individual recognition. There is a "toponymic lag" at play when Belot's marquis can party in the rue Laffitte while still calling it the rue d'Artois, a lag made possible by the dual nature of streets and their names: they are at once sites of collective memory and living locations, places where individuals walk, talk, mingle, and murder.

In *L'Invention du quotidien*, Michel de Certeau calls street names and addresses "symbolizing nodes" precisely because they combine state-decreed sense with the connotations of deep personal meaning.[10] They are both public and private, communal and individual, like the crimes that are committed on city streets and move inevitably between the personal domain of domestic trauma and the public screen of media exposure, government action, and judiciary fiction. But more than vaguely oscillating between private scene and public address, street names signal a deeper unease in fin de siècle crime writing, a desire to isolate individual acts of violence from broader networks of political upheaval. While later writers from Malet to Daeninckx explicitly link urban crime to its political underpinnings, their nineteenth-century predecessors often displayed ambivalence, even denial, toward the idea of their mutual interference.

Belot's *Le Drame de la rue de la Paix* provides a clear example of the repression and return of national violence found in popular urban crime fiction. The serial novel begins, after all, by setting up a distinction between political insurrection and domestic drama:

> L'intérêt politique absorba tellement notre attention, pendant les premiers mois de l'année 1848, que peu de personnes se souviennent aujourd'hui des catastrophes privées ou judiciaires arrivées en grand nombre durant cette époque tourmentée. En effet, ce qui, en temps de calme, suffit à alimenter notre insatiable curiosité parisienne, ne saurait convenir dans les jours de troubles et de révolution. Comment s'intéresser au drame qui se déroule entre les murs d'une maison ou derrière la porte d'une cour d'assises, lorsqu'il se passe sous nos yeux un drame bien autrement palpitant auquel nous sommes directement mêlés, car il met en question nos intérêts les plus chers? Le rappel, la fusillade, le canon couvrent les autres bruits et nous rendent sourds à tous les cris qui ne montent pas de la rue.

> [Political concerns absorbed our attention so thoroughly, in those first months of the year 1848, that few today remember the many private or judiciary catastrophes during that turbulent era. Indeed, what suffices to feed our insatiable Parisian curiosity in calmer days would not do at all in days of trouble and revolution. Why take

interest in dramas unfolding within the walls of a house or behind the doors of a courtroom when before our very eyes appears a drama, thrilling in a far different way, in which we are directly involved? The trumpet call, the bullet fire, the cannons drown out other noises and render us deaf to all cries that do not rise up from the street.] (1)

Here, "political concerns" serve as a mass distraction from the domestic drama that Belot plans to expose. But if "private or judiciary" cases are those that occur within a house or a courtroom, rather than in the restless streets, why does Belot conventionally identify the eponymous private crime of his novel by its location on the most ironically named rue de la Paix?[11]

By progressively disavowing his initial claim, Belot renders street insurrection and domestic drama inseparable, not by pointing out that all crime is political (as his twentieth-century counterparts might), but by forcing their parallel spaces to collide. Despite having said at first that political violence distracts from private crime, Belot's narrator suggests halfway through the novel that street politics and home events may be directly related to each other by the very contiguity of the spaces in which they occur:

On dirait que cette affaire de la rue de la Paix suit la même marche que les événements dont Paris est le théâtre depuis le 22 février 1848. Elle est entraînée, pour ainsi dire, dans le mouvement politique. Rue de Grammont, les incidents vont succéder aux incidents, comme aux Tuileries les ministères succèdent aux ministères. . . . Cette corrélation ne nous étonne pas. Le grand entraîne toujours le petit. L'agitation des masses se communique aux individus; la fièvre qui court dans les rues monte dans les maisons.

[It would seem that this nasty business of the rue de la Paix is following the same path as the course of events for which Paris has acted as theater since February 22, 1848. The affair is being swept along, as it were, in the political current. On the rue de Grammont, incident will follow upon incident, just as in the Tuileries ministry will follow upon ministry. This correlation is hardly surprising. The great always carries along with it the small. The unrest of the masses spreads to the individuals; the fever

that races through the streets [dans les rues] rises up into the
homes.] (338–39)

This time, rather than drown out the cries of the home, the revolutionary noise
of the street enters the private space and infects it like a fever. The story's female protagonist, a young widow named Julia, experiences the encroachment
of political onto private space when she tries to pray for her dead husband at
the église Saint-Roch and cimetière du Père-Lachaise; with Paris "in full
insurrection," the personal itinerary of Julia's pilgrimage is hampered by
the movement of national guard patrols, the songs and shouts of rebelling
students, and the chilling sounds of "une vive fusillade" [a gun battle]
(339–40).

Even more strikingly, by the story's end the interior space of the "drame
de la rue de la Paix," which Belot had announced as walled-in and private, will
be literally invaded by political insurrection. The novel's dénouement begins
with a decisive tête-à-tête inside the bourgeois salon of a house on the rue de
Grammont. At this key moment, Julia has just unknowingly agreed to marry
her husband's murderer, Savari, but their domestic love scene is interrupted:

En ce moment le salon de Julia fut subitement illuminé. Une
troupe d'hommes portant des torches traversaient la rue de
Grammont pour gagner les boulevards. Ils étaient précédés et suivis
d'une foule immense chantant la *Marseillaise*. Des tambours et des
clairons accompagnaient les voix. Tous célébraient à l'envi la
victoire que le peuple avait remportée dans la journée sur la royauté.
Les réformes demandées étaient accordées, le ministère venait
d'être changé. On quittait les barricades, les troupes rentraient
dans les casernes, la circulation se rétablissait, on fraternisait et on
illuminait de toutes parts, sans se douter qu'une heure après, on
allait s'égorger sur le boulevard des Capucines.

[At this moment, Julia's salon was suddenly lit up. A troop of men
carrying torches was crossing the rue de Grammont to reach
the boulevards. They were joined by an enormous crowd singing
the Marseillaise. Drums and bugles accompanied their voices. The
people outdid each other in celebrating the victory they had won
that day over the monarchy. . . . Folks were leaving the barricades,
troops were returning to their barracks, traffic was resuming its

course, people were fraternizing and lighting up the town, with not
a hint of suspicion that an hour later their throats would be slit on
the boulevard des Capucines.] (342)[12]

When public insurrection enters the space of private crime, it changes
everything: after two hundred pages of keeping his secret, the handsome murderer Savari is so profoundly affected by the revolutionary shouts and songs
from the street that he blurts out a confession in the salon, loses the love of
his life, runs downstairs to the corner of rue and boulevard, and gets swept
away with the patriotic crowd only to become a political martyr when gunned
down by soldiers in the street. The quickening pace of the story's dénouement
echoes the tumult of the crowd: Savari gets caught in the flow of the street
and receives his punishment through the communal violence of a political
shoot-out rather than at the hands of the justice system, focused as it is on the
individual criminal. Mortally wounded, he asks to be taken back to the rue
de Grammont (a metonymic stand-in for Julia's apartment), but finds his
beloved gone. He dies at the door of her building, on the threshold between
political and personal space.[13]

Rather than serve merely as dramatic background or echo to private crime,
revolution here refuses to stay on the street. Not only bourgeois salons, but
institutional interiors are invaded: "Lorsque la grande voix de l'émeute gronde
dans Paris, l'agitation qui règne au milieu des rues franchit les plus hautes mu-
railles et pénètre dans les prisons" [When the loud voice of riot rumbles in
Paris, the civil unrest that reigns in the streets will climb the highest walls
and penetrate into the prisons] (351). In the story's second (and final) dénouement, the violent criminal Langlade takes advantage of the revolt's chaos to
escape from his prison cell. He joins the insurgents in the streets, fighting
alongside random groups with no concern for what side he is on. What does
matter to him is revenge: he goes to his lover's house, evicts her British par-
amour, rapes her, then throws her over the balcony and kills himself too. Like
the other architectural thresholds in this tale, the balcony is no mere static
opening; it is a real space of violent exchange. With bodies flung from house
to street, or dying between street and house, Belot's novel undoes its initial
distinction between communal uprising and private drama; in the end, the
personal and political cannot be torn apart.

Street addresses are always private and public, indicating both domestic
interiority and public accessibility (a stranger can find "13, rue Marlot" on a
map). And as "anachronistic toponyms," they allow the cyclical politics of past

governments to intrude on the present space of habitation. Street-names in late nineteenth-century crime stories forge an uncanny link between the urban crimes they profess to display and the political context they try to repress: for despite disavowals, "les drames *de* la rue" end up "*dans* la rue."

Street-Name Mysteries in the Twentieth and Twenty-first Centuries

If nineteenth-century street-name mysteries are at pains to distinguish private crime from the politics of "la rue," such is not the case with their latter-day counterparts. In these, the titular street name explicitly intersects private with public space, with domestic dramas always revealed to be marked by contemporary political strife, as in Léo Malet's 1943 classic *120, rue de la Gare*—or by the resurgence of past national violence, as in Daeninckx's *12, rue Meckert* (2001) and Radoman's *6, rue Bonaparte* (2000). The thesis of the following sections is that urban toponymics—specifically, changing street names—literalize in these texts the intrusion of time into space, of political history into domestic topography, in such a way as to reveal a generic consciousness in the *noir engagé* of its own splitting off from the apolitical parlor-game whodunits of the classic era that replaced the fin-de-siècle's *feuilletonesque* sensationalism.

Whether as still-menacing presence or haunting past, World War II inhabits the urban streets of Malet's and Daeninckx's texts, thus politicizing their central topographies of detection; and in Radoman's novel, the city itself externalizes the schizophrenic split of the narrative subject through its political street-name repressions. In these texts, the detective's urban "labyrinth"—an image associated with static spatiality—is infused with the jagged time of violent history, so that the detective's work can only be visualized along a double axis of past-present and here-there. The street acts as literal intersection of space and time, while the titular address—a sign of both interior life and public access—reconnects the private crimes of the whodunit tradition to the political engagement of the modern-age *noir*.

Malet's Muddled Map of Occupation

Perhaps the most famous French street-title mystery is Léo Malet's *120, rue de la Gare*, commonly understood to have revived a slumping genre and redirected it toward the conventional alleyways, private dicks, and buxom bimbos of the *noir*.[14] In Malet's novel, the politically motivated name change of the titular street leads to hermeneutic delays in the investigation of a murky crime involving private property; by weaving that crime into the national politics of France during World War II, Malet makes explicit the connection between urban nomenclature and ideological power.

The novel's title is also its central clue, a coded key to the story's solution that appears first as an enigmatic phrase and only later as an anchored location. At the start, the investigator Nestor Burma is held prisoner in a German stalag with a fellow POW who has mysteriously lost his memory and is dying. The amnesiac's last words are "Dites à Helene . . . 120, rue de la Gare" [tell Helen . . . 120, rue de la Gare], to which Burma replies with a request for geographical precision: "Paris?" The man is able to give him only an unspecified "affirmative sign" before he dies.[15] The reader, like Burma, assumes that the dying man's gesture has located the rue de la Gare in the capital city, but in fact he has only responded to the sound of his own homophonous surname, Parry. Thus the whole novel is based on an aural slip between person and place.

Undoubtedly, the jewel thief Georges Parry, whose nickname Jo Tour Eiffel confirms his connection to the city, can be read as allegory for Paris's own amnesia during World War II. His loss of memory coincides with the story's setting during the German occupation, and the temporary forgetting of his own identity marker inevitably calls our attention to the implications of urban names and their erasure for political ends.[16]

For Claire Gorrara, place names in *120, rue de la Gare* function as fantasmatic signifiers that detach the story from its realist setting:

> Unconscious processes of deduction are . . . projected onto
> the layout of the city as street names carry further clues for
> the investigation. Bob lives in Rue de la monnaie, hinting at the
> reasons for his murder, while . . . Montbrison . . . lives in Rue
> Alfred Jarry, an allusion to the grotesque figure of Ubu Roi,
> responsible for murder and mayhem in Jarry's Absurdist play.
> It would seem that the resolution of Bob's murder lies not in the
> deduction of the classic whodunit but in the possibilities of
> wordplay and free association. (29)

Gorrara is right to invoke linguistic free play, for her examples are joined in Malet's text by other street names, like the rue de Lyon, read alternately as

Lyon the city and lion the animal. In fact, one might go even farther by turning to Jacques Derrida's well-known reflections on the *nom propre*, the proper
name indicative not only of identity, but also of propriety, ownership, cleanli-
ness, and the metaphysical illusion of self-presence.[17] There is no doubt that
Malet's story of amnesia, theft, and occupied zones replaces stable presence
with slippery word play and the *mise-en-question* of private property. After
all, Parry is a thief, and Burma's inquiry takes place in a territory in flux, the
"interzone" of occupied Paris, where nothing is "proper" or properly situated.
Much of the story revolves around delays and displacements of the "cartes
interzones" that characters send and try to receive; political flux intercepts
direct communication and stalls free circulation (75).

       Yet proper names in Malet's text are not merely unanchored sites of free
association or *Nadja*-like spurs to spatial vagabondage.[18] No surrealist wanderer, Burma actually uncovers a truth—not by surfing the slip of the signifier but by facing the political history of a French location. When he is told
by an informant in Paris that 120, rue de la Gare does not exist, he tries to
decode the address name with fanciful wordplay and associations, but in the
end he realizes that the Parry/Paris mistake has led him falsely to the capital
city. The field of possible locations is now opened up to the entire nation, since
"des rues de la Gare, ce n'est pas ce qui manque en France. Il doit y en avoir
une par agglomération" [there's no shortage of rues de la Gare in France. There
must be one in every urban area] (76). In order to narrow down the real address, Burma consults the Bureau Géographique de l'Armée, but this official
resource proves useless, for in the end it takes idiosyncratic associations (involving the Marquis de Sade and a lion's statue near the childhood home of
Burma's colleague) to direct the investigator toward the correct address in the
Paris suburb of Châtillon. What had led him astray? A politically motivated
name change. As Burma learns from his assistant Hélène, Châtillon's rue de
la Gare shows up on no current maps. She explains: "La rue Raoul-Ubac est
la nouvelle dénomination de la dernière portion de la rue de la Gare. Jusqu'à
hier, j'ignorais ce détail. Avant l'armistice, cela s'appelait encore rue de la Gare"
[The rue Raoul-Ubac is the new name for the last section of the rue de la Gare.
Until yesterday, I wasn't aware of that. Before the armistice, it was still called
the rue de la Gare] (90). So political events have marred the spatial legibility
that might have cleared up the mystery much sooner.

       This red herring is of course is narratologically useful, but is the German
occupation merely a background distraction from the private crime of property theft? Burma would have one think so, when he contrasts Parry's jewel

thievery with "la fausse piste du crime politique" [the wrong track [or red herring] of a political crime] (59). War apparently has nothing to do with a robber's venal motivations. Yet how can one fail to connect Parry's appropriation of the name of a public monument as his own sobriquet, Jo Tour Eiffel, with the invading army's appropriation of France's national sites? In the end, Malet fuses the private and the political through geographic coincidence in the scene that causes Parry's amnesia. After being tortured in his own home by money-hungry accomplices, Parry wanders into an adjacent field, where German soldiers capture him as a political prisoner and replace his civilian clothes with an army uniform. But even before then, the location of his house in the occupied terrain of La Ferté Combettes has precluded his seclusion from wartime interests. Indeed, Burma recounts this household scene as an ironic conjunction of personal suffering with national trauma: the "tac-tac-tac des mitrailleuses" [rat-a-tat of machine guns] muffles the cries of Parry's "troisième degré renouvelé du XVIIIe siècle" [third degree revived from the eighteenth century] (83). Anachronistic torture (the past surging into the present) aligns with spatial contiguity (the soldier's field next to the house) to displace Parry's very body from the realm of private crime to political prison. The linguistic play on Paris and Parry has tipped the reader off to the disquieting mobility of the proper name, for if a human subject and an urban location may have the same aural signifier, how can private identities and actions be kept separate from the web of public interests? The contrived nature of Parry's in extremis suffering—private torture followed by political capture—signals Malet's manipulation of the genre's conventional distinction between civic and political violence.

As with the palimpsest of street names, a double axis—temporal and spatial—is broken here: Parry's personal trajectory is derailed by the geographic contiguity between home and field, while his loss of memory cuts the connection between present and past, initiating a novel-length inquiry in which political crime seems nothing but a red herring. Malet's novel is a *noir* not only because of its World War II atmospherics but also because it insistently reminds us of the *forgetting* that classic detective fiction causes when it reduces crime to an apolitical puzzle. When S. S. Van Dine, who defined the detective story as an "intellectual game," codified the genre into twenty rules, he insisted that "The motives for all crimes . . . should be personal. International plottings and war politics belong in a different category of fiction."[19] With an ironic wink, Malet follows this rule—in the end, the motive *is* personal—but only by exposing its amnesiac relation to politics and time. The novel's titular street name is not just the site for horizontal homophonous play; it is more essentially marked by history, by the disruptive substitution of one proper name by another.

Michel de Certeau calls the "proper" a victory of space over time, but in this novel of property theft, impropriety, and slippage of the *nom propre*, time (history, politics, war, national violence) will always intrude on a mapped and ordered space in which addresses stably denote private domiciles. As a *noir* alternative to contemporary whodunits, Malet's novel plays with the tropes of clever deduction while concluding that historical consciousness must return to puncture the associative surface of a cryptogrammatic crime novel.

In this way Malet's street name mystery acts as a hinge between its nineteenth-century predecessors (which disavow connections between domestic crime and street violence) and today's more directly *engagé* novels of Daeninckx's ilk (which make national history the key to contemporary crime-solving). The street-name motif reveals an increasing historical dimension to the central tension between private crime and political violence. When René de Pont-Jest complains that revolutions have changed nothing beyond street names, he implies that these changes are nonessential, bringing about no real reform. And when Belot allows the cries of a street insurrection to infiltrate the space of a domestic drama, he leaves his victim on the threshold of an unchanged address. But in Malet's novel, the change of a street name because of political upheaval does have consequences, both private and public: it keeps a daughter from claiming her (ill-gotten) inheritance while concurrently creating confusion in the official maps of the nation. Malet hints at—through the anachronistic torture scene and the theme of recovering an amnesiac's past—a temporal axis of disorientation, but his mystery rests primarily on the contiguity of Parry's crimes with the contemporary Occupation. In Daeninckx's work, on the other hand, history has a long arm: crimes in the streets can only be explained through investigation of the guilty secrets of a long-buried national past.

Napoleon's Reach: Daeninckx

In Didier Daeninckx's *12, rue Meckert* (2001), the journalist Maxime Lisbonne investigates a former colleague's murder at his own apartment, located at the eponymous address. The street name is also a proper name (Meckert was a historical figure from the eighteenth century). Yet in this novel, as in Malet's, there is an "improper" slippage of signifiers, this time not from person to place but also back in time, when Maxime Lisbonne becomes intrigued by his Communard namesake, a political hero and the inventor a century earlier of the striptease show on the rue des Martyrs. The story's central mystery may revolve around "les disparues" [the missing girls] of Châteauroux, but Lisbonne's investigation more insistently stumbles against the joint histories of places and names.

Daeninckx draws attention to urban nomenclature through Lisbonne's girlfriend Eléonore, a real estate agent whose deep knowledge of Paris streets helps her sell apartments to intellectuals and history buffs.

Elle prenait le temps de se renseigner sur le quartier, sur la rue, sur l'immeuble, afin d'ancrer le trois-pièces qu'elle était chargée de vendre dans l'histoire de la ville. Elle savait ainsi que sous la Révolution, la rue Montmartre avait été rebaptisée Mont-Marat, que les Francs-Bourgeois s'étaient, un temps, métamorphosés en Francs-Citoyens et que le Cirque d'Hiver s'appelait Cirque Napoléon lors de son inauguration par le troisième du nom."

[She took the time to learn about each neighborhood, each street, each building, to anchor the three-room apartment she was selling in the history of the city. So she knew that during the Revolution, the rue Montmartre had been rebaptized Mont-Marat, that the Francs-Bourgeois had once been transformed into Francs-Citoyens, and that the Cirque d'Hiver was christened Cirque Napoléon at the time of his inauguration by the third holder of that name].[20]

These political renamings are the key to Eléonore's salesmanship, but they also signal Lisbonne's interest in the archival layers that cut into urban space. To know that la rue Montmartre contains the near-anagrammatic memory of a revolutionary Mont-Marat is to know, as Daeninckx's detective does, that crimes in the streets of Paris are never fully severed from their historical precedents. And to revive the ghost of Napoleon by recalling the Cirque d'Hiver's former name is to refuse a spatialized erasure of the past.

This acknowledgment of the past-in-present of urban space warrants pride of place for Daeninckx's pride in Kristin Ross's well-known essay "Watching the Detectives."[21] For Ross, Daeninckx's fiction captures a postmodern spatial dialectic described by Henri Lefebvre as an explosion of uneven development in which history is translated into spatial contradiction (55–56). That new pre-fab structures in the *banlieux cités* are already crumbling, for example, repre-sents a short circuit of historical development. Ross focuses on the suburban landscape as the site of history's collapse into the present, but Daeninckx's depictions of city centers also support her general point that a postmodern interest in space reinscribes, rather than merely excludes, time and history.[22] In *12, rue Meckert*, Eléonore's present-day use of street name history for eco-nomic gain compresses time into space, bringing toponymics from the past to bear on the current city map, while Lisbonne's investigation reveals his-torical crimes as direct motivators of modern-day violence.

When a street name is changed, it is no longer visible on a plaque or sign; it is removed to the archival recesses of libraries and government offices or kept alive in oral tradition. For her part, Eléonore turns to a nineteenth-century edition of the *Dictionnaire des rues de Paris écrit par Guillot* to sell a place to an academic whose daydreams are embroidered with the evocative names of its medieval occupants: "Ysabeau l'Espinète, Agnès aux Blanches Mains, Edeline l'Enragée" (35). A nineteenth-century book revives the ghosts of the Middle Ages in the streets of twentieth-century Paris—and a woman, Eléonore, holds the key to this image of spatialized time. In this way she, like Hélène in Malet's *120, rue de la Gare*, acts less as sidekick to the protagonist detective than as Ariadne to his Theseus, leading him through the city's labyrinthine streets to the criminal monster at the story's center. But to the mythical space of the labyrinth, Lisbonne's girlfriend adds the dimension of time, for her "thread" is history itself. As archival layers of the past are revealed in the spatial layout of the urban present, crime fiction itself is exposed as caught in a double tempo-rality: on the one hand, the mythical eternity of a recurrent epistemological quest; on the other, the time-laden investigation as archival discovery. Along with other modern and postmodern *noir* writers, Daeninckx doubly refuses historical amnesia, both intradiegetically—through stories of past violence af-fecting present crime—and at a "meta" level, by reflecting on political violence as the return of what the classic detective genre had striven to repress.

More Napoleons: Radoman

The spatiotemporal implications of such an anti-amnesiac project come through dramatically in Vladan Radoman's *6, rue Bonaparte*, an unnerving novel in which urban toponymics reveal the psychopathology of space, time, and the human subject. In Chapter 8 of this book, I will explore Radoman's "schizo-cartographies" in more detail, but for now let me introduce the ways in which his novel's titular street address imprints a violent national history onto the fragmented space of the postmodern city.

Part of a series called "La ballade d'un Yougo," *6, rue Bonaparte* gives away its politicized content in the nationalistic street name of the title—but only through the ironic lens of its anything-but-French-patriot protagonist. Radoman's dystopic novel is narrated in the first, second, and third person by a paranoid schizophrenic named Vic Toar—*victoire*, "victory." His identities include Serbian hitman, alcoholic doctor, published poet, and avocational rapist-killer.

Vic's displacement from the Balkans to the streets of Nice has created a split relation to space and time. When he leaves a psychiatric prison to walk in the city, the Belgrade of his past penetrates Nice's urban grid—or devours it, as Vic puts it. At one point, after being set down randomly at a street corner at night, he watches a hooker (delicately named Sucette) take her client to the rue de la Buffa, a name whose alimentary overtones suggests hunger to one of Vic's two personalities: "L'autre abruti qui partage ma carcasse, qui m'emmerde, . . . réclame sa pitance. . . . Il avait faim. Moi, pas vraiment" [The other asshole who shares my carcass, who gets on my fucking nerves, . . . claims his pittance. He was hungry. Me, not really].[23] Yet Vic follows another street whose name evokes food, the rue Maccarani, as though his walking were determined by what de Certeau calls the "semantic tropisms" of a poetic geography, a superimposed map that orients the subject's itinerary according to the subconscious drift of metaphorical association.[24] While one of Vic's selves is guided by bodily hunger, the other, the narrating self, reflects on the names of the streets as he walks them:

> je pris la rue du Commandant-Raffal. J'ignorais tout de ce 'héros niçois, 1913–1952,' et j'aurais préféré que cette ruelle porte encore son ancien nom, celui de la Paix.

> [I took the rue du Commandant-Raffal. I knew nothing of this "Niçois hero, 1913–1952" and I would've preferred that the alleyway had kept its former name, of Peace (*de la Paix*).] (25)

Why this nostalgia for an Edenic peace that never existed? (Even in the crime novel tradition, as we have seen, the rue de la Paix was a site for violence and crime.) That Vic prefers the street's former name to the present one suggests a desire to substitute peace for military violence and thus acts as a mise en abyme of the novel's narrative repression.

This tension between military violence and a pacific whitewashing of the past is central to Radoman's novel. For the whole story—two hundred pages of a partly typical *noir*, with Vic as a maverick detective tracking down city killers—is in fact a cover story for an *un*narrated return to the Balkans, where Vic takes on the identity of a Serbian soldier on a sadistic killing spree. For most of the book, Vic is in denial about this militaristic reality; he has rejected the boundless violence of his fragmented nation-state and chosen to live in a peacetime France in which crimes can be imagined as merely personal, even random, apolitical events. But they are neither random—he himself has systematically murdered the victims whose deaths he is meant to investigate—nor apolitical: the vengeance and passion of Vic the individual are overshadowed by his sense of himself as a Serbian nationalistic avenger. So his nostalgia for the street's former "peaceful" name is hardly disingenuous; it is part and parcel of his psychotic break with the military reality of his own history.

In *6, rue Bonaparte* the disjunctions of urban toponymics are mapped onto psychic pathology, with the typical sequence of repression of recall reversed: it is not the narrator's past but his present (featuring the Serbian killings) that he represses and replaces with an episode that floats outside time and grounded place. In Vic's deluded mind and in the reader's reception of his skewed reality, the narrative replacement for the Serbian episode consists of a vague, nightmarish, destination-less voyage in the Mediterranean Sea, outside national waters and purely mythical in nature (Vic calls himself Ulysses in Ithaka). Nothing happens in this place. And time loses all meaning: "Y avait-il encore un intérêt à mesurer le temps en ce lieu? Perdu, flottant sur une mer morte, . . . qui, sauf un fou, se soucierait encore d'un passé, d'un présent, d'un avenir?" [Was there any point in measuring time in this place? Lost, floating on a dead sea, . . . who but a madman would still care about a past, a present, a future?] (184). Time has gone mad, space is out of joint.

At sea, Vic has lost all sense of chronology (257), but already earlier, in the Nice psychiatric ward, time had been stretched beyond measure: "Pendant au moins un siècle, les jours sans matins avaient coulé dans ma tête, en poursuivant un million de nuits aveugles, dépourvues de rêves" [During at least a century, the days without mornings had flowed through my mind, chasing a million blind and dreamless nights] (33). The flattened temporality of

Vic's drugged and psychotic mind might be read in contrast with his doctors' historicist rationality, for on their office walls hangs a spatially ordered marker of the past: the framed reproduction of a seventeenth-century world map (30). But this anachronistic incursion into the space of forward-thinking science itself reveals the doctors' primitive brutality, just as a "décor d'un mystère moyenâgeux" [stage set of a medieval mystery play]— dirt, shadows, black torches—will reveal that post-apocalyptic Nice is itself defined by the violence of time immemorial: "Était-ce la même guerre qui durait depuis des millénaires, depuis la nuit des temps?" [Was this the same war that had been waged for millennia, since the end of time?] (266). As past collapses into present, the sickening chaos of the wartorn Balkans is displaced onto the supposedly stable French city of Nice. Is this vision just another of Vic's psychotic delusions? One cannot know, but when his repressive wall tumbles and he finally admits he had been wreaking bloody havoc in Kosovo rather than floating peacefully in a mythic sea, it becomes clear that Vic's story spatializes the mind of a madman. "Ma folie propre était un simple reflet figé, glacé, de l'immense folie du monde" [My own madness was a mere fixed and frozen reflection of the immense madness of the world], he declares (241). Well before the book's final crescendo, this global analogy has found its local precursor in the schizophrenia of city streets: the coexistence, with temporal disjunction, of the rue de la Paix and the rue du Commandant-Raffal replicates Vic's double identity. And so does the book's central address: *6, rue Bonaparte.*

Indeed, the psychotic historical crossings of (and at) this address reveal Radoman's city as itself a split subject. During the first half of the book, 6, rue Bonaparte is inhabited by an African witch doctor who reads his violent prophecies not in tea leaves but in dog shit. In the second half, after Vic's elided trip to the Balkans, 6, rue Bonaparte has a new tenant, a whole different kind of doctor: the white establishment Dr. Niaize, who secretly inoculated hospital workers with an immortality drug that allowed them to survive a cataclysmic fog that wiped out Europe's urban infrastructure. In postapocalyptic Nice, 6, rue Bonaparte is a mad dictatorship's headquarters, from which Dr. Niaize imposes martial law on the semiorganized hordes of immortals who range through the destroyed city carrying machine guns and wearing high fashion from looted shops. As Dr. Niaize shows Vic around the headquarters, he indicates the spatial entropy of his mad plan for power, from the city of Nice to the whole world: "Un plan de Nice aggrandi, une photo satellite de la région, une carte de France et une mappemonde couvraient un mur entier" [An enlarged map of Nice, a satellite photo of the region, a map of France, and a world map covered the entire wall] (228). "Impressive, isn't it?" Niaize boasts: "—Impressionnant, non? Si Bonaparte avait pu imaginer que son modeste logis niçois deviendrait un jour le centre du monde!" [If only Bonaparte had been able to imagine that his modest abode in Nice would someday become the center of the world!] (228). (And in case the reader has missed the Freudian overtones of the doctor's Napoleon complex, he adds, "if only Mommy could see me now.") Later Dr. Niaize gives a speech wearing a bicorne and holding his right hand slipped in the gap of his coat, raising in bodily form the historical ghost of his own Bonapartist address.

As the book's title and setting, the street name itself is the key to the schisms that ravage Radoman's story. If the places where private citizens live have to be marked by the official histories of violent military upheaval (rue Commandant Raffal, rue Bonaparte), it is no surprise that boundaries between private and public collapse, taking with them any coherent temporal linearity. Time here is more fraught than for Daeninckx's Lisbonne, who unearths archival layers of history because they have created a violent present. In Radoman's text, a single address can hold a black prophet of the future and a white revivalist of the past while simultaneously morphing in a schizophrenic's mind with the streets of Belgrade, where violence has lost all time: "[Nous vivions] dans un pays suspendu dans un espace hors du temps. En dehors de l'histoire" [We lived in a country suspended in space outside time. Outside history] (233).

Outside history: nothing more aptly describes the deluded Vic, whose work in Nice cuts him off from the political realities of the land he loves. But nothing less aptly describes the novel, in which repressed Balkan violence bursts through Vic's consciousness in the form of a murderous alter ego residing in streets marked by dictators' ghosts.

In his *Lieux de mémoire* essay Milo suggests that we have entered an era of "post-history" and "anti-memory," since nowadays new street names belong to the neutral categories of nature (flowers, trees) or nonpolitical culture (musicians, impressionist painters) rather than to those of ideological regimes or "héros très contestés" like Napoleon[25] (1914, 1913). But if France's city planners have gotten beyond history, the same cannot be said of its crime writers, who expose the genre's localizing conventions as necessarily historical: unlike classic whodunits, with their armchair detectives, street-name mysteries put their investigators in the place of revolution, in the site of history's insertion into the present, in the *lieu de mémoire* that is the city street.

*   *   *

In this chapter, I have proposed that all street name mysteries figure a bi-axial intersection of past/present and public/private spheres of violence. There is a difference, though, between the early and later novels on which I have chosen to focus. In the late nineteenth century, the "toponymic lag" of street names signals a failed exclusion of the revolutionary political context from the domestic sphere of crime *feuilletons*. Later, Léo Malet's *120, rue de la Gare* re-anchors private crime in the political context of World War II through the cartographic slippages of Occupied urban space. And finally, the postmodern *noirs engagés* of Daeninckx and Radoman explicitly embark on an anamnesiac project by inscribing French national history in the (psychotically) private and (economically) privatized sites of modern-day crime. Through this analysis, I have tried to add an element of historical change to Uri Eisenzweig's classic description of the detective novel as fundamentally occulting "the socio-historical dimension" of real space.[26] Citing Agatha Christie's location of inquiry in cozy estate rooms as opposed to war fronts, Eisenzweig astutely identifies the detective genre's (unsuccessful) attempts to dissociate personal crime fiction from political context and material contingency, "particularly during the 1920's and 1930's" (191). He is right to highlight that age of generic codification, for it was then that practitioners like S. S. van Dine cut off the abstract problem-solving function of detective fiction from its more sensationalistic forms.[27] But it is worth looking farther into how crime fiction beyond its most purified deductive forms has registered the genre's developing unease with national history. In Part III, I will explore maps, grids, and the classic locked room locations that act as "the spatial materialization of the detective plot's de-centering in relation to contemporary social reality" (Eisenzweig, 207). But here, I have emphasized the city street as locus of inquiry into the crime genre's grappling with the history of France's politicized urban nomenclature; as royal and Napoleonic specters have jostled with laic and civic labels on city maps, the public/private split of criminal investigation has moved from the unease of contiguity to the archival probe of anachronistic space.

PART III

CARTOGRAPHIES

CHAPTER 6

Terrains Vagues: Gaboriau and the Birth of the Cartographic Mystery

When Emile Gaboriau extended a Poe-like crime story to novel length in his 1863 *L'Affaire Lerouge*, he became the "father of French detective fiction." Among the direct imitators of *L'Affaire Lerouge*, which frames a long historical flashback within a present-day mystery's investigation, were Arthur Conan Doyle in England, Anna Katherine Green in America, and Fortuné de Boisgobey in France. But beyond his direct descendants, Gaboriau was to influence the *roman policier* tradition by positing a particularly French disjunction between revolutionary politics (associated with provincial space and temporal regress) and domestic crime (associated with Paris streets and contemporary culture). Indeed, his spatial imagination continued to haunt twentieth-century French crime fiction and its "mappings," both textual and literal.

This chapter focuses on Gaboriau as the founder of a particular feature of many crime novels: the inclusion of a printed map. The tradition spans the twentieth century: from Gaston Leroux's maps of crime scenes in *Le Mystère de la chambre jaune* (1907), through Malet's *arrondissement* by *arrondissement* mysteries of the 1950s, to the Ouvroir de Littérature Potentielle Policière (OuLiPoPo) fascination with fictionalized crime maps in the 1970s and 1980s. But Gaboriau came first: the fifth chapter of his 1869 novel *Monsieur Lecoq* includes a visual diagram of the story's cabaret crime scene, complete with iconic footprints, a coded layout of the building, and the *terrains vagues* that separate the seedy bar from the cross streets of "civilization."

In 1974, Henri Lefebvre wrote that if society were deprived of the possibility of true revolution, "Le terrain vague serait l'ultime recours de la vitalité irréductible" [the vacant lot would be the last recourse for irreducible vitality.][1] In other words, there would only be spasmodic upheavals in a dominant capitalist State. Lefebvre's comment, part of his larger argument on the social production of space, uses the *terrain vague* as a site that represents the end of History—but also one that registers a recurring violence on the national body. If that violence has no "bite" (i.e., if it cannot lead to real political change), it may be because the *terrain vague* has acquired an association with vagueness and periphery, with the impotent volatility of local violent acts. By analyzing Gaboriau's fictional map of 1863, I want to consider the modern origins of these associations. How does the *"terrain vague"* spatialize the marginalization of the criminal class in the context of Second Empire urbanization? How does the *local clos* motif intersect with allegorizations of cultural porosity? And how does Gaboriau's coded image inaugurate a foundational conception of space for the *roman policier*?

The *Terrains Vagues* of *Monsieur Lecoq*

Before Émile Gaboriau became known as the father of French detective fiction, he was a successful "chroniqueur," a journalist who contributed verses, anecdotes, and *comptes rendus* to a number of Parisian papers. Throughout the year 1857, the young Gaboriau wrote a weekly column for *La Vérité Contemporaine*, a satirical newspaper previously called *Les Contemporains*, a title meant to evoke its up-to-date topicality.[2] Gaboriau's contributions were indeed timely, as he submitted news and stories of Parisian life that went no further back than the previous week—thus his column title, "Echos de la semaine" (akin, perhaps, to "Talk of the Town" or "Shouts and Murmurs" in the *New Yorker* today). Gaboriau's subsequent newspaper chronicles, in *Le Tintamarre* and *Le Progrès* carry titles just as evocative of ephemeral today-ness: "Cancans, Echos, Bibelots, Bigarrures, Choses et autres, Babas et risettes, Nouvelles à la main, Mauvais propos [etc.]" [Gossip, Chatter, Curios, Miscellany, Things and others, Marvels and chuckles, Gazettes, Scandals, etc.] (Bonniot, 43). These weekly musings, as well as the articles Gaboriau wrote in 1859 and 1860 for *Le Journal à 5 centimes*, display the future novelist's interest not only in human types—from the picturesque *zoave* to the ambitious *demi-mondain*—but in their physical surroundings, with Paris taking pride of place.

In 1859, for example, Gaboriau reacted to the administrative establishment of the city's 20 *arrondissements* by contributing a short essay on each.[3] Not surprisingly, in this high era of Haussmannization, he devoted many of his comments to the topographic changes currently underway in the capital city: "Ainsi," he writes, "les limites de Paris vont être portées au pied de l'enceinte fortifiée" [In this way, the borders of Paris will extend to the base of the fortified wall], adding that major building projects will isolate the Jardin du Luxembourg and that construction around the canal Saint-Martin will include the cultivation of a large "terre-plein" planted with four parallel rows of trees (Bonniot, 53). This *terre-plein*, I would suggest, might be contrasted with the far less civilized *terrains vagues* that escape urban renewal, for though Gaboriau keeps a neutral tone in his press column, his critical voice emerges in the following decade through the judiciary crime novels for which he became famous.

Indeed, the uneven topography of Paris sets the stage for his detective novel *Monsieur Lecoq* (1868), which begins as a loud cry attracts the attention of a police patrol making its rounds by the "ancienne barrière d'Italie." The story begins, but not before the narrator has indulged in some sociological commentary on the dangers of this "vaste quartier qui s'étend de la route de Fontainebleau à la Seine, depuis les boulevards extérieurs jusqu'aux fortifications" [vast area that extends from the Fontainebleau road to the Seine, from the outer boulevards to the fortifications]—that is, in what is now the Eastern part of the *13e arrondissement* and what then Gaboriau described as a deserted region with a bad reputation. The narrator explains why the *quartier* is dangerous: "C'est que *les terrains vagues*, encore nombreux, devenaient, passé minuit, le domaine de cette tourbe de misérables sans aveu et sans asile" [The reason is that the *terrains vagues*, of which there were still many, were overrun after midnight by the muck of godless and homeless wretches] who refuse the formalities of modest lodgings, along with the vagabonds and ex-cons who remain despite energetic measures by city police.[4]

The term *terrain vague* refers to any uncultivated space ("vide de cultures et de constructions" [devoid of cultivation and construction], according to the *Petit Robert*), but in the nineteenth century, it appeared with notable frequency in crime gazettes and novels of the underworld. Ponson du Terrail's *Rocambole*, for example, identifies the *terrains vagues* of Paris (one between the rue Courcelles and the rue de Laborde; another circumscribed by the rue du Château-d'eau and that of the Faubourg-du-temple) as handy places for the shady dealings of criminals and street buskers (*saltimbanques*).[5] Although Gaboriau personally hated Ponson du Terrail, his novels would echo his rival's interest in socially marginal characters (the *saltimbanque* serves as disguise for

Monsieur Lecoq's central suspect)—and in the *terrain vague* as their liminal habitus, a space where unlit fog provides cover for less civilized acts. Neither urban nor rural, the *terrain vague* metaphorically transforms even the great city Paris into a sinister wasteland: "On se serait cru à mille lieues de Paris, sans ce bruit profond et continu qui monte de la grande ville comme le mugissement d'un torrent au fond d'un gouffre" [One could imagine oneself a thousand miles from Paris, if it weren't for the deep, constant noise coming up from the city like the roar of a torrent from the depths of an abyss] (*Monsieur Lecoq*, 13).

Criminality is thus abetted by semi-urban location, as Gaboriau ascribes the region's danger to a mix of idiotic obstinance on the part of the "rôdeurs de barrières" [barrier tramps] and the spatial characteristics of the *terrains vagues*: "Les lumières se faisaient rares et il y avait de grands emplacements vides entre les maisons" [Lights grew fewer and there were large empty sites between the buildings] (22, 13). These are the empty spaces that facilitate the appearance of seedy *bouges* and *cabarets* like La Poivrière, the scene of a triple murder that serves as the novel's instigating mystery.

By setting his crime in the borderlands of the *barrières* rather than in center-city streets, Gaboriau shows himself to be up-to-date, for as noted earlier, two strands of crime fiction immediately followed Haussmann's dispersal of real crime from city center to periphery. One strand, exemplified by popular serial novelists like Pierre Zaccone, anachronistically continued to set their crime stories in the symbolic center of La Cité; the other, led by Gaboriau, captured what Dominique Kalifa identifies as a narrative transfer of urban danger from city center outward.[6] Whereas Eugène Sue had famously begun his 1842–43 *Mystères de Paris* in the labyrinth of dark, narrow, tortuous roads extending from the Palais de Justice to the cathedral of Notre-Dame in la Cité, Gaboriau responds to the Haussmannian decentering of contemporary crime by displacing danger to the borderlands of the *barrières*. He refuses, in other words, the nostalgia of novelistic romanticization in favor of journalistic observation of the present moment—a moment during which, historically, "Fortifications, terrains vagues et espaces incertains des marges de la ville favorisent . . . l'exercice de la violence" [fortifications, *terrains vagues*, and indeterminate spaces at the edges of the city facilitate acts of violence] (Kalifa, 36).

The peripheral displacement of urban crime was not completely new, of course; Kalifa cites the transfer in 1832 of the guillotine from the Place de Grève to the Saint-Jacques Barrier as a highly symbolic start to the center city clean-up process, adding that Sue's novel itself marks the gradual transition outward: "S'ils s'ouvrent rue aux Fèves, c'est à la barrière Saint-Jacques que s'achèvent *Les Mystères de Paris*, signalant ainsi la vigueur de ce transfert" [Though the novel opens at the rue aux Fèves, it is at the barrière Saint-Jacques that it ends, thus signalling the vigor of this relocation] (23). Nevertheless, by the 1860s and 1870s, the effects of Haussmannization had definitively shifted poverty and crime to newly sinister locales:

> A la Belle Epoque encore, la dénonciation de l'insuffisance policière en banlieue nourrit le discours sécuritaire. . . . En diminution dans les vieux quartiers du centre, les violences nocturnes se multiplient en revanche après 1860 dans les arrondissements périphériques (notamment les XVe et XIXe arrondissements, nouveaux coupe-gorge), ainsi que dans la partie orientale de la ville qui totalise alors plus de 62% des agressions.

> [As late as the Belle Epoque period, discourse on safety continued to feed on complaints about insufficient policing of the suburbs. . . . While nocturnal violence was declining in the older areas of the central Cité, it dramatically increased after 1860 in the peripheral *arrondissements* (especially the new rough areas of the fifteenth and nineteenth *arrondissements*), as well as in the eastern parts of the city in which more than 62% of attacks occurred.] (36)

Gaboriau's fictions follow the criminal topography of his time, as he sets violent acts in liminal spaces such as the edges of the *18e arrondissement* and the suburb of Batignolles—or La Jonchère, whose borderline nature in *L'Affaire Lerouge* is read by David Bell as symbolic of murder's location both inside and outside the boundaries of civilization.[7] Bell identifies the location as belonging to a specifically modern civilization whose barriers have been pierced by nascent train technology, with the increased number of routes in and out of the city leading to the disquieting mobility of criminal bodies. As with *L'Affaire Lerouge*, Gaboriau's *Monsieur Lecoq* indexes a modern shift—in this case the move outward of crime to the *terrains vagues* of the Barrières in an age of urban renewal.

The importance of the *terrain vague* is indicated in *Monsieur Lecoq* not only by the novel's introductory descriptions of the criminal and liminal space, but by the prominence of the very phrase in the map that is reproduced in chapter 5 of the book edition.[8] This diagram, the first of many printed crime scene maps to accompany a *roman policier*, is presented in the text as hand-drawn by the young detective Lecoq after he has been given the case of the La Poivrière murders (see Figure 5).[9] Oddly, though, the map appears to the reader before the description of its creation, for it is only in chapter 8 that we find Lecoq at work: "Le jeune policier s'assit devant une table et commença par esquisser le *plan du théâtre du meurtre,* plan dont la légende explicative devait aider singulièrement à l'intelligence de son récit" [The young policeman sat at a table and started to sketch out a *map of the scene of the crime,* a map with an explanatory legend designed to bring singular clarity to his account] (47). The "récit" at stake is Lecoq's police report, destined to raise his professional profile, but it also of course refers implicitly to Gaboriau's own "récit," since the "plan" and its "légende explicative" serve to orient *Monsieur Lecoq*'s readers as well. We "read" the map as a substantiating document of the fictional space.

I would warrant that what most readers first notice on the map is the very phrase "terrains vagues" as it appears in large letters in the central open space of the drawn diagram. The two words appear skewed, at an obtuse angle to one another, as though to underline the site's deviation from what is "right." And indeed the very choice of "terrains vagues"—as opposed to "Barrière," which would have emphasized civic jurisdiction—echoes the written text's introduction of this as the place for vagabonds and ne'er-do-wells, a propitious setting for the type of crime that attracts the patrol's attention: a low-class bar brawl that ended badly.

But readers of *Monsieur Lecoq* know that despite appearances, both murderer and witnesses turn out to come from the highest ranks of society—and it takes hundreds of pages for the detective Lecoq to accept what seemed sociologically *and spatially* impossible: that death at this *bouge des barrières* came at the hands of a wealthy nobleman, the duc de Sairmeuse. An early clue to that fact comes in the crime scene map itself, which inscribes the *terrain vague* as a space of potential contact between high and low society: the murder scene is framed by two roads, the relatively straight Rue du Chateau des Rentiers and the somewhat more disorderly and curvaceous Chemin sans Nom. The social allegory in these names is obvious, an intersection of property and poverty that creates a criminality specific to this time of uneven urban development.

The police agents themselves, indicated by the letter A on the map and identified in the key, are situated closer to the nameless path than to the "high road"—an appropriate location given their own socio-economic status and

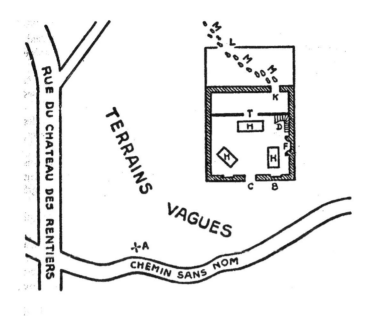

A.   ` – Point d'où la ronde commandée par l'inspecteur du service de la Sûreté, Gévrol,
          entendit les cris des victimes.
          (La distance de ce point au cabaret dit la *Poivrière* n'est que de 123 mètres, ce
          qui donne à supposer que ces cris étaient les premiers; que, par conséquent, le
          combat commençait seulement.)

B.   – Fenêtre fermée par des volets pleins, dont les ouvertures permirent à l'un des
          agents d'apercevoir la scène de l'intérieur.

C.   – Porte enfoncée par l'inspecteur de la Sûreté, Gévrol.

D.   – Escalier sur lequel était assise, pleurant, la veuve Chupin, arrêtée provisoirement.
          (C'est sur la troisième marche de cet escalier, que le tablier de la veuve Chupin
          fut plus tard retrouvé, les poches retournées.)

F.   – Cheminée.

H.H.H. – Tables.
          (Les empreintes d'un saladier et de cinq verres ont été constatées sur celle qui
          se trouve entre les points F. et B.)

T.   – Porte communiquant avec l'arrière-salle du cabaret, devant laquelle le meurtrier
          armé se tenait debout.

K.   – Seconde porte du cabaret, ouvrant sur le jardin, et par où pénétra celui des agents
          qui eut l'idée de couper la retraite du meurtrier.

L.   – Portillon du jardinet, donnant sur les terrains vagues.

M.M.M. – Empreintes de pas sur la neige, relevées par les agents restés à la *Poivrière*, après
          le départ de l'inspecteur Gévrol.

Figure 5. Émile Gaboriau, *Monsieur Lecoq*. Lecoq's map of the scene of the
crime. Liana Levi.

their mandate to venture into lawless lands. Or rather, *semi*-lawless lands, since the *terrain vague* sits at the exact intersection of a nameless path and a recently-annexed official road: the Rue du Chateau des Rentiers had been part of the suburban *commune d'Ivry* in 1855 but was re-classified in 1863 as belonging to the *voirie parisienne*. Once again, Gaboriau demonstrates an up-to-date awareness of the capital city's changing topography, a trait that combined with the titillating exposure of behind-the-scenes judiciary process to all but guarantee commercial success for this follow-up to *L'Affaire Lerouge* and *Le Crime d'Orcival*.

Blank Space

So far, I have identified the *terrains vagues* in *Monsieur Lecoq* as a journalistic detail that supports the contemporary characterization of Gaboriau's work as "le tableau du Paris actuel, pris sur le vif."[10] But that is just one side of the interpretive coin, one that emphasizes *Monsieur Lecoq*'s feuilletonesque lineage over its status as early *roman policier*. Though the novel retains the vestigial "péripéties compliquées" [complicated twists and turns] that allow purists like Fereydoun Hoveyda and Boileau-Narcejac to distinguish it from the pared-down classics of a Doyle or Christie, it also establishes an investigative order that will become the spine of the genre's narrative formula.[11] And I would argue that the novel's *terrains vagues* do double duty, having as much to do with narrative form as with sociological reality. For when Lecoq arrives on the scene of the crime, he does not muse—as had the narrator—on the *terrains vagues* as junkyard of the homeless and recidivists; rather, he wipes away any distractions from the crime at hand and takes the terrain as a text to be read by the detective deciphering clues—in this case, a line of footprints in the snow leading out from *La Poivrière*:

> Ce terrain vague, couvert de neige, est comme <u>une immense page blanche où les gens</u> que nous recherchons <u>ont écrit</u>, non seulement leurs mouvements et leurs démarches, mais encore leurs secrètes pensées, les espérances et les angoisses qui les agitaient.

> [This snow-covered *terrain vague* is like a vast blank page on which the people we seek have written not only their movements and their actions, but also their secret thoughts, the hopes and fears that motivated them.] (32, my emphases)

Through the intervention of the fictional detective Lecoq, the *terrains vagues* are taken out of their sociohistorical context and rendered abstract. They become a purely epistemological "field," a space of inscription and interpretation. Lecoq's analogy between vague terrain and blank page holds an undeniable appeal for the kind of textual criticism that dominated the study of the detective genre in the 1970s and 1980s, inspired by Todorov's formal analyses of the genre's temporal sequences and by Lacan's and Derrida's readings of Poe's "The Purloined Letter," which emphasized the displacements of a pure signifier in a symbolic system unanchored by external reference. The self-referentiality of Monsieur Lecoq's *terrain vague* as vast blank page certainly invites a post-structuralist reading. We can see the detective, scanning the snowy field for tracks, as a stand-in for the reader, as we scan the book's pages for hermeneutical indices, the black marks or traces of a scriptorial absent presence.

But the "absent presence" that Lecoq ends up identifying through his study of footprints is that of the crime's witnesses—and what is revealed is not so much their structural relation to the crime (he already knows they are witnesses) but their gender and class: the two sets of boot prints are smaller than a man's, one with flat soles indicating a servant and the other with tiny high heels indicating a wealthy noblewoman—surely out of her element in this sinister location. Indeed, Lecoq surmises that a third person, a man, has escorted the women away from the *terrain vague* and re-oriented them "dans la direction de la rue du Château-des-Rentiers"—in the direction, that is, of the crime's true source. For as a three-hundred-page flashback reveals, the murders in *La Poivrière* are the result of a Restoration era family drama involving a property dispute among the upper classes.

The novel veers away, then, from the pure textuality implied by Lecoq's blank-page analogy and re-inscribes the space of the *terrains vagues* with the social concerns that the narrator had introduced at the start. In this way, it ends up less susceptible to the "Purloined Poe" or formalist type of reading than to the alternate and parallel strand of crime genre criticism that developed out of D. A. Miller's Foucault-inflected *The Novel and the Police*, with its emphasis on historical context and changing demographics of crime in the nation. The *terrain vague* may be a blank page, but its boundary—as the map reminds us—is that of the wealth/poverty intersection and its very blankness (i.e., its legibility) derives from its uncultivated nature as liminal space between urban buildings and rural crops. Thus sociology joins textuality in this founding space of the crime fiction genre.

The map's functional duality is of particular interest if one considers the split between formalism and historicism that has characterized not only critical approaches to crime fiction but the very definition of the corpus itself: on the one hand, one finds the classic *roman d'énigme* whose logical puzzles and formal conventions are seen to pave the way to the self-referentially parodic anti-roman policier of the 1970s and 1980s (Robbe-Grillet, Butor, Ollier) and on the other hand, the more historically grounded *roman judiciaire* of the nineteenth century is understood as founding a strand of engaged detective fiction that culminates today with the sorts of néo-polars and noirs for which Didier Daeninckx is known. In histories from Boileau-Narcejac's to Stephen Knight's 2004 book, these two strands of the detective genre are posited as separate: the formal and the historical.

Gaboriau's foundational detective stories are, of course, both—both narratives of deductive ratiocination *and* glimpses into the contemporary workings of the French judicial system. With this chapter's reading of the *terrains vagues*, I hope to expose the artificiality of splitting the two strands from each other. For Gaboriau's *Monsieur Lecoq* reminds us that the space of modern crime fiction has always been both real and textual—and if the novel's journalistic narrator and enigma-solving detective seem to figure a split between history and form, its *terrains vagues* recombine the two strands by existing in the novel as both social borderland and blank page.

Moreover, the inclusion of the map reinforces this double function. For maps, as visual supplements to written text, are always necessarily both referential and abstracting. Perhaps this is why they have accompanied the detective genre into its most modern—and referentially ambiguous—forms. As we shall see in the next chapter, maps continue to haunt even those detective fictions that explore what has been defined as the quintessential postmodern space, the *banlieue*. A further look at Gaboriau's own peri-urban mapping in *Monsieur Lecoq* will remind us of the nineteenth-century roots of (1) liminal spaces of civilization as the privileged sites of criminal investigation; and (2) the crime genre's continual tug between rationalized abstraction and brutal reality.

Map

Mapping is mastery. Renaissance cartographers converted *terrae incognita* into scriptic art; Descartes grounded the myth of self-possession in perspectival space.[12] Whether manifesting themselves as sea-monsters or philosophical doubt, cultural anxieties in the West have been quelled by the act of cartography. What to do, then, in late nineteenth-century France, when faced with the anxiety of crime that continues to plague citizens despite the best efforts of urban reformers and the *police scientifique*? One perennially appealing option was to turn to the detective as mapmaker.

Gaboriau's printed diagram, complete with now-iconic footprints and a coded layout of the building in its surroundings, marks the young Lecoq as a modern-minded investigator. For as historians Marina Daniel and Virginie Berger have recently demonstrated, the use of judicial cartography burgeoned in the nineteenth century, becoming increasingly systematic in the latter half of the century as a technique for the "enquête de terrain."[13] Especially in the cases of blood crimes, magistrates began substantiating their written reports with visual representations of the "théâtre du crime" (Daniel, 109). Similarly, as we have seen, Lecoq prepares his map as a textual supplement designed to elucidate the inquiry. By italicizing the phrase *plan du théâtre du meurtre* in his description of Lecoq's mapmaking, Gaboriau signals its currency in actual judiciary procedure; indeed, Lecoq's use of a *légende explicative* accords him with the norms that were being developed in this new technique of investigation (Gaboriau, 47).

For by the 1880s, the graphic conventions for a *plan judiciaire* had been unofficially established: "Dans les cas de morts violentes, l'enquêteur devait indiquer avec méticulosité la position du cadavre, la situation des armes ou instruments découverts à sa proximité, les signes pouvant indiquer tel ou tel genre de mort, l'étendue et la localisation des indices sanglants" [In cases of violent death, the investigator was tasked with meticulously indicating the position of the corpse, the placement of any weapons or tools found nearby, the clues pointing to this or that manner of death, the extent and location of the wounds, etc.] (Daniel, 112). And by the end of the century, in 1899, the Austrian criminal jurist Hans Gross had provided written prescriptions for the proper *établissement des plans*:

Il faut indiquer l'orientation, les rapports de situation et de distances entre les bâtiments, utiliser une échelle décimale et donner des désignations aux meubles suivant la lettre qui commence leur nom, par exemple 'L' pour lit, 'T' pour table, 'A' pour armoire.

[One must indicate the positioning, the relative locations and distances between buildings, using a decimal scale and identifying each piece of furniture according to the first letter of its name, for

example "B" for bed, "T" for table, "A" for armoire.] (cited in
Berger, 100)

Although he will later deviate from these developing norms, Lecoq begins by
following the new conventions, establishing himself as an investigator to be
reckoned with, one poised to replace the old-school Gévrol with a modern spatial expertise.

In particular, the young investigator Lecoq's mapmaking demonstrates a
synthesis of the technical skills often farmed out to trained experts. In this
way, he differs from a growing norm of outsourcing: though the maps were
usually drawn by members of the judicial system and police force,

> Il arrivait aussi, surtout à la fin du XIXe siècle, que la réalisation
> des dessins judiciaires fut confiée à des spécialistes, géomètres,
> architectes, arpenteurs, agents voyeurs et même professeurs de
> dessin, nommés comme expert en vertu de l'article 43 du Code
> d'instruction criminelle de 1808.

> [Sometimes, too, especially at the end of the nineteenth century,
> the production of these judiciary drawings was entrusted to special-
> ists: land surveyors, architects, topographers, hired agents, and
> even drawing instructors, called in as experts in accordance with
> article 43 of the criminal Code of 1808.] (Daniel, 117)

The young police agent Lecoq himself uses the skills of many trades to draw
up his map.

Such professional multivalence might be attributed simply to the romanesque compression by Gaboriau of different roles into one central character,
but it also serves a more important cultural function: to invest the fictional
detective with the patina of scientific authority. Certainly in the admiring eyes
of his elderly assistant le père Absinthe, Lecoq's cartographic gesture takes on
its impressive proportions from the positivistic expertise it implies:

> Le plan, particulièrement, émerveillait le bonhomme. Il lui en était
> passé beaucoup sous les yeux, mais il s'était toujours figuré qu'il
> fallait être ingénieur, architecte, arpenteur tout au moins, pour
> exécuter un semblable travail. Point. Avec un mètre pour prendre
> quelques mesures et un bout de planche en guise de règle, ce

conscrit, son collègue se tirait d'affaire. Sa considération pour
Lecoq s'en augmenta prodigieusement.

[The map in particular filled the old man with wonder. He had
seen plenty of them before, but had always thought that one
would have to be an engineer, an architect, or at the very least a
land surveyor, to be able to produce one this well. With a tape
measure to make a few estimates and a piece of wood serving as a
ruler, this draftee, his colleague, was getting along nicely. His
respect for Lecoq increased by leaps and bounds.] (48)

Here, Lecoq's superior powers are directly linked to the technical skills of an
engineer, an architect, or a land surveyor: those who master the landscape.

In this way, Lecoq is associated with the prestige of engineering Paul
Virilio identifies as a "veritable cult" of the nineteenth century.[14] In Virilio's
dromological analysis, modern mapmaking was inextricably linked to the ideology of domination inherent in military strategy:

This military thought, that claims by functional planning to
eliminate chance (which it considers synonymous with disaster and
ruin), becomes totally confused at the end of the *ancien régime* with
the thinking of the bourgeois political class, its taste for rational
nomenclature, its tireless activity of totalitarian scribe (encyclo-
pedist), the osmosis taking place at the entrance to the cities
(permeable membrane between the highway and the street). (42–43)

Such a desire to eliminate disaster certainly jibes with the generalized bourgeois impulses of detective fiction, with its rationalist combat against the social disorder of violence.

But even more specifically, Gaboriau's novel taps into the militaristic ideology described by Virilio through its figural presentation of Lecoq's cartographic skills as weapons in the service of warfare. Lecoq's domination of the
mystery scene through mapmaking is called a "tactique . . . de bonne guerre"
[good war tactic] designed to show his deductive superiority to his rival, the
officer Gévrol (48). In writing the police report, "Il le soignait comme un jeune
général le bulletin de sa première victoire" [he drafted it as carefully as a young
general writing up the report of his first victory] (48). Like a soldier rising
through the ranks, Lecoq takes the bloodied "field" of La Poivrière as an

opportunity for advancement. His mapmaking gives him a distinct advantage over the patrol agents who first came upon the scene of the crime, for rather than establish an ordered, bird's-eye view, they had entered the confusion of snowy night by thrusting an unstable lantern into the unyielding night:

[La] lumière petite et fort brillante décrivait les plus capricieuses évolutions, . . . traçant les plus inexplicables zigzags, rasant le sol parfois, d'autres fois s'élevant, immobile par instants et la seconde d'après filant comme une balle.

[The small, bright light moved most capriciously, tracing the most inexplicable zigzags, at times grazing the ground, at others rising up high, one moment still and a second later skittering away like a bullet]. (38)

Surely, compared to this haphazard roaming, Lecoq's technically masterful mapmaking will clear the mystery up post haste.

But no, the opposite will in fact turn out to be the case. Lecoq's map does not in the end live up to its postivistic promise. As I have argued elsewhere, Lecoq is no master at the start of this six hundred-page *bildungsroman*.[15] His investigation can only progress by fits and starts and its resolution comes as much from chance encounters and the external aid of Tabaret as from Lecoq's own deduction. In this way, *Monsieur Lecoq* serves as a prime (indeed, primary) example of what Dominique Kalifa has analyzed as a key *écart* [gap] in the *roman policier* genre between theory and practice. On the one hand, the proliferation of maps and charts included in investigative reports signals the genre's reliance on rationalist, positivist systems of knowledge. But on the other hand, most judicial reports were steeped in the sensationalistic language of cliffhangers and pulp fictions; "L'emprise feuilletonesque y demeure dominante, condamnant souvent le raisonnement au profit de l'événement, l'induction au profit du hasard [The influence of serial novels remained dominant, often favoring event over intellection, chance over inductive reasoning] ("Enquête," 248). Monsieur Lecoq's map, in the end, might serve as nothing more than a generic red herring: an appeal to rational mastery that dazzles and distracts from the truly unsystematic "Enquête" (the title of the novel's first half).

After all, despite le père Absinthe's wide-eyed admiration for Lecoq's survey skills, the map turns out neither to provide the key to the solution, nor to provide a fully coherent, satisfactory view of the scene. For one thing, as scene of the crime, Lecoq's map lacks some important data: where are the bodies? From looking solely at the diagram, one would not know how many men were killed (three), nor that the gun-wielding suspect remained in the main room. This seems especially strange, given that the key does mention the cabaret's other living inhabitant, the widow Chupin, seated and sobbing on the steps. As if to underscore such gaps, the letters of the key appear in alphabetical order, but skip haphazardly forward: ABCDFHHHTKLMMM—a system seemingly unrelated to Hans Gross's code. The reasons for this order are unexplained, but the legend's effect is to undermine the very systematicity invoked by the technical sciences—engineering, architecture, and surveying—whose skills Lecoq is said to wield in his mapmaking.

Equally unsettling is the map's lack of closure. Gaboriau could have included only *La Poivrière*, but he decenters it within the *terrain vague*, itself only half-circumscribed by the two roads mentioned in the text. And the cabaret is more than penetrable; though the building is first described as hermetically sealed and its door has to be kicked in by officer Gévrol for access, it soon becomes clear that witnesses have been able to exit under the police officers' noses, out the back of the *bouge* and through the gate of the yard's latticework fence (14). Not even within the main house are spaces well-enclosed, as windows, doors, and stairways are indicated on the map by openings and indentations. Of course, within the visual vocabulary of architectural plans, these would not stand out as unusual, but the written key that Lecoq appends to the drawn map calls attention to their importance, as seven of its textual notations refer directly to liminal spaces: *fenêtre fermée; porte enfoncée; escalier; cheminée; porte communiquant avec l'arrière-salle; seconde porte du cabaret, portillon du jardinet* (37).

The porosity of the cabaret space acts as a mise-en-abyme of the larger Paris: no matter how often its Barrières are redrawn, unwanted social elements seep in and out. *Monsieur Lecoq*, one of the first detective stories (i.e., a novel that sets out to circumscribe violent crime through a ratiocinating process) designates the spaces of violence as resisting description, circumscription, closure. Ultimately, Lecoq's crime map is as vague as its central site, the *terrain vague* that is meant to separate the seedy bar from the cross-streets of civilization.

Mapping Away Matter: Leroux's *Chambre jaune*

The gap between Lecoq's aim at technical mastery and his actual cartographic practice is made even wider in Gaston Leroux's 1907 *Le Mystère de la chambre jaune*. Though the map of Leroux's titular crime scene clearly aligns itself with Rouletabille's rationalist system, it registers "despite itself" a resistance to that order, signaling in the end the ideological tensions that persist in the crime fiction genre as it enters the twentieth century.

Virtually every reader of Leroux's novel has noted that the journalist-detective Rouletabille proclaims a mathematical method of Cartesian purity that is belied by the narrative messiness of his investigation. For Uri Eisenzweig, *Le Mystère de la chambre jaune* exemplifies the early detective genre's occultation of capitalist materialism through narrative strategies of camouflage and displacement.[16] In particular, the topographic isolation of the château du Glandier constitutes a fictional space outside socioeconomic concerns and class politics; but of course, like Rouletabille's "cercle de la Raison," it is exposed as inhabiting the realm of the imaginary (206–9). While Eisenzweig sees the characters' personal passions as a screen for the actual motivations of capitalist interest, Jacques Dubois and Jon Eburne identify Rouletabille's rationality as a screen for those interpersonal relations themselves. Eburne writes that "Leroux's yellow room, despite its formulaic show of ratiocination, already recognizes the provisional and purely functional quality of this logic, insofar as all the narrator's talk about logical method serves merely as a ruse for exposing the nexus of social relations that find their symbolic articulation in the mechanics of the locked room."[17] And for Dubois, the social-symbolic mechanism at work is one of foreclosure, in both its psychoanalytical and juridical meanings: Rouletabille's efforts to create a bounded mental and topographical space of purity constitute attempts to exclude the threat of his father, Larsan.[18] Dubois sees Rouletabille as "utopiste," in the sense of wanting to clean up the world, to eradicate the messy social threat of crime.

David Platten's analysis of *Le Mystère de la chambre jaune* aligns with these types of reading, while adding the specificity of Leroux's ambivalence toward modern sciences at a fin-de-siècle moment when the objective certainty of Newtonian physics was beginning to be toppled.[19] Rouletabille clings through his avowed rationalism to a system of knowledge being challenged in the scientific world inhabited by practitioners like the Stangersons: "The value of empirical and forensic evidence is subordinated in this story, through the character and actions of Rouletabille, to the abstract realm of Cartesian reasoning" (*Origins and Beginnings*, 23). Resisting the Stangersons' empiricism, Rouletabille turns to a mathematical solution which "derives from a precise understanding of how the subject's field of vision is constantly mediated by the effects of time" (*Pleasures*, 33).

The temporality of vision may well in fact already signal a break in Rouletabille's Cartesian system, as science's larger move from Newtonian physics toward Heisenbergian uncertainty is reflected in a gradual shift from objectivity to subjectivity in specific theories of visual perception. In my own work on Leroux's novel, I have explored the ways in which epistemological tensions between abstract deduction and empirical method within the science of optics structure the visuality of the modern detective novel genre.[20] Rather than see science in this novel as a mere red herring (as does Dubois when he states that the physics-related plot is nothing but an "ersatz" pretext; 164), I suggest, following Platten, that the emerging empiricism and sensationalism of early twentieth-century scientific discourse works to undercut Rouletabille's avowed rationality. And further: that the science itself registers that central ambivalence between Reason and sensation.

What we—Eisenzweig, Eburne, Platten, Dubois—agree on is that the story "cheats": that is, there is an irreducible gap between Rouletabille's claim of pure method and the story's actual structures and motives, whether they be understood as social, symbolic, or epistemological. And that the novel's famous locked room motif spatializes that gap. For if Leroux explicitly presents the yellow room's hermetic enclosure as homologous with Rouletabille's "cercle de la Raison," it takes a readerly suspension of disbelief not to care that the entire rationalist premise of the detective's investigation is undermined by its solution: the crime was committed before the room was locked, so there was, in fact, never a *local clos*. What is surprising to me is that in all of the discussion of Rouletabille's Cartesian "espace mental" (Dubois, 164), there is no mention made of the maps that accompany Leroux's text—for they are the spatialized externalizations of that mental space. They are the visible manifestation of Rouletabille's attempts to impose a Cartesian grid onto the messy world of passion, desire, and violence. As cartographic acts, they embody the scientific authority, clarity of method, and purified rationality to which Rouletabille clings in the face of troubling modernity.

Figure 6 includes the first of two maps included in printed editions of *Le Mystère de la chambre jaune*: the yellow room in the side pavilion of Stangerson's château du Glandier. (The second is a floor plan of the estate home from which the crime's culprit has seemingly disappeared into thin air.) Both are described in the novel as having been drawn by Rouletabille and are presented as essential to the reader's comprehension of the mystery. As the narrator explains, regarding the yellow room map:

Il a été tracé par Rouletabille lui-même, et j'ai constaté qu'il n'y
manquait pas une ligne, pas une indication susceptible d'aider à la
solution du problème qui se posait alors devant la justice. Avec la
légende et le plan, les lecteurs en sauront tout autant pour arriver à
la vérité qu'en savait Rouletabille quand il pénétra dans le pavillon
pour la première fois et que chacun se demandait: "Par où l'assassin
a-t-il pu fuir de la 'Chambre Jaune'?"

[It had been drawn up by Rouletabille himself, and I could see that
it lacked not one single line, not one clue that might help solve the
judicial problem at hand. Armed with the legend and the map,
the reader will be as well prepared to find the truth as was Rouletabille when he entered the pavillion for the first time and wondered
"By what means of egress did the killer escape from the Yellow
Room?"] (87–88)

With its dark rectilinear lines and typescript key, the reproduced map does
indeed look professional; we may surmise that Leroux or his publisher employed a typesetter or cartographer to design it since in Leroux's original manuscript the map appears as a messy, bare-bones sketch on the back side of a
page.[21] Rouletabille thus shares with Gaboriau's Lecoq a technical expertise
that lends added authority to his role as journalist and amateur detective.

If we compare the two maps, we find Rouletabille's "chambre jaune" diagram technically superior to Lecoq's crime scene map. It employs more cartographic and architectural design conventions such as shading and varied
typescript in the map as well as in the explanatory legend. It thus comes closer
to the Cartesian ideal of purified abstraction that Rouletabille claims as investigative method. Of the two authors, Leroux also works harder to create
the spatial closure that makes the mystery so compelling and that reinforces
the "cercle de la Raison": the pavilion and park are bordered by a "mur de clô-
ture," a "fossé," and another triple-thick wall. Gaboriau's cabaret, on the
other hand, floats within an unframed space, so that the *terrain vague* Lecoq
compares to a "page blanche" merges into the actual, material *page blanche* of
the book. Neither directly includes human figures (no outline of a body as in
later ones, such as Willis Kent's 1931 *A Woman in Purple Pajamas*), but both do
include footprints, worth comparing.

In the legend to his map, Gaboriau identifies the drawn footprints leading out of the cabaret through an open gap as "empreintes de pas sur la neige"

pavillon pour la première fois et que chacun se demandait : « Par où l'assassin a-t-il pu fuir de la "Chambre Jaune" ? »

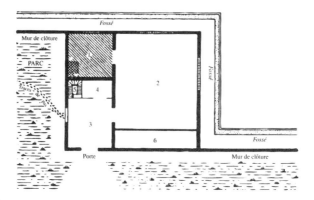

88

1. Chambre Jaune, avec son unique fenêtre grillée et son unique porte donnant sur le laboratoire. 2. Laboratoire, avec ses deux grandes fenêtres grillées et ses portes, donnant l'une sur le vestibule, l'autre sur la Chambre Jaune. 3. Vestibule, avec sa fenêtre non grillée et sa porte d'entrée donnant sur le parc. 4. Lavatory. 5. Escalier conduisant au grenier. 6. Vaste et unique cheminée du pavillon servant aux expériences de laboratoire.

Avant de gravir les trois marches de la porte du 180 pavillon, Rouletabille nous arrêta et demanda à brûle-pourpoint [1] à M. Darzac :

« Eh bien, et le mobile du crime [2] ?

– Pour moi, monsieur, il n'y a aucun doute à avoir à ce sujet, fit le fiancé de Mlle Stangerson avec une grande 185

---

1. *À brûle-pourpoint* : brusquement.
2. *Le mobile du crime* : le but, la raison du crime.

Figure 6. Gaston Leroux, *Le mystère de la chambre jaune*. G. F. Flammarion.

[footprints on the snow] [M] (and he uses the word "empreintes" again for the marks left by drink-glasses on a table [H]). Leroux, on the other hand, accompanies the footprints that hit a closed window of the pavilion with a curving phrase, "Traces de pas." The two terms are fundamentally synonymous, but "empreintes" in Gaboriau fits with the terrain as blank page, through its relation to printing processes [*gravure* and *moulage typographique*]; whereas "traces" also has a mathematical meaning as point of intersection—which is appropriate to Leroux, since Rouletabille's solution to the mystery is all about mathematical points of intersection among characters. The abstracting, "whitewashing" function of cartography is further evident in the difference between the "traces des doigts ensanglantées" (89) in Leroux's written description of the *Glandier*'s crime scene and the simple "traces de pas" of his drawn diagram. In both Gaboriau and Leroux, the map signals an impulse to ward off crime's messiness through the imposition of rational order and symbolic closure. But there is a wider gap in Rouletabille's map between those two regimes; his "Traces des pas" constitute the only curve in two diagrams of rectilinear order, as though signaling a subtle return of the repressed muck that disrupts the spatial purity of the Cartesian grid.

In this way, Leroux's *Chambre jaune* map points toward the further messiness of *Le Parfum de la femme en noir*'s map of the Château d'Hercule on France's Southern coast. As discussed in Chapter 3, the porousness of the fort and the semi-openness of the presqu'île represent both France's military vulnerability and Rouletabille's personal ghosts. The threat of the past, as both national and family history, disrupts the idealized closure of Rouletabille's "cercle de la raison," that abstracting mental space made visible through the novel's cartographic act. Leroux's detective novels are known primarily for continuing the central "local clos" [locked room] premise that runs through the murder mystery tradition, beginning with Poe's *Rue Morgue* and Conan Doyle's "Speckled Band" (in which a snake is found to have slithered into an apparently hermetically sealed room).[22] As with any "récit impossible" in this lineage, the closure in Leroux is an illusory one. And the crime scene map inevitably exposes the artificiality of its own attempt. With their compasses, rulers, and mapmaking tools, Gaboriau's and Leroux's detectives claim the "authoritative, ontological power" of cartography.[23] But despite their recourse to spatial and scientific forms of control, violence always returns.

In his *Cartographic Cinema*, Tom Conley identifies fictional maps as powerful ideological tools complicit with cartography's history of "appropriation, control, and administration of power."[24] But the modern and postmodern age exposes the rifts in cartography's totalizing ideology; "Deleuze speculates that as an implicit result of world history the cinematic image can no longer refer to a 'globalizing or synthetic situation'—as a *mappamundi* would offer an enclosed view of earthly space—but to scenes of dispersion or disruption" (Conley, 9). Just as Conley has identified a new time-image regime of postwar cinema in which a fictional map "can make visible the history of the strategies informing what a film is projecting" (14), so the analysis of crime-scene maps in modern detective fiction can expose the irreducible tensions between the genre's rationalizing impulse and its throbbing fascination with violence. With his "cercle de la raison" and rectilinear maps, Gaston Leroux's early twentieth-century detective Rouletabille is particularly effective in allowing us to visualize this pull between the ideology of Rationalism and the ragged realities of space, time, and crime. As I indicated in this Chapter 1, the maps in Leroux's early twentieth-century mark an overlap space between two modes that Derek Gregory describes in his *Geographical Imaginations*: (1) "geography and the world-as-exhibition"—the impulse to render visual a specifically modern constellation of power, knowledge, and spatiality; and (2) "cartographic anxiety," the questioning or critique of the hierarchical rationalist and nationalist premises of that impulse.[25] They thus set the stage for the mid-twentieth-century experimentations that will be explored in the following chapter: the printed maps of the Paris arrondissements in Léo Malet's *Nouveaux mystères de Paris* (1954–9), which explode the locked room motif outward, into a paradoxical "open closure" both formal and political; and the map of an English town in Michel Butor's experimental *L'Emploi du temps* (1956), which unsettles the notions of center and periphery, border and boundary, that anchor the nationalist ideology of the locked room mystery.

CHAPTER 7

Mapping the City: Malet's Mysteries and Butor's Bleston

On August 23, 1973, François Le Lionnais founded a spinoff of the experimental Oulipo (Ouvroir de littérature potentielle) dedicated to the detective genre: the Oulipopo (Ouvroir de littérature policière potentielle).[1] This collective has published issues of its journal *Enigmatika* on topics like the Série noire, characters like Arsène Lupin, and authors like Pierre Véry. Its third volume was entitled the *Atlas des plans de roman policiers* [Atlas of detective novel maps]. Unlike the Oulipo's 1981 *Atlas de littérature potentielle*, which highlights spatial form in text through the architectonics of fixed form poetry, the anagrammatic re-ordering of linear text, and the mathematical shapes (chiasmic, sinusoidal, "hélicoïdal") attributed to narrative, the Oulipopo's publication is a literal atlas: it consists of a collection of maps and diagrams that had originally appeared printed in detective novels ranging from Agatha Christie's *Murder on the Orient Express* (layout of a train compartment) to Gaston Leroux's Rouletabille stories (Chateau d'Hercule from *Parfum de la dame en noir*) and others by authors such as Willis Kent, Ellery Queen, and C. Daly King.[2] The maps are reprinted with no regard to chronological order, nationality, or type of map. We see, for example, reproduced diagrams of airplane cabins, salon interiors with furniture icons and body outlines, geographical overviews of outdoor locations, cutaways of apartment buildings, and a seating chart for a millionaire's dining table. To introduce the volume, Annie Matiquat uses the phrase "Topographie des lieux fantômes" [Topography of phantom places].

On the one hand, the notion of a *topographie des lieux fantômes* seems to veer away from the maps' concrete materiality and toward their de-realizing function, their fantasmatic status. But on the other hand, we might read this *Atlas* as literalizing Marcel Bénabou's remark: "je vois la dimension oulipienne dans l'exploration des situations impossibles" [I see the oulipian dimension in the exploration of impossible situations/locations].[3] Taking '*situation*' literally as place, we find these maps at the intersection of a generic tradition (the detective novel as "récit impossible") and of the "dimension oulipienne"—the linguistic play of formal constraints.[4] *Enigmatika*'s recirculation of these maps, cut off from their host novels, represents one form of oulipian "exploration" of impossible sites, but the representational stakes of crime fiction maps can be more fully explored by reattaching these cartographic limbs to their textual bodies—that is, by studying novels in conjunction with their maps for the interplay of textual topography and visual topology.

In this chapter, I focus on two novelistic projects that link printed city maps to narratives that play with the crime novel form: Léo Malet's *Nouveaux mystères de Paris* (1954–59) and Michel Butor's *L'Emploi du temps* (1956). Though neither of these appears in Oulipopo's *Atlas des plans des romans policiers*, they certainly could have, since both create a "phantom" urban space for the reader. Their juxtapositions of city map and crime novel necessarily raise questions of spatial representation, textual referentiality, and generic convention. And their experimentation with the *local clos* formula contributes to an entropic spatiality that marks the modern genre as explored in this book. If the maps by Lecoq and Rouletabille end up undermining their rationalist ideologies despite themselves, those featured in Malet''s and Butor's mid-twentieth-century fiction signal a growing, more explicit realization that "all that is solid melts into air." Theirs is a playfully subversive spatiality that exposes the limits of social order and investigative closure.

According to the strictest of literary histories, Malet's and Butor's texts inhabit opposite ends of the detective novel spectrum. Malet's stories are classic potboiler *noirs*, with their *détective de choc* Nestor Burma roaming the gritty streets of Paris to solve episodic crimes. Butor, on the other hand, writes an "anti-roman policier," using *Nouveau roman* techniques to undermine classic expectations of detection and closure. Like other early *Nouveau roman* detective novels (Robbe-Grillet's *Les Gommes*, Ollier's *La Mise en scène*), *L'Emploi du temps* explicitly parodies the genre through metafictional or antirepresentational effects.[5]

This contrast between a traditional Malet and a counter-detective novelist Butor seems at first glance to be upheld by their texts' spatial metaphorics. For if both authors present the city as a labyrinth, they do so in quite different

ways: Malet's Paris is a shadowy circuit of real streets and alleyways whose
criminal threats are sociologically and politically anchored—think, for example, of *120, rue de la Gare*, in which roads and communication are blocked
by the constraints of the German Occupation. Butor's labyrinth is far less
historical, as the novel's references to mythic details like Ariadne's thread
allow the fictional city of Bleston to be understood as symbolic of an urbanity at once modern and timeless.[6] Mireille Calle-Gruber, for example, calls it
a universal "Everytown for humanity."[7] We are thus faced with what appears
to be a straightforward dichotomy: Malet as a traditional detective novelist
with a realist spatiality versus Butor as an experimental novelist with a more
fictionalized spatial structure.

When we shift our attention, however, to the linguistic strategies employed by the two authors, the distinction becomes less clear. After all, in
relation to other *nouveau roman* writers, Butor is not all that audacious. As
Celia Britton has pointed out, Butor occupies an ambiguous position within
the *nouveau roman* group, having been taken to task by Ricardou and Robbe-
Grillet for his stubborn representational concerns; in the case of *L'Emploi du
temps*, the city's mythic status paradoxically recuperates while disrupting the
process of representation.[8] In Malet's case, the crime story plots appear quite
typical, but the author's insistent cryptogrammatic riddles and acronymic puns
remind us not only that he began his literary career as a surrealist but that he
came eventually to be read as an Oulipo author *avant la lettre*: in 1982, the
Oulipopo dedicated a full issue of *Enigmatika* to Malet.[9]

What happens, then, to the apparent contrast of realist Paris to
mythic Bleston if we read these authors' maps in relation to their textual
transgressions—of realist form in Malet and of generic convention in
Butor? The question is informed by the fact that cartography itself is a scientific
mode whose representational function has been put into question by modern
thinkers such as John Ruskin and postmodern theorists such as David Harvey,
Yi-Fu Tuan, and Edward Soja.[10] As discussed earlier in this book, maps are
always already fictions, visual texts to be read according to certain representational conventions. Derek Gregory identifies the modern age as one of
"cartographic anxiety" and although he is referring to the anti-essentialism
of natural space, we might note a doubling of anxiety that occurs when you
join the conventionality of mapmaking to one of the most conventionalized
of literary genres, the *roman policier*.[11] Both Malet and Butor, authors writing
at a founding moment for French formalism, destabilize reference by playing

with the formal conventions of novel and map. But they also inevitably register the puncturing of rationalized space by the chaos of crime. How, in their texts, do spatial and textual references collide over the troubling social reality of criminal violence? How does the map's atemporal spatiality work with the temporality of narration? And what can Malet's and Butor's crime scene maps tell us about modern and postmodern geographical imaginations?

Open Closure: Malet's *Nouveaux Mystères de Paris*

If Léo Malet was claimed by the Oulipo as one of its practitioners by anticipation, it was not only because of his penchant for anagrams and pun-filled pseudonyms. It was also because the *Nouveaux mystères de Paris* was organized by a self-imposed or voluntary formal constraint: the composition of one crime story set in each of Paris's 20 *arrondissements*.[12] The 1982 *Enigmatika* issue dedicated to Malet recounts twice this crime fiction's origin story: when asked how he came up with the idea for *Les Nouveaux mystères de Paris*, Malet replies that while taking a walk in the city, "L'idée me vint d'une série de romans policiers se passant chacun dans un arrondissement, sans en franchir les limites administratives. Ce serait—paradoxe—, le roman en vase clos, mais en plein air" [The idea came to me for a series of detective stories each of which takes place in one *arrondissement*, without extending beyond its administrative limits. It would be, paradoxically, a novel cut off from the world, but in open air].[13] Later he restates the idea for his series: "Ce serait une sorte de nouvelle version du *'local clos,' mais en plein air (paradoxe)*" [It would be a sort of new version of the "locked room" [mystery], but in open air (a paradox)][14] This second formulation is noteworthy because it combines one of the *roman policier* tradition's most recognizable formal conventions—the *local clos* ("locked room")—with a spatial paradox of open closure, that is, something rather hard to represent visually, though Malet did include a reproduced map with many of his arrondissement stories.

A street map of the 6th arrondissement, for example, accompanies "La Nuit de Saint-Germain-des-Prés," a story that begins with an "avis au lecteur" proclaiming: "Ceci est un roman" [This is a novel].[15] The novel's characters, continues Malet, all come from the author's typewriter and should not be confused with real people in the real world—with three exceptions (here he provides proper names): Monsieur Paul Boubal, owner of the Café de Flore;

Pascal, a waiter there; and Henri Leduc, another businessman of the *quartier*. These, writes Malet, are "personnages réels, bons et bien vivants," flesh-and-blood folks he has allowed to enter his fictional space (735). Like this textual notice, the *arrondissement* maps in *Nouveaux mystères* refer simultaneously to the realist "*hors-texte*" of Paris neighborhoods and to Malet's fictive universe, as phrases referring to the stories appear inserted into city maps ("Cave du Passage Dauphine où fut élue Miss Poubelle," for example). By combining the real space of an urban "*générateur*" with the textual self-referentiality of these typewriter-font captions, Malet's maps iconically reproduce his texts' own intermediate representational status. We should not forget, after all, that Malet's tales at once use realist spatial tropes to comment on France's sociopolitical situation in the mid-twentieth century, while simultaneously using verbal play in a way that was subsequently appropriated by Oulipo as serving anti-realist aims. The maps of *Les Nouveaux mystères* seem to support the referential illusion of an "*au-delà*" to the text, but their captions point back to the novel itself as the map's primary referent. This effect is highlighted by the humorously negative construction of some of the maps' captions: "Nestor Burma ne s'y rendit jamais" [Nestor Burma never went there] (referring to a place that exists whether or not the detective shows up, yet one that is identified in reference to the fictional Burma); or "aucun cadavre ne trempait dans le canal St-Martin" [there was no cadaver to be found soaking in the canal St-Martin], which plays on the expectations of crime fiction convention while signaling a real location. Moreover, Malet's topos of a "local clos en plein air" is reinforced by the joint presence of open-ended roads with an artificial rectangular frame that does not conform to the arrondissement shape. Here again, we encounter a realist au-delà with a fictional closure.

Malet ended up writing a story for all but five of the *arrondissements*, from "Le Soleil naît derrière le Louvre—1er arr" (1954) to "L'Envahissant cadavre de la plaine Monceau—17e arr" (1959). This latter title, with its spooky attribution of "spreading invasion" to a murdered body, signals a spatial expansion of urban crime that manifests itself already textually in the first of the mysteries, "Le Soleil naît derrière le Louvre"—the story on which the rest of my analysis will focus. While Eugène Sue's 1842 *Mystères de Paris* confined urban crime primarily to the pre-Haussmann space of "la Cité," Malet's new *Mystères* disperses violence throughout all the Paris *quartiers*. And even within the uneasy confines of a particular neighborhood, the first, we find allegorized a broader shift from stable urban consolidation to the networked spatiality of an age of global expansion.

"Le Soleil nait derrière le Louvre" begins with a description of the *quartier* that emphasizes the "clos" side of *local clos*—its stink of "viandes mortes" [dead meats], its dead-end shops for the "classes laborieuses," the stifling effect of the Ministère des Finances, and finally, the perfect symbol of enclosure: a collection of caged birds for sale on the quai next to the Tuileries: "Et sur les quais, les oiseaux sont en cage. Ils sifflent. Ils appellent au secours. Polop" [And along the riverbanks, the birds are in cages. They whistle. They call for help. Plop" (425). In case the reader is tempted to contrast the plight of the caged birds with that of the "free" ones that fly about in the nearby park, Malet reminds us that that supposedly open space is itself nothing but a prison:

> Les oiseaux des Tuileries ne sont pas plus libres. Ils n'en bougent
> pas, des Tuileries. C'est une cage un peu plus vaste, dans un
> magnifique décor, voilà tout. Pour sauver l'honneur, il reste les
> pigeons qui se soulagent sans vergogne sur les bonshommes de
> pierre mal abrités dans leurs niches de la rue de Rivoli, ou sur
> les touristes qui sortent du Louvre, les yeux perdus d'admiration.
> N'empêche que tout cela, c'est quand même de la rigolade sinis-
> tre. Et les vols pratiqués dans les collections du musée (*La Joconde*,
> avant la guerre de 14; *L'Indifférent*, avant celle de 39, et, ces jours-ci—
> avant celle de quand?, un portrait par Raphaël) constituent des
> divertissements qui tournent court.

> [The birds of the Tuileries gardens are no freer. They never leave the
> place. The Tuileries: it's a cage, too—a bit bigger, and in a magnifi-
> cent setting, but that's all. To keep up appearances, you've got the
> pigeons who relieve themselves without shame on the defenseless
> statues in their half-alcoves on the rue de Rivoli, or on the tourists
> leaving the Louvre with their eyes lost in admiration. Even so, it's a
> grim bit of fun. And the thefts from the museum collections (the
> Mona Lisa, before the War of '14; the Indifférent, before the one
> of '39, and nowadays—before which war?—a portrait by Raphaël)
> constitute dead-end amusements.] (425)

Here, pigeons rebel to no effect, statues remain immobile and shit upon, and tourists circulate dumbfounded within the metaphorically claustral space of this inert arrondissement. Even when art theft seems to pry open the Louvre's locked walls, Malet's sentence contains the disruption, through the visual

enclosure of parentheses—a typographical *"lieu clos ouvert"*—and by ending with the phrase "tournent court," as though such shenanigans could do
nothing but circle back on themselves, re-contained by the first arrondissement's essential nature as open-air *local clos*.

But, as readers familiar with the locked room mystery tradition know, the
fictionalized crime spaces of the *roman policier* never actually fulfill their promise of hermetic closure. In Poe's *Rue morgue*, the orangutan slips out through
a fire escape; in Doyle's "The Speckled Band," the room has an opening big
enough to allow a serpent to enter; and in Leroux's *Mystère de la chambre jaune*,
the narrative cheat consists in placing the crime at a time before the Yellow
Room has been locked. In Malet's case, the avowed closure of the Louvre
quartier is undermined by the crime story's dependence on the continual penetration of its borders: telegrams come in and out, boats from as far away as
Tahiti dock at the ports of the Seine, and the two brother criminals—a jet-
setter and a provincial boob—roam in and out of hotels whose names (Le
Transocéan and l'Hôtel des Provinces) reflect the brothers' external origins
while reinforcing the *quartier*'s porosity, its openness to external transients. If
the *premier arrondissement* is an open-air cage, it is one whose birds can fly.
Security is threatened by the communication of words, yachts, and stolen
goods across *arrondissement* borders that are, after all, purely notional. (As
Barthes reminds us, a neighborhood's functionality does not preclude exceeding
its boundaries, since its semantic content relies not only on the abstraction of
the urban map that constitutes it but on the different uses and perceptions
of its inhabitants.)[16]

Still, it is more than just the arbitrary definition of the *arrondissement* that
makes this space an open-air *local clos*. I would suggest that Malet's mid-
century city in particular is at a crossroads, veering toward an economic
dispersal that is thematized in both the topology and the crime (theft) of the
story. This becomes clearer if we read Malet's *premier arrondissement* in conjunction with Michel Serres's 1994 book *Atlas*, a reflection on how space in
our day can no longer be defined univocally as either local or global.[17] Serres's
Atlas proposes to draw a map of the city's move toward postmodernity, its
entrance into a global network whose virtual sites mobilize (in the sense both
of calling up for action and of rendering mobile) the traditional city's squares,
streets, and monuments. The Paris locations that Serres chooses as exemplary
of this transition from local urbanity to global *réseau* are the exact settings of
Malet's first *Mystère de Paris*: the Louvre and the coin shops that line the first
arrondissement's rue Richelieu. Michel Serres calls the rue Richelieu (rich site)

aptly named because it stockholds wealth: the Bibliothèque Nationale Française conserves books, the Louvre contains fine art. and the coin shops store old money.

But these spaces of conservation are not made to remain static:

> remarquons qu'une bibliothèque, un musée, une vidéothèque . . .
> ne jouent pas seulement le rôle de dépôt, immobile, mais aussi et,
> sans doute, surtout de lieu de consultation, donc de mouvement.
> Le rappel réveille ce qui dort dans la mémoire, inutile et encombrante sans le souvenir vivace. Celle-là stocke, protège de l'usure
> ou de l'oubli ce qu'elle conserve, pour que la remembrance réunisse
> ou ressuscite, quelque jour, ce qu'elle désigne, aveuglément, comme
> les membres épars d'un cadavre dépecé.

> [We should note that a library, a museum, or a videothèque plays
> not only the role of an immobile warehouse, but also—and
> doubtless, especially—that of a place of consultation, and thus
> of movement. The recall awakens what is sleeping in the memory, useless and cumbersome without the vivid act of recollection.
> Memory stocks, protects from decay or oblivion what it conserves,
> so that the act of remembering can eventually reunite or revive
> what it blindly identifies as the scattered parts of a dismembered
> corpse.] (Serres, 145)

Serres's cadavers, though metaphorical, return us to the crime novel, in which a detective revives inert stock, recirculating the past through the narrative of deduction. But in Malet's text, circulation and movement are always juxtaposed with bodily enclosure: we get the displacements of art and the shifty wanderings of criminals, but they imprison their victims in subterranean caves or tie them in the bird cage shops. The story abounds with images of open closure: not just the bird cages, but also art frames and mirrors, a suitcase whose contents spill out, and most notably the story's final sentence, "Le soleil naissait derrière le Louvre" [The sun was rising behind the Louvre], a phrase that suggests the opening of a new day while circling back to the initial textual gesture of the title itself. There is a continual interplay of conservation and flux, closure and circulation, economic accumulation and dispersal that keeps Malet's city poised between the constraints of the traditional polity and the networked open-ness of an emergent global economy.

Nestor Burma is an ambivalent figure here. As an independent investigator, he can exceed the boundaries of a judiciary system organized by *arrondissement*, but he is also perpetually stopping, apprehending the troubling
circulation of criminals and stolen goods. Burma's Fiat Lux agency is located
on the rue des Petits Champs, which intersects the rue Richelieu between the
Louvre and the Bourse—between what Michel Serres identifies as the poles
of conservation and circulation that mark the city's transition from modernity to postmodernity. In the end, this ambivalent location recalls the author
Malet's own formal intermediacy between the "closed conventions" of the traditional *roman policier* form and the "open constraints" of the Oulipo's linguistic play.[18]

The Mark of Cain: Criminality in Butor's Bleston

Michel Butor's 1956 novel *L'Emploi du temps* thematizes an open closure of another sort, as its narrator Revel finds himself incapable of leaving the English
town of Bleston during the entire year he has come from France to work there.[19]
A literal "local clos en plein air," the fictional city of Bleston appears as a map,
printed in frontispiece form before the novel's first journal entry (Figure 7).
The map has no extratextual referent, since Bleston is not a real city.[20] But it
does make use of the realist tropes of *vraisemblance* in its layout and coded
details: the crosses that designate churches and cemeteries, the inclusion of
both architectural and natural forms, the differentiated lines to depict railways, streets, and rivers. It looks like a typical map of a typical English
town. Moreover, it supports the novel's referential illusion by posing as an
anchor, as the background reality for the narrator's urban wanderings; many
readers have followed Revel's described itineraries along the streets of this
printed map. At once realistic and not real, Butor's Bleston joins topoi like
Hardy's Wessex and Faulkner's Yoknapatawhta county as lying somewhere
along a spectrum from real to fantastic—from the actual Paris arrondissements that Malet uses to Tolkien's Middle Earth, for example, with its elven
homes and mythic landscape. But of course these two poles are neither clear
nor stable. After all, even without their captions, Malet's real Paris maps are
guilty of the ideological distortions and topographic fictionality that postmodern spatial theory reveals in all cartographic acts. And conversely, Tolkien's Middle Earth maps rely for their legibility on the conventional rules of
orientation and rural landscape depiction. Indeed, I would agree with Hillis

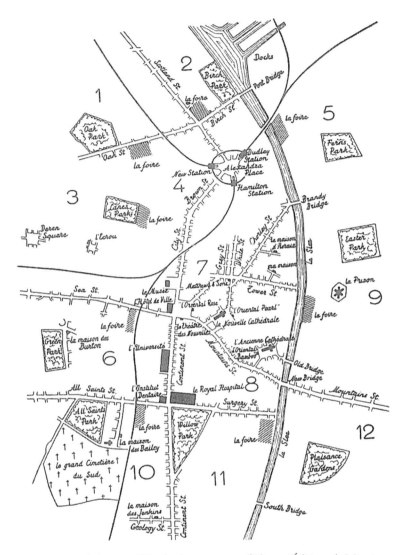

Figure 7. Michel Butor, *L'Emploi du temps*, map of Bleston. Éditions de Minuit.

Miller, who writes in *Topographies* (1995) that taking maps as background texts for literary fictions is problematic not just because cartography itself is problematic, but because there exists no literary text that is either purely mimetic or purely self-referential.[21]

If any text stands at equipoise between these two impossible representational projects, it may well be *L'Emploi du temps*, as becomes evident when we look at the details of his map in relation to the novel. The first thing to notice is that the place-names on this map of an English town are bilingual: some English (Birch Street, Dudley Station, South Bridge) and others French (le musée, l'Hôtel de Ville, l'Institut Dentaire). But beyond these public sites, we also find indicated in French the homes of the narrator and his friends: "ma maison," "la maison d'Horace," "la maison des Burton"; it thus becomes clear that this is not some pre-existing map of Bleston. It is, rather, a map of *Revel's* Bleston, of the city as he has come to know it, complete with the disorientation that comes from a clash of two linguistic cultures. Indeed, some of the odder place names combine English and French, but with French as the grammatical frame—le Royal Hospital, l'Oriental Pearl—as though the English toponyms were being presented through the linguistic lens of the Frenchman. Of course, the resulting subjectivity of this map does nothing to undermine the referential illusion. On the contrary, it could be said merely to replace a Balzacian or "objective" model of realism with the phenomenological realism that characterized much mid-twentieth century French fiction. When Butor's narrator says, for example, that his faulty mental image of the city gains in clarity as he discovers its streets and orients himself to its dimensions, he is upholding a realist spatiality, asking the reader to suspend disbelief of Bleston's real existence as object of his experience (28).

On the other hand, the map-plus-narrative text itself thematizes self-referentiality as a way to signal its very constructedness and therefore to call into doubt its founding illusion of reference. When Revel asks for directions to the town center, for example, he is asked, "What do you mean by center?," to which he answers "Alexandra Place," but then admits to himself: "C'était le premier exemple qui m'était venu à l'esprit; j'aurais pu lui dire tout aussi bien: "l'Ancienne Cathédrale," ou "l'Hôtel de Ville" [It was the first example that came to mind; I could just as easily have told him: the Old Cathedral, or the Hôtel de Ville] (29)." The spatial notion of a center is thus exposed as unmotivated, purely linguistic and subjective. Certainly, if we look to the map for referential substantiation, we also find that though a mathematical center could be determined, an actual town center and its related concept of periphery are hardly self-evident.

Textual/visual reference is further destabilized in a second element of the Bleston map: the fair, or carnival, rendered on the map as "la foire" [fair/carnival], a phrase abutting a shadow-box of diagonals with no clear boundaries, and located in eight different spots on the town. The article "la" is singular, because this is in fact one fair, itinerant and circulating through the town, like Revel himself. The novel emphasizes the fair's movement, its seasonal and circular displacement. The fair is a "parasitical microcosm" of the town itself, one that is chained to its eight-month trajectory around the town center, like a planet in orbit (again, a kind of open-air closure.) In June, Revel goes to the fair in the 5th arrondissement, in August, the 8th, and so on. But on the map, the fair's successive locations are represented as simultaneous. The uncanny juxtaposition of multiple icons with the singular article ("la" foire) signals to the reader the static instantaneity of visual—as opposed to narrative— representation. This distinction, so important to New Novelists such as Robbe-Grillet and Claude Simon in the 1970s, was reprised by Michel de Certeau as two different symbolic languages of space: the itinerary ("a discursive series of operations") and the map ("a plane projection totalizing observations").[22] To a certain extent, the distinction seems to hold up here, since in the written text the fair moves around as time passes, while on the map, it is halted and pinned down. But on the other hand, its very multiplication—the refraction of one fair into eight icons—undermines whatever totalizing illusion the map is meant to have. The fair is like a parasite, an interloper in the social field that, like its low-class carnies, poses a threat to urban stability.

In fact, a second notable aspect of the fair is its insistent link in the text to a series of fires set by an arsonist at various locations in the town, throughout Revel's year-long visit. The repeated narrative juxtaposition of the fair with the fires, along with the novel's bilingualism, allows us to see the English word "fire" within the French "foire" and to note the differential "o," an opening or blank space we might even read as a linguistic return on the map of what it has repressed: circulation, orientation, the temporal reality of the wandering subject.

A final noteworthy element of the Bleston map is its Prison, indicated by a hexagonal shape framing a six-pointed star or asterisk. In the novel, Revel burns a map of Bleston and watches as the six-pointed star that represents the prison disappears into a blackened, ashy hole. Elsewhere, when describing the city (not its map), he says that the prison building is hexagonal. The map itself represents the Prison with a certain redundancy: it includes both the hexagon, iconic because of its physical resemblance to its referent, *and* the star, a purely conventional symbol that refers to the map-within-the-text rather than to the prison itself. The result is a double referentiality, to the town of Bleston and to its spatial representation in the form of a map. The prison's double use

of icon and symbol is further paired with the linguistic sign "la Prison" whose
own indeterminacy—(is the French definite article followed by an English or
French noun?)—exposes the arbitrary nature of representational form.

But Butor's Prison is perhaps even more interesting in its combination of
the *nouveau roman*'s referential questioning with the *roman policier*'s interest
in the real social space of criminal justice. The following passage about the
Prison of Bleston exposes this uneasy clash of formalism and social realism:

> je marchais à peu près parallèlement à la Slee, depuis Daisy Fields
> où la foire était déjà en partie installée vers le terrain vague du
> cinquième qu'elle achevait de quitter, rencontrant l'un des angles de
> l'enceinte hexagonale de la Prison, je me suis détourné de mon
> chemin pour faire le tour de cette région dangereuse, rasant, dans
> le crépuscule, son haut rempart à la cime hérissée de tessons, le tour
> de cette région qui est comme un trou, Bleston, à l'intérieur de ton
> tissu, un trou dans lequel tu rassembles, telle une amibe dans sa
> vacuole, les corps que tu n'as pas assimilés, ne pouvant pas les
> rejeter à l'extérieur parce que tes limites sont trop imprécises, cette
> région en résonance avec ce qui est le plus lointain, et qui apporte
> sa menace jusqu'en ton cœur, avec le bâtiment pénitentiaire au
> centre, en forme d'étoile à six branches, à la fois ta condamna-
> tion et ta sauvegarde, Bleston, dont la représentation sur ton plan,
> semblable à un cristal de neige noire, m'était apparue à la fin
> d'avril, lorsque je te brûlais en effigie, comme une sorte de négatif
> de la marque éblouissante imprimée au front de Caïn.

> [I was walking pretty much parallel to the Slee [River], from Daisy
> Fields where the fair was still partly installed toward the open field
> [*terrain vague*] that it had just left, meeting up with one of the
> angles of the hexagonal enclosure of the Prison, I deviated from my
> path to go round this dangerous region, this region that is like a
> hole, Bleston, in your very fabric, a hole into which you gather,
> like an amoeba into its vacuole, the bodies that you haven't
> assimilated, being unable to cast them out because your limits are
> too imprecise, this region which brings its threat into your very
> heart, with the penitentiary building at its center, in the form of a
> six-pointed star, . . . whose representation on your map, like a black
> crystal of snow, appeared to me at the end of April, when I was

burning you in effigy, like a kind of negative of the dazzling mark imprinted on the brow of Cain.] (346–47)

The passage begins with the phenomenological experience of the city walker in a *parcours* that we can trace: "depuis Daisy Fields où la foire était déjà en partie installée vers le terrain vague du cinquième qu'elle achevait de quitter."[23] But here Revel reverses the trajectory of Bleston's other itinerant, the fair, which cannot be represented on the map as "partly installed" and which is located in a space unmarked on the map, though identified in the text: the *terrain vague*, a phrase that hearkens back to the first-ever detective novel map, the crime scene in Gaboriau's *Monsieur Lecoq* of 1868.[24]

As discussed in the previous chapter, in Gaboriau's foundational detective story, the *terrain vague*—uncultivated land—is what separates civilized society from the criminal underworld. Its location at the *barrières* of Paris allowing for the parasitical circulation of the city's unwanted—just as in Butor's Bleston 100 years later, the *terrain vague* hosts both itinerant fair and set penitentiary in an "open closure" that rends the city's social fabric. Like the carnies and the prisoners, Revel is granted semi-official status and his urban wanderings but up against the spatial contours of that status: "rencontrant l'un des angles de l'enceinte hexagonale de la Prison, je me suis détourné de mon chemin pour faire le tour de cette région dangeureuse, [. . .] cette région qui est comme un trou." Again we encounter a hole or a gap, not the temporal gap of the journal's missing date, but a spatial gap.[25] The "trou" at once weaves and unweaves the city's own fabric ("à l'intérieur de ton tissu") by attempting to contain "les corps que tu n'as pas assimilés, ne pouvant pas les rejeter à l'extérieur parce que tes limites sont trop imprécises"; the "open closure" of the city, its cartographic imprecision, leads to a parasitic incorporation/ incarceration of a criminality "qui apporte sa menace jusqu'en ton cœur, avec le bâtiment pénitentiaire au centre, en forme d'étoile à six branches."

Here, the narrator switches back from the city as referent to the map: "dont la représentation sur ton plan, semblable à un cristal de neige noire, m'était apparue à la fin d'avril, lorsque je te brûlais en effigie, comme une sorte de négatif de la marque éblouissante imprimée au front de Caïn." Concerning this complex passage we should note the idea of criminal bodies as inhabiting an uncanny region that exists on the map while constituting a gap in its very fabric. With the mark of Cain, we return to a mythic or fantasmatic city, but one whose original sin is revealed through a cartographic other, the map whose imprecise borders and gaping black hole expose the violence done to unassimilable bodies in the social space. The map reveals, in other words, what the experimental novel's formal play seeks to suppress: the real "terrains vagues" of the *roman policier*, its groundedness in an urban topography marked by social as well as symbolic violence.

In the end, then, both Malet and Butor use the double "open closure" of their maps and textual projects to reconnect linguistic play to the kind of urban dispersal that characterizes postmodern geographies. Butor's own interest in the fluid and changing boundaries of today's "mégapoles," the urban "monsters" of expansion like São Paulo, Cairo, Mexico City, and New York, echoes the discussions in Serres's *Atlas* that I emphasized in my reading of Malet as well as the "post-metropolis" theorized by Edward Soja.[26] Butor writes:

> Parlait-on de la municipalité, notion de plus en plus juridique et dans la plupart des cas périmée, ou de la région tout entière, et comment fixer les limites de celle-ci puisque justement les faubourgs des faubourgs s'effilochent au long des voies d'accès?

> [Was the discussion about the municipality, a concept that was becoming more and more legalistic and in most cases outdated, or about the entire region? and how would one go about determining its boundaries, since the very suburbs of suburbs weave their way along the access roads?] (cited in Calle-Gruber, 9)

Thus the mid-twentieth-century revival of peripheral terrains as privileged site of criminality is deeply connected to the growing awareness of the fictionality (and dying ideology) of a closed and coherent urban space.

Both Malet and Butor can be seen to usher in what David Harvey, among many, has identified as the rise of postmodernist cultural forms and spatial organization. In *The Condition of Postmodernity*, Harvey cites Jonathan Raban's 1974 *Soft City* as representative of an oppositional strain of writing, which grew out of 1960s collectivist idealism into a critique of the rationalized, automated systems of mass production and urban planning. "To the supposed domination of rational planning," writes Harvey, Raban opposed an image of the city as an emporium in which all sense of hierarchy and homogeneity of values was in the course of dissolution (4–5). And he cites Raban: "The city as we imagine it, the soft city of illusion, myth, aspiration, nightmare, is as real, maybe more real, than the hard city one can locate in maps and statistics, in monographs on urban sociology and demography and architecture" (Harvey, 5). One would think that Malet's and Butor's urban maps would fall on the side of the "hard city" in this equation. Like Lecoq's and Rouletabille's maps before them, they tap into the cartographic desire for mastery and rationalized order. But as the readings in this chapter suggest, those visual add-ons interact with the textual fabric of the novels to destabilize notions of social, political, and spatial order. Harvey reminds us that the anti-authoritarianism of the "soft city" is not simply a positive, idealistic vision of hand-holding community: "Beneath all that, lay the grumbling threat of inexplicable violence, the inevitable companion of that omni-present tendency for social life to dissolve into total chaos" (6). In a way, crime novelists are the best-placed to map this "hard" truth of the "soft city." By inscribing the refractory and dispersive messiness of violence into the fabric of supposedly clear cartographies, experimental crime fiction novelists like Malet and Butor expose and explore the continuing social struggle between reason and disorder.

CHAPTER 8

Zéropa-Land: Balkanization and the Schizocartographies of Dantec and Radoman

In the past quarter-century, technological acceleration and global networking possibilities have combined with geopolitical instability in the minds of spatial theorists to result in a less-than-sunny "supermodern space": themes of dystopia and dissolution dominate concepts from Marc Augé's *"non-lieux"* to Bruce Bégout's "Zeropolis" and even Michel Serres's "blank/white space."[1] Despair has dominated spatial thought in the late capitalist moment, writes Patricia Yaeger: "Space is a fragmentary field of action, a jurisdiction scattered and deranged, which appears to be negotiable or continuous but is actually peppered with chasms of economic and cultural disjunctions."[2] It is not surprising that the "dark side" of the shrinking world has left its mark on the French *noir*, a genre in which location means everything and whose classic form relies on the simultaneous manipulation by criminals and crime-solvers of communication and transportation networks. If trains and telegraphs created contact nodes and escape routes in nineteenth-century crime fiction, modern informatics have extended the genre's narrative reach—into the realms, for example, of international data trafficking and mass-mediated global violence.

But globalization has not merely extended crimes and detection into ever-larger settings, seamlessly expanding the crime scene map from room . . . to city . . . to nation . . . to globe . . . to virtual reality. No, between Auguste Dupin strolling onto the rue Morgue in Poe's 1841 short story and the postmodern detective Case jacking into cyberspace in Gibson's 1984 *Neuromancer*, we find intermediate geographies: spaces that are difficult to map because they simultaneously crash and recuperate illusions of national and ethnic identities. The late twentieth-century cyber-*noir* is marked by technological dystopias, networks of nightmarish criminality, and—most important for the purposes of this study—jarring reflections on the dissolution of comforting spatial boundaries.

One victim of globalization's "growing pains" is the France of the 1990s, which suffered a territorial identity crisis as many citizens of *la patrie* watched, with varying levels of investment, the near-neighbor Yugoslavian nations break up and cartographic confusion ensue. Among the many fictional and nonfictional responses to this crisis, two popular crime novels implicitly connected political violence to shattered spatiality by setting their stories in a transnational Western Europe (called "Zéropa-land" by one author) whose "civilized" nations (France, Holland, England) are indirectly affected by the fragmentation and violence of the Balkans. In Maurice Dantec's 1993 *La Sirène rouge*, the ideological mercenary Toorop crisscrosses Europe's highways to resolve a crime that is both domestic (a young girl flees her murderous mother) and global (the mother runs an international snuff film industry); Dantec's temporary focus on an apparently apolitical matter is underwritten in its very violence by Toorop's alternate role as an undercover fighter for the Bosnian cause.[3] In Vladan Radoman's 2000 *Ballade d'un Yougo*, a Serbian hit man named Vic Toar ("victoire") restarts his life as a poet-doctor in Nice but soon devolves into murderous schizophrenia in the streets of the post-apocalyptic Southern city.[4]

These two authors come from opposite ends of the political spectrum. Dantec's bellicose commitment to the Bosnian cause made global news when he moved to Quebec in self-exile from the European continent and his native France; while Belgrade-born Serb Radoman moved to France and co-founded the humanitarian agency Médecins sans Frontières.[5] But through their fictions, both Dantec and Radoman displace the violent fragmentation of the Balkans onto new cartographies of Western European social space. Dantec's highway nodes and virus metaphors, Radoman's subterranean street life and schizophrenic ocean-space: both imaginaries inscribe the *noir* with the topographical psychopathology of the "supermodern" world map.

Blogs, the Balkans, and a little country called *Poldévie*

In 2003, an English blogger named Tom Coates called for the "Balkanization of the blogosphere" as a response to the current aggregation of sites by link frequency, which gave too much exposure to entries from the United States and filtered out blogs from other countries.[6] Coates proposed that the best solution to the aggregation problem would be to geocode weblogs by "balkani[zing] our aggregators—slic[ing] their responses on the basis of meta-data," in order for visitors to sites like Blogdex and Daypop to find links by country or time zone. This popular blogger's use of the term "Balkanization" did not raise many virtual eyebrows. Although one respondent complained that the word choice brought up ugly visions of ethnic cleansing (albeit "of links," not people), the majority of posters simply continued to use it as a syn-onym for fragmentation or filtering, asking for example, "Is geography really the best divider in this day and age? How about balkanizing by interest?"

The linguistic transfer of the term "Balkanization" from a geopolitical his-tory to the abstract space of the internet was not itself put into question. Why not? Perhaps first of all, because the web has always been troped as a "space" complete with the geographic characteristics of orientation and navigation, scapes, and sites. But certainly also because the very concept of the "Balkans" is itself already a fictionalizing spatial abstraction. As Alexander Kiossev writes in his article on Balkan maps and identities, the label "Balkans" is "a geographic metonym that presupposes the existence of a non-geographical referent"[7] (165). As a plural rendered conceptually singular, the term "the Balkans" covers over what are essentially "uncertain and dynamic relations between names, territorial spans, borders, social groups, individuals, and identities" (165). A perfect metaphor, then, for the blogosphere. And indeed, undefined territories, social groups, individuals, and identities are exactly what is at stake in Tom Coates's call for the world-wide web's "Balkanization."

They are also what is at stake in another 2003 blogger's use of the term, this time as a negative description of the web. Whereas Coates called for Bal-kanization to counteract U.S. dominance of the blogosphere, a Frenchman named Tristan Nitot writes on the Open Web group that until 2003, search engine incompatibilities have been a "nightmare" of Balkanization and that unified Web standards will put an end to this "balkanisation du Web."[8] Again, the spatialized metaphor seems to evacuate the actual violent content of Bal-kan history, but of perhaps of more interest in this value-switch from positive to negative is the national difference: an English blogger sees balkanization as a good thing, while the Frenchman sees it as a nightmare, from which tech-nological standardization will allow us to awaken.

If, as suggested earlier, the term "Balkans" has always served as an un-stable referent, it can thereby be mobilized for different interests and through different national lenses. In her now-classic 1997 book *Imagining the Balkans*, Maria Todorova notes that the "use of Balkan as an ascriptive category in different languages" reflects different national ideologies.[9] Among the main European languages that "have been decisive in forming a 'hardened' Balkanist discourse," French stands out for having both a singular and a plural form: *le Balkan* for the mountain range and *les Balkans* for the peninsula. Todorova also points out that the French adjective "balkanique" is often used as a pejorative (32). This should not surprise anyone familiar with France: the Balkans have long served as a national target for ethical hand-wringing, disdain, pity, anxiety, and outright condemnation.

The Balkans hold mythic power as an "Other" to many Western nations, of course, but the exceptional intensity of France's culturopsychic investment in the region is perhaps evidenced by the invention of its own Balkan nation, the imaginary country of Poldévie (Poldavia). The nation began as a political hoax in 1929, when the right-wing journalist Alain Mellet publicly called for the socialist and communist Left to send missionary help to the oppressed peoples of Poldévie, on behalf of the fanciful Committee for Poldavian Defense.[10] The mystification was soon exposed, but Poldévie's charm persisted through fiction. It returned, for example, in Hergé's 1935 comic book *Tintin and the Blue Lotus*, in which the Poldavian consul appears as Tintin's hostile doppelgänger.[11] And the Oulipo playfully revived Poldavia's language and people in their novels of the 1970s and 1980s: Raymond Queneau's *Pierrot mon ami* (1972), Georges Perec's *La Vie mode d'emploi* (1978), and Jacques Roubaud's *L'Exil d'Hortense* (1990).[12]

The persistence of this semi-comic hoax both feeds and draws on France's long-lasting stereotypes about the Balkans. If, as Hervé Le Tellier suggests, the nation-state of Poldévie occupies a privileged place among chimerical geographies, it is because the cliché of a "mosaic" of Balkan peoples makes it easy to imagine one more small slavic nation hidden in the regional patchwork (213). Bertrand Westphal invokes an image both banal and phantasmatic, a Poldévie of mountain-men who might be benign princes, dangerous felons, or both at once (7). The phrasing reminds us that geography and crime have always been interconnected in the French cultural imaginary of the Balkans. Moreover, the Balkan geography-crime nexus refuses to remain safely exoticized in the form of Poldavian cartoon characters and linguistic games; note the tone of anxiety in Roubaud's *L'Enlèvement d'Hortense* (1987):

Les Poldèves sont partout. Et ils sont vivants, bien vivants. Ils sont
en Poldévie, bien sûr, leur patrie. Ils occupent depuis les temps

228 CHAPTER 8

mêlés indéfinissables, une région montagneuse et autochtone, qu'ils peuplent de bandits et de moustaches (souvent co-présents dans les mêmes visages). Mais ils sont aussi parmi nous, en petit nombre, certes, mais actifs . . . Leur influence est-elle bénéfique? maléfique? Devons-nous craindre les Poldèves? Sont-ils notre avenir, notre audace, notre espoir? Je ne sais, et je m'interroge?

[The Poldavians are everywhere. And they are alive and well. They are, of course, in Poldavia, their homeland. From time vague and immemorial, they have inhabited the native mountainous region, peopling it with bandits and mustaches (often on the same face). But they are also among us—in small numbers, yes, but active nonetheless. Are they forces of good? or of evil? Should we fear the Poldavians? Are they our future, our audacity, our hope? I do not know, and I ask myself that very question.] (cited in Westphal, 7)

This slightly facetious passage slides from a quaint "Otherland," populated by moustachioed bandits, to a French interrogation of its own identity. The fictional Poldévie thus serves as a marker of the way in which the real Balkans' multiply imagined instabilities—political, territorial, epistemological—have spilled over to invade France's own self-image throughout the twentieth century and perhaps most critically during the ethnic conflicts of the 1990s.

The 1990s conflict in Yugoslavia was generalized in the eyes of Western Europe as a "Balkan tragedy" (Todorova, 161), a category that both erased historical differences among nation-states and brought to the fore a deep anxiety about the disintegration of cartographic boundaries. There have been recent scholarly attempts to avoid such generalizations, such as the 2002 volume *Balkan as Metaphor: Between Globalization and Fragmentation*, which explores ways the Balkans have been troped in an age of global networks and political instability. In their Introduction to the volume, the editors write that "The . . . authors [here] resist any representational strategy that leads to the decomposition of the Balkans into functional fragments—as NATO army bases, as digital maps, or as the 'Mall of the Balkans'" (19). The idea, resisted by these authors, of "functional fragments" already reduces a rich set of cultures to stereotypical use, but it perhaps covers over the more disturbing trope of "dysfunctional fragments." There is no doubt that through Western European eyes, the Balkans have persistently stood for the threat of fragmentation. The "bloody Balkan wars, political intrigues and irrationality, nationalist hysteria, [and] senseless fragmentation into weak small states" result in a "dark Balkans" (Kiossev, 179–80) that haunted (and perhaps still haunts) the cultural imaginary. Both Dantec and Radoman, *noir* novelists publishing in France at the end of the twentieth century, present dystopic visions of Europe menaced by the Balkans as a "shadow-space" of cartographic disorder, brutality, and crime.

Dantec's Zéropa-Land

Maurice Dantec is the "bad boy" of French cyberpunk, a loudmouth *agent provocateur* whose website (called, in English, "Welcome to the Black Box, Baby!") opens with a self-aggrandizing music video that combines images of American soldiers with Dantec's own quotes about his heroic resistance to censorship. His words are grenades, he proclaims, and among the many targets of his vitriolic lobs is the Western Europe whose non-intervention in the Serbian-Bosnian conflict inspired Dantec's self-imposed exile to Canada in 1997. Though his later novels like *Les Racines du mal*, *Babylon Babies*, and *Villa Vortex* more directly engage questions of cybertechnology and the "post-human" (a term Dantec himself uses frequently), his first published novel, *La Sirène rouge* (1993) explicitly connects pro-Bosnian sentiment to a newly emerging European topography. Filled with disgust for his country's ineffectual lefty response to Serbian atrocities, Dantec prophesies the dissolution of France as a nation: "The failure to prevent the destruction of Yugoslavia demonstrates, for Dantec, the terminal decadence of the 'Old Continent', i.e. Europe."[13] The redefinition of borders in the Balkans announces an inevitable devolution of European nation-states into an array of territories disputed by "armed factions of nihilists and regionalists" (Morrey, 297). Already in his "metaphysical and polemical journal of 1999," entitled *Le Théâtre des opérations*, Dantec refuses to grant Europe spatial cohesion, describing the composition of *La Sirène rouge* as a transplant of hardboiled genre conventions from the strong, militaristic American soil to "our European space, or rather to this *non-space*"[14] (427, my emphasis)

La Sirène rouge, made into a movie in 2002, "stars" as its adult protagonist a tough-guy loner named Hugo Toorop. His patronym sounds like a contraction of *tout Europe*, and indeed the character surpasses the limits of a singular national identity: he was born in France, lives in Amsterdam, speaks many languages with no accent, and regularly crosses the Austrian, Slovenian, and Croatian borders to smuggle arms into "what's left of the Bosnian republic" in 1993. The novel's other characters are no less pan-European: at the story's start, Toorop encounters a young adolescent girl named Alice Kristensen, whose mother is Dutch, stepfather is Austrian, and birth father is British-born but peripatetic, boating between Barcelona and the coast of Portugal. At the same time, Alice's mother Eva extends her powers beyond Europe: she runs an international snuff film ring, videotaping the lurid sexual tortures and murders of young girls, often immigrants like Alice's tutor from Sri Lanka. As Toorop and Alice pair up to escape Eva's sadistic grasp, the reader becomes aware of two apparently unrelated networks of international proportions—both called le Réseau. Eva's network of blood-lust and capitalism employs a Dutchman trained in South African mercenary camps, neo-Nazis using U.S. marine corps methods, and a host of connections from Dakar to Venezuela with shell companies and accounts in Barbados and Switzerland. (Eva has even socialized on a yacht with Donald Trump!)

Paralleling Eva, but on the other side of the moral compass, Toorop belongs to an anti-Serbian "réseau," the Liberty Bell Network, which also imports agents and methods from all over the world: Toorop's mentor, Ari Moskiewicz, is a former Nazi hunter and member of the Israeli intelligence agency Mossad who shares Italian-American mafia secrets learned from William Burroughs, Jr.; another key player, the gifted computer programmer Vitali Guzmann, uses his informatic genius to help Western European arms smugglers navigate ex-Yugoslavian territories. Even the objects in this novel testify to the new global mobility of bodies and capital: characters sit on sofas from Sweden and drive imported cars like the aptly-named Chrysler Voyager. All of this mobility and flux is quite decisively presented as dystopic, for unstable borders are what allow the tentacular reach of both Eva's evil and the Serbian violence. Interpol, which is supposed to be pan-European, can do nothing, as it butts up against Swiss bureaucracy; cartographically central, but politically neutral, Switzerland becomes a sort of black hole or blank spot around which the networks buzz and circulate. As a result, the only way to save Alice from her mother's clandestine Réseau is for Toorop to insert her into his parallel network, whose mobile nodes and vectors have been established by the programmer Vitali according to the rhizomatic branchings of an actual European road map.

Although not reproduced visually, the map is described in the text as fully material. Toorop keeps unfolding the large, unwieldy road map onto the passenger seat of his car as he escorts Alice from Amsterdam to the Algarve. As though anticipating today's crime stories told through Google Maps, Dantec provides enough detail for the reader to follow along the routes, chosen and alternate:

> Cent cinquante kilomètres plus bas environ, la N630 croisait la N5, en direction de Badajoz. . . . Obliquer tout de suite vers Badajoz puis rejoindre Evora et piquer sur l'Argave. Ou continuer à suivre la N630 jusqu'à Séville puis prendre l'A49 en direction de Vila Real de Santo Antonio, à la frontière, avant de poursuivre plein ouest vers Faro."

> [About a hundred and fifty kilometers to the South, the N630 intersects with the N5, in the direction of Badajoz. Turn immediately toward Badajoz, then rejoin Evora and cut over to the Argave. Or keep following the N630 all the way to Seville, then take the A49 toward Vila Real de Santo Antonio, on the border, before continuing due West toward Faro.] (304)

Eventually, though, and perhaps predictably for an author infatuated with the tropes of the macho maverick, Toorop goes off-map, "empruntant de petites routes qui n'étaient même pas indiquées sur sa carte routière" [taking smaller roads that weren't even on the road map] (488). As the story enters its climactic finale on boats floating at sea, nationally bounded territories give way to uncharted space: "A un moment donné, [Toorop] quitta la nationale et emprunta une petite piste sablonneuse qui longeait la mer" [At one point, Toorop left the stateway and took a small sandy path along the coastline] (514). The road map is discarded and primal battle ensues. In the end, if *La Sirène rouge* is a politicized chase fantasy, it is also a sustained reflection on the question of mapping human subjects who exist at the brink of a de-territorialized space— the space of "Zéropa-land," Dantec's word for a Europe that will be nullified, zeroed (*zéropé*) by Serbian atrocity and cartographic chaos (*Théâtre*, 429).

The mapping of human subjects is literal, as from the novel's start, it is cartographic nomination that constitutes identity. Toorop's only childhood memories are of learning place names on the train route between Paris and Amsterdam. Alice's middle name is Barcelona because her father loved the place. And the entire peoples of the Balkans are described not as having been killed, but as having been erased from a map:

> [Toorop] n'était qu'un type de trente-trois ans qui avait un jour cessé de supporter que des populations entières soient quotidiennement

rayées de la carte à Sarajevo, Olovo, Prijedor, Alisic, Bosansky
Brod, Gorazde, Srebrenica ou Bihac, Bosnie-Herzégovine.

[Toorop was just a thirty-three year old guy who got fed up with
the fact that on a daily basis entire populations were being struck
off the map of Sarajevo, Olovo, Prijedor, Alisic, Bosansky Brod,
Gorazde, Srebrenica or Bihac, Bosnie-Herzégovine.] (12)

Crossed off the map of Europe, the Bosnians leave a gap that results in a narrative that is all about mapping. The Amsterdam police even uses the term
cartographier as a synonym for "to identify," as they try to track Eva's actions:
"le couple Kristensen-Brunner commençait à être sérieusement cartographié"
[the Kristensen-Brunner couple was beginning to be mapped in earnest]
(119–20).

Dantec's novel repeatedly invokes actual maps, as in an unsettling scene
in Eva's *réseau* headquarters that evokes both military strategy and border-
line (and "border-line") psychosis. In the flush of battle, Eva posts maps on
the walls of her house and pins color-coded pegs onto them to mark the
European search routes taken by her henchmen, reducing her human subjects to cartographic points. She then spreads an enormous map of the world
onto a table and, in a husky voice, invites her passive, lust-filled husband to
look at it with her. He watches, hypnotized and immobilized "telle une mari-
onnette" as her blood-red fingernail scratches the paper and stabs at colored
territories on the map (144). A long passage follows the disembodied fingernail (the "red oval") across the map's multiple named countries and as the
husband watches, he becomes sexually aroused by the metonymical slippage
of red nail, red territories, and red blood of their past and future victims:

L'ongle rouge se ficha sur un endroit du vaste puzzle multicolore.
La Suisse, reconnut-il. Le grattement de l'ongle sur le papier. Le
sud de l'Espagne maintenant. L'ovale rouge traversa le détroit de
Gibraltar et franchit la frontière du Maroc espanol. Stoppa un
instant au sud-ouest de Marrakech, sur la côte. Ensuite une longue
ligne droite plein sud jusqu'à un point à l'ouest de l'Afrique. Dakar,
lut-il à l'extrême pointe du continent, et de l'ongle. L'océan maintenant. Vernis écarlate sur le bleu roi de l'Atlantique. De petites
taches jaunes et orange. Les Caraïbes, les Antilles. La Jamaïque.

Panama. Le Venezuela. Le paradis. Le paradis sur terre. . . . La robe rouge d'Eva prit soudainement cette couleur qu'il aimait tant. Oh, putain oui, le paradis sur terre.

[The red nail jabbed at a spot on the vast, multicolored puzzle. He recognized Switzerland. The scratch of the nail on the paper. The south of Spain now. The red oval crossed the strait of Gibraltar and reached the border of Spanish Morocco. Stopped for a moment at the south-west of Marrakesh, on the coast. Then a long straight line due south all the way to a point in West Africa. Dakkar, he read, at the very tip of the continent, and of the nail. The ocean, now. Scarlet polish on the royal blue of the Atlantic. Small spots of yellow and orange. The Caribbean, the Antilles. Jamaica. Panama. Venezuela. Heaven. Heaven on earth. . . . Eva's red dress suddenly took on that color that he loved so much. Oh, fuck yeah, heaven on earth.] (144–45)

Though Eva is tracing an itinerary here, her agency is supplanted by her parts, while the flow of a transnational voyage is transformed rhythmically into a series of spasmodic jumps. Indeed, the passage's parataxic style—verbless phrases juxtaposed side-by-side—mimes the map's visual assemblage of un-linked color-patches, with the brisk punctuation of periods functioning like the sharp jabs of Eva's nail as it enters the Southern (hotter, moister, . . .) lati-tudes. In this way, the cartographic space becomes the externalized stage for Eva's global theater of sexual-sadistic control.

One might even read the discomposite zones of Eva's world map as an allegory of the hellish fragmentation of Dantec's prophesied *Zérope*, in con-trast to the linked spaces of Toorop's road map, which represents a Europe that retains (up to a point) a unifying, sinuous network of avenues. In Toorop's parallel *Réseau*, maps allow the navigation of "Autobahn City," Dantec's nickname for the pan-European road space and *La Sirène rouge*'s original ti-tle (*Théâtre*, 427). Whereas Eva jabbed at the map from above, Toorop enters the space of "tout Europe," foregoing the mastering *survol* for the vehicular version of the *Wandersmänner* experience on the ground.[15] Still, his is no lu-dic *dérive*; Toorop is on the run with Alice from killers and cops and must follow an itinerary mapped out for him by the Réseau. As the voyage pro-ceeds, the reader gets treated to scenes in which computer programmer Vitali unfolds paper road maps and traces alternate branching routes on them with felt-tip pens whose colored ink smells vaguely of the gasoline left on the real roads the maps replicate. As with the passage on Eva's world map, there is a theatricality to these scenes, with Toorop and Alice often watching wide-eyed as Vitali switches maps like the virtual space magician he is. This is a war, and cartographic space its *"théâtre des opérations."*

It has to be a computer programmer (Vitali) who masters the space, for, as Lawrence R. Schehr has observed, Dantec's universe is fundamentally structured by the computer metaphors of network and link, replication, and virus.[16] Dantec's apocalyptic vision of computer virology is based on the medical analogy of opportunistic infections like those of AIDS, shingles, and the retro virus (Schehr, 93). Schehr is right to emphasize the biological/machinic nexus of the virus metaphor in Dantec, for even in *La Sirène rouge*, which predates his later "post-human" fictions, Dantec presents Europe's (criminal and counter-criminal) networks as fueled jointly by blood and gasoline, bodies and cars. We might add here that *La Sirène rouge* attributes to that viral infection a very particular location in the Europea—or Zéropean— body/machine: the Balkans as its origin-point. "L'enfer s'était déplacé," thinks Toorop as he realizes the parallels between videotaped Serbian atrocities and Eva's snuff-film industry. He continues:

> Non, il proliférait, comme un virus. . . . L'Europe succombait à ses virus, le monde occidental moderne à ses limites, montrant là son vrai visage, annonciateur d'un crépuscule redoutablement tangible, encore une fois.

> [No, [not displaced]: it was proliferating, like a virus. All of Europe was succumbing to the virus, the modern western world at its limit, showing its true face, the warning sign once again of a tangible, dreaded dusk.] (439)

Dantec's use of the term slips and slides between technology and biology: cyber-virus, information-virus, Vitali's "viral strategies," Toorop's "identity-virus," Liberty Network as antivirus, fighting the virus of "lies and ethnic purification." As the chase-scene of this suspense novel draws toward its cinematic dénouement, Toorop wonders: "Et maintenant . . . , les choses en étaient-elles arrivées au point que puisse se développer une sorte de réplique 'capitaliste' du virus totalitaire?" [And now, he thought, had things really gotten to the point of developing a capitalist *réplique* of the totalitarian virus?] (517). Here the term "réplique" should be understood as a response, but also as a replica, for the political topography of Europe stands poised to repeat the fragmentation of Yugoslavian "territoires de l'ombre" (*Théâtre*, 429). As indicated at the start of this chapter, the Balkans exist as a "shadow-space," one that haunts Dantec's novel as the political background to an apparently personal, even familial, set of crimes—and one whose cartographic confusion announces the apocalyptic deterritorialization of Europe.

Radoman's Post-Apocalypse

Serbian-born Vladan Radoman is less well known than Maurice Dantec, but his trilogy *La ballade d'un Yougo* (2000, Série Noire) packs as dramatic a wallop as *La Sirène rouge* while adding a disturbing and intriguing reflection on the psychoanalytic reverberations of territorial conflict. Radoman's triptych recounts the odyssey of Vic Toar, a Serbian hit-man who seems to have left behind his violent past as rapist-killer-special agent in Belgrade to restart life as a poet-doctor in the city of Nice, in the South of France. But his brutal impulses will not lie dormant and *Bleu mistral*, the trilogy's first volume, ends with the protagonist interned in a psychiatric prison for violent criminals. In the second volume, *Orphelin de mer* followed by *6, rue Bonaparte*, he is released from the prison hospital by a shady (and perhaps hallucinated) team of secret agents who involve him in a complex scheme that results in murder victims galore. Using a Bulgarian alias, Vic Toar acts as both detective, investigating the criminal network, and as psychotic contributor to the carnage. As discussed briefly in Chapter 5 of this book, Vic's mental space is a double one, split between the literate doctor and the Serbian beast. In fact, as the novel progresses, the first-person narration exposes Vic's schizophrenia through the play of personal pronouns: "nous" is literally a double agent, a single bounded body inhabited by two Vics, "moi" and "l'autre."

Not content to haunt merely a mental space, the psychotic split of Radoman's narrator manifests itself in the actual urban space of Vic's adoptive city. From the beginning, Nice acts as a present-day template for the shadow-space of Vic's remembered Belgrade. As he rambles, for example, through the streets and squares of Nice, Vic indulges in an unsettling vision

that substitutes his native land and waterways for the French geography of
the Mediterranean:

> La folie des nuits belgradoises n'était plus loin. Le nez en l'air je
> humais les effluves charriés par la brise de mer. J'aurais pu le jurer:
> là-bas, au bout de la rue Halévy, ne somnolait plus cette grosse
> baignoire emplie d'eau salée. C'est mon Danube vivant, carnivore
> et cruel, qui s'étirait, soupirait d'aise et, s'apprêtant à inonder, à
> dévorer la ville, se faisait les dents sur les galets de la plage.

> [The madness of the Belgrade nights was not far. With my nose in
> the air, I breathed in the stench brought over by the sea breeze. I
> could have sworn it: down there, at the end of Halévy Street, it was
> no longer that fat, slumbering bath of briny broth. [No], it was my
> living Danube, carnivorous and cruel, that stretched itself out,
> sighing with ease and readying itself to flood, to devour the city,
> cutting its teeth on the pebbles of the shore.] (23)

Personified into a bloodthirsty creature, the Balkan region threatens to burst
out of its own boundaries in a hostile takeover of Europe. In Vic's deranged
mind, the cruelties of war are often displaced from human carnage onto a
geographical register, culminating in his complaints about cartographic absurdity: "Un orage de feu et de haine a ravagé pendant cinq ans ma patrie.
Elle n'existe plus. La mer Adriatique . . . n'est plus la mienne. Des nouvelles
frontières ont été dessinées par des hommes stupides" [A storm of fire and
hatred had ravaged my motherland for five years. She no longer exists. The
Adriatic Sea is no longer mine. New borders have been drawn by stupid
men] (37).

Vic's violent fantasy of a Balkan menace to French territory eventually
becomes a narrative reality, for at the novel's turning point, a mysterious cataclysm hits all of Western Europe with massive death and infrastructural
collapse, leaving only a post-apocalyptic wasteland peopled by ranging hordes
of underground armies and sadistic doctors. The seaside town of Nice, "ce
havre de paix et de luxe saxon" [that Saxon haven of peace and luxury] (81), is
transformed for the final installment of La Ballade d'un Yougo into a catastrophic replica of the Balkan states, its skies blackened by smoke and its
streets littered with corpses. Indeed, the sci-fi plot of the power-crazed
Dr. Niaize, who vaccinates hospital lackeys with an immortality drug and

hires Vic to kill a rival dictator, seems a mere diversion from the novel's true interest: the psychic and geographic ravages of the Balkan conflict.

Vic learns of the destruction of Western Europe only after the fact, as he returns from a months-long odyssey on a boat in the Mediterranean. Arriving at the silenced coast of Nice, he discovers the smoky ruins of a ravaged city and a rare survivor explains that one day the sky had mysteriously darkened and rained down death on the dogs and people of the region. "Font chier, les Serbes . . . .Tout ça est arrivé à cause de ces cons" [They're pains in the ass, those Serbs . . . All this shit happened because of those assholes], declares the bitter man (209). And Vic Toar comes to understand that somehow the bombing of the Balkan states by a European alliance has catapulted the entire region into a new era of pustulence, smoke, and primal brutality. This is not the chance for a new Eden, for "il faudrait . . . davantage qu'une apocalypse pour changer la nature humaine" [We'd need more than an apocalypse to change human nature] (232). No, the feral societies of men that now roam the burned streets of Nice only repeat their predecessors' sins, displacing them from the Balkans to the southern French coast. Vic makes the connection explicit when he points out to Dr. Niaize the absurdity of his Napoleonic claims to territorial power:

Au pays des aveugles les sourds sont rois. Qui, à part nous et ces pauvres diables en bas, est au courant de votre indépendence? Combien d'autres provinces françaises ou de pays d'Europe ont precedé ou suivi votre exemple? Ici même, n'y a-t-il pas des tentatives de morcellement . . . Autrefois, vous appeliez ça de la balkanization . . . Je ne sais . . . Les quartiers de l'Ariane ou de la Trinité, par exemple, partagent-ils votre élan micropatriotique?

[In the land of the blind, the deaf man is king. Who, other than these poor devils down there, even knows about your independence? How many other provinces in France or other European countries have came before or have followed your example? Even here, aren't there attempts at subdivision? You used to call that balkanization . . . I don't know . . . The neighborhoods of Ariane or Trinity, for example, do they share your micropatriotic fervor?] (234)

Though quite different from Dantec, Radoman shares with him a dark vision of the Balkans' cartographic fragmentation as leading to catastrophe for Europe. One might even borrow Dantec's term *Zéropaland*, with its nullifying echo of Disneyland, to describe the hell of post-apocalyptic Europe, as it is presented to intrepid tourists from Latin America (which, apparently, has been spared); when Vic Toar finds a pamphlet washed ashore from a cruise ship in the harbor, he sees a picture of the cindered and fallen Eiffel Tower, accompanied by prose:

> L'agence de tourisme tous risques vous invite à une voyage exceptionnel. Visitez les décombres de l'Ancien Monde. Faites connaissance avec les autochtones survivants, des sauvages pratiquant une nouvelle religion de l'immortalité. Plus excitant que le trekking dans l'Himalaya, plus dangereux qu'un voyage lunaire. . . . Offrez-vous un sejour en *Enfer* pour la modique somme de 10 000$ par personne en cabine particulière. Réduction de 30% pour les seniors et les jeunes mariés.

> [Our comprehensive tourist agency invites you on an exceptional journey. Visit the ruins of the Old World. Get to know surviving natives, savage worshippers at the new church of immortality. More exciting than a Himalayan trek, more dangerous than a moon voyage. Treat yourself to a stay in Hell for the modest sum of $10,000 per person, with private cabin. 30% discount for seniors and newlyweds.] (285)

Like Dantec in *La Sirène rouge*, Radoman taps into the "cartographic anxiety" of our postmodern age by evoking maps in their materiality as central to the representation of psychotic delusion. Maps like the maritime chart consulted by Vic during his absence from Nice:

> [Il] se pencha sur une carte marine, aligna la règle de Cras et, pour la troisième fois en trois jours, entoura au crayon la même position, 44°22'N et 7°43'E. Il repoussa la carte et la règle, se redressa et cria un juron. Une injure terrible en serbe.

> [He bent over a sea chart, lined up the Cras ruler and, for the third time in three days, circled in pencil the same location, 44°22'N et 7°43'E. He pushed away the map and the ruler, sat up and swore loudly. A foul curse word in Serbian.] (184)

By confirming his boat's immobility, the map and navigational tools propel Vic's state of nervous tension into violence, the verbal irruption of his Serbian self. The latitude and longitude refer to a spot in the Mediterranean Sea below Entrarque, Italy, where Vic has slaughtered a man for having informed him of 5,000 Serbian deaths from bombings by the "Alliance." "Il avait aussi parlé d'une immense indifférence des peuples de l'Occident pour les souffrances du peuple serbe. . . . Si Belgrade, mon Ithaque à moi, était détruite, je n'avais plus où aller. Sauf à Nice" [He had also spoken of the Westerners' immense indifference to the suffering of the Serbian people. If Belgrade, my own Ithaca, had been destroyed, I would have had nowhere to go. Except Nice] (201–2). The Southern French city returns as the mythical counterpart to Belgrade—and as the cartographic center of the new post-apocalyptic world.

In Chapter 5, we saw that power-hungry Dr. Niaize externalizes his Napoleonic hopes for world conquest from his headquarters on the well-named rue Bonaparte. Let us look once again at the series of maps that extend his delusional empire outward from the center: "Un plan de Nice agrandi, une photo satellite de la région, une carte de France et une mappemonde couvraient un mur entier. Chaque document était surchargé de signaux, de flèches, de croix dessinés au feutre de différentes couleurs" [An enlarged map of Nice, a satellite photo of the region, a map of France, and a world map covered the entire wall. Each document was filled with notes, arrows, crosses drawn with different colored markers] (228). We find here an uncanny echo of Dantec's evil Eva, with her own territorial ambitions extending beyond Europe. In Dr. Niaize's case, the quest for mastery depends on a deterritorialized Europe that has lost all national and rational borders.

In response to a collapse of territorial order, both crime novelists turn to an oceanic nonspace in their novel's dénouements: *La Sirène rouge* ends with a dramatic chase scene on two boats (Eva's and Toorop's) in the coastal waters off Portugal, while Radoman's trilogy ends with Vic Toar realizing that his memory of a mythic voyage through uncharted seas was actually just a schizophrenic screen for what he had actually done, which was to return to the Balkans and carry out a series of atrocities on countless victims. "Il faudra l'admettre, nous étions bien au Kosovo, et non pas à Ithaque, et nous y avons commis des choses abominables" [It couldn't be denied, we were actually in Kosovo, not Ithaca, and there we had done abominable things] (288). The violence of his Balkan self has broken through the psychic borders of his mind, just as the Danube threatened to devour southern

France and just as the cataclysm of Serbian violence had actually, it turns out, crashed across the frontiers of civilization, bringing down the entirety of Western Europe. The sea in Radoman is no supermodern "non-lieu," in Augé's sense of a State-controlled transit space; rather, it serves as an illusion of timelessness, of a mythic return to a pre-catastrophic era, a pause in the narrator's confrontations with (his own and Europe's) brutality and dissolution.

But it is also a "non-space" in the sense of a wrinkle or fold in the continent's map. For the Mediterranean Sea, which actually separates Southern France from its Eastern neighbors, loses its comforting function of separation; it is figuratively "devoured" by the blood-soaked waters of the Balkan lands, allowing Belgrade and Nice to be conflated as equivalent sites of disaster. Near the end of Radoman's novel, Vic asks, "Le cauchemar qui se déroulait sous le soleil éteint de la Côte d'Azur était-il une simple réplique de celui de Kosovo?" [Was this nightmare that was unfolding under the dull sun of the Côte d'Azur simply a *réplique* of the one in Kosovo?] (266). Again, as in Dantec, we have the word "réplique," rich with connotation: "une réplique" is a copy, a reply, a response, a retort, a counter-attack, an aftershock, a replica—a viral and violent replication on Western Europe's cartographic body of the Balkans' disturbing disintegration.

In Dantec's *La Sirène Rouge* and Radoman's trilogy, then, the Balkans become a shadow-space whose cartographic fragmentation directly threatens French identity, as its contoured maplines fall victim to the figural terrors of cyber-technology and globalized crime. More generally, these authors' 1990s *néo-polar* explorations of rhizomatic networks and schizoid criminal splits belong to a larger entropic tendency that extends into the post-9/11 world of violence, a world crisscrossed by networks so radically globalized that it no longer makes any sense to distinguish between crime and terrorism or to discuss identity in terms of nation-states. In order to explore that exploded "nonspace," let us turn to Dantec's 1999 *Babylon Babies*. Although that novel was written before the 9/11 attacks of 2001, it proposes a postmodern topography that goes beyond globalization and into interplanetary, cybernetic, psychic, and neuromolecular territories. Using Deleuze and Guattari's notions of schizoanalytic cartography, *Babylon Babies* undercuts the very possibility of mapping criminal terrain that had served as the fundamental epistemological condition for the modern detective novel from Poe to 2000.[17] In a way, it is the ultimate anti-"crime novel," bursting out of national, individual, and generic boundaries while reflecting on the traces of the *policier* genre.

Schizocartographies of Crime: *Babylon Babies*

Maurice Dantec dedicated *Babylon Babies* to Philip K. Dick, Gilles Deleuze, and Donna Haraway, as well as to a number of scientists, cyberneticists, punk rock musicians, and editors of Gallimard's Série noire.[18] The plot of this 719-page "cyberpunk" novel begins in 2013 when Hugo Cornelius Toorop, the tough mercenary veteran of the Bosnian conflict whom we have met in *La Sirène rouge*, accepts a mission to accompany a young woman named Marie Zorn from Kazakhstan to Montreal, where he will be paid to protect her from the violent attacks of Siberian mafiosos, postmillenarian cult leaders, mad scientists, and motorcycle gangs. Why is Marie Zorn so valuable? It takes a few hundred pages, but we learn that this young schizophrenic woman of French-Canadian descent is pregnant—and what she carries in her womb seems at first to be a biological weapon (a "schizo-virus" that spreads schizophrenia to the population), then possibly a transgenetically mutated animal in the DNA-strand form of a double serpent, but are actually cloned human twins who will usher in a whole new world—a post-human, post-individual world whose vision of networked unitary knowledge combines the Deleuzian human-machine with the shamanistic myth of the Cosmic Serpent. Marie Zorn is aware of the cosmic importance of her role as the New Eve of the dawning world Dantec sees growing out of the post-Tower of Babel, postmodern condition of multilingualism, its fragmentation, chaos, and conflict. As with the Genesis story, Dantec's novel is filled with destruction: from the bomb blast that turns a Montreal apartment tower to rubble, to the political dissolution of national territories, to the fragmented sense of self that our "hero" Toorop experiences as psychosis when he meets an ectoplasmic ghost who speaks to him in dozens of languages at one time. Out of that babble is born a new neural network of transnational communication; and Toorop ends up realizing that the so-called scattering of the schizophrenic subject is actually a trans-individual network of polyglot unity—that Marie Zorn combines in her own womb and mind all the globe's identities and languages. Even though she is biologically feminine, the polymorphous Marie serves as transhistorical junction point for dead male Indian chiefs and Venetian polyglots from the sixteenth century. In the twenty-first century, Marie is inextricably linked to "Joe-Jane," a post-gender artificial intelligence who speaks through various bodies and machines in long prophetic passages.

Midway through the novel, a violent clash destroys the Montreal apartment building where Toorop had brought Marie Zorn for protection. When Toorop awakens, wounded, from that apocalyptic attack, Marie has disappeared, and he has been brought to a new apartment-Tower, higher than the last one. This place is a new Babylon, complete with hanging gardens and polyglot inhabitants—but as Toorop discovers, it is no ordinary apartment building. This is, we are told, the First Autonomous Post-Human Territory, a home to the creatures of biocybernetic experimentation—biologically born humans with robotic limbs and organs as well as robot machines programmed to replicate human emotions and actions, including jealousy, copulation, and even suicide. The cyborg language comes through to Toorop as confused babble at first, but as he spends more time living (and in one case, having sex with) these biocybernetic beings, he becomes more and more connected to the universal logo-matrix embodied by Marie Zorn and Joe-Jane. By the end of the novel, the evil leader of an interplanetary millennial cult is dead and Toorop has fully connected through neurovisualization psychotechnologies with the fertile Marie Zorn. She is destined to die in childbirth, but not before having "libéré" the network of cosmic knowledge through her writing. That knowledge will live on in the form of her healthy twins, two girls of omniscient consciousness whom Toorop agrees to adopt, thus becoming the nonbiological father to the post-individual humanity of the future.

For Lawrence R. Schehr, the complex plot of *Babylon Babies* pertains to Dantec's generally "dark and dire" vision of apocalyptic neural networks and viral replication.[19] At the heart of this dark vision, writes Schehr, is the "dissolution of the male subject"—a violent fragmentation, morselization, *sparagmos* of the self, in which Dantec's cyborgian sci-fi universe brings death and destruction to individuals, replacing them with a threatening and evil collectivity. The emphasis here is on the negative side of Dantec's recurring motifs of Babylon and Babel, which Schehr connects to the destruction on 9/11 of the Twin Towers in New York City.[20] In his 1985 essay on translation, entitled "Des tours de Babel," Jacques Derrida reminds us that the Biblical story from Genesis, in which God destroys the Tower in Shinar and scatters its builders across the earth, is a story of language, of a violent shift from monolingual unity to multilingual confusion.[21] But the notion of linguistic discord as trauma relies, wrote Derrida, on an origin myth of unity in which God alone retains the power of speech as creation. Once we liberate ourselves from that origin-myth, we can think of multilingualism not only in negative terms as mere replication, repetition, and babbling confusion, but also as a new way to create—one that escapes the castrating eye of the Divine Creator and so allows a scattering of seed to bear new (sometimes monstrous) fruit across an ever-shifting network of language. With that multilingual fertility in mind, we might re-think Schehr's reading of Dantec's fiction not only in terms of waning masculinity but also in terms of new fictional alternatives to biological reproduction. *Babylon Babies* in particular explores the question of creation after destruction, by transposing the sexual and textual ambiguities of the Tower of Babel myth onto a cybernetic world of the near future. Indeed, one might take Dantec's novel as narrating the radical disempowerment of its virile protagonist in order to imagine the liberatory possibilities for that dissolution of the phallic self. In other words: yes, the phallic male subject has been dispersed and has lost his authoritative powers, but at his novel's end, Dantec fictionally re-plugs him into a translinguistic network or "neuromatrix" of textual and post-sexual reproduction.

But more specifically, and more directly relevant to this study, that dissolution of the phallic self manifests itself also through the novel's self-referential narrativization of the eclipse of the *roman policier*'s mastering protagonist: the male detective. If Hugo Cornélius Toorop was the tough hero of *La Sirène rouge,* successfully navigating young Alice out of danger in the 1993 novel, he loses all footholds of authority, orientation, and power in the world of *Babylon Babies* (published in 1999, but set futuristically in 2013). A mercenary killer in war zones too complex to comprehend, Toorop tries (along with the reader) to understand the various agents affecting a criss-crossing network of military, paramilitary, and civilian actions. As he marches through Kyrgyzstan's Terskey Alatau range, he distracts himself at nightfall by glancing at a few pages of a Russian-language newspaper, in which sports commentary rubs elbows with true crime:

> L'autre page traitait essentiellement de faits divers et d'affaires criminelles. Un serial killer sévissait dans la région de Krasnoïarsk, en deux petites années, il avait tué et dépecé une bonne dizaine de jeunes femmes, laissant à chaque fois les cadavres à proximité d'un poste de police, ou d'un service administratif.

[On the next page, it was basically local news and crime reports.
A serial killer was brutalizing victims in the Krasnoïarsk region; in
two short years, he had killed and dismembered ten or so young
women, leaving their bodies each time near a police station or
administrative agency.] (95)

Appearing near the start, as does the *fait divers* that announces the murders
of the Rue Morgue to Dupin in Poe's 1841 tale, this news story of a serial killer's grotesque exploits would seem to readers of crime fiction exactly the type
of narrative trigger that would set Toorop off on a crime-solving quest. Instead, however, our protagonist continues flipping through the newspaper's
pages with anything but reasoning lucidity; he has medicated himself with a
sleeping drug skin patch and drifts to sleep before awakening to continue the
journey whose psychotropic effects leave him moving through the mountains
like a "machine vivante." (96) After reading the *fait divers* about the serial killer
who chops his victims into pieces, Toorop glances at two more items: one about
a Russian federal police investigation into the mysterious explosion of a private business jet, and the other about an apparently mafia-related apartment
fire. What these three news stories have in common is the theme of dispersal,
dismemberment, disaggregation.

Much later in the novel, the three seemingly unrelated events are connected to the near-apocalyptic forces of destruction at work across the globe
and into other planets, but it is not through any real investigative acumen on
the part of Toorop that branches of the enormous network of criminal, military, mafia, activist, political, scientific, and terrorist activity are exposed.
In fact, our protagonist is bounced around the globe by forces beyond his
control and understanding; along with Marie Zorn and other members of
his team, Toorop is subjected to the same entropic, explosive forces glimpsed
in the newspaper's *faits divers*.

Unable to comprehend the trans-individual, techno-biological constellation of agents at work around him, this tough-guy adventurer who solved the
mysteries of *La Sirène rouge* feels completely out of his element: "Toorop se
dit que du rocambolesque, on passait à la science-fiction" [Torop told himself
that things were moving beyond the rocambolesque and into Sci Fi territory]
(108). Unlike Ponson du Terrail's Rocambole, who remains the focal point of
the 1857–1871 adventure series even as he transitions from juvenile delinquent
to mastermind, Toorop is displaced from the narrative center for much of the
increasingly fragmented second part of the novel. He is certainly no Dupin

or Sherlock Holmes: Toorop's many attempts to deduce who is in power or what Marie Zorn is carrying in her womb turn out to be dead ends and red herrings, with the truth revealed by circumstances beyond his control. One reason for this is that Toorop relies on outdated investigative methods like unfolding paper maps on a kitchen table and researching Marie's past through public on-line university libraries: "Mais ça ne le conduisait que vers d'autres ramifications, au cœur d'un labyrinthe dont il ne saisissait aucunement la topographie" [But all this did was lead him toward other branchings, at the heart of a labyrinth whose topography he couldn't at all understand] (299).

As this phrase suggests, the transition from masculine hero to post-individual network is figured throughout the novel as a loss of cartographic mastery. From the very start, Dantec's narration disorients both Toorop and the reader. The action begins *in medias res* in the Taklamakan desert of Northwest China, near the Tchinguiz steppes, with Toorop the mercenary soldier engaging in what appear to be skirmishes of various territorial wars. The conflicts involve a confusing number of interested parties, from the Ouïghor guérilleros to Russian and Kirghizistani smugglers, Kazakh mafiosos, Islamic fundamentalists, Chinese dissidents, Turkestani liberation forces, Tibetan guerrillas, Manchu independence fighters, and Inner Mongolia secessionists. The theme of schizophrenia appears in a discreet verbal hint in the first pages, when Toorop pulls out his assault weapon, a Russion "schiskov"; at this point, the text splits itself off into a footnote to explain that the weapon's nickname was given by the Moudjahidin Afghans. The "schiskov" is linked metonymically to the deterritorializing effects of globalized capitalism, as in the first pages we encounter British-trained Kazakhstanis who employ decoding technologies made in underground Sichuan factories, paid for with funds of the Japanese organized crime syndicate Yakuza. As he hikes through the Chinese steppes, the Balkan-born Toorop himself holds French-made grenades and Kool cigarettes packaged in Peking, which he plans to trade for Indian Camels or Russian Marlboros (21–22). Manufactured objects and human subjects are displaced across the vast logistical field of what Paul Virilio identifies as the dromocratic time-space: "The countryside, the earth is henceforth given over, definitively consecrated to war by the cosmopolitan mass of workers, an army of laborers speaking every language, the Babel of logistics."[22]

Like a twenty-first century Fabrice at Waterloo, Toorop is deprived of any mastering overview that would allow him to comprehend the big picture of these military and para-military conflicts. Even in the flashbacks to the 1990s ex-Yugoslavia, Toorop yearns for a cartographic mastery of the scene—as evidenced by his desire for the modern *carte d'état-major*:[23]

> Il avait envie de voir les cartes d'état-major. Il avait envie de comprendre les mécanismes stratégiques qui avaient œuvré, invisibles, tandis qu'il courait sous la mitraille.
>
> [He wanted to see the ordnance survey map. He wanted to comprehend the strategic mechanisms that had been invisibly at work while he was running through shellfire.] (32)

But when Toorop does succeed in acquiring a series of maps that illustrate the shifting fronts of combat, their complexity and divergence from his lived experience only frustrate him desperately. Perspectival mastery comes no closer in the narrative present of the Chinese steppes. Toorop studies military strategy manuals and Sun Tzu's *L'Art de la guerre*, doing his best to understand "la coordination opérationnelle et stratégique" of the different warring elements (44). But as he traces a map of China in the sand, adding arrows to indicate the multiple vectors of assault, the design ends up looking like nothing but a monstrous animal (45). Cartographic coherence is also the unreachable fantasy of another character, the corrupt Russian minister of foreign affairs, Romanenko. He has acquired a war simulation computer software program, "Kriegspiel" that holds centuries of military history and creates "une carte vivante des conflits présélectionnés par l'utilisateur humain" [a map of conflicts preselected by the human user] so that he can visualize the conflicts as a co-ordinated "état-major virtuel" (77, 81). But the shifting and disordered army positions at the borders resist his machinic mastery and, in the end, entropy wins out again as Romanenko is shot to pieces.

In the first part of the novel, Toorop clings to notions of mapped mastery, as when he asks Romanenko for an operational map of the terrain in order to plan an escape route with Marie Zorn from Kazakhstan to Montreal. When Romanenko skeptically asks why, Toorop responds with (deluded) confidence about his own centrality to and control of the mission: "Pour que vous me montriez toutes les possibilités en question. Je suis le responsable opérationnel" [So that you can show me all available possibilities. I am in charge of operations] (141). Just as he had done in *La Sirène rouge*, Toorop consults an actual paper roadmap, as he navigates through sixteen hundred kilometers of chaos with a female protectee in the car; "Ils venaient de passer le

Balkhach, ils n'allaient pas tarder à sortir de la grand-route pour prendre la piste coloriée en rouge sur la carte que tenait Toorop sur ses genoux" [They'd just passed Balkhach, it wouldn't be long before they would pull off the highway to take the road colored in red on the map on Toorop's lap] (145). But Dantec's text indicates quickly to the reader the roadmap's obsolescence, through the playful juxtaposition—within two pages—of Toorop's "carte" to newer technologies that go by the same name: the embedded "carte à puce" [computer chip], the airplane boarding-pass "carte d'embarquement," and the virtual "carte technique de l'avion" through which one reserves seats on the plane. Without fully realizing it, Toorop is entering a much more complex world in which the old-school networks of black market drugs and weapons are superseded by the clandestine trafficking across "zones frontalières" of mutant animal species, clones, genomically altered humans, and Deleuzian "schizoma chines" that traverse biological and technological categories of distinction.

With a whole new world comes a whole new kind of cartography. Marie Zorn's consciousness, from her adolescent psychotic visions of extraterrestrial kidnapping to the guided hallucinations that mark her adult entry into networks that transcend a unitary conception of the self, is described in terms of maps:

Puis elle se diffracta dans une galaxie de tunnels fulgurants, qui tracèrent la carte d'un cerveau à l'échelle de l'univers. Elle était ce quasar balbutiant, ce big-bang psycho; la sensation/connaissance désormais bien connue, *le corps sans organe, devint cartographie structurale de sa propre neurologie,* elle était son propre cerveau, ce réseau de neurones que déployait son corps cosmique dans l'espace-machine de ce rêve dont elle savait qu'il n'était pas le sien.

[Then she was diffracted into a galaxy of shooting tunnels that traced the map of a brain on the scale of the universe. She was this infant quasar, this psycho big bang; that soon to be well-known sensation-consciousness, the body without organs; she became the structural cartography of her own neurology, she was her own mind, this network of neurons unfurled by her cosmic body into the space-machine of this dream that she knew wasn't her own.] (170)

Dantec is using here the Deleuzian language of schizoanalytic cartography, as Marie becomes a body-without-organs, unlimited by the physical time-space grids of socio-political geography. Through this new cartography, Marie can

navigate the infinite strata of human (sub)consciousness and history, plugging
into alternate identities, from a Native American warrior to the biomechani-
cal "schizomatrix" of Joe-Jane.

Some shadowy scientists in the novel have figured out how to *cartographier* Marie's genetic code to detect her schizophrenic anomaly through the
hallucinogenic neuronal and transgenetic viral biotechnologies that mark this
new-world terrain (332–34). But not Toorop. Even after the reader has surfed
with Marie her multidimensional visions, we find Toorop trying to orient himself in the old mode: "Il déplia une carte de la ville sur la table de la cuisine et
traça au Stabilo le trajet à suivre" [He unfolded a city map onto the kitchen
table and traced out the planned route with a magic marker] (188). It's no use,
of course. The fragmentary world-view will eventually force Toorop to abandon his two-dimensional cartography. But the realization comes slowly. Two
hundred pages in, he accepts that the contours of the nation-state model no
longer apply: "A ce que Toorop comprenait, les vieux clivages politico-culturels
s'étaient évanouis comme des mirages au-dessus du nouveau désert de l'univers"
[Toorop was starting to see that the old politico-cultural rifts had faded away
like mirages above the new desert of the universe] (233). But it is only much
later (in Part III, "Amerika on Ice") that he is able fully to enter the new world
space, guided by the hallucinated phantom of Ari Moskiewicz, who had—
ironically—been the mapmaker and Toorop's mentor in *La Sirène rouge*. At
this point, Toorop has been rendered unconscious by the violent blast that
destroyed the Montreal apartment building where he'd been protecting Marie Zorn; he has no idea where she or the rest of his team may be, nor can he
explain how his hallucinated self can be walking the streets of the Canadian
city in the company of his friend who had died a decade earlier in Australia.
Ari, the "vieux routier," is no longer giving him maps to follow on the highways of Europe; he is now the spectral angel-guide of a different sort of
"trip," in which Toorop enters an undefined time-space of gradual, glimpsed
enlightenment: "Le monde n'était plus qu'un voile brumeux, Ari lui-même
une structure diaphane, spectrale, un nuage de gaz ectoplasmique qui se di-
latait lentement dans l'habitacle" [The world was nothing but a veil of mist,
and Ari himself just a diaphanous, spectral shape, a cloud of ectoplasmic gas-
ses slowly dilating in the passenger compartment] (437). Whereas in *La
Sirène Rouge* Toorop was in the driver's seat of Alice's flight to safety, in
Babylon Babies he is separated from Marie Zorn, who drives herself up the
Northern Coast of Canada along the "routes du futur" that open up from the
North American highway into dizzying, three-dimensional space: "Au bout

d'un moment elle avait vu le ciel s'ouvrir devant elle, l'autoroute s'était dédoublée, puis ramifiée en un réseau de béton aux dimensions infinies. Chaque embranchement conduisait à une des étoiles du ciel" [At one point she had seen the sky open ahead of her, the highway had split in two, then branched out into a concrete network of infinite dimension. Each branch led to one of the stars in the sky] (442).

When Toorop awakens, wounded, from his hallucinatory voyage, the first image invoked is one of mapping: "Enfin une cartographie cohérente apparut, avant même que ne surgissent quelques formes à peine distinctes derrière le voile tendu entre lui et les objets" [Finally a coherent cartography appeared, even before some barely visible forms began to arise behind the veil that separated him from the objects of the world] (485). But this is no color-coded map of his location on a city grid; finally, with the help of the spectral Ari, Toorop has entered into the new schizocartographic space of the human animal-machine or body-without-organs: "La cartographie conscience-sensation était formelle. Sa main était une machine" [The consciousness-sensation cartography was clear. His hand was a machine] (486). Toorop's shattered hand has been replaced by a bionic prosthetic and it is at this point, in a section entitled "Homo sapiens neuromatrix," that Toorop enters the "premier Territoire Post-Humain Autonome" of biocybernetic experimentation (504). Here, Toorop allows himself to meld into the other, as when he has sex with a cyborg (a biologically born woman embedded with various machinic grafts and hologram decorations); their union is also described in terms of a new cartography, one that has nothing to do with Cartesian mind/body or self/other distinctions of the perspectival grid: "Ils s'étaient enlacés et embrassés en silence, commençant à tracer leurs cartographies corporelles-mutuelles." [They embraced and intertwined in silence, starting to trace their mutual-body mappings] (519).

In the novel's climactic final scenes, Toorop accepts his own marginalization and allows his mind to be plugged through a neurovisualization transmittor into Marie Zorn's consciousness as she journeys into the northern reaches of Canada just before giving birth. He follows her, psychically and virtually, as she encounters apocalyptic rains that force her from her car and leave her clinging to an ancient, rhizomatic tree:

L'arbre aux racines mises à nu et lavées par la pluie formait un nouveau diagramme, ... Déconnecté de son lieu d'origine, *déterritorialisé* par le flot chaotique des éléments. . . .

[The tree, whose roots had been exposed and washed by rain, formed a new diagram. Disconnected from its birthplace, *deterritorialized* by the chaotic flow of the elements, . . .] (567, emphasis in text)

Toorop's own deterritorialization is subordinated to Marie's Christic sacrifice, as she realizes that she will have to die in the storm in order to give birth to a new post-human race. (Dantec's adult conversion to conservative Catholicism is evident in the symbolism here as well as in a fantasy passage about the floating souls of aborted fetuses.)[24] Toorop has no primary control over the outcome, as he is guided by the neuromatrix Joe-Jane in a simultaneous vision experience of Marie's journey. Again, the mastering terms of cartographic science are turned to radically new use, as Toorop is oriented in virtual space by Joe-Jane: "je vais le guider droit sur la zone en positionnant les pointeurs de son néocortex dans la bonne direction, il n'ira pas se perdre à l'autre bout de la galaxie" [I'm going to guide him straight into the zone by positioning his neocortex pointers in the right direction so he won't get lost at the other end of the galaxy] (583). And: "Lorsque la neuromatrice sera revenue de son voyage à elle, elle aura vu une fenêtre sur le futur, et elle ramènera sûrement des coordonnées topographiques de premier ordre" [As soon as the neuromatrix comes back from her own voyage, she will have seen a window into the future and she will surely bring back first-rate topographic coordinates] (588). This is no carte *d'état-major*, no totalizing, globalizing, and dominating *mappemonde* of the sort we saw in *La Sirène rouge* or in Radoman's *6, rue Bonaparte. Babylon Babies* announces a new world order of trans-individual dispersal that has no place for the reasoning, male detective who had anchored the *policier* genre for over a century. At the end of Dantec's 1999 novel, Toorop—once the musclebound hero of the *néo-polar*—becomes, basically, a nanny. He adopts Marie Zorn's twin baby girls with the awareness that he will never fully understand their superior consciousness and that they represent an end to human centrality on the universe's map: "Les jumelles . . . étaient l'explosif divin et fatal qui raierait l'humanité de la carte" [The twins were the divine and fatal explosive that would strike mankind off the map] (717). An end to cartography; an end to humanity; an end, perhaps, to crime? An end to crime fiction?

*   *   *

In the chapters of this book, I have emphasized the ways scientific discourse intersects with the representational rifts and fissures in the national terrain of France. From the geological turbulence under the modern space of Second Empire Paris to the deterritorialized networks of twenty-first-century cyberpunk fiction, we have seen the cut of (political and personal) violence increasingly dispel the illusions of cartographic coherence and mapping mastery. And yet, while an author like Dantec is spinning his hero off into the starry *réseaux* of postmodern and posthuman time-space, Gallica's Série Noire continues to publish hundreds of detective novels and hardboiled thrillers; the *New York Times Book Review* continues to devote a weekly section to crime fiction; mystery novels from Sweden to Chile continue to make the best-seller lists all over the globe; writers continue to add new twists to the detective model (blind investigators, lesbian cops, housebound psychics); and fictional crime stories continue to evoke for readers the regional specificity of locations from high-tech Hong Kong to regional villages in the badlands of South America.

These variations are still being explored, even as the world's territories shape-shift and cartography enters a new age of virtual possibilities. What global crime fiction has inherited from Poe's rue Morgue and the long French tradition from 1860s *feuilletons* to today's *néo-polars* is a spatial imaginary that anchors formal tensions between reason and disorder in the violently cracked terrains of home, city, and nation.

NOTES

PROLOGUE: POE

1. Laura Lee Downs and Stéphane Gerson, eds., *Why France? American Historians Reflect on an Enduring Fascination* (Ithaca, N.Y.: Cornell University Press, 2006). Citations from "The Murders in the Rue Morgue" are from *The Selected Writings of Edgar Allan Poe*, ed. G. R. Thompson (New York: Norton, 2004).

2. The story's original title was "The Murders in the Rue Trianon-Bas"; Poe crossed out that street name to replace it with "Morgue." In his 1943 study of Poe's manuscript, Ernest Boll writes that readers in France found the new title overly literal, but that "upon English-speaking readers the French phrase has the primary effect of a macabre figure of speech and profoundly deepens the emotional suggestiveness of the original title with a chill of horrible anticipation." "The Manuscript of *The Murders in the Rue Morgue* and Poe's Revisions," *Modern Philology* 40, 4 (1943): 302–15, 305. The transatlantic Anglo-French crisscrossings continue to this day: see Pierre Verdaguer, "Borrowed Settings: Frenchness in Anglo-American Detective Fiction," *Yale French Studies* 108 (hereafter, *YFS 108*) Special Issue on "Crime Fictions," ed. Andrea Goulet and Susanna Lee (2005): 146–59. See also Pim Higginson, *The Noir Atlantic: Chester Himes and the Birth of the Francophone African Crime Novel* (Liverpool: Liverpool University Press, 2011). Higginson's identification of Chester Himes as the inspiration for twentieth-century French African fiction serves as a fascinating reminder of early America's own postcolonial status in relation to the production of a literary genre that cuts across high/low distinctions.

3. Jules Verne also pointed out the inexactitude of Poe's urban descriptions: "Edgard Poë [sic] ne semble pas avoir visité Paris, dont il décrit inexactement certaines rues dans l'une de ses Nouvelles." Verne, *Edgar Allan Poe et ses œuvres* (Reims: Éditions à l'Écart, 1978), 2.

4. See G. R. Thompson's Introduction to the Norton Critical Edition of Poe's writings: "Edgar A. Poe: An American Life (1809–1849)," in *The Selected Writings of Edgar Allan Poe*. See also Jeffrey Meyers, *Edgar Allan Poe: His Life and Legacy* (New York: Scribner's, 1992), 38, in which he cites Alexandre Dumas, "Account of a Visit by Poe to Paris," *Saturday Review of Literature* 6 (December 21, 1929): 594–95.

5. 2,500 copies of *La Gazette des tribunaux* and over 22,000 copies of *La Presse* were printed in 1846. C. Belanger, J. Godechot, P. Guiral, and F. Terrou, eds., *Histoire générale de la presse française*, vol. 2, *De 1815 à 1871* (Paris: PUF, 1969), 146. For more on the important context of the nineteenth-century popular press, see Anne-Marie Thiesse, *Le Roman du quotidien: Lecteurs et lectures populaires à la belle époque* (Paris: Chemin Vert, 1984); and Dominique Kalifa, Philippe Régnier, Marie-Ève Thérenty, and Alain Vaillant, eds., *La Civilisation du journal: Histoire culturelle et littéraire de la presse française au XIXe siècle* (Paris: Nouveau Monde, 2011).

6. Eugène François Vidocq's ghostwritten memoirs, published in 1828 with the support of Hugo, Dumas, and Balzac (who based the character Vautrin on Vidocq), are available through the Bibliothèque Nationale de France, http://gallica.bnf.fr/ark:/12148/bpt6k510007 .notice.

7. On the "glocal" characteristic of contemporary crime fiction, see Marieke Krajenbrink and Kate M. Quinn, eds., *Investigating Identities: Questions of Identity in Contemporary International Crime Fiction* (Amsterdam: Rodopi, 2009), especially Eva Erdmann's "Nationality International: Detective Fiction in the Late Twentieth Century," 11–26. See also Claire Gorrara, *French Crime Fiction* (Cardiff: University of Wales Press, 2009), 3: "It is [the] notion of the intersection of the global and the local that is one of the most persistent markers of European crime traditions into the twenty-first century, highlighting the myriad ways in which regional cultures and traditions are being slowly but irresistibly eroded by the growing internationalization of commerce and crime."

8. Dominique Kalifa, *Naissance de la police privée: Détectives et agences de recherches en France, 1832–1942* (Paris: Plon, 2000); and Clive Emsley and Haia Shpayer-Makov, eds., *Police Detectives in History, 1750–1950* (Aldershot: Ashgate, 2006).

9. See Laura Otis, *Membranes: Metaphors of Invasion in Nineteenth-Century Literature, Science, and Politics* (Baltimore: Johns Hopkins University Press, 2000); Ronald R. Thomas, "The Fingerprint of the Foreigner: Colonizing the Criminal Body in 1890s Detective Fiction and Criminal Anthropology," *ELH* 61, 3 (Fall 1994): 655–83; Nanette Fornabai, "Criminal Factors: *Fantômas*, Anthropometrics, and the Numerical Fictions of Modern Criminal Identity," *YFS 108*, 60–73; Oliver Gaycken, *Devices of Curiosity: Cinema and the Scientific Vernacular* (Oxford: Oxford University Press, 2015); Andrea Goulet, "South Sea Daggers and the Dead Man's Eye: Foreign Invasion in Fin-de-Siècle Fictions," *Cahiers Victoriens et Edouardiens* 61 (April 2005): 317–33; and Andrea Goulet, "Curiosity's Killer Instinct: Bibliophilia and the Myth of the Rational Detective," *YFS 108*: 48–59.

10. Fereydoun Hoveyda, "D'Archimède à Arsène Lupin en passant par le Juge Ti," *Histoire du roman policier* (Paris: Pavillon, 1965); and for a more nuanced discussion of the classical roots of the modern genre, Page Dubois, "Œdipus as Detective: Sophocles, Simenon, Robbe-Grillet," *YFS 108*: 102–15.

11. Marc Lits, *Le Roman policier: Introduction à la théorie et à l'histoire d'un genre* (Liège: Céfal, 1999); Jacques Dubois, *Le Roman policier ou la modernité* (Paris: Armand Colin, 2006); and David Platten, *The Pleasures of Crime: Reading Modern French Crime Fiction* (Amsterdam: Rodopi, 2011).

12. Bruno Latour, *The Pasteurization of France*, trans. Alan Sheridan and John Law (Cambridge, Mass.: Harvard University Press, 1988).

13. Kevin J. Hayes, "Mrs. Gore and 'The Murders in the Rue Morgue,'" *Notes and Queries* 58, 1 (March 2011), 85–87.

14. Thomas Cragin, *Murder in Parisian Streets: Manufacturing Crime and Justice in the Popular Press, 1830–1900* (Lewisburg, Pa.: Bucknell University Press, 2006).

15. The trope of an urban forest appears, for example, in Honoré de Balzac's *Les Chouans* (1829), Alexandre Dumas's *Les Mohicans de Paris* (1854–9), Victor Hugo's *Les Misérables* (1862), and Paul Féval's *Jean Diable* (1862) and *Les Habits noirs* (1863).

16. See Robert A. Nye, *Crime, Madness, and Politics in Modern France: The Medical Concept of National Decline* (Princeton, N.J.: Princeton University Press, 1984); and, on the Anglo-American tradition, Ronald R. Thomas, *Detective Fiction and the Rise of Forensic Science* (London: Cambridge University Press, 1999).

17. In 1856, the Frères Goncourt declared Poe's work to be something critics had never before encountered, a "new literary world" and early harbinger of the twentieth century (cited in Dubois, *Le Roman policier ou la modernité*, 38). Gaboriau, father of French detective fiction, explicitly acknowledged his debt to the American; and Barbey d'Aurevilly identified the analytical approach as "[l']originalité vraie d'Edgar Poe." See Léon Lemonnier, "Edgar Poe et les origines du roman policier," *Mercure de France*, 15 octobre 1925, and Lemonnier, *Edgar Poe et la critique française de 1845 à 1875* (Paris: PUF, 1928), 151. Later, Pierre Véry shuffled chronology in his Holy Trinity of detective fiction: "Gaboriau is the father of the detective novel, Edgar Poe, the son and G. K. Chesterton, the Holy Spirit. We owe everything to Gaboriau." Cited in Roger Bonniot, *Émile Gaboriau ou la naissance du roman policier* (Paris: Vrin, 1984), 443. Gaboriau's admiring biographer Bonniot concedes that Poe was an innovator of the *roman policier* form, but adds that Poe's algebraic dryness and lack of material "fonds" keeps him from being the true inventor of the genre (*Émile Gaboriau*, 165).

18. See the Introduction to Jean-Claude Farcy, Dominique Kalifa and Jean-Noël Luc, eds., *L'Enquête judiciaire en Europe au XIXe siècle: Acteurs, imaginaires, pratiques* (Paris: Créaphis, 2007).

19. James, Clive. "Blood on the Borders: Crime fiction from all over," *New Yorker*, April 9, 2007.

20. David Geherin, *Scene of the Crime: The Importance of Place in Crime and Mystery Fiction* (Jefferson, N.C.: McFarland, 2008); Norbert Spehner, *Scènes de crimes: Enquêtes sur le roman policier contemporain* (Québec: Alire, 2007); and Nina King et al., *Crimes of the Scene: A Mystery Novel Guide for the International Traveler* (New York: St. Martin's, 1997). See also Gary Hausladen, "Where the Bodies Lie: Sense of Place and Police Procedurals," *Journal of Cultural Geography* 16, 1 (Fall/Winter 1996): 45–64. Stephen Knight's *Crime Fiction, 1800–2000: Detection, Death, Diversity* (New York: Palgrave Macmillan, 2004) includes chapters on African and American detective traditions. The split between mental abstraction and corporeality is not limited to the Western sphere; see, for example, Yoshikuni Igarashi, "Edogawa Rampo and the Excess of Vision: An Ocular Critique of Modernity in 1920s Japan," *positions* 13, 2 (Fall 2005): 299–327.

21. Michel de Certeau, *The Practice of Everyday Life*, ed. Steven Rendall (Berkeley: University of California Press, 1984), 92–93.

22. While proposing that the imbrication of textuality and architecture is to be found in all literature, Philippe Hamon nevertheless highlights two genres as exemplary: "The two literary genres that were, by all accounts, first 'invented' in the nineteenth century—the detective story (Poe, Émile Gaboriau) and the prose poem (Aloysius Bertrand, Baudelaire)—both feature intricate and most often urban decors that stand out by their architectural specificity." *Expositions: Literature and Architecture in Nineteenth-Century France*, trans. Katia Sainson-Frank and Lisa Maguire (Berkeley: University of California Press, 1992), 6.

23. Boileau-Narcejac. *Le Roman policier: Essai théorique et historique sur le genre policier* (Paris: PUF, 1974).

24. Maurizio Ascari, *A Counter-History of Crime Fiction: Supernatural, Gothic, Sensational* (New York: Palgrave Macmillan, 2007), 8.

25. In Marie Bonaparte's classic Freudian reading of the *Rue Morgue*, Poe's tale works through the distorting mechanisms of the unconscious, so that the window and chimney become apertures through which the phallic ape violates the cloacal room. "Selections from the Life and Works of Edgar Allan Poe: A Psycho-Analytic Interpretation," reprinted in *Purloined Poe: Lacan, Derrida, and Psychoanalytic Reading*, ed. John P. Muller and William J. Richardson

(Baltimore: Johns Hopkins University Press, 1987), 101–32, 118–19. Rob Rushing provides a sophisticated update of Bonaparte's reading, one that takes socio-historical context into account by identifying the "prior" colonial violence of the Borneo primate's abduction from its native land and sale in Europe; through the intellectualization of the traumatic scene, the text enacts a "forgetting" of violence. *Resisting Arrest: Detective Fiction and Popular Culture* (New York: Other Press, 2007), 128.

26. David Platten in "Reading-Glasses, Guns and Robots: A History of Science in French Crime Fiction," *French Cultural Studies* 12, 36 (October 2001): 253–70, considers the use of Cartesian logic and empirical science in Gaston Leroux's *Le Mystère de la chambre jaune* (1908). See also my *Optiques: The Science of the Eye and the Birth of Modern French Crime Fiction* (Philadelphia: University of Pennsylvania Press, 2006).

27. Priestman, Martin. *Detective Fiction and Literature: The Figure on the Carpet* (London: Macmillan, 1990), 6. In this classic study, Priestman argues that the horror of the *Rue Morgue*'s grisly corpses is well-controlled, "seen" only through the mediation of newspaper clippings and therefore sublimated, abstracted. Priestman's more recent work has moved beyond this purified conception of the genre (see Ascari, *A Counter-History of Crime Fiction*, 7).

28. Martin Priestman, *Crime Fiction from Poe to the Present* (Plymouth: Northcote, 1998), 9.

29. The polar toggle between spatial abstraction and material place has imprinted not only the work of fictional detectives, but also the methodological approaches of literary critics who analyze them. In the late 1980s and early 1990s, especially, there was an apparent divide between mathematical or formal models, from the Derrida/Lacan debate reprinted in *The Purloined Poe* to John Irwin's *The Mystery to a Solution: Poe, Borges, and the Analytic Detective Story* (Baltimore: Johns Hopkins University Press, 1994) and a more historically anchored, Foucauldian line of genre criticism typified by D. A. Miller's *The Novel and the Police* (Berkeley: University of California Press, 1989). The analyses proposed in this book cut across those critical categories by attending to textual intersections between space and place, between diagrammatical thought and embodied setting.

30. In *Detective Fiction and the Rise of Forensic Science* (Cambridge: Cambridge University Press, 1999), Ronald R. Thomas connects Dupin's consultation of Cuvier to contemporary reforms in criminal law. Platten points out, however, that the use of science in Poe is a bit more ambivalent, less positivistic than Thomas's reading might suggest ("Reading-Glasses"). In "Detective Fiction, Psychoanalysis, and the Analytic Sublime," Shawn Rosenheim argues that "the description of the orangutan virtually reverses Cuvier's actual claims," in *The American Face of Edgar Allan Poe*, ed. Shawn Rosenheim and Stephen Rachman (Baltimore: Johns Hopkins University Press, 1995), 161.

31. Other critics have pointed out ways Dupin's tale undercuts its own rationalist premises. See, for example, Peter Thoms, "Poe's Dupin and the Power of Deduction," in *The Cambridge Companion to Edgar Allan Poe*, ed. Kevin J. Hayes (London: Cambridge University Press, 2002), 133, which sees Poe's texts as transgressive and productive of mystery, rather than drily resolvent. My aim is to explore this tension in relation to a post-Cartesian spatiality in scientific discourse.

32. On the importance of the postcolonial context to reading this genre, see also Pim Higginson, "Mayhem at the Crossroads: Francophone African Fiction and the Rise of the Crime Novel," *YFS 108*: 160–76; Nancy A. Harrowitz, "Criminality and Poe's Orangutan: The Question of Race in Detection," in *Agonistics: Arenas of Creative Contest*, ed. Janet Lungstrum and Elizabeth Sauer (Albany: State University of New York Press, 1997); J. Gerald Kennedy and

Liliane Weissberg, eds., *Romancing the Shadow: Poe and Race* (London: Oxford University Press, 2001); and Jon Thompson, *Fiction, Crime, and Empire: Clues to Modernity and Postmodernism* (Urbana: University of Illinois Press, 1993).

33. In her recent study of the locked room motif in Norwegian crime fiction, Anna Stenport situates *The Ice Palace* by Tarjei Vesaas in the context of experimental, international modernism associated with Paul Auster, Jorge Luis Borges, and Thomas Pynchon. But it is Poe's *Rue Morgue* that anchors Stenport's thesis: "By analyzing modes of entry and exit into the victims' apartment on a quiet back street in Paris, Dupin's analysis also affirms how a geographical context of colonialism, transnational travel, and multilingualism is part not only of nineteenth-century European modernity, but also of how a thematic emphasis on geography illuminates the function of the genre's essential narrative device of the locked room." "The Nature of Locked Rooms: Tarjei Vesaas' Novel *The Ice Palace* and Experimental Crime Fiction," *Studies of the Novel* 42, 3 (Fall 2010): 305–20.

CHAPTER I. INTRODUCTION: MAPPING MURDER

Epigraph: Franco Moretti, *Atlas of the European Novel 1800–1900* (London: Verso, 1999), 8.

1. The theoretical contours of this spatial shift are synthesized in Verena Andermatt Conley's *Spatial Ecologies: Urban Sites, State and World-Space in French Cultural Theory* (Liverpool: Liverpool University Press, 2012). I have found her book's chapters on Lefebvre, de Certeau, Baudrillard, Augé, Virilio, Deleuze and Guattari, Latour, and Balibar invaluable in crystallizing these thinkers' spatial theories in relation to the modern politics of France.

2. Edward Casey, *Representing Place: Landscape Painting and Maps* (Minneapolis: University of Minnesota Press, 2002).

3. Praising Cuvier as the greatest poet of his century, Balzac wrote in *La Peau de chagrin* (1831) of the breathtaking, vertiginous, even frightening effect of glimpsing the deep past in the underground layers below France's agricultural terrain. One might see this famous "Ode to Cuvier" as a poetic answer to the question asked much later by Yi-Fu Tuan, in *Dear Colleague: Common and Uncommon Observations* (Minneapolis: University of Minnesota Press, 2002): "Vertigo of space is common enough. Stand at the edge of a cliff and one can suddenly feel dizzy, about to fall—about to be drawn into the yawning space. Do people ever experience vertigo of time?" (2)

4. Cuvier's 1812 Preface to *Recherches sur les ossemens fossiles des quadrupèdes* presents his cataclysmic theory of torrential seas that deposit bones in cliffside geological strata. Martin Rudwick explains that "Cuvier and his mineralogist collaborator Alexandre Brongniart first worked out how to transform 'stratigraphical' piles of rock formations . . . into nature's 'documents' for tracing the sequence of events in nature's history. Cuvier and Brongniart's joint field survey of what they termed the 'Paris Basin' became the most widely admired model for turning stratigraphy into geohistory," *The New Science of Geology: Studies in the Earth Sciences in the Age of Revolution* (Aldershot: Ashgate, 2004), ix. Kenneth Taylor also provides some useful history: "Speaking strictly, there was *no* geology in 1776. The term itself had not yet been coined, at least not with the scientific meaning it was shortly to acquire. . . . only in the early nineteenth century did the word gain something approaching universal recognition and acceptance"; "the science of geology as it came to be conceived in the train of the term's invention was not a direct, lineal descendent of a more primitive eighteenth-century version of the same thing. Instead, the late eighteenth-century developments that set the stage for the emergence

of geology as a new discipline included a reordering or reorganization of the sciences, making room in a new way for a distinct science of the earth." "Geology in 1776: Some Notes on the Character of an Incipient Science," in Taylor, *The Earth Sciences in the Enlightenment: Studies on the Early Development of Geology* (Aldershot: Ashgate, 2008), 78, 83.

    5. In Gaboriau's 1869 *Monsieur Lecoq,* the young detective "s'extasiait devant les surprenantes facultés d'investigation de cet excentrique policier [Tabaret], qui . . . reconstruisait le drame de la vérité, pareil en cela à ces naturalistes qui, sur la seule inspection de deux ou trois os, dessinent l'animal auquel ils ont appartenu" [went into raptures over the astounding investigative faculties of this eccentric agent who could reconstruct drama and truth, just like those naturalists who, upon the mere inspection of two or three bones, were able to draw the animal to which they had belonged] (Paris: Liana Levi, 1992), 414. And in his 1891 "The Five Orange Pips," Arthur Conan Doyle identifies Cuvier as the paleontologist model for criminal detection: "The ideal reasoner . . . would, when he had once been shown a single fact in all its bearings, deduce from it not only all the chain of events which led up to it, but also all the results which would follow from it. As Cuvier could correctly describe a whole animal by the contemplation of a single bone, so the observer who has thoroughly understood one link in a series of incidents, should be able to accurately state all the other ones, both before and after." Arthur Conan Doyle, *The Adventures of Sherlock Holmes* and *The Memoirs of Sherlock Holmes* (New York: Penguin, 2001), 105. By the twentieth century, the trope was so well known that Leroi-Gourhan turned the analogy back on itself, advising his fellow paleontologists to approach underground evidence as though they were fictional detectives: "Les personnes préhistoriques ont leur manière de se faire comprendre, qui n'est pas dénuée de coquetterie. On ne perce pas leurs secrets à coups de pioche. Elles ne se livrent que par allusions et, comme dans un roman policier, on ne peut plus retrouver la filière si l'on a vidé par mégarde le cendrier qui contenait le bout de cigarette révélateur" [Prehistoric peoples have their own, coquettish, way of making themselves understood. One doesn't pierce their secrets with a pickaxe. They only reveal themselves through hints and, as in a detective novel, one can only pick up the traces if one has inadvertently emptied the ashtray containing the telling tip of the cigarette]. A. Leroi-Gourhan, *Les Chasseurs de la préhistoire* (1955; Paris: Métailié, 1983), 12.

    6. Claudine Cohen, *La Méthode de Zadig: La trace, le fossile, la preuve* (Paris: Seuil, 2011).

    7. Carlo Ginzburg, "Clues: Roots of an Evidential Paradigm," in *Clues, Myths, and the Historical Method*, trans. John and Anne C. Tedeschi (Baltimore: Johns Hopkins University Press, 1989).

    8. Like Cohen, Ginzburg cites Voltaire's retelling in *Zadig* of the Persian tale of the Brothers Serendip as well as Cuvier's paleontological method as a direct influence on Poe, Gaboriau, and Conan Doyle. While Ginzburg's example of Cuvier is above ground (the hoofprint in the dirt that tells us what an animal ate and the shape of its thigh bone), my chapters trace Cuvierian verticality, with the *roman policier* sending its protagonists underground, to uncover the mysteries of earth and bone.

    9. Colin Jones, "Theodore Vacquer and the Archaeology of Modernity in Haussmann's Paris," *Transactions of the RHS* 17 (2007): 157–83, 170.

    10. Darwin's theory of evolution entered the French public imaginary at the same time as paleontological finds were opening up the dizzying perspective of "deep time," the geologic history that spans back for millennia and whose strata were deemed inhabited by man only after fossil evidence emerged in the mid-nineteenth century. See Martin Rudwick, *Scenes from Deep Time: Early Pictorial Representations of the Prehistoric World* (Chicago: University of

Chicago Press, 1995); and Ralph O'Connor, *The Earth on Show: Fossils and the Poetics of Popular Science, 1802–1856* (Chicago: University of Chicago Press, 2007).

11. In "The Natural History of Poe's Orangutan," Robert W. Mitchell carefully refutes earlier claims that Poe derived his story from newspaper accounts of thieving monkeys and folklore about murderous apes; Mitchell writes that Poe directly consulted the writings of Cuvier and other naturalists as primary sources for his tale. *The Selected Writings of Edgar Allan Poe*, 260.

12. Jacques Derrida, *The Animal That Therefore I Am*, ed. Marie-Louise Mallet, trans. David Wills (New York: Fordham University Press, 2008). Cary Wolfe provides a useful overview of the stakes of current animal studies: "Rather than treat the animal as primarily a theme, trope, metaphor, analogy, representation, or sociological datum (in which, say, relations of class, or race, or gender get played out and negotiated through the symbolic currency of animality and species difference), scholars in animal studies, whatever their home disciplines, now appear to be challenged not only by the discourses and conceptual schemata that have shaped our understanding of and relations to animals but also by the specificity of nonhuman animals, their nongeneric nature . . . . And that irreducibility of the question of the animal is linked complexly to the problem of animals' ethical standing as direct or indirect subjects of justice." Wolfe, " 'Human, All Too Human': Animal Studies' and the Humanities," *PMLA* 124, 2 (March 2009): 564–75, 567.

13. The word orangutan derives from the Malay and Indonesian words for "person" and "forest," used first for human forest-dwellers, then for apes.

14. David Bell, "Technologies of Speed, Technologies of Crime," *YFS 108*: 8–19; Dominique Kalifa, "Crime Scenes: Criminal Topography and Social Imaginary in Nineteenth-Century Paris," *French Historical Studies* 27 (2004): 175–94.

15. Daniel Compère, "Le Roman d'aventures policières au XIXe siècle," in *Poétiques du roman d'aventures*, ed. Alain-Michel Boyer and Daniel Couégnas (Nantes: Cécile Defaut, 2004); and *Dictionnaire du roman populaire francophone*, ed. Compère (Paris: Nouveau Monde, 2007).

16. The late nineteenth-century criminological use of phrenology, with the human skull as living site of legible information about brutal tendencies, has been well documented. But the skulls and bones of the dead and long dead also influenced popular theories of criminality, atavism, and human nature. See Dorian Bell, "Cavemen Among us: Genealogies of Atavism from Zola's *La Bête humaine* to Chabrol's *Le Boucher*," *French Studies* 62, 1 (January 2008): 53–64. As for the geological and paleontological sciences, they had far-reaching effects on the French cultural and literary imaginary. See, for example, Louise Lyle and David McCallam, eds., *Histoires de la Terre: Earth Sciences and French Culture, 1740–1940* (Amsterdam: Rodopi, 2008); Scott M. Sprenger, "Balzac, archéologue de la conscience," in *La mémoire en ruines: Le modèle archéologique dans l'imaginaire moderne et contemporain*, ed. Valérie-Angélique Deshoulières and Pascal Vacher (Clermont Ferrand: Presses Universitaires Blaise Pascal, 2000), 97–114; and Nigel Harkness, " '*Textes fossiles*': The Metatextual Geology of Verne's *Voyage au centre de la terre*," *Modern Language Review* 107, 4 (October 2012): 1047–63.

17. Christopher Prendergast, *Paris and the Nineteenth Century* (Cambridge, Mass.: Blackwell, 1992); Kathryn Grossman, *Figuring Transcendence in Les Misérables: Hugo's Romantic Sublime* (Carbondale: Southern Illinois University Press, 1994); Göran Blix, *From Paris to Pompeii: French Romanticism and the Cultural Politics of Archaeology* (Philadelphia: University of Pennsylvania Press, 2008).

18. Victor Hugo, *Les Misérables*, vol. 2 (Paris: Librairie Générale Française, 1998), 1702. Unless otherwise noted, all translations are mine.

19. On Freud as archaeologist and on the haunted house and being buried alive as the two quintessential tropes of the nineteenth-century uncanny, see Anthony Vidler, *The Architectural Uncanny: Essays in the Modern Unhomely* (Cambridge, Mass.: MIT Press, 1992).

20. Claude Lévi-Strauss, *Tristes tropiques* (Paris: Plon, 1955), trans. John and Doreen Weightman (New York: Penguin, 1992), 56–57.

21. Gaston Bachelard, *La Poétique de l'espace* (Paris: PUF, 1957), 37.

22. Bernard Stiegler and Jean-Paul Demoule, *L'Avenir du passé: Modernité de l'archéologie* (Paris: Découverte, 2008), 6.

23. Michel Serres, *Atlas* (Paris: Flammarion, 1997).

24. Two recently published books analyze post-World War II French crime fiction in relation to Rousso's "Vichy Syndrome" model of traumatic repression and return in the national consciousness: Claire Gorrara, *French Crime Fiction and the Second World War: Past Crimes, Present Memories* (Manchester: Manchester University Press, 2012); and Margaret-Anne Hutton, *French Crime Fiction 1945–2005: Investigating World War II* (Aldershot: Ashgate, 2013).

25. Claire Gorrara, *The Roman Noir in Post-War French Culture* (New York: Oxford University Press, 2003). See also Donald Reid, "Didier Daeninckx: Raconteur of History," *South Central Review* 27, 1-2 (Spring-Summer 2010): 39–60.

26. Dominique Viart and Bruno Vercier, *La Littérature française au présent: Héritage et mutations de la modernité* (Paris: Bordas, 2005).

27. Jacques Derrida, *Spectres de Marx* (Paris: Galilée, 1993).

28. Nicolas Abraham, and Maria Torok. *L'Écorce et le noyau* (1978; Paris: Flammarion, 1987). Colin Davis provides a cogent discussion of the differences between Derrida's broader *hantologie* and Abraham and Torok's theory of the transgenerational phantom in "*État présent:* Hauntology, Spectres and Phantoms," *French Studies* 59, 3 (2005): 373–79.

29. "Polarchéologies" is the title of an interview of Anne de Leseleuc by Fred Vargas, in *813: Les Amis de la littérature policière* 55 (May 1996): 13–15. Both authors trained in the field of archaeology and use historical layering in their historical and contemporary mystery novels.

30. Simenon's *Maigret et le fantôme* (1964), for example, has nothing even vaguely or symbolically supernatural about it.

31. "Avec 'Un lieu incertain,' Fred Vargas revisite une vieille histoire de vampire," *Le Monde,* June 24, 2008.

32. Cited in Alfu, *Léo Malet: Parcours d'une œuvre* (Amiens: Encrage, 1998), 74.

33. J. Hillis Miller, *Topographies* (Palo Alto, Calif.: Stanford University Press, 1995).

34. On Walter Benjamin's association of the rise of the detective novel with the development of the bourgeois interior, see David F. Bell,"Reading Corpses: Interpretive Violence," *Substance* 27:2 (1998): 92–105; and Tom Gunning, "The Exterior as Intérieur: Benjamin's Optical Detective," *boundary 2* 30, 1 (Spring 2003): 105–30.

35. See Paul Virilio, *Speed and Politics: An Essay on Dromology*, trans. Mark Polizotti (New York: Semiotext(e), 1986).

36. Kristin Ross, "Watching the Detectives," in *Postmodernism and the Re-Reading of Modernity*, ed. Francis Barker, Peter Hulme, and Margaret Iverson (Manchester: Manchester University Press, 1992), 46–65.

37. Muller and Richardson, eds., *The Purloined Poe*, 185.

38. Jacques Derrida, "The Purveyor of Truth," trans, Alan Bass in *The Purloined Poe*, 199.

39. David Canter, *Mapping Murder: The Secrets of Geographical Profiling* (London: Virgin Books, 2003).

NOTES TO PAGES 28–31

40. See Mark Monmonier, *How to Lie with Maps*, 2nd ed. (Chicago: University of Chicago Press, 1996). An entertaining guide to cartographic deception, Monmonier's book details ways in which distortions of scale, projection, symbols, color, and icon size in maps can reflect deliberate falsification or subtle ideological propaganda.

41. See Robert Champigny, *What Will Have Happened: A Philosophical and Technical Essay on Mystery Stories* (Bloomington: Indiana University Press, 1977).

42. August 1846 letter to Philip P. Cooke, *The Selected Writings of Edgar Allan Poe*, 684.

43. John Merriman called attention to the geographical peripheralization of urban crime in *The Margins of City Life: Explorations on the French Urban Frontier, 1815–1851* (Oxford: Oxford University Press, 1991).

44. Christian Jacob, *The Sovereign Map: Theoretical Approaches in Cartography throughout History*, trans. Tom Conley, ed. Edward H. Dahl (Chicago: University of Chicago Press, 2006). The work of thinkers like Edward Soja, *Postmodern Geographies: The Reassertion of Space in Critical Social Theory* (London: Verso, 1989) and Derek Gregory, *Geographical Imaginations* (Cambridge, Mass.: Blackwell, 1994) has revived critical focus on the ideological underpinnings of cartography.

45. See Tom Conley, *The Self-Made Map: Cartographic Writing in Early Modern France* (Minneapolis: University of Minnesota Press), 1996.

46. Haussmann bragged about having eliminated criminal sites, such as the rue Transnonain, where the army murdered innocent residents in 1832. David P. Jordan, *Transforming Paris: The Life and Labors of Baron Haussmann* (Chicago: University of Chicago Press, 1995), 265. Photographic identification, fingerprinting, and anthropometric methods of tracking criminals emerged around 1888, with Alphonse Bertillon's *Service d'identification*; on the methods and institutional history of *la police scientifique*; see Ilsen About, "La Police scientifique en quête de modèles: Institutions et controverses en France et en Italie (1900–1930), in *L'Enquête judiciaire en Europe au XIXe siècle*, 257–69; and Thomas, *Detective Fiction and the Rise of Forensic Science*.

47. David Platten, "Reading-Glasses, Guns and Robots: A History of Science in French Crime Fiction," *French Cultural Studies* 12, 36 (2001): 253–70: "the value of empirical and forensic evidence is subordinated in this story, through the character and actions of Rouletabille, to the abstract realm of Cartesian reasoning" (260).

48. "Robinson and Petchenik comment that maps 'do not fit clearly into the categories of either discursive [verbal] or presentational [pictorial] symbolism.' I would put it differently: maps are *at once* discursive and presentational symbols." Edward S. Casey, *Representing Place: Landscape Painting and Maps* (Minneapolis: University of Minnesota Press, 2002), 174.

49. *Spatial Machineries and Local Materializations of Fiction*, http://spacefiction.wordpress.com/, is a bilingual French/English blog featuring posts about maps of both fictional and real spaces in fiction, film, and virtual narratives. These are often connected to crime, as in Fritz Lang's 1931 movie *M*, which includes an animated map sequence. See Patrick Bray on the broader philosophical implications of the text-map: *The Novel Map: Space and Subjectivity in Nineteenth-Century French Fiction* (Evanston, Ill.: Northwestern University Press, 2013); and on maps in film: Tom Conley, *Cartographic Cinema* (Minneapolis: University of Minnesota Press, 2007).

50. Michael Marrinan and John Bender, *The Culture of Diagram* (Palo Alto, Calif.: Stanford University Press, 2010).

51. Derek Gregory, *Geographical Imaginations* (Cambridge, Mass.: Blackwell, 1994).

52. Marx's phrase is used by Marshall Berman to describe how capitalism "liquefies" the social and spatial relations of a city. *All That Is Solid Melts into Air: The Experience of Modernity* (New York: Penguin, 1988).

53. On Pennac and Michel Steiner, see Susanna Lee, "Punk *Noir*: Anarchy in Two Idioms," *YFS 108*. Izzo is considered a top detective novelist of the new French regionalism; "total chaos" is the English translation of the slang title of the Marseille trilogy's first installment, *Total Kheops* (1995).

54. Roland Barthes, "Sémiologie et urbanisme," in *L'Aventure sémiologique* (Paris: Seuil, 1985); Michel de Certeau, *L'Invention du quotidien*, vol. 1, *Arts de faire* (Paris: Gallimard, 1990), 179 (English version: *The Practice of Everyday Life*, 121).

55. Georges Perec, *Espèces d'espaces* (Paris: Galilée, 1974). Perec begins with a description of French colonial history that privileges cartography over political events: "il n'y a pas un espace, . . . il y a plein de petits bouts d'espaces . . . . Un autre [de ces bouts d'espace], vaguement hexagonal, a été entouré d'un gros pointillé . . . et il a été décidé que tout ce qui se trouvait *à l'intérieur* du pointillé serait colorié en violet et s'appellerait France, alors que tout ce qui se trouvait *à l'extérieur* du pointillé serait colorié d'une façon différente . . . et s'appellerait autrement (en fait, pendant pas mal d'années, on a beaucoup insisté pour colorier en violet—et du même coup appeler France—des morceaux d'espace qui n'appartenaient pas au susdit hexagone, et souvent même en étaient fort éloignés, mais, en général, ça a beaucoup moins bien tenu)" [There is no "space" in the singular, . . . there are lots of little bits of spaces. One of them, vaguely hexagonal, was once circled by a big dotted line . . . and it was decided that everything that happened to be *inside* the dotted line would be colored in violet and called France, while everything *outside* the dotted line would be colored differently . . . and would be given a different name (in fact, for quite a few years, there was a strong insistence on coloring violet—and thereby calling France—some bits of space that weren't part of that hexagon, and were even often quite far away from it, but in general, that didn't last so long] (14). By suggesting somewhat facetiously that aesthetic form determines national boundaries, Perec not only exposes spatial organization as fundamentally arbitrary, he also makes a statement about realism and mapping, for here, representation itself supplants the external "real" as referent—as though it were the map that determines reality and not the other way around.

56. See also Edward S. Casey, *The Fate of Place: A Philosophical History* (Berkeley: University of California Press, 1997). In a broad discussion of place in Western thought, Casey notes that contemporary thinkers do not attempt to define place as fixed and essential; rather, authors attempt to explore place "at work": "in the course of history (Braudel, Foucault), in the natural world (Berry, Snyder), in the political realm (Nancy, Lefebvre), in gender relations and sexual difference (Irigaray), in the productions of poetic imagination (Bachelard, Otto), in geographic experience and reality (Foucault, Tuan, Soja, Relph, Entrekin), in the sociology of the *polis* and the city (Benamin, Arendt, Walter), in nomadism (Deleuze and Guattari), in architecture (Derrida, Eisenman, Tscjhumi), in religion (Irigaray, Nancy)" (286). On gender, I would add Doreen Massey's *Space, Place, and Gender* (Minneapolis: University of Minnesota Press, 1994).

57. Patricia Yaeger, "Introduction: Narrating Space," in *The Geography of Identity*, ed. Patricia Yaeger (Ann Arbor: University of Michigan Press, 1996), 4.

58. Dantec's first foray into crime fiction was as contributor to "Le Poulpe," an Éditions Baleine collection begun in 1995 in which various authors add to the adventures of the private investigator "Gabriel Lecouvreur dit le Poulpe." The ludic aspect of this experiment in collective

authorship is reflected in the frequent use of puns in the novel's titles (Dessaint's *Les Pis rennais*, Lefort's *Vomi soit qui malle y pense*, etc.).

59. Scholarship on the crime genre in postcolonial and non-Western contexts includes Pim Higginson's *The Noir Atlantic: Chester Himes and the Birth of the Francophone African Crime Novel*, Sari Kawana's *Murder Most Modern: Detective Fiction and Japanese Culture* (Minneapolis: University of Minnesota Press, 2008), and Persephone Braham's *Crimes Against the State, Crimes Against Persons: Detective Fiction in Cuba and Mexico* (Minneapolis: University of Minnesota Press, 2004). On geocriticism and spatiality, see for example *Geocritical Explorations: Space, Place, and Mapping in Literary and Cultural Studies*, ed. Robert T. Tally (New York: Palgrave Macmillan, 2011); and Robert T. Tally, *Spatiality* (New York: Routledge, 2013).

60. Luc Boltanski, *Énigmes et complots: Une enquête à propos d'enquêtes* (Paris: Gallimard, 2012); the English title is *Mysteries and Conspiracies: Detective Stories, Spy Novels and the Making of Modern Societies*, trans. Catherine Porter (Cambridge: Polity, 2014).

61. Many scholars, of course, do not set Poe aside. In *Le Roman policier: Introduction à la théorie et à l'histoire d'un genre littéraire* (Liège: Céfal, 1999), Marc Lits defines the crime genre's four-pronged imaginary according to the elements in Baudelaire's translation of the title of Poe's story: "Double"=the genre's structural duality; "assassinat"=its criminal theme; "dans la rue"=its sociological dimension; and "Morgue"=the role of imagination and the specularity of death (73–86).

CHAPTER 2. QUARRIES AND CATACOMBS: UNDERGROUND CRIME IN SECOND EMPIRE *ROMANS-FEUILLETONS*

Epigraph: Doreen Massey, *For Space* (London: Sage, 2005), 133.

1. Georges Verpraet, *Paris, capitale souterraine* (Paris: Plon, 1964), 40–41.

2. Colin Jones, *Paris: The Biography of a City* (New York: Penguin, 2004), 12.

3. See Gilles Thomas, *The Catacombs of Paris* (Paris: Parigramme, 2011); Alain Clément and Gilles Thomas, *L'Atlas du Paris souterrain* (Paris: Parigramme, 2001); Jean-Didier Urbain, "Les Catanautes des cryptocombs—des iconoclastes de l'ailleurs," *Nottingham French Studies* 39, 1 (Spring 2000): 7–16; and Barbara Glowczewski et al., *La Cité des cataphiles: Mission anthropologique dans les souterrains de Paris* (Paris: Klincksieck, 1983). Gilles Thomas is currently preparing a book on catacomb fiction that promises to be useful and pertinent: *Les Catacombes. Histoire du Paris souterrain, "Promenades littéraires dans les catacombes"* (Édition Le Passage, forthcoming).

4. David L. Pike, *Subterranean Cities: The World Beneath Paris and London, 1800–1945* (Ithaca, N.Y.: Cornell University Press, 2005).

5. Colin Jones, "Theodore Vacquer and the Archaeology of Modernity in Haussmann's Paris," *Transactions of the Royal Historical Society* 17 (2007): 157–83, 170.

6. Interestingly, Haussmann's lieutenant Eugène Belgrand, who was largely responsible for the engineering of the Paris sewer system, was also a paleolithic scholar, author of works like *La Seine*, vol. 1, *Le Bassin parisien aux âges préhistoriques* (1869) (Jones, "Vauquer," 169)

7. Göran Blix, *From Paris to Pompeii*, "The Romantics, Heirs to the Revolution, Were Born Catastrophists" (165); Michael Shortland, "Darkness visible: Underground Culture in the Golden Age of Geology," *History of Science* 32 (1994): 1–61.

8. "Le compte rendu de l'Académie des sciences" (*Constitutionnel* du 28 juin 1881), cited in Élie Berthet, *Paris avant l'histoire* (Paris: Jouvet et Cie., 1885), 76.

9. The tiny rue Pagevin, now named rue d'Argout, is in the Châtelet-les-Halles district (2e *arrondissement*).

10. Claudine Cohen, *The Fate of the Mammoth: Fossils, Myth, and History*, trans. William Rodarmor (Chicago: University of Chicago Press, 2002). Original *Le Destin du mammouth* (Paris: Seuil, 1994).

11. On the scientific evidence of violence in prehistory, see Jean Guilaine, and Jean Zammit. *Le Sentier de la guerre: Visages de la violence préhistorique* (Paris: Seuil, 2001).

12. Other prehistoric fictions include Edmond Haraucourt, *Daâh, le premier homme* (1914), Adrien Cranile, *Solutré, ou Les chasseurs de rennes de la France centrale: Histoire préhistorique* (1872), J. H. Rosny Aîné, *Vamireh* (1892), *Eyrimah* (1893), and *La Guerre du feu* (1909), and Jules Lermina, *L'Effrayante aventure* (1910). For an extensive list that goes beyond the French corpus, see Marc Angenot and Nadia Khouri, "An International Bibliography of Prehistoric Fiction," *Science Fiction Studies* 23, 8, pt. 1 (March 1981): 38–53; Gordon Chamberlain, "Notes and Correspondence," *Science-Fiction Studies* 28, 9, pt. 3 (November 1982), 342–46; and Khouri and Angenot, "The Discourse of Prehistoric Anthropology: Emergence, Narrative, Paradigms, Ideology," *Minnesota Review* 19 (1982): 117.

13. In his Preface, Berthet notes that "L'Immortel Cuvier, l'inventeur de la paléontologie, ne voulait même admettre que l'homme eût existé à cette antiquité prodigieuse. Les savants de l'Europe refusaient de croire que les silex, trouvés dans les terrains quaternaires par l'illustre Boucher de Perthes, fussent des produits de l'industrie humaine. C'est seulement depuis quelques années que des découvertes nouvelles, incontestables, éclatantes, ont dégagé cette période des nuages mystérieux qui la voilaient" [The immortal Cuvier, inventor of paleontology, did not even admit the possibility that man might have existed during that prodigiously ancient era. The learned men of Europe refused to believe that the flintstones found in quaternary terrains by the illustrious Boucher de Perthes were the products of human industry. It has been only recently, in the last few years, that new incontestable and powerful discoveries have drawn back the mysterious curtain keeping that period in the shadows] (5).

14. Berthet cites here the French archaeologist Gabriel de Mortillet, among the first to formulate a chronological classification of the epochs of man's prehistoric cultural development. Mortillet's *Le Préhistorique: Antiquité de l'homme* was published in 1882.

15. In a "Petit dictionnaire des idées reçues en vigueur dans le roman populaire" of 1900–1914, Anne-Marie Thiesse includes the following associations as commonplace in serial fiction: "*Rousse*. Nourrit de noirs desseins.—*Voir Blonde*." And under *Brune*: "Entre blonde et rousse, ange et démon" [*Redhaired woman*: harbors dark plots, *see Blonde. Brunette*: between blonde and redhaired, angel and demon]. *Le Roman du quotidien: Lecteurs et lectures populaires à la Belle Epoque* (Paris: Le Chemin vert), 145.

16. Élie Berthet, *Les Catacombes de Paris*, vols. 1, 2 (Paris: Hachette, 1863) [Consulted at the Bibliothèque des littératures policières (BiLiPo)].

17. Louis Sébastien Mercier, "Tableau de Paris" in Mercier and Restif de la Bretonne, *Paris le jour, Paris la nuit* (Paris: Laffont, 1990). For a brief history of the Paris quarries, see Fierro, Alfred. *Histoire et dictionnaire de Paris* (Paris: Laffont, 1996), 751–72. In the 1770s, the discovery of vast subterranean tunnels, which contrary to law had not been filled in, caused grave concern to the city's inhabitants; on September 15, a royal edict called for inspection and repair of the quarries. Fierro cites René Suttel, *Catacombes et carrières de Paris* and Émile Gérard, *Paris souterrain* as indispensable resources on the subject.

18. Thomas Cragin's argument in *Murder in Parisian Streets: Manufacturing Crime and Justice in the Popular Press, 1830–1900* (Lewisburg, Pa.: Bucknell University Press, 2006) offers a useful context for thinking about these superstitious responses. Writing about nineteenth-century crime *canards*, Cragin suggests that modern rational explanations for criminality raised by literary, political, legal, and political elites of the time had less impact on popular thought than did surviving traditional notions of morality; even as late as 1868, *canards* ascribed the murderous impulse to a "monster" or "sorceress" with a "black soul" administering "products of the Devil" (145–46).

19. Berthet's "Fantôme de Montsouris" (i.e., Médard) has been compared to Leroux's "Fantôme de l'Opéra" as incarnating a subterranean version of the *Beauty and the Beast* story: both are "solitary monsters" who undergo a mythic/symbolic death through love for an unattainable woman (Glowczewski et al., *La Cité des cataphiles*, 182–83).

20. Rosalind Williams, *Notes on the Underground: An Essay on Technology, Society, and the Imagination* (Cambridge, Mass.: MIT Press, 1990). Because Williams's emphasis in this book is on the technological, rather than naturally formed, underground, she cites geological history only to explain that by the end of the nineteenth century it was no longer feasible to imagine discovering unknown worlds under the Earth's surface (chap.1, "The Underworld as a Vision of the Technological Future," 1–21).

21. For background on the geological debates of the nineteenth century, see Martin Rudwick, *Georges Cuvier, Fossil Bones, and Geological Catastrophes: New Translations and Interpretations of the Primary Texts* (Chicago: University of Chicago Press, 1997).

22. The dating of these serial novels can be tricky. Publication announcements in *Le Siècle Illustré* suggest that early episodes of Labourieu's *Les Carrières d'Amérique* appeared earlier in the decade, but for my citations I use the C. Vanier 1868 edition scanned in Gallica: http://gallica.bnf.fr/ark:/12148/bpt6k56614409.r=Labourieu+carrières+de+paris.langEN. Zaccone's *Les Drames des catacombes* first appeared in *Le Roger-Bontemps* 241, 20 août 1861–258, 17 déc. 1861; I consulted the serial publication at the BiLiPo, but am using page numbers from Gallica's scanned volume version (Paris: Ballay Aîné, 1863), http://gallica.bnf.fr/ark:/12148/bpt6k56523185.image.r=jardins.f1.langFR. On a related note, another contemporary book shares Berthet's title: Pierre-Léonce Imbert, *Les Catacombes de Paris* (1867). Imbert's book is not crime fiction; it presents itself, rather, as a "Guide" in which the narrator and his friends explore quarries and catacombs while providing the reader with a brief history of Paris's underground space. That history does include the well-known brigands of the Montsouris plains, but more suggestive for our purposes are the metaphorical implications of violence in Imbert's description of the geological properties of Parisian rock: "Je signalerai, rue du Port-Royal, sous la Maternité, une particularité fort curieuse. La pierre est recouverte de carbonate de chaux, coloré par des décompositions de pyrites (fer sulfuré), qui font tout d'abord croire à du sang figé" [I will point out, on Port-Royal street under the maternity wing of the hospital, a very curious particularity: the stone is covered in lime carbonate and colored by pyrite (iron sulfur) decay, which makes one at first imagine it is clotted blood] (28) Pierre-Léonce Imbert, *Les Catacombes de Paris: Guide illustré de vingt planches hors texte* (Paris: Lacroix, 1867), http://www.catanaute.com/CATANAUTE.COM/Dwld_Livres_anciens_p1.html.

23. Section names for Leroux's *La Résurrection de Rocambole* are variable; the 1866 Dentu edition used the title "Le Souterrain" for the section called "Rédemption" in the 1992 Robert Laffont edition. In this section, a complex and melodramatic (i.e., "Rocambolesque") plot includes the imprisonment of a character next to the skeleton of an earlier victim in an underground cavern, which itself is doubled by a second cave in which a series of mirrors create a

phantasmagoric spying device. On the Rocambolesque, see Robin Walz, "The Rocambolesque and the Modern Enchantment of Popular Fiction," in *The Re-Enchantment of the World: Secular Magic in a Rational Age*, ed. Joshua Landy and Michael T. Saler (Palo Alto, Calif.: Stanford University Press, 2009).

24. Dominique Kalifa, "Les Lieux du crime: Topographie criminelle et imaginaire social à Paris au XIXe siècle," *Sociétés et Représentations* 17 (2004): 131–50, 136.

25. "Dans les catacombes de Paris," *Lord Lister, #17 Le Grand Inconnu* (Paris: Eichler, n.d.). [Coll. BiLiPo] The Lord Lister series was apparently of German origin but capitalized on anglophilia/phobia and was published by A. Eichler in Paris between 1908 and 1914.

26. On the carnavalesque and political implications of the nobleman/commoner disguise motif in Sue and Dumas, see Dominique Jullien, "Travestissement et contre-pouvoir dans le roman-feuilleton," *Littérature* 153 (mars 2009): 50–60.

27. See Dominique Kalifa, *Les Bas-fonds: Histoire d'un imaginaire* (Seuil, 2013).

28. The gypsum quarries called Carrières d'Amérique (because their product was exported to the U.S.) were closed by 1860 and became part of the Buttes Chaumont park, planned under Napoléon III, after a short stint in 1879 as a horse-trading site.

29. By tying the serial crime genre to a Cuvierian "geochronology," I am trying to go beyond an initial association of the Parisian underground with Revolution. I want to explore that connection in terms of narrative structure and the topographic morphology revealed by the stratigraphic maps of the Paris Basin Cuvier and Brongniart produced in 1808 and 1811. See Martin Rudwick, "Cuvier and Brongniart, William Smith, and the Reconstruction of Geohistory," in *The New Science of Geology*. Rudwick explains that Cuvier and Brongniart introduced in the early 1800s a newly *historical* geological understanding based on their observation of the Paris Basin. Their narrative reconstruction of the Earth's successive convulsions (as opposed to one sole Biblical deluge) invited comparison to the region's above-ground upheavals: "Cuvier and Brongniart presented a geohistory of the Paris region that was as complex and—even in retrospect—as unpredictable as the bewildering twists and turns, the war and peace, the sudden coups d'état and quieter interludes, of the Revolutionary and Napoleonic politics they had both lived through in the past two decades. Furthermore, just as the politics of those years had been different, though related, in other parts of Europe, so the geohistory Cuvier and Brongniart offered for the Paris region could be expected to be related, but not identical, to that of other regions" (19). Similarly, in *Scenes from Deep Time* Rudwick explains how the stratigraphical branch of geology, which studies the layering of sedimentary and volcanic rock, led to a new, retroactive way of reading past eras (92).

30. Cuvierian cataclysm contrasts in this way with transformism. For Stephen Kern, Lyell's 1830 *Principles of Geology* "demonstrated that geological phenomena are caused by gradual and uniform forces acting according to continuously operating laws" and are thus in accord with a deterministic causal order of nature as seen by Comte and others: *A Cultural History of Causality: Science, Murder Novels, and Systems of Thought* (Princeton, N.J.: Princeton University Press, 2004), 6. A cataclysmic model, then, implies that brutality still holds, while the more peaceful transformism would imply progress from a primitive violence toward an ever-increasing civility in the modern world.

31. Félix Nadar, *Le Paris souterrain* (Paris, 1861; Caisse nationale des monuments historiques et des sites, 1982).

32. On the public and spectacular nature of popularized geology in the nineteenth century, see Ralph O'Connor, *The Earth on Show*; and Rudwick, *Scenes from Deep Time*.

33. The titles of some of Labourieu's other works reveal his political investments: *Mystères de l'Empire par un espion politique et militaire* (1874); *La Colonne Vendôme, roman historique* (1872); *Mémoires d'un déporté* (1881).

34. Eugène Sue, *Les Mystères de Paris* (Paris: Gallimard, 2009), 138.

35. Constant Guéroult and Paul de Couder, *Les Étrangleurs de Paris* (Paris: Louis Chappe, 1859), 171, http://gallica.bnf.fr/ark:/12148/bpt6k5610605v.

36. Jules Lermina, *Les Loups de Paris* (Paris: Boulanger, 1883), http://gallica.bnf.fr/ark: /12148/bpt6k5578711t.r=Lermina+loups+de+paris.langEN.

37. Pierre Souvestre and Marcel Allain, *Fantômas XXIII: Le Bouquet tragique* (Paris: Fayard, 1912), 179.

38. Gaston Leroux, *La Double vie de Théophraste Longuet* (Paris: Flammarion, 1904), chap. 30. The novel first appeared in *Le Matin*, 5 octobre–22 novembre 1903, under the title *Le Chercheur de trésors*.

CHAPTER 3. SKULLS AND BONES:
PALEOHISTORY IN LEROUX AND LEBLANC

1. Though some aspects of its broad argument have been contested, Eugen Weber's classic study of a Third Republic shift from regionalism to nationhood remains a touchstone for thought on this period. *Peasants into Frenchmen: The Modernization of Rural France, 1870–1914* (Stanford, Calif.: Stanford University Press, 1976).

2. Stephen Knight, *Form and Ideology in Crime Fiction* (Bloomington: Indiana University Press, 1980).

3. Stéphane Gerson, *The Pride of Place: Local Memories and Political Culture in Nineteenth-century France* (Ithaca, N.Y.: Cornell University Press, 2003), 7. Although some saw the provinces as backward and barbarous, writes Gerson, many understood regionalist culture as key to modern interests in tourism and marketing. Indeed, he argues that there was more to the early nineteenth century's cult of local memories than mere nostalgia or fear of progress: "[it] also contributed to processes we associate with Western modernity, from the rise of science and state building to civic participation and the formation of new modes of territorial identity" (4).

4. Arsène Lupin's patriotism is often linked to water, whether in the coastal setting of *L'Aiguille creuse* (1909) or the military submarine he retrieves for France in *Le Sept de cœur* (1907). For his part, Rouletabille represents France in his transnational adventures in Russia (*Rouletabille chez le tsar*, 1913) and Germany (*Rouletabille chez Krupp*, 1917).

5. Michel Mollat du Jourdin, "Le front de mer," *Les Lieux de mémoire, T.2,* Pierre Nora, ed. (Paris: Gallimard, 1997), 2721–64, 2721.

6. Gaston Leroux, *Le Parfum de la dame en noir* (Paris: Le Livre de Poche, 1960). The novel first appeared in serial form in *L'Illustration* from September 26, 1908 to January 2, 1909.

7. See Dubois, *Le roman policier ou la modernité*; Daniel Couegnas, *Fictions, énigmes, images: Lectures (para?) littéraires* (Limoges: Pulim, 2001); and Jean-Claude Vareille, *L'Homme masqué, le justicier et le détective* (Lyon: Presses Universitaires de Lyon, 1998)

8. Jean-Philippe Marty links Rouletabille's physiognomy (a closed and rounded face) to his faith in Cartesian thought and to his Oedipal fight against the paternal, criminal threat of Larsan. Marty, "Présentation," in Gaston Leroux, *Le Mystère de la chambre jaune* (Paris: Flammarion, 2003), 7–24.

9. I am not distinguishing here between an "antiquarian" (scriptural) and an "archaeological" (secular) perspective, as I don't believe Leroux was invoking that debate, already settled by then. See Lawrence Frank, *Victorian Detective Fiction and the Nature of Evidence: The Scientific Investigations of Poe, Dickens, and Doyle* (London: Palgrave Macmillan, 2003), 102–6.

10. See my *Optiques*, 141–42, 247.

11. The work done in the field of archaeology also reminds us that museum visualizations of the (prehistoric) past are shot through with ideology; see Sam Smiles and Stephanie Moser, eds., *Envisioning the Past: Archaeology and the Image* (Malden, Mass.: Blackwell, 2005).

12. On Lupin's nationalism, see Francis Lacassin, "L'Art de cambrioler . . . l'histoire de France," *Europe: Revue Littéraire Mensuelle* 604–5 (Août–Septembre, 1979): 24–34; Dominique Jullien, "'De Cesar à Lupin': Patrimoine et cambriolage dans *L'Aiguille creuse* de Maurice Leblanc," *Romanic Review* 81, 1 (January 1990): 105–18; and Colette J. Windish, "Arsène Lupin: Une certaine idée de la France?," *French Cultural Studies* 12, 2, 35 (2001): 123–232.

13. Maurice Leblanc, "Herlock Sholmes arrive trop tard," in *Les Aventures d'Arsène Lupin, gentleman-cambrioleur* (Paris: Hachette, 1960), 457.

14. David Platten, "Origins and Beginnings: The Emergence of Detective Fiction in France," in *French Crime Fiction*, ed. Claire Gorrara (Cardiff: University of Wales Press, 2009), 14–35, 29.

15. On the bicycle as a fin-de-siècle symbol of progress, see Eugen Weber, *France, Fin de Siècle* (Cambridge, Mass.: Belknap Press of Harvard University Press, 1988); and Rosemary Lloyd, "Reinventing Pegasus: Bicycles and the Fin-de-Siècle Imagination," *Dix-Neuf* 4 (April 2005).

16. Claudine Cohen, *Un Néandertalien dans le métro* (Paris: Seuil, 2007).

17. "'Ardi,' Oldest Human Ancestor, Unveiled," *Discovery News @DNews*, November 27, 2012: http://news.discovery.com/history/archaeology/ardi-human-ancestor.htm.

18. Pierre Boitard, *Études antédiluviennes: Paris avant les hommes. L'homme fossile, etc.* (Paris: Passard, 1861), 3.

19. Rae Beth Gordon, *Dances with Darwin, 1875–1910: Vernacular Modernity in France* (Burlington, Vt.: Ashgate, 2009), 83–84.

20. On Paul Broca's "topographie cérébrale," see also Nélia Dias, *La Mesure des sens: Les anthropologues et le corps humain au XIXe siècle* (Paris: Flammarion, 2004).

21. See Cragin, *Murder in the Parisian Streets*, 151; and Robert A. Nye, *Crime, Madness, and Politics in Modern France: The Medical Concept of National Decline* (Princeton, N.J.: Princeton University Press, 1984).

22. Régis Messac, *Les Romans de l'homme-singe* (1935; Le Teich: Ex Nihilo, 2007), 22. See also Lantelme, Michel, and André Benhaïm, eds., *Écrivains de la préhistoire* (Toulouse: Presses Universitaires du Mirail, 2004).

23. Gaston Leroux, *Balaoo* (Paris: Presses de la Renaissance, 1977). The novel first appeared in serial form in *Le Matin* in 1911. Leroux explains his scientific term in a footnote: "Du grec *anthropos*, homme, et *pithekos*, singe: animaux qui tiennent le milieu entre le singe et l'homme, et qui auraient été comme une transition de celui-là à celui-ci. Quelques savants, dont Gabriel de Mortillet principalement, ont relevé, dans les terrains tertiaires, la trace et les débris fossiles de ces animaux intelligents, et aussi la preuve de leur intelligence. D'autres, sur la foi des récits de voyageurs, affirment que cette espèce de singe existe encore et qu'on peut en retrouver quelques spécimens au fond des forêts de Java" [From the Greek *anthropos*, man, and *pithekos*, ape: animals existing between the human and the ape, and who supposedly existed as the transition from the latter to the former. Some scientists, among them principally Gabriel de

Mortillet, have unearthed, in tertiary strata, the traces and fossil remains of these intelligent beasts, as well as proof of their intelligence. Others, on the strength of travelers' accounts, maintain that this primate species exists still today and that some of its specimens can be found deep in the forests of Java] (109).

24. Balzac's criminal-turned-police chief Vautrin is an obvious textual model, but Leroux may be playing instead on the echo with "vaurien." The Vautrin siblings also fit the crime-novel cliché of the criminal underground, as they use a long-deserted quarry under the forest canopy for storage and hiding.

25. Jacques Derrida, *The Animal That Therefore I Am*, ed. Marie-Louise Mallet, trans. David Wills (New York: Fordham University Press, 2008).

26. In her analysis of Edgar Rice Burroughs's *Tarzan of the Apes* (1912), Marianna Torgovnick writes that the popular fiction's abduction scenes "suggest certain rules: qualities like lust belong to animals and blacks, not to Euro-Americans, except when they are renegade, outcast." *Gone Primitive: Savage Intellects, Modern Lives* (Chicago: University of Chicago Press, 1990), 53. Jules Lermina's 1905 "To-Ho le tueur d'or," while not following a crime novel format, does feature intermediate ape-men of Sumatra: the violent and barbaric "Orang-Aceh," who fight off Dutch invaders; as the novel's plot progresses and the main characters move deeper into the forest, they discover a series of increasingly ape-like transition species.

27. Laura Otis, *Membranes: Metaphors of Invasion in Nineteenth-Century Literature, Science, and Politics* (Baltimore: Johns Hopkins University Press, 1999).

28. Among the skull and catacomb-themed crime novels housed at the BiLiPo, we find these: Erik J. Certön, *Le Carillon des catacombes*, Série Mon Roman Policier III (Paris: Ferenczi et fils, 1849); Léo.Gestelys, *Le Gang des catacombes*, La Loupe, Série Policière 82 (Lyon: Jacquier, 1959); Max-André.Dazergues, *L'Âme habite le crâne?* Série Police et Mystère 343 (Paris: Ferenczi et fils, 1938–39); Jean Campocasso, *Le Crâne dans la poubelle*, Série Espionnage Aventure Police (Chevilly-Larue: Éditions des Roses, 1954); Edmond Romazières, *La Clef dans le crâne*. Roman Policier, Collection Rex 9 (Paris: Agence Parisienne de Distribution, 1939); George Maxwell, *Tous des pourris!* Collection Noire Franco-Américaine (Paris: Trotteur, 1953).

CHAPTER 4. CRYPTS AND GHOSTS: TERRAINS
OF NATIONAL TRAUMA IN JAPRISOT AND VARGAS

Epigraph: "And beneath the city lie the other cities, the trampled history of men and women from the past and the homes of today have pushed onto their cellars and the flesh of today has reared up on the bones in the earth." François Bon, *Impatience* (Paris: Minuit, 1998), cited in Alexandre Dauge-Roth, "Du non-lieu au lieu-dit: Plaidoyers de François Bon pour une urbanité contemporaine," in *Discursive Geographies: Writing Space and Place in French*, ed. Jeanne Garane (Amsterdam: Rodopi, 2005), 237–66, 62.

1. Claire Gorrara, "Forgotten Crimes?: Representing Jewish Experience of the Second World War in French Crime Fiction," *South Central Review* 27, 1/2 (Spring/Summer 2010): 3–20.

2. "[T]oute l'écriture policière de Daeninckx s'organise autour du principe de la remontée dans le temps, jusqu'aux origines du souvenir traumatisant" [All Daeninckx's detective fiction is organized around the theme of going back in time, back to the origin-point of traumatic memory]. Verdaguer, Pierre. "Mauvais genre et B.C.-B.G. policiers," *Sites: The Journal of 20th-Century/Contemporary French Studies* 1, 1 (Spring 1997): 31–50, 47. See also Donald Reid,

"Didier Daeninckx: Raconteur of History," *South Central Review* 27, 1/2 (Spring/Summer 2010): 39–60.

3. Nicolas Abraham and Maria Torok. *L'Écorce et le noyau* (Paris: Flammarion, 1999). Abraham and Torok's psychoanalytical work has inspired compelling studies of fiction, including especially Esther Rashkin's *Family Secrets and the Psychonalysis of Narrative* (Princeton, N.J.: Princeton University Press, 1992), the first full-length study to apply the concepts of "the phantom, cryptonomy, symbol, symbolic operation, trauma, and anasemia" to texts ranging from Balzac's "Facino cane" to Poe's "Fall of the House of Usher" (9). See also Rashkin's *Unspeakable Secrets and the Psychoanalysis of Culture* (Albany, N.Y.: SUNY Press, 2008).

4. See, for example, Christine Berthin, *Gothic Hauntings: Melancholy Crypts and Textual Ghosts* (New York: Palgrave Macmillan, 2010) and Carla Jodey Castriciano, *Cryptomimesis and Jacques Derrida's Ghost Writing* (Montreal: McGill-Queens University Press, 2001).

5. See the Editor's Note to "New Perspectives in Metaphsychology: Cryptic Mourning and Secret Love," in Abraham and Torok, *The Shell and the Kernel*, ed. Nicholas T. Rand (Chicago: University of Chicago Press, 1994), 99–106.

6. Martin Hurcombe and Simon Kemp, eds. *Sébastien Japrisot: The Art of Crime*, Faux Titre, vol. 329 (Amsterdam: Rodopi, 2009), 24.

7. David Bellos, "The Lessons of *L'été meurtrier*," in *Art of Crime*, 139–49.

8. Pierre Verdaguer, *La Séduction policière: signes de croissance d'un genre réputé mineur* (Birmingham, Ala.: Summa, 1999), 14.

9. Jacques Dubois, *Le Roman policier ou la modernité*, 64. The three "utopic" authors analyzed in Dubois's book are Gaston Leroux, Georges Simenon, and Sébastien Japrisot.

10. Simon Kemp, "Japrisot on Film," in Hurcombe and Kemp, *Sébastien Japrisot*, 67.

11. Bellos, "The Lessons of *L'Été meurtrier*," 140.

12. Sébastien Japrisot, *Un long dimanche de fiançailles* (Paris: Denoël, 1991), 13.

13. Japrisot translates the following passage from *Alice in Wonderland*: "I see nobody on the road," said Alice. "I only wish *I* had such eyes," the king remarked in a fretful tone. "To be able to see Nobody! And at that distance too! It's as much as *I* can do to see real people, by this light!" On playful fictionality as a key element of Japrisot's earlier novels, see Claire Gorrara, "Through the Looking Glass: Defeats of Detection in Sébastien Japrisot's *L'Éte meurtrier*," in Hurcombe and Kemp, *Sébastien Japrisot*, 151–64. Lewis Carroll is a recurring reference point, with logical conundrums and absurdities that transform the traditional mystery story into "a fictional universe of imploding narrative structures and identities."

14. For most translations in this section, I am using Japrisot, *A Very Long Engagement*, trans. Linda Coverdale (London: Picador, 1993). I have made some changes where literal translation of word play was required; and I have kept the original French edition's page numbers.

15. Jacques Derrida, "Fors," in Abraham, Nicolas, and Maria Torok. *The Wolf Man's Magic Word: A Cryptonymy*, trans. Nicholas Rand. (Minneapolis: University of Minnesota Press, 1986); orig. *Cryptonymie: Le Verbier de l'homme aux loups* (Paris: Flammarion, 1976).

16. Esther Rashkin, "Nicolas Abraham and Maria Torok," in *The Columbia History of Twentieth-Century Thought*, ed. Lawrence D. Kritzman (New York: Columbia University Press, 2006), 378.

17. Martin Hurcombe usefully identifies Mathilde's mahogany box as itself constituting an archive, a repository of testimony whose fragmentary and partial contents reveal the irreducible discontinuity between past and present in the novel. "The Passing of Things Remembered: Sébastien Japrisot's *Un long dimanche de fiançailles*," *Romance Studies* 25, 2 (April, 2007): 85–94, 88, 90.

18. Shoshana Felman identifies the reconstructive logic of psychoanalysis as that which structures crime fiction in general and Japrisot's *Piège pour Cendrillon* in particular. "De Sophocle à Japrisot (via Freud), ou Pourquoi le policier?," *Littérature* 49 (Février 1983): 23–42. Like *Un long dimanche*, Japrisot's earlier detective novel *Piège* revolves around the multiple substitutions of identities, bodies, and names. According to Felman, murder itself becomes a narrative "figure of substitution," with its own spatial logic of displacement and movement; and she concludes that the novel functions as "le récit même du déplacement des énigmes" [the narration of the very displacement of enigmas]—that is, if the reader is placed in the position of analyst, it is not with an unambiguous, univocal solution as the outcome (39). *Un long dimanche*, on the other hand, might seem to resolve itself unambiguously through the identification of Manech and his reunion with Mathilde, but I would argue that it actually has more in common with *Piège* than one might think, particularly in its spatial logic of substitution.

19. Fred Vargas is the pseudonym of Frédérique Audoin-Rouzeau, a trained medieval historian and archaeologist who has also written scholarly works on the epidemiology of the bubonic plague and eukaryotic archaeology. Vargas has encountered phenomenal success as a crime novelist, especially since her unprecedented double win of the Duncan Lawrie International Dagger for best crime novel translated into English. See Véronique Denain, "Women in French Crime Writing," in *French Crime Fiction*, ed. Claire Gorrara (Cardiff: University of Wales Press, 2009).

20. Stéphane Audoin-Rouzeau, Leonard V. Smith, and Annette Becker. *France and the Great War 1914–1918* (Cambridge: Cambridge University Press, 2003), 55–56.

21. Verdaguer, "Mauvais genre et B.C.-B.G. policiers," 46.

22. Susanna Lee, "Scruple and State Sovereignty: Fred Vargas's Romantic *Étatisme*," *Contemporary French Civilization* 34, 1 (2010): 73–96, 74.

23. Nicolas Abraham and Maria Torok, *The Shell and the Kernel: Renewals of Psychoanalysis*, ed. and trans. Nicholas Rand (Chicago: University of Chicago Press, 1994), 171.

24. Ascari, Maurizio. *A Counter-History of Crime Fiction*. One of the early texts Ascari connects to the burgeoning crime genre is the anonymous tale "Le Revenant," published with a French title in an 1827 Edinburgh periodical (94). One might note, in support of Ascari's thesis, that René Belleto's prize-winning crime novel of 1981 is also called *Le Revenant*, and continues—at the end of the twentieth century—to mix elements of the fantastic with the detective genre.

CHAPTER 5. STREET-NAME MYSTERIES
AND PRIVATE/PUBLIC VIOLENCE, 1867–2001

1. René Réouven, *La Vérité sur la rue Morgue* (Paris: Flammarion, 2002); Robert Deleuse, *La Véritable affaire de la rue Morgue* (Paris: Eden, 2004).

2. Dominique Kalifa, "Les lieux du crime: Topographie criminelle et imaginaire social à Paris au XIXe siècle," *Sociétés & Représentations* 1, 17 (2004): 131–50. See also chap. 4 of Kalifa's *L'Encre et le sang: Récits de crimes et société à la Belle Epoque* (Paris: Fayard, 1995), 109–19.

3. Dominique Kalifa, "Crime Scenes: Criminal Topography and Social Imaginary in Nineteenth-Century Paris," *French Historical Studies* 27, 1 (2004), 175–94.

4. Uri Eisenzweig, "Violence Untold: The Birth of a Modern Fascination," *YFS 108*: 20–35.

5. Pont-Jest, René de. *Le No. 13 de la Rue Marlot* (Paris: F. Rouff, 1877) [Coll. BiLiPo], 1.

6. Victor Hugo, *Notre-Dame de Paris* (Paris: Larousse, 2003), 515–16. (*Coupe-Gorge* is merely a less vulgar term for *Coupe-Gueule*, "cut-throat"—so the joke is that polite language hasn't changed the location's basic threat to life and wallet.)

7. See Priscilla Parkhurst Ferguson, *Paris as Revolution: Writing the Nineteenth-Century City* (Berkeley: University of California Press, 1994), especially her chapter on "Mapping the City," which describes the spatial inscription of a proliferating "city of revolution" whose fragmentation and continual changes undermine any aesthetic of integration or nostalgia for coherence.

8. Adolphe Belot, *Le Drame de la rue de la Paix* (1866) [Coll. BiLiPo], 96. Belot wrote many plays and novels, including the scandalous lesbian story of 1870, *Mademoiselle Giraud, ma femme*. A theatrical version of *Le Drame de la rue de la Paix* was playing at the Odéon in 1883. See *Courrier de l'art: Chronique hebdomadaire des ateliers, des musées, des expositions, des ventes publiques, etc.*, No. 52: 27 (Décembre 1883). [Gallica]

9. Daniel Milo, "Le Nom des rues," in *Les Lieux de mémoire*, ed. Pierre Nora (Paris: Gallimard, 1997), 2: 1887–1918. Street names warrant an entire entry in Nora's *Lieux de mémoire* collection precisely because they signify temporal as well as spatial identity, in that street names act as repository of collective memory. Daniel Milo traces a historical shift in street naming from the spontaneous and communal "mémoire collective" of the Middle Ages to the governmentally decreed "mémoire officielle" of the nineteenth century.

10. Michel de Certeau, "Pratiques d'espace," in *L'Invention du quotidien* (Paris: Union Générale, 1980), 190–91. For de Certeau, the multiple associations of a street name allow it to surpass the State government's decrees; they can resist as polysemic "noyaux de signification" that allow for liberatory promenades (190–91).

11. In 1896, Aristide Bruant wrote the following verses, imagined as the words of Napoleon: "La ru'd'la Paix ça n'va guère / Avec un nom comm'le mien. // Qu'on l'appell'la ru'd'la Guerre / Et je n'réclam'rai plus rien" ["Peace Street don't go one bit / Wit' a name like mine. // Let them call it War Street/ And I'll leave 'em alone"]; cited in Julia Przybos, *Zoom sur les décadents* (Paris: José Corti, 2002), 40. Przybos points out the symbolic force of politically inspired name changes: "Rues, places et squares se voient 'renommés' à chaque bouleversement politique. . . . Ce sont là gestes politiques et magiques à la fois: en effaçant les marques du pouvoir passé, on croit affermir le pouvoir présent" [Streets, squares, and public parks find themselves "renamed" at every moment of political upheaval. . . . These gestures are at once political and magical: by erasing the marks of past power, [new leaders] imagine they are strengthening present power] (39).

12. This is, in a way, the antithesis of Baudelaire's willful (though ironized) retreat into an interior, depoliticized space in "Paysage": "L'Émeute, tempêtant vainement à ma vitre, / Ne fera pas lever mon front de mon pupitre" [Riot, storming vainly at my window, / Will not make me raise my head from my desk]. Belot's novel exposes the porous borders between insurrection and private activity.

13. The motif of threshold space recurs obsessively not only in the texts of nineteenth-century crime *feuilletons*, but also in the visual images that accompany them. Lurid illustrations in crime gazettes abound with the framing device of the doorway—as in Pont-Jest's "La Duchesse Claude" (reproduced in Thiesse, *Le Roman du quotidien*, 121). Liminality is thematized throughout the popular genre: walls are used for eavesdropping, bodies are flung from balconies, chases occur at town barriers and bridges, and murders take place in doorways or on the landings (*paliers*) of urban apartment buildings. The *palier* is a particularly suggestive space, as it marks the intersection of vertical stairway and horizontal apartment life in the

multistory *maisons* typical of pre-Haussmann Paris. In *Apartment Stories: City and Home in Nineteenth-Century Paris and London* (Berkeley: University of California Press, 1999), Sharon Marcus analyzes the class-crossing culture of *paliers* and the ways they functioned architecturally and socially as a threshold of private and public space. See also François Loyer, who writes that nineteenth-century French urban architecture was fundamentally structured by an inside/outside dichotomy, *Paris XIXe siècle: L'immeuble et la rue* (Paris: Hazan, 1987).

14. In most literary histories of the detective/crime genre, the early twentieth century is dominated by "the big Three": Gaston Leroux's Rouletabille novels, Maurice Leblanc's Arsène Lupin stories, and Souvestre and Allain's Fantômas series, all of which thematize the urban center/rural margins dichotomy in the establishment of national identity without directly engaging with pressing issues of political violence. In the interwar years, considered the Golden Age for anglophone crime fiction, things were relatively quiet in France; see, for example, Fereydoun Hoveyda's *Petite histoire du roman policier* (Paris: Pavillon, 1956), 49. World War II provided a resurgence in the genre, with Malet's *120, rue de la Gare*; a "critical dossier" testifying to Malet's role as innovator in French crime fiction can be found in *Enigmatika 18, Spéciale 81* [Ou.Li.Po.Po.] (Paris: Butte aux Cailles, 1982).

15. Léo Malet, *120, rue de la Gare* (Paris: SEPE, 1943).

16. This goes in both directions: Germans imposed new names, which were often ignored by locals; but also French resistance put false street signs up or changed their directions to confuse invading armies. In Tardi's well-known comic book version of Malet's novel, a partially hidden series of street signs reveals French names in small font below large block letters in German, as though to signal typographically the logic of occupation: "Kommandant von Gross-Paris" above "Rue de Rivoli", ". . . u. Unfallmeldestelle" above Rond Point des Champs-Elysées," etc. Tardi, with Léo Malet, *120, rue de la Gare* (Tournai, Belgium: Casterman, 1988), 167.

17. See especially the chapter "La Violence de la lettre: De Lévi-Strauss à Rousseau," in Jacques Derrida, *De la grammatologie* (Paris: Minuit, 1967), 159–62.

18. Malet was famously intrigued by surrealist art and associated himself at times with the movement, but not in this case. On surrealism and the noir, see Robin Walz, *Pulp Surrealism* (Berkeley: University of California Press, 2000); Jonathan Eburne, *Surrealism and the Art of Crime* (Cornell University Press, 2008); and Andrea Goulet, "*Le Soleil naît derrière le Louvre*: Malet, Surrealism, and the Modern Explosion of Paris," *L'Esprit Créateur* 54, 2 (2014), 141–158.

19. S. S. Van Dine, "Twenty Rules for Writing Detective Stories," *American Magazine* (September 1928), http://gaslight.mtroyal.ca/vandine.htm.

20. Didier Daeninckx, *12, rue Meckert* (Paris: Gallimard, 2001), 34.

21. Kristen Ross, "Watching the Detectives," in *Postmodernism and the Re-Reading of Modernity*, ed. Francis Barker, Peter Hulme, and Margaret Iversen (Manchester: Manchester University Press, 1992), 55–56.

22. This is part of Ross's larger questioning of a dichotomy between modernism as time-oriented versus postmodernism as spatial (48–49). Ross writes: "The detective's privileged access to spatial contradictions of the present allows history to emerge: not with the purpose of giving the French 'images' of their past—but rather to defamiliarise and restructure their experience of their own present"; she sees Daeninckx's detective fiction as a "response to the postmodern crisis in narrative," a crisis of economic collapse linked to spatial entropy (61).

23. Vladan Radoman, *Orphelin de mer suivi de 6, rue Bonaparte: La ballade d'un Yougo*, vol. 2, Série Noire (Paris: Gallimard, 2000), 24–25.

24. Michel de Certeau, *The Practice of Everyday Life* (Berkeley: University of California Press, 1984). For de Certeau, proper names orient the drift: "Walking is in fact determined by semantic tropisms" (103). Often, the names of city streets work on the subconscious, so that a second, poetic geography [orientation, itinerary] is superimposed on the literal map, thus allowing the wanderer to elude urbanistic systematicity.

25. Politically neutral designations like Acacia would be the equivalent of the Elm or Maple Streets in U.S. towns.

26. Uri Eisenzweig, *Le récit impossible: Forme et sens du roman policier* (Paris: Christian Bourgeois, 1986), 189.

27. See, for example, Boileau-Narcejac on mathematical abstraction and Stephen Knight on the "clue-puzzle form." Boileau-Narcejac, *Le roman policier: Que sais-je?* (Paris: PUF, 1975); Stephen Knight, *Crime Fiction 1800–2000: Detection, Death, Diversity* (New York: Palgrave Macmillan, 2004).

CHAPTER 6. TERRAINS VAGUES: GABORIAU AND THE BIRTH
OF THE CARTOGRAPHIC MYSTERY

1. Henri Lefebvre, *La production de l'espace* (Paris: Anthropos, 1974), 64.

2. Bonniot, *Emile Gaboriau ou la naissance du roman policier*, 32.

3. These essays are unsigned, but Bonniot attributes them to Gaboriau (*Émile Gaboriau*, 52–53).

4. Emile Gaboriau, *Monsieur Lecoq* (Paris: Liana Levi, 1992), 11.

5. Ponson du Terrail, *Rocambole* (Monaco: Rocher, 1963), 2: 132, 4: 31.

6. Dominique Kalifa, *Crime et culture au XIXe siècle*, 22.

7. David F. Bell, "Reading Corpses: Interpretive Violence," *Substance: A Review of Theory and Literary Criticism* 27, 2 (1998): 92 105, 95. Bell's essay usefully articulates the way in which local topography grounded the early detective novel's appeals to scientific authority in grisly reality. Bell analyzes Gaboriau's 1866 *L'Affaire Lerouge* as fundamentally structured by the logic of the threshold; "Crime, especially its most violent manifestation—murder—is located simultaneously inside and outside of the boundaries of civilization" (95). The fictional detective attempts to neutralize violence symbolically through an appeal to increasingly sophisticated scientific methodologies, but in practice, the activity of the detective is less abstract and more like that of the scientist "of the terrain"—an activity described by Isabelle Stengers as "gathering traces, *rassembler les indices*" (Bell, 99).

8. *Monsieur Lecoq* was first published in serial form in *Le Petit Journal*, May 27–July 31, 1868.

9. This was the first map appended to a modern detective story, but it was not, of course, the first crime-scene map. An early example is Antonio Cospi's 1643 *Il Givdice criminalista*, a manual on criminal investigation with sections on poison, physiognomy, and forensics that includes a drawn plan of a house, complete with secret passages and concealed staircases which could facilitate crime. The map is reprinted in Bradin Cormack and Carla Mazzio, eds., *Book Use, Book Theory 1500–1700* (Chicago: University of Chicago Library, 2005). My thanks to Karen Fresco for this reference.

10. The phrase is taken from press publicity for one of Gaboriau's lesser-known novels, *La Vie infernale* (1870). Cited in Bonniot, 151.

11. See Hoveyda, *Histoire du roman policier*, 52.

12. Conley, *The Self-Made Map*.

13. Virginie Berger, "Les plans de l'enquête dans la seconde moitié du XIXe siècle"; and Marina Daniel,. "Découverte du crime et besoins de l'enquête. Le dessin judiciaire en Seine-inférieure au XIXe siècle," in *Sociétés & Représentations: La Justice en images*, ed. Frédéric Chauvaud (Paris: CREDHESS, 2004).

14. Paul Virilio, *Speed and Politics*, trans. Marc Polizzotti (Los Angeles: Semiotext(e) 2006), 41–42.

15. Goulet, *Optiques*.

16. Uri Eisenzweig, *Le récit impossible*. For Eisenzweig, the locked room motif should be read neither as mere symbolic game nor as an anxiety-response to the chaotic complexities of a dangerous world, but rather as a paradigmatic instantiation of the ruptures inherent in the ideological construction of the modern Nation-state as unified space (229–30). See also Eisenzweig's "L'Instance du policier dans le romanesque: Balzac, Poe et le mystère de la chambre close," *Poétique* 51 (September 1982): 279–302.

17. Jonathan P. Eburne, *Surrealism and the Art of Crime*, 43–44.

18. Jacques Dubois, *Le Roman policier ou la modernité*, 157–70, 162.

19. David Platten, *The Pleasures of Crime*, 31–33; Platten, "Origins and Beginnings: The Emergence of Detective Fiction in France," in *French Crime Fiction*, ed, Claire Gorrara, 14–35.

20. Andrea Goulet, "The Yellow Spot: Ocular Pathology and Empirical Method in Gaston Leroux's *Le Mystère de la chambre jaune*," *SubStance* 107, 34.2 (2005): 27–46.

21. Page 11 verso, notes for *Le Mystère de la chambre jaune*, in "Fonds Gaston Leroux: Romans, théâtre, scénarios," http://gallica.bnf.fr/ark:/12148/btv1b5506356n/f45.image.r=.langEN.

22. See Robert Adey, *Locked Room Murders* (London: Ferret Fantasy, 1979); Roland Lecourbe, and Robert Adey, *99 chambres closes: Guide de lecture du crime impossible* (Amiens: Encrage, 1991).

23. Christian Jacob, *The Sovereign Map*, xiii.

24. Tom Conley, *Cartographic Cinema* (Minneapolis: University of Minnesota Press, 2007), 9.

25. Derek Gregory, *Geographical Imaginations*.

CHAPTER 7. MAPPING THE CITY: MALET'S *NOUVEAUX MYSTÈRES DE PARIS* AND BUTOR'S BLESTON

1. See Warren F. Motte, Jr., ed., *Oulipo: A Primer of Potential Literature* (Lincoln: University of Nebraska Press, 1986).

2. *Enigmatika* No. 3: "Atlas des plans de romans policiers," *Ouvroir de Littérature Policière Potentielle*, ed. Annie Matiquat (n.d.) [BiLiPo coll.]

3. Marcel Benabou, "Vers une théorie de la lecture du texte oulipien—Fragments d'un débat," in *Oulipo Poétiques*, ed. Peter Kuon (Tübingen: Gunter Narr, 1999), 211.

4. Raymond Queneau identifies the *roman policier* as the highest form of *littérature potentielle* in his epilogue to *Pierrot mon ami* (Oulipo *Atlas*, 27).

5. Ollier's *La Mise en scène* also includes a fold-out map, though not of city space. See Sjef Houppermans, *Claude Ollier Cartographe* (Amsterdam: Rodopi, 1997).

6. See, for example, Pierre Brunel, *Butor: L'emploi du temps, Le texte et le labyrinthe* (Paris: Presses Universitaires de France, 1995); and Michael Sheringham, "City Space, Mental Space, Poetic Space: Paris in Breton, Benjamin and Réda," in *Parisian Fields*, ed. Michael Sheringham (London: Reaktion, 1996).

7. Mireille Calle-Gruber, *La Ville dans l'emploi du temps de Michel Butor* (Paris: Librairie A.-G. Nizet, 1995).

8. Celia Britton, "The status of representation in Michel Butor's *L'emploi du temps* and *La modification*," *Journal of Beckett Studies* 3 (Summer 1978).

9. *Enigmatika 18 Spéciale 81* (Léo Malet). OU.LI.PO.PO, ed. Jacques Baudou (Paris: la Butte aux Cailles, 1982).

10. David Harvey, *The Condition of Postmodernity: An Enquiry into the Origins of Cultural Change* (Cambridge, Mass,: Blackwell, 1990); John Ruskin, "The Bible of Amiens," cited in Georges Raillard's Postface to Butor, Michel. *L'Emploi du Temps* (Paris: Union Générale d'Éditions, 1966), 444–5; Edward W.Soja, *Postmodern Geographies*; Yi-Fu Tuan, *Topophilia: A Study of Environmental Perception, Attitudes, and Values* (Englewood Cliffs, N.J.: Prentice-Hall, 1974).

11. Derek Gregory, *Geographical Imaginations*.

12. On the modern and ludic spatiality of *Les Nouveaux mystères de Paris*, see Peter Schulman, "Paris en jeu de l'oie: les fantômes de Nestor Burma," *French Review* 73, 6 (May 2000): 1155–64.

13. "Treize questions à Léo Malet," *Enigmatika 18 Spéciale 81* (Léo Malet). OU.LI.PO.PO. (Paris: Butte aux Cailles, 1982), 15–22, 19.

14. "Rencontres: Bernard Drupt s'entretient avec . . . Léo Malet," *Revue Indépendante* 147, 135–40, 137–38.

15. Léo Malet, *Les Enquêtes de Nestor Burma et les nouveaux mystères de Paris* (Paris: Robert Laffont, 1985), T. I, 735. "La Nuit de Saint-Germain-des-Près" first appeared in 1955 under the title "Le Sapin pousse dans les caves."

16. Roland Barthes, "Sémiologie et urbanisme," in *L'Aventure sémiologique* (Paris: Seuil, 1985), paraphrased by Jean-Xavier Ridon in his Introduction to "Errances urbaines," a special issue of *Nottingham French Studies* 39, 1 (Spring 2000): 2. In *Espèces d'espaces*, Georges Perec writes along similar lines, "Ça a vraiment quelque chose d'amorphe, le quartier: une manière de paroisse ou, à strictement parler, le quart d'un arrondissement, le petit morceau de ville dépendant d'un commissariat de police" [It really has something amorphous about it, the *quartier (*neighborhood): an air of the parish or, strictly speaking, the quarter of an *arrondissement*, the little bit of city that depends on a police station] (79).

17. Michel Serres, *Atlas* (Paris: Julliard, 1994).

18. It is useful to keep in mind the distinction Chris Andrews makes between constraints (rules) and conventions (generic regularity). Andrews, "Constraint and Convention: the Formalism of the OULIPO," *Neophilologus* 87 (2003): 223–32.

19. Michel Butor, *L'Emploi du temps* (1956; Paris: Minuit, 1995).

20. Many critics have identified Bleston with Manchester, the English city Butor knew as well as Revel knows Bleston. See, for example, Jack Kolbert, "The Image of the City in Michel Butor's Texts," *Kentucky Romance Quarterly* 32, 1 (1985): 13–22, 13. Despite the biographical link, however, a cursory glance at a map of Manchester reveals no formal correlation to Butor's Bleston.

21. J. Hillis Miller, *Topographies* (Palo Alto, Calif.: Stanford University Press, 1995), 11.

22. Michel de Certeau, *The Practice of Everyday Life*, 119.

23. The de Certelian analogy of linguistic grammar to the act of walking is suggestively echoed in some Oulipo statements: "Suivre une règle, c'est un parcours" (Oulipo) and "J'écris pour me parcourir" (Perec), both cited in *Oulipo poétiques*, ed. Peter Kuon (Tübingen: Gunter Narr (1999), 214, 195.

24. See Chapter 6. By setting his story in a *terrain vague*, Gaboriau inaugurates an important topos: the representation of peripheral urban zones Michel Sirvent identifies as central to the genre in his article on space in modern detective fiction. Michel Sirvent, "Représentations de l'espace urbain dans le roman policier d'aujourd'hui," *Nottingham French Studies* 39, 1 (Spring 2000): 79–95. Sirvent notes the use of the phrase *terrains vagues* in novels like Robbe-Grillet's *Les Gommes* and Jonquet's *Moloch* (83). Also of interest is Sirvent's "Reader-Investigators in the Post-Nouveau Roman: Lahougue, Peeters, and Perec," *Romanic Review* 88, 2 (March 1997): 315–35, reprinted in *Detecting Texts: The Metaphysical Detective Story from Poe to Postmodernism*, ed. Patricia Merivale and Elizabeth Sweeney (Philadelphia: University of Pennsylvania Press, 1999), 157–78.

25. For Butor, the traditional *roman policier* fills in its gaps: "Ce qui est très important c'est que des lacunes aient été comblées, qu'il y ait une explication sur chaque trou qui a été décelé" [What's crucial is that the gaps be filled in, that each exposed hole be explained]. In the *nouveau roman policier*, on the other hand, "il y reste des trous" [holes remain], cited in Laura Rice-Sayre, "Le roman policier et le nouveau roman: Entretien avec Michel Butor," *French-American Review* 1, 2 (Spring 1977): 101–14, 109, 112.

26. Edward Soja, *Postmetropolis: Critical Studies of Cities and Regions* (Oxford: Blackwell, 2000).

CHAPTER 8. ZÉROPA-LAND: BALKANIZATION AND
THE SCHIZOCARTOGRAPHIES OF DANTEC AND RADOMAN

1. Marc Augé, *Non-Places: Introduction to an Anthropology of Supermodernity*, trans. John Howe (London: Verso), 1995; Bruce Bégout, *Zeropolis: The Experience of Las Vegas* (London: Reaktion, 2004); Michel Serres, *Atlas* (Paris: Julliard, 1994).

2. Patricia Yaeger, ed., *The Geography of Identity* (Ann Arbor: University of Michigan Press, 1996), 4.

3. Maurice G. Dantec, *La Sirène rouge* (Paris: Gallimard, 1993).

4. Vladan Radoman, *Orphelin de mer*, suivi de *6, rue Bonaparte: La Ballade d'un Yougo*, vol. 2, Série Noire (Paris: Gallimard, 2000).

5. Dantec, two of whose prize-winning novels have been adapted as blockbuster-style movies (Olivier Megaton's 2002 *The Red Siren* and Mathieu Kassovitz's 2008 *Babylon A.D.*), is better known internationally than Radoman. Claire Gorrara cites Dantec as a key contributor to "a reconfigured literary landscape" that crosses national and generic boundaries, *The Roman Noir in Post-War French Culture: Dark Fictions* (Oxford: Oxford University Press, 2003), 18–19.

6. Tom Coates, "The Balkanisation of Blogdex," http://www.plasticbag.org/archives/2003/07/the_balkanisation_of_blogdex/, Posted July 29, 2003.

7. Alexander Kiossev, "The Dark Intimacy: Maps, Identities, Acts of Identification," in *Balkan as Metaphor: Between Globalization and Fragmentation*, ed. Dusan I. Bjelic and Obrad Savic (Cambridge, Mass.: MIT Press), 2002.

8. Tristan Nitot, "La fin de la balkanisation du Web," http://openweb.eu.org/humeurs/balkanisation/, March 21, 2003.

9. Maria Todorova, *Imagining the Balkans* (New York: Oxford University Press, 1997), 31.

10. Bertrand Westphal, "La Poldévie ou les Balkans près de chez vous: Un stéréotype français," *Neohelicon* 32 (2005): 1, 7–16, 8.

11. Hergé. *Les Aventures de Tintin: Le Lotus bleu* (1936; Paris: Casterman, 1999).

12. Hervé Le Tellier, *Esthétique de l'Oulipo* (Bordeaux: Castor Astral, 2006), 113–214. More recently, three Australian authors have put out a well-known fake travel guide to "Molvania, a land untouched by modern dentistry," whose precursor was certainly the French Poldévie. Santo Cilauro, Tom Gleisner, and Rob Sitch. *Molvanîa (Jetlag Travel Guide)* (New York: Overlook Press, 2004).

13. Douglas Morrey, "Dr Schizo: Religion, reaction and Maurice G. Dantec," *Journal of European Studies* 37, 3 (2007): 295–312, 295–96. On new scientific thought in *Babylon Babies*, see also Morrey's "Natural and Anti-Natural Evolution: Genetics and Schizophrenia in Maurice G. Dantec's *Babylon Babies*," *L'Esprit Créateur* 52, 2 (2012): 114–26.

14. Maurice G. Dantec, *Le Théâtre des opérations: Journal métaphysique et polémique 1999* (Paris Gallimard, 2000).

15. Michel de Certeau, *L'Invention du quotidien*, 1: 139–42.

16. Lawrence R. Schehr, "Dantec's Inferno," in *Novels of the Contemporary Extreme*, ed. Alain-Philippe Durand and Naomi Mandel (London: Continuum, 2006), 89–99.

17. Félix Guattari, *Cartographies schizoanalytiques* (Paris: Galilée, 1989); and *Mille Plateaux: Capitalisme et schizophrénie*, vol. 2 (Paris: Minuit, 1980). See also Eleanor Kaufman and Kevin Jon Heller, eds., *Deleuze and Guattari: New Mappings in Politics, Philosophy, and Culture* (Minneapolis: University of Minnesota Press, 1998). Kaufman's introduction explains how Deleuze and Guattari link schizoanalytic cartography to a "deindividualized restructuring of subjectivity" (7).

18. The novel is classified by the editors as science fiction, published in Gallimard's Folio SF line rather than its Folio policier series, which had featured Dantec's *La Sirène rouge* and *Les Racines du mal*.

19. Schehr, "Dantec's Inferno."

20. See also Schehr's essay on Derrida and 9/11: "Kaddish," *Contemporary French Civilization*, 29, 2 (2005): 71–87.

21. Jacques Derrida, "Des Tours de Babel," in *Difference in Translation*, trans. Joseph F. Graham (Ithaca, N.Y.: Cornell University Press, 1985).

22. Paul Virilio, *Speed and Politics,* 85.

23. The *carte d'état major* appeared in the early nineteenth century and was seen as progress over the eighteenth-century Cassini map, to which it was topographically superior. See Michael J. Blakemore and J. Brian Harley, *Concepts in the History of Cartography: A Review and Perspective* (Toronto: University of Toronto Press, 1980); J. Brian Harley and David Woodward, eds., *The History of Cartography*, 6 vols. (Chicago: University of Chicago Press, 1987); Norman J. W. Thrower, *Maps and Civilization: Cartography in Culture and Society*, 2nd ed. (Chicago: University of Chicago Press, 1995); and David Woodward, ed., *Art and Cartography: Six Historical Essays* (Chicago: University of Chicago Press, 1987).

24. See Jean-Louis Hippolyte, "Paranoia and Christianity in Maurice Dantec's Crime Fiction," *Studies in 20th and 21st Century Literature* 33, 1 (2009): 86–101.

INDEX

ACKNOWLEDGMENTS

This book has been a number of years in the making, and along the way I have benefited beyond measure from the generosity of colleagues, friends, family, and institutions. Many of my intellectual guides appear as proper names in the Index and I thank them for having carved out paths to explore.

I began work on *Legacies of the Rue Morgue* at the University of Illinois at Urbana-Champaign, where I was given research support in the form of an Illinois Program for Research in the Humanities fellowship, an Andrew W. Mellon Faculty fellowship, and a summer travel grant from the William and Flora Hewlett Foundation. Among the many friends and colleagues who contributed directly to my thinking on this project, I want especially to mention Rob Rushing, my partner in crime at the IPRH; Anna Stenport and William Castro, who joined Rob and me in a caffeine-fueled international crime writing group; Maggie Flinn and Jordana Mendelson, who encouraged me to branch out in new directions; Joe Valente, who has inspired me to keep moving forward; Larry Schehr, whose bountiful energy I sorely miss; and Patrick Bray and Armine Mortimer, both of whom read earlier drafts of my book with exquisite patience and expertise.

I have been lucky to have the friendship of Ania Loomba, Suvir Kaul, and Zack Lesser to serve as a bridge between my two professional homes, UIUC and the University of Pennsylvania. At Penn, my book project took on a wider scope and deeper precision with the help of Rare Book and Manuscript librarians John Pollack and Lynne Farrington; research assistants Sara Phenix and Said Gahia; and supportive colleagues, including Gerald Prince, Michèle Richman, Lydie Moudileno, Jean-Michel Rabaté, John Tresch, André Dombrowski, Paul Saint-Amour, Jim English, Kevin Platt, and many others. I am very grateful to Jeffrey Kallberg, Rebecca Bushnell, and Penn's School of Arts and Sciences (SAS) for the Weiler Fellowship that allowed me to complete my manuscript; and to Ayako Kano, David Barnes, and Jennifer Moore, whose organization of faculty writing retreats sponsored by SAS and the Graduate School of Education helped kickstart two summers of productive writing. More recently, I have been inspired to think beyond disciplinary boundaries through participation in the Mellon-sponsored Humanities, Urbanism, and Design initiative, led by Penn colleagues Eugenie Birch and David Brownlee.

Beyond my home institutions, numerous colleagues have contributed to this book through conference conversations, lecture invitations, e-mail exchanges, collaborations, corrections, and warm fellowship. I cannot hope to name them all, but they include Susanna Lee, Seth Whidden, Corry Cropper, Daryl Lee, Pim Higginson, Ora Avni, Julia Przybos, Catherine Nesci, Dominique Kalifa, Marie-Ève Thérenty, Françoise Gaillard, David F. Bell, Tom Conley, Alison James, Marshall Brown, Gayle Zachmann, Sonya Stephens, Andrea Thomas, Oliver Gaycken, Robin Walz, Mary Vogl, Arthur Evans, Melanie Hawthorne, Bruno Chaouat, Christophe Wall-Romana, and Kevin J. Hayes. I want to make special mention of Catherine Chauchard, director of the Bibliothèque des Littératures Policières (BiLiPo) in Paris. It is true that a number of the nineteenth-century texts I consulted at the BiLiPo in the early years of research for this book have been recently digitized through the Bibliothèque Nationale de France Gallica project. But while their broader accessibility is undoubtedly welcome, I continue to cherish my time at the BiLiPo, as it allowed me to experience the wonderful expertise and generosity of the library staff there, as well as to "*feuilleter* les *feuilletons*," as had the first readers of these popular fictions.

Let me thank, too, the editors and publishers who have granted me permission to reprint some of the material in this book. Versions of the following chapters have previously appeared: the Japrisot section of Chapter 4 in *Sébastien Japrisot: The Art of Crime*, ed. Martin Hurcombe and Simon Kemp (Rodopi, 2009); Chapter 5 in *Modern Language Quarterly* (March 2007); Chapter 6 in *Romantisme* (March 2010) [French version] and *Formules: Revue des créations formelles no. 14* [English version]; Chapter 7 in *L'Esprit Créateur* (Summer 2008); and the Balkans sections of Chapter 8 in *Contemporary French Civilization* (Summer 2009). I am immensely grateful to the two external readers of my manuscript for their expert advice, and to Eric Halpern, Alison Anderson, and the staff of the University of Pennsylvania Press for their excellent work in turning this manuscript into a book.

Finally, I cannot imagine having had the motivation to bring this project to fruition without the constant support of my close friends and extended family. Thank you to Goulets, Reynaldos, Estys, Andersons, and Leders—and especially to Jed, Jonah, and Maya, to whom I dedicate this book with much love. I want also to dedicate it to the memory of Josué Harari, who somehow and with great generosity found the energy to cheer, steer, and champion the project even in the final months of his life. Thank you, Josué.